D1374534

Christmas in Germany

Christmas in Germany

A Cultural History

JOE PERRY

UNIVERSITY OF NORTH CAROLINA PRESS
Chapel Hill

© 2010 The University of North Carolina Press

All rights reserved
Designed and set in Garamond Premier Pro with
MT Goudy Text Lombardic Capitals by Rebecca Evans
Manufactured in the United States of America

The paper in this book meets the guidelines for permanence
and durability of the Committee on Production Guidelines for
Book Longevity of the Council on Library Resources.

The University of North Carolina Press has been a member
of the Green Press Initiative since 2003.

Library of Congress Cataloging-in-Publication Data
Perry, Joe.
Christmas in Germany: a cultural history / Joe Perry.
p. cm. Includes bibliographical references and index.
ISBN 978-0-8078-3364-3 (cloth: alk. paper)
1. Christmas—German—History.
2. Germany—Social life and customs. I. Title.
GT4987.49.C453 2010
394.26630943—dc22   2010010137

Portions of chapter 5 are revised versions of material that appeared in
"The Nazification of Christmas: Politics and Popular Celebration in the Third
Reich," *Central European History* 38 (December 2005): 572–605; portions of
chapter 6 are revised versions of material that appeared in "The Madonna of
Stalingrad: Mastering the (Christmas) Past and West German National Identity
after World War II," *Radical History Review* 83 (Spring 2002): 6–27.

cloth   14 13 12 11 10   5 4 3 2 1

FOR
Joe & Frances

Contents

Figures

Acknowledgments

THIS BOOK HAS MUCH TO SAY about the generous spirit of the Christmas mood, and perhaps it was contagious: many friends, colleagues, and institutions supported my work on this book in many ways, and it is a real pleasure to thank them here. It is impossible to note everyone who helped along the way, but I will always recognize this as a collective project. Any errors that remain, despite this gracious assistance, are of course my own.

A number of institutions provided the research and travel support that made this book a possibility. A grant from the German Academic Exchange Service (DAAD) allowed me to spend eighteen months in Germany conducting research. I also received invaluable aid from the College of Arts and Sciences and the Department of History at Georgia State University; the College of Liberal Arts and Sciences and the Department of History at the University of Illinois at Urbana-Champaign (UIUC); the DAAD (again); the American Historical Association; the Council of European Studies; and the German Historical Institute.

I am deeply indebted to those who read and commented on substantial portions of the book or gave other invaluable support. Rudy Koshar and Paul Lerner reviewed the manuscript for the University of North Carolina Press, and their sage advice pushed me to consider the full implications of the history of German Christmas. Peter Fritzsche has been on board since the beginning and read drafts "again and again"; his mentorship strengthened the study in countless ways. Alf Lüdtke and Bernd Wegner made fundamental contributions to this work as it was taking shape, and Alon Confino, who supported this project early and often, interceded at crucial moments along the way. Doris Foitzik, whose own book on German Christmas I deeply admire, shared copies of her original sources, an act of remarkable generosity that I will long remember; Timothy C. Dowling did the same. Sven

Reichardt, Katherine Pence, Rolf Dieter Müller, and Christian Gerlach also shared sources. I am grateful for permission to reprint the revised portions of this book that previously appeared in *Central European History* and *Radical History Review*. I am also thankful for the encouragement and help extended by Chuck Grench, Jay Mazzocchi, Katy O'Brien, and the rest of the team at the University of North Carolina Press.

Archivists and librarians across Germany facilitated my research. The friendly interest of Katerina Rentmeister at the Children's Book Section of Stabi-Ost/Berlin encouraged me in the early days of my research. I was amazed and delighted when Dr. Peter Kunzl of the Evangelisches Zentralarchiv (EZA) in Berlin dug up an entire file labeled "Weihnachten." His help, and that of Dr. Peter Beier and Barbara Lehman, made the EZA the friendliest archive in all of Germany. Sabine Schumann at the Bildarchiv-Preussicher Kulturbesitz went out of her way to make sure I had the best possible illustrations for the book. The congenial staff of the Bundesarchiv, the Bayerische Hauptstaatsarchiv, the always astonishing Deutsches Bibliothek in Leipzig, and the other archives and institutions where I worked provided indispensable assistance.

Over the years, colleagues and friends read drafts and offered encouragement of many kinds. Knowing Karsten Borgmann, Eve Duffy, Ingo Haar, LeeAnna Kieth, Anna Minta, Brian Plane, Sven Reichardt, and Maria Paz Squella made my stay in Germany exciting and productive. When I was working in Atlanta, Jeanette Brabanetz and Alexandra Pfeiff tracked down missing materials in Germany. Mike Allen, Jennifer Evans, David J. Fine, Michael Galchinsky, Giles Knox, Tom Lekan, Rob Nelson, Stephen Nissenbaum, Jack Santino, and Anthony Steinhoff read and commented on chapter drafts, and their constructive criticism greatly improved the book. I've also benefited from more informal exchanges with Omer Bartov, Andrew Bergerson, Benita Blessing, P. C. "Buddy" Boyd, Paul Breines, Belinda Davis, Wilhelm Deist, Andrew Donson, Heide Fehrehnbach, David Goldberg, Jeffrey Herf, Gerhard Hirschfeld, Jennifer Jenkins, Eric Jensen, Brett Klopp, Jennifer Kopf, Urte Lietz, Anne Lipp, Christa Lorenz, Denise Messick, George Mosse, Armin Nolzen, Till van Rahden, Cory Ross, Richard Steigmann-Gall, and Eric Weitz; all shared insightful ideas about contacts, sources, and interpretations.

The history department at Georgia State University (GSU) has offered a stimulating environment for my intellectual endeavors. Isa Blumi, Kevin Baker, Duane Corpis, Denise Davidson, Ian Fletcher, Richard Laub, Jared

Poley, and Christine Skwiot all read chapters; their comments pushed me to think of Christmas in new ways. I'm also grateful to Rob Baker, Michelle Brattain, Hugh Hudson, Matt Lasner, Alecia Long, David McCreery, Doug Reynolds, Jake Selwood, Chuck Steffan, Nick Wilding, Larry Youngs, and my other colleagues for their support over the years. At GSU I further benefited from the work of several fine research assistants, including Mindy Clegg, Kevin Goldberg, David Gross, Christopher Huffman, and Jon Schmitt. They quickly found out, as I did early on, that Christmas is always at the end of the reel.

My associates at the University of Illinois, where this project began, gave indispensable support in its early stages. I am particularly grateful for the encouragement of Peter Fritzsche, Matti Bunzl, Harry Liebersohn, and Sonya Michel. All showed insight and patience as they challenged me to develop my interpretations. A lively and dedicated group of graduate students and faculty made UIUC an amazing place to learn how to do history. Special thanks are due to Glenn Penny, who was always ready for some informal advising; and to Masha Bucur, Clare Crowston, and Rose Holz for their friendly support. Rose, Kathy Mapes, and Michelle Moran shared valuable insights on the writing process; participants in the University of Illinois German Colloquium did the same. I furthermore gained much from the company of people like Jim Barret, Dave Bielanski, Eric Buhs, Antoinette Burton, Dawn Flood, Bryan Ganaway, Irina Gigova, Toby Higbie, Keith Hitchins, Craig Koslofsky, Dave Krugler, Mark Leff, Brent Maner, Michelle May, John McKay, Mark Micale, Elisa Miller, Andrew Nolan, Eva Plach, David Prochaska, Brian Sandberg, Adam Sutcliffe, Christine G. Varga-Harris, Steve Vaughn, John Wedge, Molly Wilkenson, Mila Yasko, and Jonathan York, to name just a few. Though they had little to do with this project, I am also indebted to the history faculty at the University of Colorado at Boulder—especially Professors David Gross, Robert Pois, Larry Silverman, and William Wei—whose enthusiasm for the study of the past first inspired my own.

Writing this book has constantly reminded me that intellectual work is a collective product, shaped by any number of personal as well as scholarly interactions. With that knowledge, I would like to thank my close friends and family. It would be impossible to adequately express my gratitude to Joyce de Vries, who read and commented on entire drafts several times and provided unstinting moral support; without her, there would be no book. My parents, Joe and Frances, believed in my academic career long before I did. This book is for them.

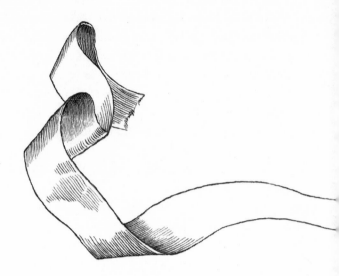

Christmas in Germany

Introduction
Germany's Favorite Holiday

Every spiritual experience of the German people since the fourteenth
century is reflected in its way in the history of German Christmas,
sometimes more clearly, sometimes more opaquely, but rarely entirely
unrecognizably.

—⟡ Alexander Tille, *Die Geschichte der deutschen Weihnacht* (1893)

GERMANS ACROSS GENERATIONS would have concurred with philosopher and literary scholar Alexander Tille when he described the close connections between Christmas and the German soul. Tille and his contemporaries—professors and poets, priests and politicians—recognized that
Christmas was an international phenomenon, the most important festival
in what they called Western Christendom. At the same time, they believed
that there was something particularly German about the holiday. "German
Christmas," they believed, was organic and unique, a synthesis of the winter
solstice rituals of primeval Teutonic tribes, the Christian celebration of the
birth of Jesus, and the age-old customs that defined German character. The
Christmas tree glittering with candles and decorations, a trip to the Christmas market, the mysterious Christmas Eve visit of Father Christmas, feasts of
roast goose with red cabbage, the uncanny scent of pine boughs indoors; all
were tokens of a specifically national festival that thrilled and fascinated Germans and non-Germans alike. The aura of ancient folk tradition and associations with family love and social harmony lent Christmas sentimental appeal
and a sense of historical depth. Yet, as this book shows, German Christmas
was never a set of timeless traditions anchored in an authentic folk culture
or a deep Germanic past. Rather, the symbols and rituals of Germany's most
popular holiday composed a fluid and permeable sign system, available for
appropriation by a variety of competing interests and groups. Each year,

Germans enacted a set of Christmas scripts that exhibited formal stability but invited improvisation and at times radical transformation. The players included family patriarchs, bourgeois matrons, and domestic servants; pastors and rabbis; famous authors and hack writers; political propagandists and national leaders; businessmen, scholars, and movie stars; and, most importantly, countless German families. All used annual celebrations to define and contest the deepest values that held the German community together: faith, family, and love to be sure, but also civic responsibility, material prosperity, and national belonging.[1]

Despite its venerable appearance, German Christmas is a relatively recent invention. The holiday as we know it took shape in the decades surrounding 1800 in the family parlors of enlightened aristocrats and bourgeois intellectuals. Recoiling from the upheaval of the French Revolution and the Napoleonic Wars, they refocused the holiday's central rituals on family and private life in order to regain a sense of stability and connect to romanticized trajectories of cultural continuity.[2] As the nineteenth century unfolded and the tempo of industrialization increased, Christmas celebrations across Western Europe and the United States helped reconcile the competitive and acquisitive culture of consumer capitalism with the requirements of the modern nation-state, which demanded a national collective built on fraternity and belonging even as it challenged familiar modes of belonging based on regional networks or religious community. Christmas was more than an escape from the burdens of political and economic crisis. At least once a year, the holiday offered a satisfying set of resolutions to two of the central dilemmas of the modern age: the desire for a stable sense of self in a rapidly changing society and the search for lasting morals in an increasingly commercialized and sacrilegious world.

The reinvented Christmas was one of the foundational practices in what philosopher Charles Taylor has termed the "expressive revolution," the great shift in conceptions of self and identity that accompanied the political and social transformations of the Napoleonic era. The sources of the modern self were set in late eighteenth-century Western Europe, Taylor and others argue, when the very core of what we are became increasingly linked to family and private life and to a new willingness to reveal our most intimate emotions to others.[3] Christmas became immensely popular throughout the Western world because the moral imperatives at the center of the holiday celebrated the basic features of modern selfhood: the "affirmation of ordinary life" embodied in middle-class family values and domestic comforts; and the choice to be good, to express feelings of love and faith and engage in acts of (Christian) charity.[4] On one level, this book uses Christmas to explore the history of the modern self across the nineteenth and twentieth centuries. It does not, however, focus on the intellectual history of this process, as do scholars such as Taylor and Jerrold Siegel. Rather, I use Christmas to show how the changing nature of the self is rooted in and transformed through everyday cultural practices, which informed and were informed in turn by grander ideas about morality, the sacred, family love, and the search for community.[5] As I hope this history makes clear, Christmas did much cultural work in the nineteenth and twentieth centuries. The modern self was hardly a static category, though Christmas lent the bourgeois personality a sense of timelessness. Holiday rituals affirmed and naturalized a middle-class subjectivity that was, after all, a mutable historical construction shaped by the ever-changing vectors of family and ethnicity, class and status, religious affiliation and political identification.

The nineteenth-century (re)invention of Christmas was a transatlantic phenomenon, closely tied to the emergence and consolidation of the nation-state. Though the holiday's central features were shared across borders, by midcentury Christmas had acquired distinct national characteristics shaped by regional customs. Contemporaries enjoyed trading opinions about "American traditions" or the "Englishness of Christmas."[6] An anonymous German author, writing in the 1844 holiday issue of one of Germany's first illustrated family magazines, recognized that Christmas brought "its joy to all the peoples of Christendom." His cosmopolitan descriptions of the unique traditions of the French, Scandinavians, and British bolstered this claim. Yet respect for the great diversity of observances hardly precluded assertions of pride in one's own national customs. Only Germans plumbed the holiday to its depths, the author continued; only Germans truly experienced "the colorful, dazzling, luminous, and rambunctious world of Christmas in the Fatherland."[7] Foreign observers agreed. American philanthropist Charles Loring Brace concluded in 1853 that "there is something about this German Festival, which one would seldom see in *our* home enjoyments"; British novelist, traveler, and journalist Ida A. R. Wylie reported in 1911 that "there is no country in the world where Christmas is so intensely 'Christmasy,' as in the Fatherland"; and in his authoritative *Christmas in Ritual and Tradition* (1912), British folklorist Clement Miles noted that "many people, indeed, maintain that no other Christmas can compare with the German *Weihnacht*."[8] Such comments played on a common theme: Christmas was somehow naturally

German, and no other nation celebrated the holiday with such heartfelt joy and enthusiasm.

Emotions, too, had national characteristics. At the heart of German Christmas was what celebrants called the *Weihnachtsstimmung*, or Christmas mood, a feeling that only Germans experienced during their semisacred moments of family festivity. Observers like Wylie pondered the mysteries of what she called "this great and untranslatable German word," which made Christmas German. "*Stimmung*," she mused, "means the 'something' which can unite an immense assembly of strangers in one bond of enthusiasm, or joy, or of sorrow. It is the longed-for guest at all festivities, the silent companion in every hour of general mourning and at Christmas—why, at Christmas it is everywhere, everything."[9] In her exuberant attempt to describe the Christmas mood as peculiarly German, Ida Wylie struggled to explain something historians of modern Germany have only begun to unravel: the history of the senses and emotions, and their power to define and reproduce social norms and identities.[10] Christmas is an excellent site for an investigation into this rich and complex history. As countless prescriptive texts admonished, a proper German Christmas required the proper sensory environment and the correct emotional response. As one anonymous but typical mid-nineteenth-century German poet enthused, "the sweet air of Christmas" brought "joy to Christendom/souls full of glory [and] breasts free of care."[11]

Writing the history of the senses and emotions is a tricky endeavor, and a general sense of my interpretative methodology may help clarify the material that follows. The goal is not so much to differentiate between "authentic" expressions of emotion and the cultural codes that told Germans what to feel. Rather, I attempt to reconstruct the rituals and customs, the stories, songs, and images—in other words, the systems of practice and representation—that made shared feelings imaginable and desirable.[12] During the holiday season, Germans participated in a range of ritualized activities that contributed to the construction of what historian Barbara Rosenwein has labeled an "emotional community." As Rosenwein explains, emotional communities, like other social communities rooted in ideas about family, ethnicity, confession, or nation, offer individuals a source of mutual recognition determined by shared values and experiences. Historically constructed "systems of feeling" define acceptable forms of emotional expression and shape the affective ties that bind people together in groups. And like other forms of identification, Rosenwein concludes, emotional communities are never mutually exclusive of other sorts of belonging. People can identify with shared affective systems temporarily, and emotions may readily support and/or contradict other forms of identity based, for example, on class, gender, or politics.[13] When Germans talked about or experienced the Christmas mood, I suggest, they joined an emotional community rooted in feelings of family love, joy, and concern for others. Such emotions have become basic to modern identities and indeed to Western culture writ large. Yet the very ubiquity of such emotions tends to mask their historical rootedness in the domestic culture of the nineteenth-century bourgeoisie.

By 1900 a vibrant commercial culture and an ever-expanding mass media had appropriated and standardized the feelings and customs of German Christmas and sold them back to broad sectors of the German population. The commercialization of the holiday changed the tempo of private celebration and helped reframe the sources of the self. Working- and middle-class Germans alike increasingly used the material goods and media products of modern society to organize their leisure-time activities, express their feelings, and assert their social-emotional affiliations. The consolidation of a modern consumer regime hardly destroyed German traditions, as many feared; rather, the commercial marketplace inspired and indeed profited from a sense of nostalgia for "Christmas as it was," even if it had never really been that way.[14] The mass production, marketing, and consumption of sentimental decorations, toys, cards, and holiday literature, however kitschy, further linked family celebration to national markets and identities.[15] By the late nineteenth century, the material goods that defined German Christmas were increasingly available to ever-greater numbers of people—if they had the cash—though the democratization of the holiday hardly leveled social hierarchies. The range of commercial products and indeed experiences that Germans enjoyed "around the Christmas tree" created cultural solidarity. At the same time, they were diverse enough to reinforce class, confessional, and political differences, a process that continues to play out in the early twenty-first century.[16]

Nationalization and commercialization in the German context were never far removed from conflicts over faith and piety. The history of Christmas is a revealing place to explore confessional conflict, secularization, and church-state relations in nineteenth- and twentieth-century Germany. From the start, the central traditions that now define "German" Christmas, such as the Christmas tree and the *Weihnachtsmann*, or Father Christmas, were products of an urban, enlightened, and primarily Protestant milieu. In a century of growing confessional tension, the choice of celebratory symbols and practices shaped divergent and competing Protestant, Catholic, and Jewish lifestyles and identities; German Catholics in particular used the holiday to shape a "socio-cultural world of their own."[17] Traditions of faith and processes of modernity were never mutually exclusive. Instead they coexisted in complex and sometimes ambiguous exchanges, as the religious aspects of the holiday profited from and gave way before bourgeois domesticity, nationalist theology, and consumer hedonism. While business interests used holiday marketing campaigns to increase sales and shoppers mobbed decorated department stores and outdoor Christmas markets, church leaders worked to protect German-Christian values from rampant commercialization and the decadent forces of "modern life." Ordinary parishioners, for their part, used the goods purveyed by consumer culture to sacralize middle-class notions of domesticity. And even if they rarely attended formal services during the rest of the year, annual recognition of the Christian elements of Christmas festivities reaffirmed a sense of religiosity and loyalty to the church. Religious traditions were also politicized. Modern Protestant celebration, like liberal Protestantism at large, was particularly open to penetration by the peculiar pseudosacred, Germanic-Völkisch ideology of Germany's nationalist political culture. This process, already evident in bourgeois family celebrations in the late nineteenth century, played out with logical if radical force in the Nazi period, as clergy and laypeople grappled with the intensely politicized relationship between church and state. As Germany's foremost national but also Christian holiday, Christmas was continually on the front line, so to speak, in ideological-political battles and church-state struggles, whether in the late imperial period, the Third Reich, or the divided Germany of the Cold War.[18]

Historians of Germany have long recognized public ritual and celebration as essential to the dramatic display of power relationships and the cultural construction of social communities and patriotic identities. They have not always appreciated the ways domestic or private celebration contributed to this process. Standard works that focus on official holidays and public festivities tend to equate national belonging with the well-articulated goals expressed in political symbols and rhetoric. This approach posits an artificial separation between public and private forms of festivity and assumes, at least tacitly, that domestic celebrations lacked political or public meaning. On this view, national holidays in nineteenth- and twentieth-century Germany were at best temporary or regional successes but failures on the broader level; they never seemed to inspire a durable sense of popular patriotism. There are numerous examples. Germans celebrated railroad openings in the Rhineland in the early 1840s, any number of city centenaries across the century, and the kaiser's birthday in 1907, but such festivities made only a partial contribution to an enduring German identity.[19] According to Alon Confino, Sedan Day, first celebrated in 1872 as a commemoration of German victory in the Franco-Prussian War, was "a national holiday without a nation" that encouraged division rather than integration and faded away in the 1890s; Weimar-era Constitution Day festivities and veterans commemorations likewise celebrated a "republic without republicans." National Socialist stagings of "religious form[s] of mythopoeia" were perhaps more successful but still short-lived.[20] Moreover, according to some historians, the supposed lack of popular national holidays reveals the general weakness of bourgeois political culture in the nineteenth century: the celebrations of the middle class represented authoritarian, monarchical symbols and ideals in a supposed betrayal of liberal class interests.[21] In short, much of the scholarship on celebration in modern Germany emphasizes the top-down work of dominant institutions, obscures both the vibrancy and the political content of domestic celebration, and assumes that private celebration had little resonance in conceptions of public, civil society. Few have addressed the challenge of ethnologist Hermann Bausinger, who urged scholars to examine the porosity of the boundaries between public and private celebration.[22]

This book moves beyond public/private dichotomies to argue that Christmas, supposedly a private family celebration, was and is Germany's national holiday. Looking at the politics of Christmas testifies to the remarkable originality and expansiveness of the domestic culture of the nineteenth-century German middle classes and at the same time underscores the political resonance of domesticity. By the twentieth century, Christmas, an invention of Germany's middle classes, had become an archetypal symbol of a German nation united above class, religion, region, or ideology—and therefore a tendentious site of political conflict. Competing groups struggled to define the holiday and control its observance. Social Democrats, National Socialists, Cold War liberals, and Communists—each appropriated German Christmas as a celebration of national harmony. Their competing holidays were more than propaganda vehicles. Politicized celebrations could and sometimes did harness a sense of shared belonging produced in the most intimate spaces of private life, and Germans used the holiday to embed themselves in political collectives. When manipulation went too far, ordinary Germans used Christmas traditions to police the nation-state from below.

My analysis seeks to highlight the importance of family festivity in the shaping of German national identity by unpacking the close ties between domestic celebration, popular piety, and consumerist desire. Scholars often code these fields of human behavior as feminine and private, which perhaps helps account for their relative absence in studies of nationalism and public politics.[23] Conventional historical narratives explain national identity in general, and German nationalism in particular, as a manly construction that moves from the public to private sphere, exemplified in the masculine rhetoric of the Pan-German League or grandiose structures like the Monument to the Battle of Peoples in Leipzig. In standard accounts, Germans line up behind a series of great male leaders—from Bismarck to Kaiser Wilhelm II, from Adolf Hitler to Adenauer and Ulbricht—leaving an impression of a German identity defined by masculine and militarist values. "The nation was a manly cause," writes David Blackbourn in what is now the standard textbook on Germany's long nineteenth century. Another historian asserts: "The nationalism of the Germans . . . depended on triumphs, marches, victories, and expectations for the same."[24] No one can seriously deny that German nationalism included exaggerated and sometimes tragic notions of masculinist militarism. The history of German Christmas shows, however, that the trajectories of German nationalism were more complex. From the German Empire (1871–1918) to the economic miracle of the 1960s, private holiday rituals evoked intimate and domesticated feelings of Germanness that were as deep as and more enduring than public celebrations or political rhetoric. To be sure, the production of the private, sentimental nation and the articulation of public, more masculine national sentiments were overlapping and mutually sustaining projects. Assertive, chauvinist nationalist discourse repeatedly permeated family celebration; the enduring popularity of war toys as gifts suggests as much. Nevertheless, the annual performance of genuinely popular holiday rituals, increasingly mediated through consumer goods, let ordinary Germans enact personal scripts of national incorporation rooted in the tender emotions of private life.[25]

Despite a shared emotional regime that celebrated visions of "Good Will Toward All Men," Christmas hardly succeeded in integrating Germans. The oft-cited project of universal social and national harmony based on shared feelings and values remained a fantasy. There was never one "German Christmas"; it makes more sense to speak of "German Christmases." Yet the ideal of a people joined together through the ideals of middle-class domesticity was remarkably powerful in a nation-state where the search for a viable community was as fractious as it was obsessive.

THE CHAPTERS THAT FOLLOW are organized thematically and chronologically. The first four return repeatedly to the formative decades surrounding 1900 to show how German Christmas was invented, stabilized, and contested in these crucial years. Chapter 1 describes the emergence of the key features of what we now see as a traditional German Christmas: the Christmas tree, the Weihnachtsmann, and the "Christmas mood." Though such traditions continue to define an authentic German holiday, they were initially Protestant, Prussian customs, and their growing popularity testified to the presence of soft but powerful forms of hegemonic Prusso-Protestant nationalism in a unified German Empire. Catholics resisted what they perceived as "modern," Protestant versions of the holiday even as they argued that shared Christian observance meant that they, too, were members of the Christian nation. Catholics and Protestants likewise shared the cult of domestic piety that grew up around the holiday in the last third of the nineteenth century. By 1900 public Christmas celebrations and private observances in middle-class family parlors had become sentimental talismans of the links among family, *Volk*, and nation. German Christmas in fact celebrated a predominantly Protestant vision of universal German community that supposedly subsumed class, religious, and regional conflicts—at least once a year.

Though the mainstream Christmas turned on visions of universal harmony embodied in the evangelical message "Peace on Earth, Good Will to Men," chapter 2 suggests that the holiday opened space for the construction and enactment of social and political difference. In the late nineteenth century, German Jews, Social Democrats, and working-class Germans shaped their own versions of Christmas. The alternative narratives and celebrations devised by these outsider groups drew on but also challenged the assumptions of bourgeois festivity. Chapter 3 examines what Germans called *Kriegsweihnachten*, or War Christmas, during the Franco-Prussian War (1870–71) and World War I. Celebrations of War Christmas effectively merged official agendas and private needs to mobilize the networks of social belonging already established by families, military units, and religious and civic associations. Despite the propagandistic nature of War Christmas, it was an effective moment for constructing national solidarity from below—an important lesson in the holiday's ability to absorb national politics that would not be lost on National Socialist and Cold War propagandists.

Chapter 4 bridges the nineteenth and twentieth centuries to chart continuities that might be obscured by the dramatic events of the war. It opens in the 1890s, when the consolidation of an increasingly ubiquitous consumer culture made obvious inroads into holiday observances, and follows that story into the Weimar years (1918–33). Christmas, according to contemporaries across this period, inspired uncontrolled outbreaks of mass *Kauflust*—the "desire to buy." The resulting profit potential enticed marketing professionals and large retailers, and the rationalization of sales organization and marketing techniques reached a fever pitch during the holiday season. Commercialization penetrated everyday celebration. It linked private life to national markets and meanings, commodified folk culture for the masses, and turned urban shopping districts into holiday spectacles. It also upset clergymen and cultural critics, who decried its effects on the authenticity of German traditions. In the Weimar Republic, economic crises and political conflict made Christmas "joy" based on prosperity a fleeting experience. The inadequacies of private celebration, exacerbated by ongoing social, economic, and political crises, invited public and political appropriation. The early years of the 1930s witnessed a determined political struggle over the meaning and use of the holiday.

The last two chapters deal more explicitly with the politics of popular celebration: National Socialists, West German liberals, and East German Communists each restructured German Christmas to shape competing ideals of citizenship and national belonging. Chapter 5 explores the tensions at the core of the so-called People's Christmas in Nazi Germany. Regime propagandists and intellectual cadres enthused by National Socialist ideologies drew on the supposed practices of pre-Christian, Nordic-Germanic tribes, familiar from ethnographic literature, to shape public and private rituals that would promote the exclusionary agendas of the racial state. Celebration in the Third Reich, like other aspects of Nazi cultural policy, was not a simple matter of top-down control that evoked passive submission or private resistance. Instead, state orchestration met with an active and enthusiastic popular response because participation in Nazi political rituals such as Christmas offered Germans attractive material and symbolic rewards. The holiday also exposed the fault lines in National Socialist political culture. Nazification exacerbated preexisting tensions between church and state, public festivities and private celebration, and modern consumerism and the more sober claims of German authenticity. The invented rituals of "People's Christmas" furthermore blurred the boundaries between Christian observance and the pseudosacred nationalist inventions favored by committed Nazis. As a result, competing religious and political groups pulled the holiday in radically different directions. On balance, Christmas was a successful celebration of the Nazi *Volksgemeinschaft* (People's Community)—at least so long as everyday life under the "national revolution" remained promising. The pressures of political radicalization and defeat in World War II exacerbated the tensions at the heart of the Nazi holiday.

The final chapter argues that Christmas was a central vehicle for the reconstruction of private and public identities in East and West Germany during the Cold War. In fiction, film, and everyday celebration, Christmas offered Germans ways to manage the moral ambiguities of the Nazi past and the ideological struggles of the present. The Cold War engendered a final spasm of intense politicization, again focused on the Christian ethos of the holiday. Growing prosperity on both sides of the Berlin Wall, however, made Cold War propaganda increasingly irrelevant. The arrival of a full-blown consumer culture challenged and undermined familiar religious traditions as well as overt political appropriations of the family holiday.

Writing about the ways Germans remade Christmas over the past 200 years is, in the end, an attempt to write about the ways Germans continually rethought the connections between themselves and their society. The history of the holiday itself, with its rich symbols and traditions, is central to this effort: Christmas was and is the Western world's foremost celebration, and the German version is quintessential. Yet this book is about more than folklore or family custom. The history of Christmas, I hope, has something to say about the German sense of self and about how Germans grappled with the transformative challenges of the nineteenth and twentieth centuries. To return to Alexander Tille's conceptualization, which opened this introduction, this book seeks to explain the ways Christmas shaped and reflected the "spiritual experience" of being German.[26]

FIGURE I.I
Cover of Hugo Elm's *Golden Christmas Book*, 1878. (© bpk Berlin
2009/SBB/Carola Siefert, Kinder- und Jugendbuchabteilung,
Staatsbibliothek zu Berlin-Preußischer Kulturbesitz)

Scripting a National Holiday

Und der Engel sprach zu ihnen: Fürchtet euch nicht! Siehe, ich
verkündige euch große Freude, die allem Volk widerfahren wird;

    denn euch ist heute der Heiland geboren, welcher ist Christus,
der HERR, in der Stadt Davids.

    Und das habt zum Zeichen: ihr werdet finden das Kind in
Windeln gewickelt und in einer Krippe liegen.

    Und alsbald war da bei dem Engel die Menge der himmlischen
Heerscharen, die lobten Gott und sprachen:

    Ehre sei Gott in der Höhe und Frieden auf Erden und den
Menschen ein Wohlgefallen.

—∞ St. Luke, chapter 2, verses 10–14, Luther Bible (1912 edition)

Dear, sweet heart! Christmas Eve is certainly an *ideé fixe* among
the Berliners, because not just children but everyone in the family
and close friends as well exchange a jumble of gifts. There is always
something sweet in this desire to give each other so much joy.

—∞ Caroline von Humboldt to Wilhelm von Humboldt,
    23 December 1815

IN 1815 CAROLINE VON HUMBOLDT, wife of Wilhelm von Humboldt,
the enlightened educator, philosopher, and Prussian diplomat, set up Christmas trees in her parlor on Unter den Linden, the main thoroughfare in the
Prussian capital of Berlin. Caroline described the scene and the family's
Christmas Eve celebration in letters to Wilhelm, who was in Frankfurt to
negotiate territorial realignments in the aftermath of Napoleon's defeat. "On
both ends of a long table, two small Christmas trees burn brightly with lit
candles," Caroline wrote, trying to include her husband in the festivities,
however far away he might be. "The Countess Dübin surrounded one with

all types of presents for her little ones, I used the other for Hermann." The children, who the day before had been "beside themselves with impatience," now found satisfaction. Hermann's "main gifts" included "a theater, a very nice construction set, a squadron of Cossacks, and so on," and "there was hardly room" for the many presents for Caroline, Adelheid, Gabriella, August, and the rest of the company. The mood was set by the glow of the "many candles and small lights" and the illuminated chandelier, which "made the atmosphere unusually pleasant." The holiday was a success, Caroline assured her husband. Despite his absence, the family and friends found "so much joy" in the holiday experience.[1]

Later claims that Caroline's was "the first Christmas tree in Berlin" call attention to the origin myths of what would become a set of very German holiday traditions.[2] The remade Christmas celebrated by the Humboldts and other members of the German Bildungsbürgertum, the upper strata of bourgeois society who valued cultivation and education as the key indicator of self-identity, reflected a broader transformation of the Early Modern festival cycle. Across the seventeenth and eighteenth centuries, Baroque celebration became increasingly bourgeois, enlightened, and politicized.[3] Like other modern festivals, the German Christmas we know today is a hybrid, a blend of distinct but interrelated celebrations once observed in church, popular culture, and court society. The 25th of December was the high point of a series of religious holidays, including Advent Sundays, a number of saint's days, and "Holy Eve," when observant Christians attended midnight or early-morning mass. Religious traditions coexisted, sometimes uneasily, with diverse superstitions and customs. From 30 November, St. Andrew's Day, to Epiphany on 6 January, popular celebration was shot through with what British ethnographer Clement Miles in 1912 called "pagan survivals." In rural areas, elves and spirits visited village farmyards on Christmas Eve, animals spoke, and young girls dropped molten lead into water to predict their future marriage partners.[4] In towns and cities, burghers and artisans celebrated with carnivalesque parades, mumming, and charivaris, fueled by profligate drinking and feasting. At court, New Year's Eve dominated the cycle of early-winter feasts and parties; aristocrats and courtiers exchanged small presents as tokens of admiration and friendship.

Though local practices persisted well into the twentieth century, particularly in rural areas, the diversity of popular celebration slowly gave way before a great wave of cultural innovation. "German Christmas" became more singular, standardized, domesticated, and sentimental, as its now-familiar features spread out from the households of the Bildungsbürgertum in a complicated process of cultural transmission. During the long nineteenth century, the modern holiday moved indoors and adopted a tamer set of rituals, embodied in the new symbols of the Christmas tree and the Weihnachtsmann (Father Christmas). The emotional charge of sacred observance was transferred to sentimental feelings of family love. Rowdy public rituals of overindulgence became private family feasts. Aristocratic gifts of sociability turned into tokens of affection between middle-class husbands, wives, and children. The result was a reinvented celebration that turned on sensory pleasure and emotional depth—the hallmarks of a modern, expressive individual at home in "a self-enclosed family of feeling."[5] Once a year, family members became the central players in private dramas of love and affection as they enacted sentimental scripts of domestic intimacy around the Christmas tree. "Christmas has turned out to be most beautiful," Caroline von Humboldt wrote to her husband. "Oh, only you are missing, dear heart!"[6] It was no mistake that Goethe's Young Werther, in one of the foundational texts of modern Western love, commits suicide on the day before Christmas Eve. The holiday was an emotionally laden celebration of emergent bourgeois lifestyles, and Goethe's novella introduced a generation of German readers to its rituals and meaning.[7]

German speakers seemed to have a special aptitude for Christmas. By the middle of the nineteenth century, locals and foreigners alike believed that the German holiday was a "ritual of Gemütlichkeit," or domestic comfort and coziness, and that Gemütlichkeit itself was a character trait that was typically German.[8] Observers began to speak of a special German Christmas mood, the Weihnachtsstimmung, an enthusiastic display of affection and happiness, piety and reverence, surprise and gratitude. The mood was encoded in a set of holiday scripts—a body of Christmas stories by famous authors like Goethe, Friedrich Schleiermacher, and E. T. A. Hoffmann, which all stressed the intense feelings of "paradisical joy" and *Innerlichkeit*, or inwardness, that enveloped the family on Christmas Eve. These classic texts were joined by a profuse number of less-famous Christmas stories written by a veritable army of churchmen, teachers, and children's authors. According to this ever-growing prescriptive literature, Christmas was supposed to be profound; yet it was also sentimental, an exaggerated celebration of middle-class family feeling. Personal diaries, memoirs, and letters suggest that Germans tried to act the part. Christmas Eve was "the most beautiful time of every year," remembered Friedrich von Bodelschwingh in a typical comment about his childhood in the early 1880s. The sight of the decorated tree evoked "deep amazement" and brought his family to "the threshold of paradise."[9]

These family performances were richly productive. Holiday observances shaped and expressed ideas about the boundaries between public and private lives, social status, confessional difference, regional particularities, and national solidarities. When Germans gathered around the Christmas tree in the nineteenth century, they envisioned themselves members of a society built on shared values and traditions. The family Christmas literature read by the middle classes portrayed celebration as a moment of national incorporation in which the rich joined the poor in a harmonious yet hierarchical civic community. If this remained an imaginary—and quite bourgeois—resolution to all manner of stubborn social antagonisms, the holiday nonetheless became a powerful symbol of the nation united. In this way, the holiday helped transform differentiated social groups based on estates and local allegiances into a middle-class "national citizenry."[10]

The publication of Professor Hugo Elm's finely wrought *Goldene Weihnachtsbuch* (*Golden Christmas Book*) in 1878, seven years after German unification, testified to the consolidation of national Christmas customs. In Elm's hands, the now resolutely German holiday was inseparably linked to visions of faith, family, Volk, and fatherland—all portrayed with sentimental sympathy on the book's cover (see Figure 1.1). "Under all corners of heaven, this consecrated, Holy Night will be celebrated with the same feelings," Elm wrote. "The German-Christian customs, closely attached to this marvelous festival, will conquer hearts everywhere and after their introduction will captivate everyone with their particular tenderness."[11] Elm was hardly alone. A generation of theologians and ethnographers reported that a specifically German Christmas combined the winter solstice rituals of Nordic tribes with the solemn pieties of Christian observance, evidence of the deep historical roots of the national Volk. Christmas songs, stories, decorations, foods, and gifts became symbols of a uniquely German identity, and by 1900 the holiday was arguably Germany's most successful national celebration.

The construction of universal Germanness around the Christmas tree was a contested project. The holiday drew much of its charge from its ability to combine the sacred and the secular, and its history across the nineteenth century was deeply entangled in the religious conflicts of the period. From the start, Christmas evolved out of a culture of reform Protestantism, which emphasized family intimacy and forged new links between piety and bourgeois domesticity; it was no mistake that the Luther Bible became German national literature, and Luther's translation of Luke's verses became the Christmas story for millions of Germans.[12] The Christmas tree, the Weihnachtsmann, even opening presents on Christmas Eve—these mainstream features of "German" Christmas had a distinct Protestant cast, and Catholic clergymen responded by repeatedly calling on parishioners to remain faithful to the holiday traditions of the true church. At the same time, Christmas anchored a national Christian culture that could include Catholics as well as Protestants; unlike German Jews or supposedly atheistic socialists, clergy and laity in both Christian denominations celebrated the birth of Christ. In the ongoing project of making Germans, Catholics could use Christmas to claim a place in the Christian nation—even as they struggled to come to terms with the predominantly Protestant national culture.[13] The growth of a mass consumer culture further blurred religious differences. The new material goods sold in national markets could reinforce denominational separatism, but they also proved conducive to the construction of a cult of domestic piety enjoyed by Catholics and Protestants alike.

Despite confessional tensions, contemporaries repeatedly claimed that the German Christmas celebrated social and national unity. The emergence of a shared culture of sentimentalism and domestic piety, embedded in family ritual and material culture, suggests that they were at least partially correct.

INVENTING THE CHRISTMAS MOOD

Buffeted by the Napoleonic Wars and the Revolutions of 1848, Germans experienced the first half of the nineteenth century as a period of crisis and transition, driven by territorial reorganization, political reaction and reform, and protoindustrialization. The Biedermeier years also witnessed the "awakening of the bourgeois world," as German families experimented with changing notions of parenting, familial affections, and gendered separate spheres.[14] The corresponding reinvention of Christmas as a family holiday drew sustenance from and helped fashion these private values and structures. A burst of popular creativity reworked existing holiday observances, producing new family rituals and classic carols like "Silent Night" (1818), "O How Joyfully" (1819), and "Oh Christmas Tree" (1826)—the latter being the first song to mention this now-indispensable decoration.[15]

The early nineteenth century also brought intense emotional innovation. This "was the golden age of private life," writes historian Michelle Perrot, "a time when the vocabulary and reality of private life took shape."[16] Gathered around the Christmas tree, German families affirmed ordinary life and all its pleasures. Family observances domesticated notions of Christian morality and charity and celebrated the ideal of a free and expressive individual, whose ability to access and articulate emotional depths came to define the very essence of humanity.[17] The ability to share such feelings and activities—to be a self in this newly formed emotional community—was at first limited to an elite stratum of the educated and, for the most part, Protestant bourgeoisie. As early as the 1850s, however, commentators asserted that the Christmas mood was universal, at least in German-speaking central Europe. As a bourgeois editorialist proclaimed in December 1844, Christmas turned the German lands into the *Heimath der Innigkeit und Gemüthlichkeit* (*sic*), the homeland of inwardness and coziness.[18]

How can we account for this rapid cultural transfusion? Two widely read texts from the first decades of the nineteenth century—Friedrich Schleiermacher's *The Christmas Celebration: A Conversation* (1806) and E. T. A. Hoffmann's *The Nutcracker and the Mouse King* (1816)—allow one to unpack, as it were, the constituent elements of the Christmas mood. In *The Christmas Celebration*, Schleiermacher used the holiday as a setting to explore the interpenetration of faith, piety, and family life. His move to locate the sacred in everyday life and love rather than in formal ritual or liturgy, expressed with some subtlety in the book, reinvigorated Protestantism in the first decades of the nineteenth century and informed the *Kulturprotestantismus*, or cultural Protestantism, of the nineteenth century.[19] Hoffmann's famous romantic fairy tale, on the other hand, contains an early and in-depth description of the family rituals that would become increasingly widespread in the years to come. Hoffmann's evocative prose captures the intense emotional excitement generated by family festivities and reveals the way Christmas made space for the play of the senses. Taken together, these classic Christmas stories show one way that the intertwined feelings of piety and intimacy were woven into the Christmas mood. *The Christmas Celebration* and *The Nutcracker* furthermore suggest that the hallmarks of what later observers would label "a good German Christmas" took shape in a specific social strata. Schleiermacher and Hoffmann were both educated cosmopolitans, living in the Prussian and Protestant territories of Berlin-Brandenburg. Though the feelings and rituals they described became popular across region, class, and confession over the course of the long nineteenth century, they never lost the specific marks of their milieu-based origins.

In 1806, when *The Christmas Celebration* appeared, the thirty-eight-year-old Schleiermacher was already one of the leading Protestant intellectuals of his time. Trained as a theologian, philosopher, and classicist, Schleiermacher had studied at the University of Halle; worked as a chaplain and pastor in Berlin, Halle, and Stolpe; and written books on religion, ethics, and church-state relations. His circle of acquaintances included Goethe and the Humboldts, and by his death at age sixty-five, he had produced an extensive body of work that cemented his reputation as a central figure in the evolution of modern Protestant theology.

Schleiermacher's Christmas novella presented contemporary readers with a "conversation" or dialogue in which the characters—enlightened bourgeois intellectuals comfortable in a salon-style atmosphere—debate the meaning of the birth of Jesus. The conversation takes place among family and friends gathered to celebrate Christmas Eve in the home of Eduard and Ernestine, and it repeatedly underscores the importance of Christmas as a celebration of Christ, whose birth turned the word of God into flesh and promised human redemption. Yet Schleiermacher's great contribution to modern theology was to move this familiar catechism beyond the boundaries of formal Christian observance. For Schleiermacher, the love expressed between spouses and between parents and children was sacred, and Christmas demonstrated this with heightened clarity and force. The novella was, in the end, didactic. Schleiermacher wanted his readers to rejoice in the realization of faith, to celebrate family values and private life, and to speak openly about the deep feelings of love and piety and the sublime mood evoked by the holiday's festivities. The novella thus offered readers a condensed and accessible version of Schleiermacher's enlightened theology. It furthermore testifies to the close connections between reformist Protestant theology and more secular ideas about modern individualism.[20]

Schleiermacher's description of the holiday rituals celebrated by his characters is somewhat underdeveloped and serves primarily as a backdrop for theological debate. It nonetheless includes telling insights into the Christmas festivities of the German-speaking Bildungsbürgertum on the cusp of the nineteenth century. The text presents a holiday in flux. Remnants of aristocratic gifting rituals at year's end combine with elements of the family celebration that would come to define Christmas in the following decades. Christmas Eve brings together the nuclear family but also friends and familiars, revealing the persistence of salon sociability. Ernestine, the presiding motherly spirit of the house, has secretly hidden the gifts brought by the guests in a richly decorated parlor. The room does not include a Christmas tree, but Ernestine has installed other fine decorations, including flowers and special lanterns. She paid particular attention to the presentation of the gifts, which she surrounded with ivy, myrtle, and amaranths, as well as fine linens and colorful textiles. At a signal from Ernestine, the invitees enter the room, express gratitude for her preparations, and open their presents (27–29). Later in the evening, a roving group of acquaintances stop in for a brief visit. In an already tamed version of Early Modern mumming parades, they play the role of *Weihnachtsknechte*, Christmas trolls who quiz the children on their behavior and hand out treats as rewards (68).

These good-spirited festivities frame a series of six dialogues, in which Schleiermacher champions the piety of everyday life over dogmatic expressions of faith.[21] First, the three adult women tell Christmas stories from their own lives, centered on the spiritual love engendered by the bonds between mother and child. After these intimate narratives, the three men engage in a more formal, intellectual debate on the theological meaning of the holiday. Here, Schleiermacher gives a sympathetic hearing to Leonhardt, who represents the secular voice of the Enlightenment and challenges the veracity of biblical accounts of the life of Jesus. In a lucid appraisal of the power of ritual, Leonhardt maintains that in a world without religious certainties, festive practices are the only way to preserve a sense of popular faith (71–75). The following speakers likewise do not make a case for the historical accuracy of the Bible. As the family patriarch, Eduard clinches the argument, stating that the object of Christmas is not to revere any particular, actual child but rather to appreciate the mystical gospel of John, which, he admits, "lacks almost entirely any historical reference." For Eduard, Christmas nonetheless means recognizing "the word become flesh, which was God and is with God." He continues to develop the argument, suggesting that "the flesh . . . is nothing but finite, limited, sensible nature" and that "the word to the contrary is the idea, apprehension." In short, Eduard suggests that the idea of the word becoming flesh refers to the moment when each individual recognizes the presence of God in nature and in humanity. "What we celebrate," he concludes, "is nothing other than our selves, as we are in total, or human nature, or however you would otherwise like to name it, accepted and recognized from the Godly principle of the divine."[22]

As Schleiermacher later wrote in *The Christian Faith* (1821), the religious impulse had a psychological basis, closely related to the "tendency of the human mind in general to give rise to religious emotions."[23] This was a founding idea in his enlightened theology, and indeed, much of the Christmas novella explores the way love, marriage, and childbirth naturally evoke a sense of faith. For German Protestants, understanding family relationships as a reflection of the sacred was not new. Historian Lyndal Roper has shown that the Reformation brought with it a new theology of gender, anchored in a patriarchal "household moralism" that reinforced rigid gender hierarchies in marriage and the family.[24]

Schleiermacher hardly mounted a critique of Christian patriarchy or the idea of distinctly separate spheres for men and women. He nonetheless revised the household moralism of the Early Modern period in ways that reinforced the values of the emergent bourgeois family life, and women were central to his reformist vision. In the words of one his characters, women perform the "holy service" of child rearing and "dwell within the temple, vestals watching over the sacred fire." Men, by contrast, "venture out into the world . . . practicing discipline or preaching penance" (37). Because women were more childlike than men, they are more able to experience religious joy; the stories told by the three women are simple tales about mothers and children during the Christmas season, but they are unabashedly spiritual. "A mother's love is what is eternal in us," remarks one of the women. "It is the fundamental chord of our being" (48). As Ernestine explains, "even when [women], in our own way, come to an understanding of God and of the world, we tend to express our most sublime, most tender feelings over and over again in those same trifles and with that same gentle demeanor which put us on friendly terms with the world in our childhood days" (55). Women (and indeed children) were no longer silent, secondary members of a male-dominated household; they were active partners in companionate relationships with a central and indispensable role in family and spiritual life.[25]

The natural exuberance of the love between mother and child exemplified for Schleiermacher the very real presence of God's love for humanity, and he drew explicit parallels between Mary and Jesus and the bourgeois mother-child relationship. Contemplating her model Nativity scene, Sophie, the precocious eldest daughter, muses: "Mother, you might just as well be the mother of the sacred baby . . . is this why women wish to give birth to sons?" (33). The adults take these ideas most seriously. "Her few words have fairly transported me just now," states Ernestine, Sophie's mother, pondering the rapturous feelings evoked by her daughter's statement. "[Sophie's] heart opened up like an angel's, so marvelous and pure, [and] in her feeling there was such a deep and basic understanding, expressed in such a simple, spontaneous way. . . . In a way I feel she did not say too much when she thought that I might well be the mother of the blessed child. For I can in all humility honor the pure revelation of the divine in my daughter, as Mary did in her son, without in the least disturbing the proper relation of mother to child" (36). For Schleiermacher, the joy of the bond between mother and child—unmitigated, transparent, pure, and unironic—expressed the deepest possible level of human happiness and revealed the divinity of God.

The tender observances of the family holiday gave adults a way to recover a childlike sense of wonder and receptivity and thus allowed them to feel the connections between the sacred and the secular. "The mood which our festival is meant to incite is joy," asserts one of the men. "That this mood is very widely and vividly aroused through the Christmas festival is so obvious that nothing more need be said on that score" (77). The custom of giving gifts was a spiritual act, according to Eduard, because "the great gift in which we all rejoice together is reflected in our lesser gifts; and the more this whole mood stands out, the more strikingly is our awareness affected by it" (45). Family singing and music were crucial for the construction of this vision of domestic bliss. Musical performances punctuate the evening's events, and the carols sung in the intimate circle on Christmas Eve "inspired as always . . . a quiet contentment and inner satisfaction" (34). Indeed, the closing words in *The Christmas Celebration*, spoken by Josef, an eagerly awaited guest who joins the party only at the very end of the novella, refer to the sensory and sacred pleasures of music. "Come, then, and above all bring the child if she is not yet asleep, and let me see your glories, and let us be glad and sing something pious and joyful" (*Frommes und Fröliches*), he announces to the company (86).

The Christmas mood was divine, Schleiermacher makes clear, though his conception of divinity moved away from traditional understandings of faith. His celebrants reject the ritual of Communion and hardly see a formal Christmas service as the locus of the sacred; the family speaks of attending mass on Christmas Day, but as Leonhard observes, "piety . . . must be an inward thing" (41). Catholic practice is accordingly cast as excessive and consistently denigrated as external, shallow, and overly ritualistic (41, 71–72). In comparison, Eduard's bold assertion that "what we celebrate is nothing other than our selves" underscores the reformist, even revolutionary aspects of this work. *The Christmas Celebration* was a primer for the modernization of piety. Following historian Lucian Hölscher, Protestant devotional culture after the Enlightenment was increasingly characterized by "the individualization of belief," which stressed individual faith and "subjective truthfulness" rather than "objective religious truth" and formal liturgical observance. While this stance was still limited primarily to educated, bourgeois Protestants in the early nineteenth century—individualizing tendencies were much less prevalent among Catholics—such ideas would increasingly define popular religious attitudes in the following decades.[26]

Modern piety was more inward, more personal—and more national. While Schleiermacher makes no overt reference in the Christmas novella to the idea that the holiday was somehow uniquely German, his larger work clearly supported the idea that Germans were specially marked for religious revival. "Here in my ancestral land is the fortunate climate that denies no fruit completely," he had written in *On Religion* (1799). "Here, therefore, [Christianity] must find a refuge from the coarse barbarism and the cold earthly sense of the age."[27]

E. T. A. Hoffmann's *The Nutcracker and the Mouse King* embedded the emotional intensity described by theologians like Schleiermacher in a secularized culture of domestic ritual. *The Nutcracker* is essential in many ways, not least because it includes a thorough description of what became the typical family celebration in modern Germany. This product of Berlin salon culture from 1816, reprinted in countless anthologies and turned into a ballet by Tchaikovsky in 1892, marked a key moment in the development of Christmas and, moreover, in the history of the senses and emotions. Hoffmann's fairy tale foreshadowed the way the relatively austere emotional styles of the Biedermeier period would give way to the sentimental family intimacies of the late nineteenth-century middle classes. *The Nutcracker* located the obsessions of the German Romantics in the nascent middle-class family parlor: nostalgic yearnings for a magical but vanished childhood, obsession with the hidden but intense realm of the senses, longings for romantic love and friendship, absorption in a mystical and sensuous appreciation of nature. Authors like Hoffmann, Achim von Arnim, and Ludwig Tieck—participants in Berlin salon culture—and neo-Romantics such as Adalbert Stifter and Theodor Storm later in the century all used the holiday as a literary setting. Their stories became canonical Christmas texts, which taught generations of readers about the sensory delights and special inwardness that awaited them under the German Christmas tree.[28]

The action in *The Nutcracker* takes place on Christmas Eve in the household of a wealthy Prussian state physician. The adults have decorated a majestic Christmas tree in secret and surrounded it with toys, and their children, Marie and Fritz, wait impatiently for their gifts—they are only allowed to enter the so-called Christmas room and see the tree and presents at the penultimate moment. The elaborate scene captures the tender feelings that bond parents and children, as well as the special sensory environment created by the aural and visual frames of the holiday: "At that moment a crystal-clear tone rang out: klingling, klingling, the doors burst open, and such a glow beamed out from the large room, that the children, with a loud cry of 'Oh! Oh!' stood still as if frozen on the threshold. But papa and mama entered through the doors, took the children by the hand, and said 'just come along, just come along, dear children, and see what the Holy Christ has given you.'" In the room they see a "huge fir tree" decorated with golden and silver apples, candies, and "most beautiful of all . . . hundreds of little candles [that] twinkled like stars in its dark branches." Around the tree lay wonderful toys: animals and soldiers for Fritz; dolls and, of course, the Nutcracker for Marie.[29] This Christmas Eve ritual encapsulates the essential elements of the German family Christmas. With minor variations, it is still celebrated like this today.

The complicated fairy tale that follows describes Marie's successful intercession in the war between the armies of the Nutcracker and the Mouse King. As the main character, Marie engages in a secret process of self-realization. She overcomes frightening and, indeed, life-threatening challenges without the aid of adults. The various scenes—the hard-fought battles, the spells placed on Drosselmeyer and the Nutcracker, the search for the "hard nut" Krakatuk and the man who has never shaved or worn boots, the command to walk seven steps backward from the beautiful princess Pirlipat without turning around—demonstrate Hoffmann's ability to effectively combine folk tales, classical mythology, and Old Testament tests of faith in a convincing if somewhat complicated story. On another level, Hoffmann gives a frightening if fanciful reading of the Napoleonic Wars, in which the forces of good triumph in the end, but only after great trials. The idea of mythic combat, Prussian arms, and victory were subtly layered into the story and, by extension, the Christmas mood itself.

The scenes of delight and joy described by Hoffmann reveal much about the way the Christmas mood legitimized nascent ideas about bourgeois domesticity and familial affection. Christmas was not the only moment for what historian John Gillis calls the "ritualization of middle-class family life." Weddings, funerals, birthdays—even daily events like crossing the threshold after work or sitting down to dinner in the evening—were evocative events that affirmed the feelings and lifestyles of the middle classes.[30] Christmas, however, stands out as the high point of the ritual cycle. The holiday's rigidly scripted and evocative set of observances cast men, women, and children in specific roles that recapitulated their place in family hierarchies. Mothers cooked and decorated the home, fathers controlled the ritual action, children voiced ardent enthusiasm and obedient gratitude. In short, the family gathered around the Christmas tree in an exaggerated demonstration of love and harmony and a show of proper age and gender roles.

Historian Gunilla-Friederike Budde has convincingly shown that bourgeois family life was emotionally cold in the nineteenth century and that the closeness described by writers like Hoffmann may have masked a lack of true feeling among family members. Wealthy parents had relatively little contact with their children; nannies, tutors, and domestic servants provided most child care; and men and women spent much of their time apart in homosocial separate spheres. The energy and money that went into preparing gifts helped atone for the affection that went lacking the rest of the year, and the excessive expression of intimacy during the holiday season, according to Budde, made the distance of everyday family relationships more palatable.[31]

Bourgeois family customs like those described in *The Nutcracker* taught children the pleasures of duty and delayed gratification. Gift bringers like Father Christmas or St. Nicholas and his minions, after all, rewarded good children and punished the bad. As Hoffmann noted, Marie and Fritz must have been "especially well behaved and pious the entire year," since they had received such wondrous gifts.[32] Children typically had to wait for hours outside the Christmas room and were often compelled to sing a song or recite a memorized Bible verse before opening their presents. Part of the appeal of Christmas Eve was the pleasure of this controlled performance, both for parents, who prepared the minute rituals of subjection, and for "good" children, who received rewards after passing the test. Even in *The Nutcracker*, certainly a story pitched at youths, Marie can only triumph after she demonstrates discipline and moral probity. She breaks the evil spell when she swears to marry the Nutcracker, despite his ugliness; only true love frees the Nutcracker from the tragedy of his enchanted disfigurement. The resolution confirmed the middle-class cult of love as well as the bourgeois-Protestant ethic of sacrifice in the moment for the larger good to come. The toys children found around the tree, as historian David Hamlin suggests, taught the values associated with a modern consumerist ethos to "posttraditional individuals." The cycles of desire and deference elicited by toys and play, Hamlin writes, "naturalized the utilitarian values of self-assertion, self-control, and the domination of nature and the environment."[33] A dialectic of renunciation and reward helped children develop the modern individuality required for success in the emotional economy of industrial capitalism, in which a satisfying rush of material acquisition (and, with luck, love and marriage) follows a period of goodness, discipline, and hard work.

The Christmas mood offered far more than compensation for the relative coldness of bourgeois familial affection or training for participation in a capitalist exchange economy. Because of its emotional charge, associations with faith and family intimacy, and central role in the annual cycle of passing time, Christmas became a core element in the historicization of family life. In the stable space of the bourgeois home, the holiday helped family members recall the past and anticipate the future. Christmas (and other domestic rituals) thus reshaped the eighteenth-century household, where inhabitants shared space with nonrelated people and experienced time in the moment. In John Gillis's words, "life flowed through the [Early Modern] house, but it was not yet the special place of beginnings and endings that it would later be imagined to be" by the nineteenth-century middle classes.[34] As adult time was divided from childhood, nostalgia for a personal past of innocence and youth, embodied in exemplary experience of a "real Christmas," increased. Seen in longer historical continuities, open displays of feeling around the Christmas tree helped define the boundaries between the ideals of love espoused by the emerging middle classes and the courtship practices of the supposedly primitive peasantry or the decadent aristocracy. In a time when marriage based on affection was still relatively experimental and practiced by a small elite, celebration crystallized codes of intimacy and strengthened this novel and inherently uncertain relationship. The convincing performance of holiday rituals offered a source of instant recognition for others who shared the same values and allegiances, and, as Charles Taylor argued, such practices led to a "new understanding of marriage [that] naturally goes along with further individualization and internalization."[35]

The emotional commitment to spouse and children was inseparable from a new appreciation of the senses. In numerous accounts, Christmas gave celebrants access to their innermost feelings, and it would be a mistake to trivialize the way carols or the sight of candles on the tree evoked family love and the mysteries of inwardness, whether secular or sacred. Hoffman's *Nutcracker* again showed the way. Tender descriptions of the sights, sounds, and scents of the holiday dominate the climax of the story, in which the Nutcracker takes Marie on a tour of his magic empire. She looks on in awe as the "sweetest scent wafted over from a wonderful forest. . . . In the dark leaves it glowed and glittered so brightly that one could clearly see how gold and silver fruits hung down from brightly colored stems, and trunks and branches were decorated with ribbons and bouquets of flowers . . . and when the orange-scent wafted through on the soft breeze, it rustled through the twigs and leaves and the gold leaf jingled and jangled, it rang out like joyous music, to which the twinkling little lights had to jump and dance."[36] Marie's dreamscape of color and sound is a heightened description of the decorated family room, with the fragrant Christmas tree at its center. Indeed the oft-recalled *Duft* or aroma of the Tannenbaum signaled a new bourgeois appreciation of the olfactory. As Alain Corbain suggested, such scents were "perfumes of intimacy" that defined the hygienic delicacy of the bourgeois-feminine private sphere.[37] Aromas were of course only one aspect of a new appreciation of the senses and emotions described by writers like Hoffmann and Schleiermacher: the Christmas mood opened individuals to a range of new experiences and led to reveries of faith, affection, and wonder that played on the depths of the soul.

In the early nineteenth century, the ability to speak of such senses and emotions—and indeed to observe an indoor holiday with all its trappings—marked out distinct boundaries of class and confession. Christmas in its modern form was in many ways an elite Protestant invention, yet Catholic reformers shared an interest in the way attention to the senses opened new realms of spirituality. The emerging Ultramontane movement, which stressed liturgical discipline and obedience to the pope and revitalized popular Catholicism, was driven by a turn to sentiment and the emotions.[38] Like their Protestant coconfessionalists, Catholic theologians fostered the notion that Christmas was an emotive high point in the cycle of Christian celebration and indeed in the individual's relationship to the divine. For Catholics, however, piety would be realized in a holiday service under institutional guidance, not at home, and in the embrace of the collective spiritual community, not on an individual basis.

The insistence on the leading role of Catholic institutions could be somewhat defensive, foreshadowing the great confessional debates over Christmas that emerged later in the century. As Catholic revivalist Marcus Adam Nickel put it in his 1834 multivolume book on the history and observance of Catholic celebration, Christmas was "the most joyful of Church holidays." Yet it was specifically "our Catholic church . . . in its deep, profound wisdom" that embodied the holiday's highest spiritual qualities. A prolific author and spiritual adviser and regent at the Catholic seminary in Mainz, Nickel placed liturgy, official ritual, and prayer at the center of the Christmas mood. "Great and wonderful is our Catholic church in its liturgical appearance," he insisted. "In its songs of praise, it is able to collect all the heavenly impressions, which Christmas must impress upon us." His text included material clergymen could adapt for use in holiday sermons, and its repetitive and evocative cadences were clearly meant to transport parishioners into the raptures of the sacred. When Nickel explained that "the Church lays the word in the mouth and the sigh in the heart, in the prayer for sacrifice, in silent prayer, in communion and with the same word, prayer, and sigh, and so brings true Christmas joy" and that "the Christian heart in glowing heated desire perceives the longing for the appearance of the Lord, for his mercy and his spiritual Christmas gift," he was not only rehearsing the codified language of liturgy. Nickel's fervor expressed an emotional transformation in the practice of faith that crossed sectarian divides.[39]

As the nineteenth century unfolded, the language of the senses and emotions penetrated private accounts of the holiday. The German Bourgeoisie increasingly used Christmas as a way to speak of love and joy and to anchor the self in a stream of domestic time that stretched from childhood to old age and included close family and friends. Aristocrat Hedwig von Olfers's letters from the 1820s include extensive descriptions of the "tremendous jubilation" of celebration. "How sweet it is," she wrote her friend, "as father and mother stand together by the Christmas tree."[40] Personal accounts repeatedly brought together the familial and the spiritual. "I will never forget the way I stood trembling and breathless with expectation with my brothers and sisters outside the door of the mysterious room," remembered a resident of Meschede, in Westphalia, of his childhood holiday in the 1830s. "How the little bell chimed, and how we went in with immeasurable and unclouded delight, as only a child's heart can feel, with a show of pleasure as if paradise itself had appeared before us."[41] The young Jenny von Droste-Hülshoff included a drawing of her family Christmas in 1833 in her private sketchbook, an act of family commemoration that would become increasingly common in upper- and middle-class circles. The childish sketch, set at the moment the children enter the Christmas room, reveals the classic decorations and the gendered nature of children's toys. The setting appears modest, but the Hülshoff's were wealthy, well-established nobility with a Romantic bent—precisely the type who found the new holiday appealing (Figure 1.2).

When rituals failed, the contrast between expectations and reality could evoke nostalgic melancholy and even overwhelming sadness. Wilhelm von Kügelgen, a court painter in the principality of Anhalt-Bernburg, lamented

FIGURE I.2
Christmas Eve with the von Droste-Hülshoff family,
from the sketchbook of Jenny von Droste-Hülshoff, 1833.
(Courtesy of the Droste-Hülshoff private family archive)

in a letter to his brother in 1845: "For me Christmas is always a difficult time
... there are so many memories associated with Christmas." When his daughter Bertha died in 1853, he wrote to his brother that "the holiday was so in-
describably melancholy" that the usual observances seemed empty. "I was
so powerfully overcome by anguish that I had to go out, and for us all a veil
hung over the joy."[42] Whether marked by death and sadness or the beauty
and joy more typical of such recollections, personal diaries and correspondence described annual celebrations as special, emotional peaks in family life.
As the household became a home, with its historical biography of personal
relationships, Germans told Christmas stories about the most intimate aspects of their inner selves.

The reinvention of Christmas in the early nineteenth century was a
transatlantic event that revealed the cultural work of national awakening.

German-speaking central Europe, Britain, the Scandinavian countries, and the United States—predominantly Protestant lands—developed distinctive yet cosmopolitan celebratory forms that crossed borders in mutually sustaining encounters. Washington Irving's account of British Christmas in "Bracebridge Hall," published in the United States around 1820, was a popular success that brought together Old World and New World rituals; Charles Dickens's *A Christmas Carol* was immediately translated into German upon its publication in 1843. German customs were particularly successful in the international marketplace for holiday goods, texts, and feelings. The "German" Christmas tree and its associated rituals was an export product. In Britain, Prince Albert brought the first tree to the royal court in 1840, even as Protestant families from Alsace introduced the custom to France.[43] The most remarkable example of the international success of German Christmas was its export to the United States in the 1830s and 1840s. A group of upper-middle-class reformers living in New England, including Unitarians Harriet Martineau and Catherine Sedgwick, wrote warm, firsthand accounts of and descriptive stories about German Christmas celebrations. Along with cookbooks and magazines like *Godey's*, *Sartain's*, and *Peterson's*, their work helped popularize the German holiday in the United States and left a lasting impact on American observances.[44]

Protestant reformer and child-friendly philanthropist Charles Loring Brace summed up the American fascination with German Christmas in his travelogue *Home-Life in Germany*, published in 1853. An invitation to spend "Christmas Eve in the German fatherland" with a family in Berlin gave Brace privileged insight into native customs. He carefully described the evening's festivities, including the children's suspenseful wait outside the Christmas room, the tree "blazing with lights, gilt, and tinsel," and the fun of opening presents. At the end of the "games and various quiet amusements," he wrote, the mother "sat down to the piano, and all the little ones were made quiet, and the whole family sung one of those sweetest of old German hymns, speaking of His patient goodness—of their own unworthiness, and the gratitude which they all for ever will owe to him." What most surprised Brace was the "half-solemnity of the evening—the almost subdued happiness [of the] merrymaking." He tried to divine the source of this unique mood. The Berliners were joyful not "because it is a 'duty to be cheerful' [or] because a family gathering is a very beautiful and desirable thing," Brace surmised. "They are cheerful because they cannot help it, and because they all love one another." German behavior held valuable lessons for an American audience. The "open and unconscious affection [was] very beautiful to see" and called attention to the "selfishness and coldness in families" in the United States, where "materialism" and "hankering after pleasures" undermined civic life.[45] Brace's romanticized vision nicely summarizes the basic aspects of the Christmas mood at midcentury: an inward character driven by the sensory frames of the holiday, an open expression of family love that was both joyful and solemn, and a combination of piety and playfulness that was distinctly German.

THE SACRED AND THE SENTIMENTAL

Observers like Charles Loring Brace insisted that a well-defined German Christmas had a "hold . . . on the whole population [in] the Fatherland."[46] In fact, Brace misread a celebration that took place in a specific bourgeois, urban, and Protestant milieu as representative of the whole. In so doing, he overlooked the great diversity of holiday customs and observances that existed in the nineteenth-century German states. Certainly Germans liked to celebrate Christmas. But regional, class, and confessional identities played an important role in determining what they actually did during the holiday season; the variations in regional observance are so broad that their description fills volumes.[47] The diffusion and consolidation of what would become the standard holiday was a lengthy and conflicted process that suppressed alternative forms of revelry and, in the end, testified to the ascendance of Prussian, Protestant culture in a unified Germany.

The history of the Christmas tree is a case in point. Even the broad vocabulary nineteenth-century Germans used to describe the tree reveals its diverse roots and symbolic malleability. Though confessional terminology was never strictly bounded, by the century's end, Protestant celebrants might open gifts around a Weihnachtsbaum or Tannenbaum (Christmas tree or fir tree), the labels most used today. Catholics, if they had a tree instead of the church-approved crèche, favored a more pious terminology that included *Christbaum, Lichterbaum,* or even *Lebensbaum* (tree of Christ, light, and life, respectively; these terms were also used by pious Protestants). The establishment of the Christmas tree as the central symbol of German celebration had no obvious historical trajectory. Rather, the custom emerged out of divergent and dispersed practices, which in Early Modern central Europe included the use of indoor greenery to celebrate the various December festivals that marked the end of the harvest season.[48]

From the start, however, the tree had important links to Protestant popular culture. A chronicle from Strasbourg, written in 1604 and widely seen as the first account of a Christmas tree in German-speaking lands, records that Protestant artisans brought fir trees into their homes in the holiday season and decorated them with "roses made of colored paper, apples, wafers, tinsel, sweetmeats etc." After reciting verses memorized from the Bible, according to the chronicler, children received "one, two, three, or four pennies, and sometimes a small book." An early attempt to keep Christ in Christmas followed in 1657, when Strasbourg clergyman and Protestant theologian Johann Konrad Dannhauer angrily condemned the practice in his book *The Milk of the Catechism*. "Among the other trifles with which they commemorate Christmastime, often overtaking the word of God or holy observances, is the Christmas, or fir tree," Dannhauer fumed. "It would be much better to direct the children towards the spiritual cedar tree of Jesus Christ."[49] Claims that Martin Luther himself invented the Christmas tree, after a Christmas Eve walk in a snowy woods with his children, are apocryphal. A much-reproduced 1856 engraving of Luther and his family singing songs around a decorated tree was a historicist fantasy; it nonetheless helped popularize the tree in Protestant households.[50]

The Christmas tree spread out in German society from the top down, so to speak. It moved from elite households to broader social strata, from urban to rural areas, from the Protestant north to the Catholic south, and from Prussia to other German states. By the late eighteenth century, the tree was fairly common in the courts of German aristocrats. In the early 1800s, it became a sign of conspicuous display in the salons of the German Bildungsbürgertum. The tree was a rather odd way for the Bürgertum to commemorate the birth of Jesus, but their relatively loose connections to the official Protestant church and familiarity with Enlightenment critiques of organized religion helped make it acceptable.[51] The tree's wider dispersion took decades, as its history in the religiously divided principality of Westphalia shows. In the early nineteenth century, the Protestant officers, officials, and businessmen who moved in after the province was incorporated into Prussia at the Conference of Vienna in 1815 brought the tree with them. (A similar process took place in the East Prussian territories around Danzig.) By the middle of the century, urban merchants, apothecaries, and tavern keepers in Westphalia installed decorated trees to entice customers into their shops, but its spread to rural and Catholic districts proceeded slowly: the tree really penetrated the Catholic countryside only after World War I.[52]

The Franco-Prussian War (1870–71) accelerated the process of the tree's diffusion across the German states. On Christmas Eve 1870, the Prussian officer corps installed decorated trees in the field hospitals, canteens, and living quarters of German troops stationed in France, and stories in the popular press about military celebrations during the Siege of Paris helped popularize this increasingly indispensable and German tradition. Though numerous texts and images placed the tree at the center of German celebration, they remained expensive and relatively rare, even in big cities, until the last decades of the century. In Berlin, for example, wealthy Protestant matron Sophie Pauline Schoepplenberg could still record her delight in her diary when on Christmas Eve 1876 she saw her first Christmas tree at her grandparent's house in Potsdam.[53]

Christmas trees became more broadly popular in the last decades of the century. They embodied the new national feeling in Germany after unification in 1871; at the same time, industrialization and the growth of mass markets made commercially produced trees increasingly available. The tree's sale in the Christmas markets set up in urban centers across the nation depended, after all, on extensive rural tree farms and an efficient rail system. The 1878 publication of University of Halle professor Hugo Elm's *Golden Christmas Book* (Figure 1.1) testified to the arrival of a national market for family Christmas literature and a new, definitive script for German celebration. The tree was central. Elm's meticulous directions for its installation and decoration, and the mail-order advertisements for ornaments and decorations of all types in the book's appendix, underscore the tree's place in mass markets and the national imagination. The tree was still very much a status object for the wealthy middle classes in the late 1870s, as Elm's glowing description makes clear. "A tasteful arrangement of the various decorative objects on the Christmas tree," he advised his readers, "makes a decidedly good impression." A correctly adorned tree included an astonishing variety of homemade and commercial decorations. The "essentials" included apples (hung only on the heaviest limbs of the tree, according to Elm's directions); nuts and pinecones gilded with gold and silver (hung carefully in alternating order, two to three or three to four per branch, depending on its strength); marzipan and chocolate models; orbs and fruits made of blown glass; strips of silver and gold tinsel (*Lametta*); artificial lilies, fuchsias, and roses, with golden ribbons instead of filaments; metal spirals for the tips of branches and a large star for the top;

and a banner proclaiming "Glory to God in the Highest" to drape around the tree's center. At the same time, Elm warned families to avoid an "incomprehensible distribution" of decorations, which threatened to turn "the most bounteous tree into a meaningless collection of curiosities" (*ein nichtssagendes Sammelkurium*).[54] Few families could afford to celebrate in such style, captured by Thomas Mann in the famous Christmas scene in *Buddenbrooks* or by Berlin illustrator Edmund Brüning in his 1888 print *On Christmas Eve*. Brüning's sentimental vision of joy and abundant prosperity, with its robust family, patriotic detail, and snowy Heimat scene—all blessed by a banner announcing the glory of God—epitomizes the late century triumph of a bourgeois, Protestant, and ever-more-nationalist holiday (Figure 1.3).

The history of what Germans call the *Gabenbringer*, or gift bringer, the mythical spirit who visits families and distributes presents in the holiday season, reveals another way the consolidation of national traditions depended on but also depreciated popular, rural, and Catholic customs. The now-familiar Weihnachtsmann, the German version of Santa Claus, was unknown until the middle of the century. Children in German-speaking territories instead faced an awesome array of mysterious holiday characters, archetypal masked "wild men" who walked the streets during the Christmas season. These customs had roots in the topsy-turvy mumming rituals popular in Early Modern festival culture. In December, young men dressed up and paraded through local villages, enticing potential mates, scaring supposedly gullible children, and demanding alms from their social superiors. One of the most popular Gabenbringer was St. Nicholas (a legendary version of the fourth-century bishop of Myra, a canonized saint) who went from house to house on 6 December with miter, pastoral staff, and a bag of gifts for good children. Even this relatively harmless personage was usually assisted by his satanic doppelgänger Knecht Ruprecht, who appeared with a blackened face and goat legs and carried a whip to punish the wayward. In his authoritative *Christmas Ritual and Tradition*, published in 1912, Clement Miles suggested that Germans had a special affinity for beast-men such as "the hideous Klabauf ... a shaggy monster with horns, black face, fiery eyes, long red tongue, and chains that clank as he moves." Regional incarnations of this "horrible attendant," besides Ruprecht and the Klabauf, included Krampus, Pezlnichol, Ru Claus, Ru Paul, Joseph Claus, Claws, Bullerklaas, Pelzmärte, Bellsnichol, and Hans Trapp.[55]

German children first met the Weihnachtsmann, the rather tame relative of these man-beasts, through the auspices of the Munich-based, Romantic

FIGURE 1.3

Edward Brüning, *On Christmas Eve*, from the family magazine
Ueber Land und Meer/Deutsche Illustrirte, December 1888.

artist Moritz von Schwind. His illustrated poem "Herrn Winter," published across Germany and the European continent in 1847 by the popular *Münchener Bilderbogen*, featured a kind and generous gift bringer who bore only passing resemblance to the classic wild men. The growing popularity of the Weihnachtsmann helped move the action indoors and transformed plebian, nocturnal creatures like the Klabauf into characters more palatable for middle-class tastes; the emergence of Santa Claus in the United States followed a similar trajectory.[56]

Things were further complicated in German-speaking territories by the presence of the Christkind, or Christ Child, who also brought children presents during the holiday season. Martin Luther had originally introduced the Holy Christ as Gabenbringer during the Reformation. His attempt to shift the focus of Christmas from 6 to 25 December to commemorate the accepted date of Christ's birth and eradicate the supposedly pagan (and Catholic) influence of St. Nicholas had long-lasting effects. By the late nineteenth century, in popular observance, Luther's ascetic Holy Christ had metamorphosed into the sentimental Christkind. This androgynous being appeared in contemporary illustrations as an angel in the form of a young boy or girl sporting wings, a flowing white gown, and a halo. The Christkind usually brought children gifts, a candle, and/or a Christmas tree. By the 1880s, the Christkind and Weihnachtsmann—both midcentury reincarnations of older, more awesome characters—dominated holiday cards, poems, stories, and songs.[57]

To a certain extent, the choice of gift bringer revealed Germany's denominational differences. The Weihnachtsmann generally visited Protestant children on Christmas Eve in north-central German lands, particularly Prussia. Though the divisions were never hard and fast, St. Nicholas and his minions remained more popular in Catholic and rural regions in southern Germany and Austria. The Christkind, despite his Lutheran roots, was especially popular in Catholic households because of his lingering associations with Jesus. In 1932 the *Atlas of German Ethnography* went so far as to posit a clean division between Protestant northeast Germany, where the Weihnachtsmann reigned, and the Catholic southwest, the domain of the Christkind.[58] The reality was more complex. Around 1900 the same child might tremble at the arrival of St. Nicholas and Krampus on 6 December, write "wish-lists" for the Weihnachtsmann, and pray to the Christkind on Christmas Eve. The standardization of these secular deities and their leakage across confessional and regional boundaries capped a long process of cultural transformation.

Invented national traditions brought a more sentimental face to Early Modern holiday rituals, even as the choice of gift bringers continued to reflect local and religious preferences.

Catholics struggled to preserve their own version of Christmas from Protestant infiltration. Already in 1823 Archduke Johann of Austria complained that a tree decorated "with candles and an entire room full of toys of all kinds" threatened the sanctity of the traditional Nativity scene and disturbed the quiet moments of Christmas Eve prayer mandated by Catholic tradition.[59] By the end of the century, "modern" Christmas observances were generating a chorus of disapproval among conservative Catholic critics. In an 1888 article titled "Protestant Customs among Catholics," the *Pastoral-Blatt*, published by the Bishopric of Münster, warned that the *Verweltlichung* (secularization) of the holiday was "in sharp opposition to the truly Catholic conception of the Christmas festival." According to the *Pastoral-Blatt*, changes in terminology captured the threat. The paper claimed that observances of "so-called Holy Eve," or *heilige Abend*, a term used to describe family celebrations on Christmas Eve, with the tree and visits from the Weihnachtsmann, were undermining recognition of "Holy Night," or *heilige Nacht*, a name associated with the more sober pieties of Catholic observance. Impious family celebrations "suppressed the beautiful St. Nicholas children's holiday" and kept Catholics away from Christmas mass, while the Christmas tree threatened to replace the "the nativity scene, the embodiment of the Christmas mystery."[60] An anonymous diatribe sent by a correspondent to the same monthly paper cited the words of the popular Catholic writer Alban Stolz, who encouraged "all Christian families . . . to devote Christmas day solely to prayer" and to "give no presents and receive none." The "most beautiful and beloved Christian festival," the correspondent wrote, was desecrated by Jews and Christians alike in their search for seasonal profits.[61]

Catholic clergymen engaged in a determined effort to police the popular customs of the Catholic community. As the comments above suggest, they reserved special ire for the Christmas tree, seen as a distinctly Protestant custom that exemplified what one critic called "the modern Christmas swindle."[62] Good Christians, wrote a Catholic reporter in Cologne, knew that a crèche, not the Christmas tree, symbolized the sacrifice of the Virgin Mary and "the eternity of the Jesus child."[63] "The candles alight [on the tree] do not lead to Christ, the light of the world, but rather away from Christ," thundered Münster's *Pastoral-Blatt*, "and one would not be wrong to name them *Irrlichter* [false lights], which lead away from the pure joy of the Catholic festival of Christ into the swamp of folly and pleasure." The solution? "Retain the original Catholic festival of Christmas or return to it anew: namely to pray in one's heart for the new-born Christ child with the means of the Holy Communion, and on Christmas Eve to gather around the confessional" instead of the Christmas tree.[64] Attempts to purify Catholic observance of "modern" tendencies met with dubious success. By the end of the century, the mainstream Catholic press readily acknowledged the national importance and ubiquity of "the wondrous and dear custom of the Christmas tree . . . the most beautiful decoration of the German celebration of Christ."[65]

Catholic leaders repeatedly urged church members to attend Christmas mass to demonstrate their faith, community loyalty, and distance from "modern" Protestantism. The Latin liturgy was not the only difference between sectarian observances, and while it is impossible here to capture the variety of practices from church to church or even within denominations, some main features stand out. Catholic priests usually offered three separate but continuous masses on "Holy Night," and the service was supposed to begin at midnight. Detailed instructions for the proper administration of the service during this extended period of worship—rubrics for decorating the altar, handling the chalice, offering the sacraments, and delivering the sermons themselves—cited congregational precedents from across the century and were meant to ensure that the proceedings followed universal church law.[66] Protestants, likewise, met at night or the early hours of the morning for Christmas worship, and while their holiday celebrations relied on liturgical precedent, pastors had more leeway for organizing the service according to local proclivities. The Catholic mass was hierarchical, regulated by directives from Rome, the bishoprics, and local priests. The Christmas service was, too: the well-defined rituals and use of Latin, meant to remind the laity of the long traditions of the church, positioned parishioners as a passive audience. The Protestant congregation took a more active role in Christmas services, responding in dialogue to the officiating pastor and singing group hymns. The Catholic service likewise relied on dialogue, but this was highly scripted and took place between officiating priests; the laity looked on and rarely spoke. Music was central to both churches, though the Catholic mass relied on a special church choir that usually performed music for, not with, the congregation.[67]

The hymns themselves informed confessional identities. Catholics favored pious songs from the medieval and Early Modern periods, such as "Lo! How a Rose E'er Blooming" or "This My Spirit Exalts the Lord" (*Meine Seele erhebt den Herren*), a translation of a Latin hymn about the Virgin Mary. Unless said hymns bracketed the Christmas sermon, delivered in the vernacular, they were sung in Latin. Protestants could choose from a wider selection of songs, including those written by Martin Luther and his followers. Well-known carols such as "From Heaven Above to Earth I Come," reputedly composed by Luther for his children in 1535, were sung in German. Protestant hymns were meant for "daily use in the Church of God" (Luther) and consciously designed to "Germanize" the service.[68] In both churches, concludes historian Anthony Steinhoff, singing and praying "transformed the assembly of individuals into a community."[69] Much was shared, but God was in the details, as it were, and even minor differences in ritual observance reinforced sectarian identities.

Outside of church, family celebration on both sides of the confessional divide became increasingly commercial and sentimental as the century progressed. Christmas helped develop a culture of faith that was not directly linked to liturgy or formal worship but was sustained instead by the vague pieties of middle-class family ideology and the everyday commodities of a growing consumer culture. Domestic rituals and symbols and mass-marketed holiday goods were not distinctly confessional; they could articulate religious differences but also subsume them in shared cultures of celebration. Nonetheless, the Protestant bourgeoisie more quickly replaced traditional rites and customs, such as regular church attendance, with new semireligious domestic observances, such as Christmas.[70]

The emergence of a new set of family Christmas carols exemplifies the process. The carols written in the first half of the nineteenth century already reinforced a cult of domestic piety in ways that flattened confessional difference. The birth of Jesus is, of course, the focus of "Silent Night," written in Catholic Austria in 1818; the song also highlights the bourgeois idyll of "mother and child" and was Germany's favorite carol in the nineteenth century for both Protestants and Catholics. Other songs omitted religious references altogether. The lyrics for the widely popular "Oh Christmas Tree" (1824), or "Father Christmas Comes Tomorrow" (which focused on toys and gifts, written around 1835), envisioned the beauty of the tree and the joys of receiving gifts and made no mention of the birth of Jesus. These and many other new carols, examples of the Hausmusik beloved by the Protestant bourgeoisie, redefined the sacred. Family performance converted the community choral recitals that punctuated formal church services into private, family sing-alongs—typically accompanied by piano, the very emblem of bourgeois domesticity. Even the most secular songs replicated the liturgical melodies and cadences of the hymnal and inserted them into domestic space. Historian Ingeborg Weber-Kellermann reminds us that when these carols were written, the "family scene" they described was still somewhat rare, at least in practice.[71] Mid-nineteenth-century carols by German-speaking composers nonetheless became indispensable to a specifically national holiday culture: they helped spread the sentimental and semisacred feelings that for contemporaries defined the Christmas mood. By 1900 Christmas music, sacred and secular, embodied the "essence of Germanness," though family carols and Christian hymns could always express religious difference as well as national solidarities.[72]

The impact of national consumer markets and the growing popularity of holiday sentimentalism are further revealed in the pages of the Christmas books (*Weihnachtsbücher*) that became central to late nineteenth-century celebration. Judging from advertisements in contemporary newspapers and journals, books were already favorite presents for young and old alike in the decades following the Napoleonic Wars. But the volumes marketed as "Christmas gifts" in those years were not particularly Christmasy. Instead, they were didactic tools for introducing children to the values and ethics of the cultivated bourgeoisie. The books explicitly offered "pleasant and instructive entertainments" for "mature" children; they were marketed as rewards for youths who, as one volume put it, were "weary from the careful and dutiful completion of [their] daily tasks."[73]

The earliest so-called Christmas books were pedagogical primers that promoted the principles of their authors—usually educators and clergymen—and reinforced milieu-specific norms, Christian values, and, after the Napoleonic Wars, admiration for the German fatherland.[74] They also confirmed confessional boundaries. In Protestant Oettingen, for example, an advertisement for Christmas books from a local publisher in 1819 featured exercise books for children "learning the art of fine handwriting," while adults were offered scholarly studies of peasant traditions and pocket calendars "dedicated to love and friendship." In Lindau in the Catholic diocese of Augsburg, by contrast, a bookstore advertised religious tracts for Christmas 1814, including "stories for mature Christian youths," a *Prayerbook for the All Holy Hearts of Jesus and Mary*, and a number of other works on worship and edification.[75] The didactic angle of these selections was typical. Across the nineteenth century, Catholics continued to use Christmas to construct what historian Jeffrey Zalar calls a "self-contained reading culture of their own." Catholic Christmas texts such as almanacs and devotional literature, along with framed pictures of Jesus, reinforced a compartmentalized sense of confessional distinctiveness even as the growth of a modern mass market for printed materials helped refashion Catholic observance in accord with the culture of domestic piety.[76]

Midcentury Christmas books continued to emphasize education and discipline, although domestic motifs like St. Nicholas, the Weihnachtsmann, and the Christmas tree began to surface in the 1830s and appeared with increasing frequency in the 1840s. It would be naïve to assume that only Protestants read such books, but they do tend to express the secular ideals of cultivation favored by the Bildungsbürgertum. *Christmas Pictures* (1840), by Protestant children's author Friedrich Güll, for example, was a pedagogical primer; direct discussion of the holiday was limited to a surprisingly small number of pages, despite the title. Of the 170 pages in *The German Christmas Book for Youths* (1851), only a fraction dealt with Christmas. Children who received this book were expected to read lengthy stories about the lives of famous writers like Gutenberg, Schiller, and Goethe. This "gift" was obviously intended to improve reading skills and instill pride in German letters. *The Evergreen Christmas Book for the Young* (1850) even included the table of chemical elements.[77] The books advertised as "Christmas presents for children" in the elitist, bourgeois-Protestant *Leipziger Illustrirte*, one of the first German-language illustrated magazines, underscored the didactic nature of Protestant Christmas literature in the decade before the Revolutions of 1848. Like Catholics, Protestants had a reading culture of their own. Publishers in the Vormärz era certainly promoted their biblical studies, but books advertised as gifts did not contain what we could consider standard Christmas stories. The "pearls of European literature" instead included illustrated histories on military themes, like *Germany's Wars of Liberation* (nine volumes, sold by subscription) or *Portraits of the Most Famous Heroes of Our Time*. Such "tasteful Christmas gifts," according to advertisement copy from 1845, "will be particularly welcome to the *gebildete Stände* [educated estates]."[78]

The now-familiar Christmas book, filled with holiday poems, stories, and songs and suggestions for making decorations and wrapping presents, emerged only in the decades following German unification in 1871. These years also witnessed the industrialization of the publishing industry. The number of books printed per year grew rapidly, and the number of bookstores in Germany doubled.[79] By the 1880s, sumptuously illustrated Christmas anthologies were popular holiday gifts—at least for those who could afford them. Despite relatively extensive literacy rates (about 40 percent in the 1830s and 75 percent in the 1870s in German-speaking territories), buying and reading books still signified participation in an exclusive bourgeois and upper-middle-class culture.[80] Elm's attractively bound and richly illustrated *Golden Christmas Book* is a classic example of the genre. In it, readers found warm descriptions of the Christmas mood, historical analysis of reputedly Germanic holiday customs, and instructions for undertaking domestic celebrations.[81] Another late nineteenth-century example, Julius Lohmeyer's *German Youth-Christmas Album* (1885), featured stories typical of many Christmas books: traditional fairy tales, didactic fables about errant children saved by magic on Christmas Eve, stories about the relations between rich and poor, a puzzle page, and instructions for making Christmas wreaths from acorns and pine cones.[82] These anthologies more or less ignored the cultivated cultural values promoted by earlier books, but they offered training of a sort. The typical Christmas book now taught readers young and old about the great national traditions that defined German Christmas and the emotional codes of the middle-class holiday.

Protestant and Catholic authors alike worried that the domestication of Christmas would undermine the relevance of Christian tradition. Christmas books often included earnest explanations of the birth of Jesus and the religious symbolism of the tree and called on families in Christian households to preserve religious observances.[83] "Holidays are holy days," insisted one Protestant theologian fighting a rearguard action in 1858. "They have nothing to do with the cares of this world, nor with its joys."[84] Despite such ascetic concerns, the connections between the sacred and the domestic, articulated so thoroughly by Schleiermacher in 1806, encouraged Protestants to design alternatives to formal religious rites. The holiday was sacred, but it did not really require church. The domestic observance of German Christmas represented a special "marriage between the earthly and the heavenly," according to an anonymous but obviously Protestant writer in the 1858 Christmas issue of the exclusive *Leipziger Illustrirte*. "Behind the star that announced the birth of the world savior, the ever-green Tannenbaum glows with its candles, and the thanks for the gift of Christendom comes with that for the gifts of the earthly father." In such idealized visions of family bliss, domestic rituals were imbued with religious meaning. When the door to the Christmas room opens, the author concluded, "and the happy crowd enters with shining eyes and thankful smiles, it is a proper example of a Christian service" (*ein Gottes-dienst rechter Art*).[85]

By the 1880s, Christmas had helped Germans, and particularly Protestants, rethink their relationship to God, Jesus, and the Virgin Mary in ways that were scarcely imaginable fifty years earlier. The holiday never lost its associations with the sacred, but serious observance of religious traditions increasingly took second place to a cult of domestic piety centered on family sentimentalism rather than any profound spirituality. The new sentimentality that surrounded Christmas nurtured the feminization of religious life in the industrial age.[86] Across the nineteenth century, women comprised an ever-growing part of regular church attendees and took responsibility for teaching children about religious belief at home. In Berlin around 1900, women comprised some two-thirds of Protestant congregations in both the working and middle classes.[87] Thus it comes as no surprise that the "ideal of motherhood," described by Gunilla-Friederike Budde as the central trait of German middle-class family life, was fundamental to the cult of domestic piety.[88] Middle-class German women spent December working with servants, shopping, cleaning and decorating the home, and organizing holiday parties. Prescriptive texts surrounded this labor with a sanctified glow. Stories, images, and poems repeatedly equated the gentle care of the bourgeois mother with angelic solace, as in this short verse from a 1904 picture book written by Protestant poet and children's author Mia Holm:

> A thousand angels fly today
> Happily o'er the land,
> Each has a little Christmas tree
> Clasped firmly in her hand.
> One smiled at me most tenderly
> Came close from on afar—
> Oh, she laughed and looked just like
> My very own mama.[89]

Children took on new roles in the cult of domestic piety. They now enjoyed a new personal relationship of material give and take with once-awesome religious figures. Jesus became a marvelous friend who brought presents or rescued children in trouble, and children wrote letters or prayed to the Christkind, asking for presents, perhaps for less-fortunate neighbors.[90] The prescriptive literature encouraged children to put their own needs first, however. "Stop here! Stop here!" cried one little girl as she begged presents from

FIGURE I.4
"Your son Franz wishes
you a Merry Christmas."
Christmas "wish card,"
printed in Berlin, 1906.
(© bpk Berlin 2009/
Museum Europäischer
Kulturen-Staatliche
Museen zu Berlin)

a diminutive "Christkindlein."[91] Children begged for gifts in the most ingratiating manner:

> Holy Christ, you cherished friend
> On whom children can depend
> Oh, please make your journey swift
> and bring along some pretty gifts.[92]

Children poured out similar sentiments on the *Wunschbögen* (wish cards) they used to thank parents for presents. These beautifully wrought cards typically combined family, religious, national, and traditional motifs that were becoming increasingly generic (Figure 1.4). Such familiarity troubled committed believers, Protestant and Catholic alike. "Even children . . . know little more of Christmas, except that they will get lots of pretty things," wrote the *Kirchlicher Anzeiger*, a Protestant newspaper in Frankfurt. "For them, the Christkind becomes a bringer of games and sweets."[93]

In the late nineteenth century, images of Jesus, angels, the Holy Family,

FIGURE 1.5
The sacred and the sentimental come together in A. Zick, *Holy Night*, the frontispiece from Victor Blüthgen's *The Christmas Book*, 1899.

and the Christkind saturated the public sphere in the holiday season. They reinforced the sacralization of private life in ways that were predominantly Protestant but again washed across sectarian borders. Illustrations from children's books repeatedly show parades of cherubic angels joining the Christkind and even Jesus to reveal themselves to normal children, often bearing gifts and decorations.[94] The frontispiece of *The Christmas Book*, published in 1899, exemplifies this imagery at its most mature. The full color illustration shows a brother and sister opening an attic window to a procession of angels and cherubs lit by a stream of heavenly light. The first two angels bear the Christ child and the second pair carries a Christmas tree with toys, while a host of cherubs singing and playing guitar brings up the rear (Figure 1.5).[95] Holiday issues of daily newspapers and illustrated magazines like the tony *Illustrirte Zeitung*, the more broadly middle-class *Gartenlaube*, and the Catholic-inflected *Daheim* invariably included stories and pictures with sentimental yet pious themes. Decorations, cards, porcelain and wooden Nativity scenes, and even chocolates portrayed the semisacred figures who visited on Christmas Eve; images of the pious middle-class family circle gathered around the tree recalled the Holy Family in the manger and helped readers see themselves in a sacred light.[96]

Catholic writers shaped their own version of domestic piety, using language that strayed less far from the sacred. The theologians, writers, educators, and priests who created Catholic Christmas culture tried to preserve traditional theology while absorbing and adapting to inescapable social changes. As Jeffrey Zalar argues, the borders of the Catholic milieu, while certainly real, were more porous than generally assumed. Celebrations like Christmas allowed Catholics "to express traditional religious and modern secular identities simultaneously."[97] Holiday stories—for example, the tale of a Catholic nun who forgoes her cherished Christmas mass because she wants to take care of a mother on her sick bed—expressed familiar bourgeois sentimentalism in a pious, Catholic vocabulary.[98] The cult of (Christmas) motherhood received similar treatment. Catholic writers equated the sacrifice of earthly mothers for their children with that of the Virgin Mary, who "subsumed her entire being and essence in the rays of the eternal son Jesus Christ."[99] Their rhetoric repeatedly emphasized Mary's role as mother. "In the veneration of the Jesus child on the lap of God's mother," wrote a Catholic journalist in 1910, "the Christian mother discovers ever new love and joy in the beaming, happy faces of her own young ones."[100] Catholic prescriptive literature reminded readers to install a crèche at home, arguing that it represented the tender care of the earthly mother as well as "the eternity of the Jesus child."[101] Annual Christmas issues of popular Catholic family magazines, such as *Alte und Neue Welt* and *Deutscher Hausschatz*, were aimed at "the Volk" rather than the bourgeoisie and introduced a broad audience to the appeal of domestic piety.[102] Yet even as Catholic writers evoked the "unforgettable appeal of the family celebration around the Christmas tree, the exalted natural sentiment, the love of children, the family feelings," they subsumed worldly joys under God's revelation. "We demand to be fully entitled participants in world culture, without seeing therein our last and highest," explained an editorialist in 1910. "For us, [the highest] remains the joyful promise of the heavenly tidings of the angel, which we expect with confident hope from the redemptive mercy of the little child from Bethlehem."[103]

As the cult of domestic piety began to wear at least some of the sharp edges off cross-confessional difference, the private home on Christmas Eve became a virtual chapel, with its own sacred rituals and decorations. "The entire family gathered in my study, around the large family table," remembered one Catholic schoolteacher. "I read a selection of Bible history aloud. . . . Then everyone joined in to sing 'Oh Come, Oh Come Emmanuel.' I read further: 'The Birth of Jesus.' Then we sang 'Born in Bethlehem.' While this was going on, I lit the candles on the tree in the next room. Then [we sang] 'Come, the Christkind has arrived.' Everyone looked for their plate [of presents]. After the requisite astonishment and wonder, once more together 'There is a Rose in Bethlehem,' and then an especially good and abundant dinner."[104] Even though the writer found the correct emotional response somewhat forced, this passage nicely captures the way domestic sentimentalism redefined piety for Catholics as well as Protestants. While the songs and readings described here are particularly Catholic, the scene includes a Christmas tree, and the overall tenor of the celebration is ecumenical. Protestant as well as Catholic families read from the Bible, sang carols, opened gifts, enjoyed "good and abundant" feasts, and pondered the Christmas mood.

On the eve of World War I, Arnold Meyer, a Catholic professor in Zurich, reluctantly admitted that "many people apparently do not want meanings attached to their Christmas tree; they simply want to enjoy it and their home celebration as a refreshing pause on their journey through life."[105] As the religiously minded Meyer realized, the sacred confronted the secular with particular resonance at Christmastime, though in the end his fears of secularization were somewhat exaggerated. Feelings of religious depth may not have played a great role in day-to-day interactions, but the sacred came to life in new ways in special, ritualized moments at home. During the holiday season, mass culture and private celebration alike resonated with a domesticated religious presence. To be sure, the popularity of angels, the Christmas tree, and the Weihnachtsmann testified to the dominance of Prussian and Protestant celebratory forms in a Germany unified from above. Yet these holiday observances jumped confessional boundaries and helped construct a shared national culture rooted in the private sphere, as the memories of a Catholic priest from Bielefeld, born in 1899, remind us: "The symbolic value of the Christmas tree was still very great in my childhood, it very much defined the mystery of the celebration. We were not allowed to see how it was brought into and set up in the Christmas room, it stood tall on Christmas morning, literally enchanted by heaven."[106] The high point of German Christmas was clearly Christmas Eve, when families gathered around the tree and brought heaven down to earth. Yet the Christmas mood expanded out beyond the borders of the home. The sentimental pieties animated by the holiday spread out to embrace less-fortunate strangers in a vision of the nation united in social harmony—at least in the fables and fairy tales that filled the pages of family Christmas books.

CHRISTMAS STORIES

In 1899 journalist, children's author, and part-time theologian Victor Blüthgen published a luxurious *Christmas Book*, a large and heavy volume printed on fine, thick paper. In Blüthgen's stories, rich burghers in top hats, fair-haired mothers in flowing dresses, and beaming boys and girls dressed in their Sunday best opened presents on Christmas Eve and crossed paths with ragged beggar children, tubercular widows, and aged tailors. Each and every one, it seemed, deserved some measure of Christmas cheer.[107] In the German Empire, stories about the interactions between rich and poor were a staple of middle-class holiday fiction. Professional writers like Blüthgen, Julius Lohmeyer, and Wilhelm Kotzde; intellectuals like Ludwig Tieck and Adalbert Stifter; and numerous anonymous teachers, clergymen, and small-time authors wrote countless Christmas stories for children and adults alike. The high price of the illustrated magazines and finely wrought Christmas books in which these stories appeared no doubt limited their audience to wealthier readers, though the rise of the mass press helped create an ever-larger reading public. Whether they took place in the genteel parlors of the bourgeoisie or the shabby garrets of the poor, the stories reflected the interests of a well-heeled audience, who used these narratives to "map the terrain of the social world."[108] These simple fables performed important ideological work. "They are all babbling a rude secret, without really wanting to," as cultural critic Siegfried Kracauer wrote in another context. Like the feature films Kracauer critiqued in the 1920s, Christmas scripts "reveal how society wants to see itself."[109]

The plots and settings of family Christmas stories portrayed a voyeuristic and idealized view of poverty that confirmed the self-image of the bourgeoisie. Generic story lines returned repeatedly to the vast divide between rich and poor. At the same time, they bridged class divisions in a utopian vision of universal harmony, predicated on the peaceful management of social difference or, less often, on extraordinary examples of social ascension. In these moralistic fables, all members of the community, regardless of status, shared the cult of middle-class domestic piety; harsh social inequalities disappeared behind a veil of holiday sentimentalism, which mystified and distorted the class basis of late nineteenth-century industrial society. It was no accident that the character of the "proletarian's son" (whose father's motto was nonetheless a very proper "Keep Order in All Things!") made his first appearance in a Christmas book for youths only in the late 1860s, concurrent with a decisive upsurge in industrialization, the rapid growth and politicization of the working class, and the explosive expansion of Germany's cities.[110] Christmas stories rarely featured such realistic proletarian characters and urban landscapes. Instead, small towns and country villages replaced the gritty city settings of contemporary society. Impoverished tailors, seamstresses, or handworkers, remnants of a preindustrial artisan estate, stood in for the industrial proletariat. While disease and impoverishment tacitly reflected the costs of industrialization, the wretched characters who populated the holiday landscape were portrayed as victims of fate and happenstance. Poverty was individualized; it had little connection to dysfunctional economic structures or social realities. The emergence of a counterliterature of "proletarian" Christmas stories in the Social Democratic press after 1890 challenged the evident hypocrisy of the mainstream narratives, but it also confirmed the centrality of holiday sentimentalism and the importance of Christmas as a symbol of the collective community.

The typical bourgeois Christmas story was set in an ahistorical, fairy-tale present. The most common character was a destitute widow, surrounded, perhaps, by orphaned street urchins, whose hand-to-mouth existence was particularly distressing in the holiday season. She likely suffered from tuberculosis—seldom mentioned by name, but signified by a racking cough and an emaciated appearance. Enfeebled women figured prominently because they were innocent, malleable, and nonthreatening and so deserved the sympathy of their middle-class benefactors. Healthy but poor adult men, to the contrary, might be dangerous representatives of the politicized working class. Christmas stories resolutely avoided such characters. Strong, able men or happily married couples never appeared in the ranks of the poor; whole, healthy families lived only in middle-class households. The feminization of poverty allowed readers to empathize with capitalism's worst victims and ignore the realities that inspired working-class agitation.

Weak but sympathetic characters offered little resistance to the extension of the middle-class values of sentimentalism and piety into their lives, undertaken most obviously in missions of holiday charity.[111] Wealthy benefactors helped the poor because, under the dirt, the impoverished shared the same core values. Potentially squalid attic apartments were always clean and orderly, their tenants pious and obsequious. The dangerous classes displayed a humble regard for middle-class respectability. In short stories with variations, middle-class family members (most often women or children), motivated by generosity and/or pity, give a hand out to their social inferiors. Thus in one typical story, a poor widow gives her son her last penny to buy oil for their lamp on Christmas Eve. The boy, awed by the wax dolls of Mary and Jesus that he sees at the local Christmas market, loses the money and begins to weep. Because his mistake results from his piety, a wealthy lady passing by gives him a gold coin.[112] The rich typically gave to the poor haphazardly, acting spontaneously when confronted with a deserving case, suggesting that more organized forms of redistribution were unnecessary. "Saving individual people," as Kracauer explained, "is a convenient way to prevent the rescue of the entire class."[113] Christmas charity was doubly blessed. Such sympathy showed that worthy do-gooders and the poor all belonged to God's great family, even as acts of giving staked out the social hierarchies fundamental to middle-class identity. The sacralization of money furthermore reconciled the teachings of Jesus with the cash nexus—always a tricky project for middle-class moralists.

The fictional poor repeatedly revealed the intensity of their inner spiritual faith, proving that they indeed shared the domestic piety championed by the middle classes. Poverty somehow added spiritual depth to human existence. Widows and orphaned children might be "so poor," but, as the Romantic poet Ludwig Tieck wrote in "Christmas Eve" (1835), God nevertheless gave them "thousands and thousands of glories, treasures, and miracles."[114] Contact with the sacred in the holiday season compelled the lower classes to reform their lives, leading to miraculous examples of self-improvement. A short story by right-wing nationalist Wilhelm Kotzde features a drunken, widowed carpenter who hears church bells and carols on Christmas Eve and is moved to celebrate the holiday with his lonely daughter for the first time in ten years. His "lost orphan," however, has spent the frosty night by the grave of her mother and is only just saved from freezing to death by the anxious carpenter. He finds his daughter and God in the same moment and swears, "Now I will now really be your father!"[115] "Christmas joy" often inspired such religious epiphanies, in which emotional depth compensated for a lack of material resources—though rich monetary rewards also awaited the reformed. Middle-class readers vicariously reinforced their sense of piety in ways that ameliorated contemporary concerns with the secularizing forces of modernization. They could learn from the example of the poor that the

Christmas spirit was tied to faith, not presents or the overindulgences of commercial culture. The simple faith, love of family, and stoic forbearance displayed by the lower classes was a vision of grace, which could overcome the disenchantment of the rational capitalist competition that informed bourgeois lifestyles.

Christmas stories furthermore offered imaginary resolution of the confessional tensions that divided the German body politic, if only by ignoring them. Authors tacitly assumed that Christians—not Protestants or Catholics—populated a harmonious if socially stratified German community. At the same time, the tropes and settings used in the stories varied according to the faith of their narrators. The boundaries were hardly impermeable, but Protestant authors generally adopted a middle-class perspective, while Catholics tended to write through the eyes of the impoverished. Stories, for example, that took the point of view of an elderly, hard-hearted farmer saved by a miracle of faith on Christmas Eve, or a poor family who found comfort in Christmas despite their sorrows, appeared in Catholic texts.[116] Protestant writers told similar stories, but from the viewpoint of middle-class intermediaries. Authors may have chosen these narrative strategies to address potential audiences. In any case, the vast majority of such stories never mentioned the actual faith of the characters.

Sentimental interaction between the rich and the poor drew on the supposedly universal qualities of middle-class romantic love, which dissolved social hierarchies through acts of intimacy even as they reinforced notions of difference based on class and gender. Like fairy tales, Christmas stories frequently told how a wealthy bachelor developed a chance acquaintance with a poor woman, fell in love, and ultimately married her. The roles were never reversed. Poverty was feminized, and the wealth and status that signified success in a competitive society were masculine traits. These cases often involved a trick of hidden identity, where the woman revealed her middle-class background through physical traits (blue eyes, blond hair, a strong chin) or behavior (cleanliness, proud bearing, knowledge of social graces). "She must be from the city and a good bourgeois family, you could easily tell by the way she looked and spoke . . . really a sweet face, just careworn and too thin," thought a sea captain stranded on Christmas Eve with a widow and her tubercular daughter in a poor but "clean and orderly" farmhouse. An engagement soon followed.[117] Narratives of social ascension played on an equivocal image of the poor. Perhaps they soothed the guilty conscience of the middle-class reader or diminished fears that the vagaries of capitalism could cast one out of the upper classes into abject poverty. Fictional cases of upward mobility consistently purveyed melodramatic myths of individual achievement in a period of social fragmentation: a person with the right characteristics could always rise into the bourgeoisie and join the respectable community.

In many Christmas stories, death under the Christmas tree provided the perfect solution to ambiguous concerns with social difference. Death brought comfort to the very sick, ended their burdensome existence, and brought them into heaven, where wealth no longer determined happiness or status. Though the poor were expendable, their dying moments revealed the miraculous power of the sacred and offered further evidence that, dead or alive, they shared the sentimental proclivities of middle-class piety. In fact, the poor had such deep emotions that, despite it all, they died joyfully on Christmas Eve, a telling lesson for middle-class readers worried about their own spiritual impoverishment. Hans Christian Andersen's "Little Match Seller" is perhaps the most famous of such stories, but it is only one of many. This pathetic but ultimately blessed character is ignored by wealthy passersby and so freezes to death on New Year's Eve, after seeing powerful and consoling visions of a holiday dinner, a magnificent Christmas tree, and her dead grandmother.[118] In garrets, alleyways, and graveyards, the poor seemed to expire—happily—in record numbers during the holiday season. The dying found solace in angelic visions, in classic carols, in the sight of a decorated tree. They relived happier memories of Christmases past, before the loss of spouses or children. Consider the fate of Victor Blüthgen's impoverished and dejected "Widow Schippang," who visits the grave of her recently deceased daughter on a clear and crisp Christmas Eve. The widow sets up a small Christmas tree, falls asleep, and has a series of pleasant hallucinations about her daughter and husband. Her contented-looking corpse is discovered beside the grave on Christmas Day.[119] In numerous stories, a death on Holy Eve lent heightened poignancy to the final moments: "'A Christmas light,'" whispered a musician dying in a garret as "a melancholy smile played on his lips,—strange—and yet so beautiful.... His heart stood still. It never beat again."[120]

The Christmas cult of death marked a clear boundary between the classes, since, after all, bourgeois characters never died. Readers, however, apparently enjoyed an emotional thrill when they fantasized about the grace and thankfulness of the dying poor. To return to Siegfried Kracauer one last time, "the death that confirms the power of the ruling institutions prevents a death in the course of a struggle against those institutions."[121] Yet it is, perhaps, too easy to be hard on these simple pieties. Christmas stories after all expounded the high ideals of the late-century bourgeoisie in fictions of social reconciliation that included rich and poor. It was no doubt difficult for middle-class moralists to imagine that the sensitive selves they had so painstakingly constructed in holiday celebrations were not shared universally across social strata. The vision of a deeply fractured society united around the Christmas tree had emotional appeal, and by 1900 it had powerful political resonance as well. It would play a lasting role in the nationalization of the holiday.

CHRISTMAS IN THE FATHERLAND

In 1862 neoromantic author Theodor Storm's novella *Unter dem Tannenbaum* (Around the Christmas Tree) appeared in the *Leipziger Illustrirte Zeitung*.[122] This short classic, since reprinted in countless anthologies of Christmas stories, is typically read for its description of a romantic and melancholy Christmas mood. Yet Storm's famous Christmas story drew from and shaped a larger process: it anticipated the nationalist conventions that would increasingly circulate in German Christmas scripts and celebrations in the late nineteenth century. If politics began to work in "a new key" after German unification in 1871, nationalization began to work in a new realm: home, respectability, private life, and intimate family relations now became profound signs of a unique German identity.[123] *Unter dem Tannenbaum* takes place on a single Christmas Eve. It tells the story of a couple with a young son who live as exiles in an unfamiliar and unnamed German state. Told from the perspective of the family father, the plot loops through a series of family Christmases past to set the stage for the events of the present. In the first half of the story, a flashback, the narrator remembers how he met, wooed, and married his wife during a series of Christmas holidays. He then reflects upon his current woes. The arrival of Christmas has heightened his longings for his lost homeland (Heimat) to an unbearable extent, and during a lengthy, poetic reverie, the narrator yearns for Christmas around "our own hearth."[124] The Christmas tree is a symbol of all that is lost—the custom is unknown in this strange land, forcing the family to observe the holiday without this cherished object. Autobiography clearly intrudes into the story. Storm had indeed proposed to his wife on Christmas Eve, and his daughter Gertrude reported that the neoromantic author had a special affinity for the holiday. "I see it all," Storm once sighed as the aroma of Christmas cake filled the air. "I see father and mother; but the time that I peer into lies in such deep distance of the past! I am a boy again!" There was more: like his fictionalized narrator, Storm had immigrated to Prussia in the late 1840s, after the king of Denmark annexed Schleswig-Holstein; Christmas, Gertrude remembered, inevitably raised intense memories of the absent Heimat.[125]

Storm's fictional longings for territorial revanchism are resolved with a touch of Gemütlichkeit when the family receives a package containing a tree with fabulous decorations from an unnamed benefactor "at home." Decorated, candles lit, the tree stood in for the missing homeland and evoked feelings of wholeness and joy: now it "was truly Christmas." At the story's end, the ten-year-old son piously places a mounted cavalryman made of sugar on the branches of the tree. Germany's future, this grace note suggests, belonged to its youth, prepared to fight for national unification.[126] Here, too, Storm was prescient. Two years later, the Prussian invasion of Denmark (1864) resolved the territorial disputes over the author's beloved Schleswig-Holstein. Victory in the Franco-Prussian War and German unification under Prussian auspices soon followed. The proclamation of the German Empire at Versailles in 1871 aroused national sentiment, but in a nation divided by region, class, and confession—not to mention history—the project of making Germans required inventive sources of cultural cohesion. Christmas, in its uniquely German permutation, seemed to fit the bill. By 1900 the holiday had been thoroughly nationalized.

One crucial step in the process that turned Christmas into a celebration of Germanness took place around 1860, when theologians, ethnographers, and linguists began to explore the ancient roots of the holiday—part of a larger effort to craft an organic history for a land that had no real national past. The supposed Germanic aspects of Christmas fascinated German-speaking scholars, and the resulting flood of books and articles contributed to a "national literary canon" tied closely to Prussian-Protestant visions of national unity.[127] In one of the first full-length studies of the holiday, published in 1858, Protestant theologian Johannes Marbach laid out an explanation that would dominate understandings of "German Christmas" for the next 100 years. The German version of the holiday fused pagan and Christian belief and had deep roots in "primordial German soil," Marbach reported.[128] The Christmas tree, which embodied the spiritual beliefs of the earliest Germanic tribes and contemporary Christians in a single symbol, exemplified the process. Ignoring its rather obvious associations with modern, bourgeois culture, Marbach asserted that the Tannenbaum spanned pagan and Christian time and represented a nation with historical traditions extending back to the prehistoric. "The intimate connection of Germandom with Christendom," he wrote, "inspired a new era for the German Volk, demonstrated by the tree of Christ, with its greenery, fresh as life, and its shining lights."[129] Other scholars agreed. Paulus Cassel, a Jewish intellectual who converted to Protestantism, argued in 1861 in his own book on Christmas that the holiday's Christian antecedents were far more important than its pagan roots. Nonetheless, he concurred that a history of the "origins, customs, and superstitions" of the holiday had much to say about the ethnic and religious past of the "German Volk."[130] The prolific German philosopher-philologist Alexander Tille reported from the University of Glasgow that Christmas united Germans even beyond national borders. "The Lights of the Christmas-tree shine as far as the German tongue is spoken," he declared, "from the east of Prussia to Alsatia, from the Baltic and the German Ocean to the south of the Danube."[131] By 1900, such ideas were commonplace. As Zurich University professor of theology Arnold Meyer put it in 1912, the bond between the pagan *deutsche Weihnachten* (literally German Holy Nights) and the Christian *deutsche Christfest* (German Celebration of Christ) defined the unique characteristics of the German holiday and captured the special relationship between Christianity and German *Volkstum* (national character).[132] The rewritten holiday testified to the existence of a "full" German past: the invention of Christmas as a national tradition built on (reputedly) actual historical artifacts and customs and so lent the national project an aura of authenticity.[133]

The scholarly analysis of supposedly ancient traditions furthermore constructed apparently natural boundaries between Germans and national outsiders. Jewish celebrations, according to Marbach, were mired in the "legalism" of Judaism and would never reach the spiritual heights of the German, Christian festival.[134] Marbach was somewhat more generous to Catholics, though he nonetheless claimed that Luther's Reformation and the "seriousness and depth of Protestantism" had clearly improved upon the Catholic preference for mumming, processions, and liturgy.[135] In 1891, in a 150-page tract on the early history of Christmas, the anti-Semitic educator Paul de Lagarde claimed that the holiday was instituted by Pope Liberius in 354 as a church attack on the doctrine of "Arianism" (which held that Christ was not the Son of God). Just as the institution of Christmas once "saved" Christendom, Lagarde argued in a faintly disguised attack on contemporary Judaism, "we first have to be rid of modern Arianism before we can again conquer the Church."[136] Alexander Tille likewise suggested that Christmas testified to the superiority of German culture, again demonstrated by the history of the Christmas tree. In an 1892 article in the British journal *Folklore*, Tille reported that the tree's export from "the Fatherland" to other European nations and the United States—where "it has taken the deepest root"—degraded German tradition. The British "spoil its appearance" by hanging too many presents on its branches. Even worse, in the United States, "the spirit of invention of the 19th century has got hold of it." Americans made ersatz trees of "moulded iron . . . and instead of the modest light of the little wax candle, the glaring gas jet bursts forth from this artificial production of the ironfounder." Only in German-speaking lands, where "a Christmas without a tree is no real Christmas," did the holiday retain its authenticity.[137]

Educated readers could peruse ideas about the profound Germanness of Christmas in any number of ethnographic or cultural-historical studies written around 1900. Books that examined Christmas in German medieval art, the "tree cults of the ancient Teutons," or vanishing folk practices and superstitions were written to promote "understanding of the German character" and went through numerous editions.[138] Even the toys found in ancient tribal graves supposedly revealed links between the "Germanic past" and contemporary holiday customs.[139] This literature would have appealed most to well-heeled Bürgers (members of the middle classes) with some postsecondary education—the 20 percent of the adult population who could be considered serious readers of literature, scholarly journals, or middle-class illustrated magazines.[140] Yet ideas about the Germanness of Christmas had broad purchase. The Christmas issues of popular magazines and daily newspapers simplified the historicist fantasies of more erudite studies for a mass audience. In the December issues of the Social Democratic press, for example, working-class readers followed stories about the Christmas tree as a "characteristic Christmas custom" that drew on the "heritage of ancient Germanic belief."[141] Knowledgeable critics quickly asserted that such stories were little better than copywriter clichés. As a Frankfurt journalist wrote in 1885, "that and how the Christian holiday and many of its favorite and volkstümlichen [popular] practices are connected with ancient Germanic sacrificial festivities and other holy pagan customs; what the Christ tree is and what it means—these are the typical subjects in the conventional Christmas articles of many newspapers."[142]

The family books that flooded the holiday gift market in the late nineteenth century further popularized the connections between Christmas and national identity. Hugo Elm's *Golden Christmas Book* (Figure 1.1) again exemplifies the process of cultural transmission. This accessible prescriptive primer for organizing bourgeois celebration included a thorough history of the German holiday and extensive instructions for making appropriate decorations of all types. In proud assertions that the "mysterious magic" of the Christmas season could be traced back to the nature worship of "our Nordic-Germanic forefathers," Elm's work clarified the historicist trajectory that linked faith, folklore, and fatherland.[143] Elaborate descriptions of the Christian holiday's similarities to the Roman Saturnalia, Nordic myth, and pre-Christian Germanic solstice rituals demonstrated the myriad ways Christians had appropriated the "pagan-Germanic worldview" for their own use. "Even as the light of Christendom destroyed the pagan gods," Elm explained in typically dramatic prose, "so the first preachers of Christendom silently adopted the customs of the people in their new teachings, or the people outwardly adopted Christianity but held tightly on to their customs with a rare determination."[144] The Norse God Loki, Valhalla, Richard Wagner's Tannhäuser, Emperor Barbarossa—all contributed to Elm's syncretic descriptions of Christmas custom.

Like his more scholarly colleagues, Elm assured his readers that the Christmas tree had "pure Germanic origins" linked to the Nordic-pagan celebrations of "our primeval ancestors"—though it, too, had been Christianized. The tree, according to Elms, was a custom shared by all Germans, from the poor to "the great and powerful." It followed German immigrants to other lands, and even non-Germans had brought the "giant of the woods" into their celebrations—though "not with its ancient German Gemüthlichkeit" (*sic*).[145] Elm was well aware of the tensions between Protestant and Catholic observances and presented the holiday as an ecumenical celebration that could unite Germans above confessional differences. "It brings joy to our very heart," he wrote, "that Christians of all confessions celebrate together the holiday of holidays, the festival of love, around the ever-green son of the forest with its candle light that touches the heart, and that the Christmas tree and the crèche rest peacefully side by side."[146] The rest of the book's contents, however, paid slight attention to Catholic traditions and subsumed confessional difference in broader Protestant hegemonies. Christmas stories about Norse Gods and pagan tree worship cast a sentimental light on the mainstream, nationalist historicism that increasingly defined Germany as a Protestant Christian nation.[147]

Catholic theologians and editorialists recognized as much. The Protestant tenor of mainstream holiday texts pressured Catholics to use Christmas to explain their own place in the body politic. As we have seen, some complained about "modern" observances and argued that Catholic rituals could preserve both internal unity and confessional difference. Others recognized that Christmas was a potent symbol of Christian-based Germanness. This shared culture, they suggested, gave the lie to exclusionary Protestant nationalism. Both arguments were made in the 1870s, as the state-sponsored Kulturkampf, or "cultural struggle," against Catholics reached its height. Rather than "peace to mankind," wrote an editorialist in the Catholic newspaper *Germania* in 1874, "the modern state has used unfortunate means to sharpen religious differences, and a peaceful coexistence between the confessions has almost become impossible." Christmas peace—preserved in its purest form in "Christian-Catholic belief"—required freedom from state persecution and the recognition that Catholics were integral members of "the German Volk" and indeed good Christians, even if they followed divergent liturgical scripts.[148] Visions of a newly muscular Christ offered a role model for Catholics struggling to persevere in their faith. Lying in the manger, Jesus appeared "helpless and weak, and yet he was the strong hero, the all-powerful God" whose "arm was able to crush those who measured him for chains."[149] A poem titled "Christ's Eve in the Orphaned Community," printed in *Germania* in 1876, used the solemn atmosphere of a midnight Christmas mass to frame the stoically endured hardships of state oppression. "The hour is twelve!—hear church bells tone/Glory to God in the Highest," the poem began, evoking the mystical atmosphere of the decorated church and the humble piety of the congregants. The congregation's beloved priest cannot officiate, however, because he "stood on Jesus' side" and fled the country to escape state persecution. Prayer and acts of communion bring him back in spirit, cementing the holy bonds of community.[150]

Catholic Christmas rhetoric was less antagonistic after the relaxation of the Kulturkampf, but it continued to grapple with German nationalism "in its dominantly Protestant incarnation."[151] Catholic leaders recognized that family observances had become important signs of national belonging and softened harsh critiques of domestic custom. As the *Kölnische Volkszeitung* wrote in 1897, the Christmas tree was "the national property of the Germans" and as such was a requisite element for a good family celebration. The crèche, however, retained its "pure Catholic origins" and its use still demonstrated confessional loyalty.[152] Newspapers featured stories about the deep history of Christmas in fourth-century Jerusalem, or accounts of contemporary celebrations in the Holy Land, perhaps to counter mainstream interest in Germanic pagan rituals.[153]

Memories of the Kulturkampf and ongoing examples of Protestant chauvinism encouraged editorialists to use Christmas to assert that Catholics were Christians who also belonged to "the fatherland."[154] The state, however, was no longer the main adversary. Rather, Catholic editorialists focused their jeremiads on Protestant reformers such as Albrecht Ritschl or Adolf von Harnack, who denied the miracle of the Virgin Birth and so destroyed the "Christian sense" of the holiday altogether.[155] The list of those who "stood against Christianity" and sought to despoil the holiday seemed to grow ever longer. By 1905, according to a critic in Cologne, it included: Social Democrats who sought to "occupy" the holiday in the name of class struggle; chauvinists and jingoists who "preach hatred against all"; the adherents of the "*Herrenmoral* [master race morality] of the superman"; "new paganists"; "decadents" of all kinds; and atheists and Jews. These "pathological weaklings of modern decadence" all believed they, too, had the right to "celebrate the high festival of peace and love." They were wrong. "If the Savior appeared again today," the editorialist concluded, "he would cast them out of the temple, as he once did the money changers."[156]

Though Christmas celebrated the birth of the Prince of Peace, militarist values increasingly permeated the German version of the holiday. Prussian victories over Napoleon in 1815, over liberal revolutionaries in 1849, and over Danish, Austrian, and French forces in the Wars of Unification had left the German army in a commanding symbolic and social position. As historian Isabel Hull notes, the military represented "the quintessence of German integration."[157] By chance, the emerging nation celebrated the first of what contemporaries liked to call *Kriegsweihnachten* (War Christmas) in the final days of the Siege of Paris in December 1870, during the Franco-Prussian War.[158] Celebration under arms "at the gates of Paris" boosted the nationalism already latent in the holiday, a process expressed in the growing German fondness for war toys.[159] Late eighteenth-century descriptions of German Christmas markets already paid fond attention to the sparkling rows of toy soldiers on display in vendors' booths, and the little boys in foundational texts like Hoffmann's *Nutcracker* invariably found a "new squadron of Hussars . . . carrying numerous silver weapons" under the Christmas tree.[160] Family carols like "Father Christmas Comes Tomorrow" ("Morgen kommt der Weihnachtsmann"), composed around 1835 by Hoffmann von Fallersleben, the author of the lyrics of the German national anthem, further encouraged the domestication of Prussian militarism. The words to what would become one of the most popular German family carols recount a list of war toys like those in late nineteenth-century images and advertisements:

> Father Christmas comes tomorrow
> Comes with all his presents,
> Drums, fifes, and rifles,
> Flags and sabers and still more
> An entire army right for war,
> That's what I really want![161]

Already in the 1840s, bourgeois family prescriptive literature underscored the importance of war toys for teaching proper gender roles. Experts encouraged parents to buy toys that observed the "differences between the sexes," a division that cast girls as mothers and boys as soldiers. Girls should get dolls and dollhouses, while "everything that relates to the military pleases young boys" and "neither flintlocks, sabers, cartridge boxes, or drums" should be missing from beneath the tree.[162]

After victory over France and national unification in 1871, the militarization of Christmas gifts acquired a new urgency. If they read the Brockhaus encyclopedia of 1886, parents learned that play was an auspicious agent of socialization; toys, according to the encyclopedia, "convey certain messages to the point where one could almost speak of intellectual and physical equipment for the training of children."[163] Boys' presents now included the most modern armaments, such as miniature artillery pieces, zeppelins, air rifles, steam-powered battle ships, and national military uniforms. The Prussian "pickle-sticker" infantry helmet, worn by troops through the first years of World War I, was particularly popular (Figure 1.6). War toys were priced to sell in all markets; as David Hamlin suggests, "consumerism extended and deepened the power of militarist norms in German society."[164] In 1908 the cost of a toy saber ranged from 48 pfennig to 2.25 marks, and a simple "pickle-sticker" helmet cost 95 pfennig (the weekly wages of industrial workers averaged about 20 marks at this time).[165] Rudolf Stocknis, a journalist in Berlin, fantasized about the war games and parade drills that might occur on Christmas Day. Outfitted with the best war toys, he wrote, "our kriegslustigen Buben" (war-hungry lads) could reenact the Battle of Gravelotte, an early Prussian victory in the Franco-Prussian War. "Hurrah!" Stocknis continued. "With complete military equipment from the [toy] store of Emma Bette, in shako and cavalry uniform, with saber, drum, Little Hans greets us

FIGURE 1.6

Gifts around the Christmas Tree, lithograph, circa 1875.
(© bpk Berlin 2009/Dietmar Katz)

on Christmas morning: 'Present Arms!'"[166] War toys taught children about current events and encouraged them to view the world through military terms. Hildegard Wallich, daughter of a minor public official, remembered that her parents repeatedly gave her two brothers tin soldiers as gifts in the mid-1880s; one always got German troops, the other French. "There were infantry, cavalry, artillery regiments on both sides with officers from all ranks, with the highest ranks and generals on horses." The tidy gender segmentation advocated in prescriptive literature could break down, however, since Hildegard enjoyed playing with her brothers' gifts. The militarization of the everyday worlds of play and leisure apparently appealed to both genders.[167]

Beyond the obvious war toys, any number of family Christmas customs confirmed the Prussian-Protestant stereotypes of home and domesticity that defined German character in the late nineteenth century.[168] The national flags hung on Christmas trees or gifts of Prussian army helmets directly incorporated state symbols into private life. Other cultural practices were less blatant but nonetheless effective agents for the naturalization and domestication of national sentiment. Special holiday foods like roast goose, red cabbage, and *Lebkuchen* (gingerbread cakes) were layered with nationalist connotations. From Bach's "Christmas Oratorio" (1734–35) to Protestant hymns like Luther's "From Heaven Above to Earth I Come" and popular carols like "Silent Night," Christmas music was proudly German, and the stories read aloud on Christmas Eve drew from a century's worth of classics by German authors like Hoffmann and Storm. Children's books increasingly emphasized the national roots of the holiday after the Franco-Prussian War, with titles such as *A Christmas Album for German Youths* (1885), *The German Christmas Book* (1904), and *German Christmas* (1912).[169] Victory over the French and unification in 1871, the advance of German colonization in the 1890s, Bismarck's holiday celebrations with Kaiser Wilhelm I—all were fair game for children's holiday reading.[170] Stories often took an imperialist slant that revealed a fascination with German Christmas abroad in colonies or exotic lands. Celebrating around improvised trees and singing "Silent Night" among "our black associates" hardly inspired a proper "Christmas mood," but it nonetheless legitimized the idea that Germans were the people of culture (*Kulturvolk*).[171] Christmas cards portrayed the kaiser celebrating a regal holiday with his family and the royal court, and glass ornaments shaped like zeppelins or the head of Bismarck adorned the "German Tannenbaum." During World War I, ornaments included Big Bertha artillery shells, U-boats, and the Iron Cross, the highest German military decoration.[172]

A single Christmas story published in 1892—a song-and-verse children's play titled "A Christmas Fairy Tale Drama"—reveals the way that "almost forty years of exclusivist Protestant nationalism" could frame the most intimate celebration of family life.[173] This literal script appeared in the *Christmas Book*, an impressive, well-illustrated volume composed of poems, songs, and stories written entirely by Prussian aristocrat Philipp Prince zu Eulenburg-Hertefeld, a senior diplomat and member of Emperor Wilhelm II's closest entourage.[174] Writing a Christmas book may seem like an unusual undertaking for this elite nobleman, best known for his role in the homosexual scandals that rocked the Prussian court from 1906 to 1908. Yet Eulenburg was an accomplished author, poet, and musician who enjoyed writing poetry, fairy tales, and short stories.[175] His *Christmas Book* could draw inspiration from famous German Christmas stories, numerous scholarly texts on the Christian-Germanic roots of the holiday, and a vast generic holiday literature written by a legion of anonymous writers. On one level, Eulenberg's

Christmas stories recount familiar nineteenth-century themes of poverty and piety, family sentimentalism, and reconstructed solstice fantasies. On another, the book reveals the potential for the overt nationalization of family celebration. Eulenberg's "Christmas Fairy Tale Drama" is a pseudo-Nordic/Christian saga of battle and war that draws on the supposedly primordial cultural-historical roots of the German holiday even as it promotes the nationalist war theology of late Imperial Germany.[176] The domestic piety championed by Schleiermacher and the sensuous mood described by E. T. A. Hoffmann in the first decades of the century were now deeply submerged in a modern, sentimental holiday that was subtly but resolutely Prussian and Protestant.

Eulenburg's play pits an evil mountain king and his minions, including the monstrous Wimmelwolf, against a mother and her children. Father is away at war, so the young sons left at home take on the adult (male) duties of defending defenseless family members (mother and daughter) from these evil trolls. The Wimmelwolf has captured the youngest daughter, and the three sons take a dramatic oath to fight to the death to free her: "I will fight under the sign of redemption and will die, if it pleases God!"[177] On Christmas Eve, a "silver fairy" sent by the Christkind appears; she gives the children silver spears to use against the Wimmelwolf. As they approach his lair, brandishing their magic weapons, they sing:

> I anoint my spear with love,
> Love will my joyful battle cry be!
> With it, my victory is assured,
> Watch out!—you King of Darkness!

> I anoint my spear with loyalty,
> Loyalty will my guide and leader be!
> With it, my victory is assured,
> Protect yourself!—you King of Darkness!

> I anoint my spear with faith,
> Faith will my strong protector be!
> With it, my victory is assured,
> Watch out!—you King of Darkness![178]

Love, loyalty, and faith; the performance of this little drama around the Christmas tree evoked the Prussian-Protestant ethos of family, national allegiance, and piety that defined the Christian-German empire. Eulenberg's appeal to defense of home in the name of a Protestant-derived war theology points rehearsed roles that the child actors from 1892 would be asked to repeat as adults some twenty years later in World War I. Unlike the results of that war, the play comes to a fairy-tale close; victory is indeed assured. The children kill the Wimmelwolf with their spears and return home, where the Christmas star heals their wounds. At the very end, father arrives, as promised, for Christmas Eve. The family unit is made sound and whole through the magic of the holiday; gender and age relationships return to normal.

Few Germans would actually perform Eulenberg's play, but there were many other holiday scripts, like the "Christmas Fairy Tale Drama," that reproduced the conservative values and social codes of Prussian-Protestant nationalism. By the end of the century, mainstream assumptions about the relationship among families, state, and society were deeply embedded in the symbols and rituals that structured middle-class celebration. The Christmas mood had moved away from the refined values espoused by its inventors, enlightened intellectuals like von Humboldt, Goethe, Schleiermacher, and Hoffmann. The holiday now embraced a culture of pleasure and self-expression, driven by an abundant consumer culture and conducive to an intense experience of individuality.[179] Family ritual turned on notions of a private and "feminine" sense of cultural belonging, an intimate and appealing counterpart to the public, more masculine aspects of Germany identity. In short, Christmas had been transformed from a celebration of haute bourgeois values to those of a sentimental, national middle class.

Dominant narratives had great power to determine the holiday's meaning, to codify the shifting constellation of relationships between self and society. In recurrent annual celebrations, however, the preexisting lines of middle-class scripts proved mutable. Celebrants generally played their roles, but they also transformed them. Germans from all sectors of society actively reworked the holiday to meet their own fantasies, needs, and expectations; as the rest of this book shows, "German Christmas" was continually open to improvisation, revision, and counterscripting.

2

Contradictions in the Christmas Mood

> The concept of celebration is commonly related to the ideas of cult
> and veneration. Festivities bring together those who became separated
> and who live apart, and they feel themselves reunited in the exaltation
> of the ceremonies. Quarrels cease and community comes into its own.
> Thus the festival recalls belongingness and gives it renewed validity.
>
> ——✧ Ferdinand Tönnies, *Custom: An Essay on Social Codes* (1909)

CELEBRATIONS SUCH AS CHRISTMAS, sociologist Ferdinand Tönnies
believed, could heal the fractures in the German body politic by recovering
a sense of authentic Gemeinschaft (community) in the midst of an alienated
modern Gesellschaft (society). His thoughts on the "belongingness" created
during festivities concurred with mainstream holiday scripts, which cast
German Christmas as a universal Christian celebration of family, folk, and
fatherland. Tönnies could base his conclusions on rich empirical evidence:
the nineteenth century was a time of intense cultural invention, which added
a number of new festivals and traditions to the annual cycle of celebration. To
be sure, the feelings of piety, national pride, and family sentimentalism that
Germans expressed during Christmas observances tapped into broad structures of emotion that crossed borders of class and confession. Yet holidays in
Imperial Germany were rarely harmonious occasions that transcended social
difference or lent the community "renewed validity," as Tönnies imagined.
Festival culture in the late nineteenth century was deeply segregated, reflecting diverse and conflicted religious, political, and economic interests. There
were sharp contradictions in the Christmas mood. "Outsider" groups — German Jews, Social Democrats, and workers — contested and reworked the social and symbolic space of the holiday in attempts to carve out alternative
lifestyles and fashion identities appropriate to countercultural milieus.[1]

FIGURE 2.1
Worker's Christmas, circa 1910. (© bpk Berlin 2009)

A broadly popular holiday that celebrated Christian morality, family values, and national belonging presented German Jews with opportunities and challenges. The construction and maintenance of Jewish identity depended not just on theology or formal religious observance. In any number of activities, Jews engaged in a "daily plebiscite" that demonstrated varying degrees of commitment to Jewish traditions. Their choices resonated with particular emphasis during Jewish and Christian holidays alike, and the Jewish response to Christmas reflected the religious, political, regional, and social differences that divided the Jewish community.[2] Orthodox Jews (in the 1900s, fewer than 20 percent of the German Jewish population) usually rejected Christmas altogether, while a small percentage of converts to Christianity might celebrate an entirely mainstream holiday. For the approximately 80 percent of liberal middle-class German Jews who might support the integrative ideology of Reform Judaism, the reactions were complex. For both German Jews and Protestants, formal religious celebrations evolved into family holidays in the nineteenth century, and the cult of domestic piety associated with Christmas became a key component of family identity.[3] Celebrating Christmas also signified Germanness and national belonging. For German Jews, the decision to observe some sort of hybrid Jewish-Christian holiday—now known by the ironic name *Weihnukka*, a combination of the German words for Christmas (*Weihnachten*) and Hanukkah (*Chanukka*)—cast issues of Jewish acculturation and assimilation in high relief. The reinvigoration of Hanukkah itself in the late nineteenth century further complicated matters. Resurrected from relative obscurity by the Zionist movement, Hanukkah and so-called Maccabee celebrations appropriated many of the sentimental symbols and rituals of the Christian holiday. Hanukkah looked a lot like Christmas, even as it expressed a determined Jewish or Zionist identity and offered a concrete alternative to Christian observances.

Social Democratic counternarratives and alternative practices in lower-class milieus further contested the meaning of German Christmas. "This official Christmas holiday is churlish hypocrisy," thundered an editorialist in *Vorwärts*, the official newspaper of the Social Democratic Party of Germany (SPD), in a typical passage. "The rich bourgeoisie celebrate around the Christmas tree the birth of the Savior of the poor, the birth in the manger, with such luxury that it insults the suffering, freezing plight of the masses."[4] As such rhetoric suggests, the SPD aggressively attacked the Christian aspects of the holiday, even as they appropriated its central symbols. Germany's Christian denominations thus faced a competing and well-established organization that promoted an aggressively antireligious but nonetheless semispiritual worldview.[5] For Social Democrats, Jesus was not the Son of God but a working-class hero. Proletarian festivities observed under the star of socialism rather than the star of Bethlehem called attention to the realities of poverty and class exploitation that lay behind the rhetoric of material abundance and social harmony.

Emerging working-class cultures of leisure and mass entertainment offered a spectrum of holiday activities that cut across socialist and bourgeois forms of celebration and reinforced the deep divisions that segmented everyday life by class and milieu in Imperial Germany. Many workers could simply not afford a "traditional" Christmas. Instead, they spent the holidays in the taverns, dance halls, and club rooms frequented by the lower classes. For some, Christmas played out as a *Sauferei*, a bout of heavy drinking frowned on by government and clerical authorities. Others made the best Christmas they could, given relatively limited resources. Working-class celebration both ignored and adopted bourgeois niceties, merging with and going beyond Social Democratic attempts to shape a distinct working-class festive culture. By the early twentieth century, Christmas had indeed become Germany's national holiday. Celebrations "on the margins" had to come to terms with mainstream observances even as they revealed a deep rending of the social fabric.[6] Jews, Social Democrats, and working Germans reshaped Christmas and grappled with the cult of sentimentalism at the heart of the holiday; criticized, appropriated, lionized, dismissed, its emotional pull was contested but undeniable.

BY THE GENTLE GLOW OF THE HANUKKAH CANDLES

Though Jewish salon hostess Fanny von Arnstein reportedly set up the first Christmas tree in Vienna on Christmas Eve in 1814, celebrations of this most Christian holiday, however secular, rarely occurred in Jewish households until much later in the century.[7] By the 1880s, accelerating upward mobility, urban immigration, acculturation, and secularizing reforms—in short, the "embourgeoisement" of many German Jews—made a de-Christianized Christmas an appealing celebration of the sentimental family values shared by middle-class Christians and Jews alike. Yet Jewishness was a category subject to multiple and competing definitions, and Christmas underscored the situational aspects of ethnic identity. In the German Empire, streams of Orthodox and liberal or Reform Judaism and Zionism crosscut hierarchies of class, status, and regional affiliation, as "East Jews"—immigrants from central and south-central Europe—clashed with wealthier and more acculturated "West Jews." By the last decades of the century, a majority of German Jews had successfully climbed from the bottom to the middle and top of the social ladder—a remarkable rise to prominence by an ethnic minority—and some 80 percent of German Jews identified with the liberal stream of modern Judaism. Rooted in the Jewish Enlightenment, or Haskala, liberal Jews favored national and cultural adaptation rather than strict adherence to Judaic law and messianic hopes for a return to the Holy Land. In the eyes of both Jews and Christians, writes historian Simone Lässig, "to be bourgeois ... became the definitive *Jewish* lifestyle norm."[8] At the same time, Jews remained outsiders, subject to social ostracism and anti-Semitism. In this complex social-historical context, the Jewish response to Christmas reflected "the rich variety of Judaisms that evolved in Imperial Germany" and highlighted the paradoxical nature of Jewish life in the Diaspora.[9]

Personal accounts written by German Jews in the late nineteenth century tend to contradict historian Monika Richarz's assertion that Jewish observance of Christmas was "the most extreme expression of secularization and assimilation."[10] In wealthy Jewish households, Christmas was unavoidable, wrote Richard Koch, a professor of medical history at the University of Frankfurt. In turn-of-the-century Frankfurt, Koch remembered, "where there were children and servants, a Christmas celebration in Jewish families was almost an imperative demand, an elementary need in the course of the bourgeois year." Only strictly Orthodox Jewish families, he continued, could "avoid" the holiday altogether.[11] Jews of more modest means also adapted to Christmas. The childhood experience of Social Democratic theorist Eduard Bernstein, born in 1850, exemplifies the way the pressures of mainstream culture encouraged hybrid celebrations in lower-class Jewish families. Bernstein's parents were members of a Reform community in Berlin. The family lived in a Christian neighborhood (in Bernstein's memory, an "entirely non-Jewish world") and viewed Sunday, not the traditional Sabbath, as the weekly day of rest. The family did not observe dietary rules at home but did attend formal services on major Jewish holidays. Eduard's father, a locomotive driver, had an intellectual relationship to Judaism. His mother, like many other German Jewish women, had a "deeply religious nature" and tried to "maintain a Jewish household." The Bernsteins observed Jewish holidays, but Christmas was the family's favorite. Bernstein's father made sure they had some sort of tree and presents, even if he had to make them himself because of a tight family budget. Eduard and his siblings enjoyed Christmas Eve; as their father placed gifts around the tree, they sang Christian carols, including "Silent Night." Both Christian and Jewish carols, Bernstein wrote in 1918, still evoked nostalgic emotions and pleasant childhood memories. The celebration of the birth of the Christian savior was not entirely sanguine, however. To preserve some distance from Christian observance, Bernstein's mother reminded her children that Jesus was an important spiritual leader but not the Son of God.[12]

The cycle of public holidays in the German Empire was decidedly and unavoidably Christian. As lawyer and author Paul Mühsam noted of his childhood in late nineteenth-century Brandenburg, "the business world" was determined by the Christian calendar. "On the high Jewish holidays the business stayed open," Mühsam remembered. "The [Jewish] religious celebrations, Sabbath, Hagada, the feast of the Tabernacles etc. were for me simply concepts, and I knew exactly when Christmas took place, but not Hanukkah."[13] Beyond such public pressures, Jewish children learned about Christmas at school and from Christian friends and servants, and they begged their parents to provide gifts, if not a Christmas or "Hanukkah tree." Even if conservative parents resisted the penetration of Christmas into Jewish private life, their offspring might well decide to bring a Lichterbaum, a "richly decorated tree of light," into their own family parlors.[14] The comfort with which German Jews celebrated Christmas is captured in a contemporary joke about a young Jewish girl who, after opening fine gifts in front of a large tree, turns to her father to ask in wonder, "Oh, papa, do Christians get to celebrate Christmas too?"[15]

For some, observance of "German" Christmas was a sign of acculturation and national belonging. Breslau historian Willy Cohn's conclusion that Christmas "was not a Christian but rather a German holiday" was apparently a familiar refrain for upper-middle-class Jews around 1900.[16] Physicist Max Born's family celebrated Christmas with what he called a "Christbaum" (Tree of Christ), even though they were official members of the Jewish community. The Born family had elaborate celebrations with gifts and decorations and sang Christian carols like Luther's "O How Joyfully" without giving much thought to the religious content of the songs. Born's father saw Christmas "as the ancient Yule Fest of the Germans, and even though he was a member of a religious minority he wanted to be German."[17] The holiday could be ambiguous for more committed Jews. In 1911 philosopher Gershom Scholem's family in Berlin observed Christmas with all the trappings of a "traditional" German holiday, including visits to the Christmas market, roast goose for Christmas dinner, a large Christmas tree, family renditions of "Silent Night," and presents for servants, relatives, and friends. Scholem's father "claimed that this was a *German folk festival* and that we participated in the celebration not as Jews but rather as Germans". After Scholem converted to Zionism, however, he found such celebrations so disturbing that he fled the house on Christmas Eve.[18]

Even if Jewish celebration of Christmas was for the most part limited to urban middle- and upper-class households, it raised serious concern among conservative and Orthodox Jews. "To call oneself a Jew and to celebrate Christmas as such," Orthodox leader S. R. Hirsh complained in 1855, "this is such a dreadful irony that we shudder before it."[19] Disputes over the proprieties of so-called Christmas tree Jews appeared with increasing regularity in the Jewish press as the century continued. Christmas was an "open wound" that undermined allegiance to Jewish tradition, wrote a rabbi from Karlsbad in the mainstream *Allgemeine Zeitung des Judentums* in 1895. Yet because children were so enthralled with its sentimental charm, the rabbi concluded reluctantly, celebration in Jewish families was unavoidable—otherwise the holiday would have the appeal of "forbidden fruit." Jewish parents could "paralyze the danger" if they set up a tree and gave out gifts but explained clearly that Christmas was a foreign import. Even this rather timid concession evoked an angry response in a subsequent edition of the paper: "Christmas is now and has been for centuries an entirely Christian holiday," wrote A. Levy from Berlin. When Jews celebrated Christmas, they "slandered Judaism." No compromise was possible, only "complete rejection."[20] Another editorialist warned: "A Christmas tree in a Jewish home is simply a sign of weakness of character, ignorance, and a total lack of piety."[21] A 1904 cartoon from the Zionist humor magazine *Schlemiel*, which portrays a menorah that "Darwinistically" morphs into a decorated Christmas tree, epitomized the critique (Figure 2.2). The reference to Darwin expressed disdain for modern secularism, and the caption—"How the Hanukkah lights of goat pelt dealer *Cohn* in Pinne evolved into the Tree of Christ of financier *Conrad* on Tiergarten Street (Berlin-West)"—mocked the artifice of the social climber, who changed his profession, lost his religion, Christianized his name, and moved from the town to the city in pursuit of wealth and assimilation. The address on Tiergarten Street only twisted the knife: the acculturated Jews who lived in the wealthy suburbs of West Berlin were infamous for their avid use of the Christmas tree.

Darwinistisches.

Wie sich der Chanukaleuchler des Ziegenfellhändlers **Cohn** in Pinne zum Christbaum des Kommerzienrats **Conrad** in der Tiergartenstraße (Berlin W.) entwickelte.

FIGURE 2.2

"Darwinistic." Anti-Christmas cartoon from *Schlemiel*, 1904. (Courtesy of the Jüdisches Museum Berlin)

The emergence of Hanukkah as a major Jewish holiday was inextricably linked to the tensions surrounding German-Jewish observance of Christmas. Hanukkah, which commemorates the 167 BCE liberation of Jerusalem from Syrians by the Jewish Maccabees, declined in importance during the first half of the nineteenth century, a result of the assimilationist tendencies associated with the Jewish Enlightenment.[22] But for a Jewish minority facing social prejudice, the eight-day ritual cycle of Hanukkah was a compelling alternative to Christian observance and so became increasingly popular in the last decades of the 1800s. Like Christmas, Hanukkah evoked the intimate links between family, faith, and nation, but in a specifically Jewish mode. Viennese intellectual and Zionist Ernst Müller caught the associations precisely in 1900, when he asserted, "We grasp the doubled meaning of our homeland holiday, the prize of the Maccabees, their proud fearlessness before both life and death, and the quiet poetry of the Jewish family, which preserves the life of the people."[23] Members of the Reform movement—who favored national assimilation over Zionist calls for emigration to the Jewish "homeland" in Palestine—also promoted the holiday. Already in 1871, the Synod of Reformed Rabbis decided to promote Hanukkah as an alternative to Christmas; some twenty years later, the mainstream *Allgemeine Zeitung des Judentums* (supposedly "above party politics" but in many ways a mouthpiece for the Reform movement) was calling for "an ersatz [Christmas] for our youth, and we have one in our Hanukkah celebration."[24] The radical Jewish poet Erich Mühsam gave the irony of competing holidays a satiric slant in his 1914 verse "Holy Eve":

Ministers and agrarians,
bourgeoisie and proletarians—
thus celebrate all Aryans
at the same time and overall
the birth of Christ in the cow stall.
(Only those, whose race he was,
would rather observe Hanukkah.)[25]

As Mühsam's poem suggests, while Christmas expressed the confidence of
the vast German, "Aryan" majority (some 99 percent of the population), the
reinvention of Hanukkah gave Jews a way to deal with marginalization and
testified to growing pride in Jewish difference.[26]

Eager to bolster this process, the Zionists strove to turn Hanukkah into a
momentous Jewish holiday. Just as Christmas gave historical depth to the notion of Germanness, Hanukkah proved that the Jews had a noble and ancient
collective history linked to the homeland in Palestine. Judah Maccabee (the
Hammer), the leader of the anti-Syrian revolt commemorated in Hanukkah
festivities, was recreated as a modern Jewish hero; in the closing pages of *The
Jewish State* (1896), Theodor Herzl himself proclaimed that "the Maccabees
will rise again." Zionist leaders such as historian Willy Cohn crisscrossed
central Europe delivering "Maccabee speeches" to Jewish organizations in a
determined effort to popularize the antiassimilationist holiday.[27] Year after
year, Zionists reminded the community that the "gentle glow of the Hanukkah candles" recalled the brave deeds of their ancient ancestors, who "fought
for national independence and religious freedom against the tyrannical attempts at repression by the Syrian rulers." Jewish families should model their
own actions on the Maccabees and persevere in God's spirit, because in contemporary Germany, "many social classes combine customary brutalization
with hatred and envy, and day after day our honor as citizens is trod into
the dust and our holy religious observances are sullied."[28] Hanukkah traveled
with the Jewish émigré community to the United States. American-Jewish
newspapers, like the socialist *Vorverts* (*sic*) and the religious daily *Tageblatt*,
castigated errant Jews who still celebrated Christmas. "The same voice that
blesses the Chanukkah [*sic*] lights cannot sing the praises of the Yule-tide
and be reckoned as an honest voice," argued the *Tageblatt* in 1903. "The same
hand that lights the long yellow tapers in the Menorah cannot light the gaudy
candles on the Christmas tree and be reckoned an honest hand."[29]

Ironically, the popularity of Hanukkah as an alternative to Christmas resulted in large part from Jewish acculturation into Christian-bourgeois society. In an era in which succeeding generations observed fewer formal religious rituals, domestic celebration preserved a sense of ethnic identity and religious stability. Jewish piety was thus feminized, sentimentalized, and commercialized in ways that paralleled the trajectories of Christian religious culture; yet the differences mattered. Private celebration was crucial for maintaining a sense of Jewishness in a hostile public environment.[30] Hanukkah, like Christmas, celebrated the family values central to the lifestyles of the German middle classes. The symbols and rituals of the Jewish holiday—such as lighting candles at the peak moment of family celebration—paralleled Christmas customs centered on family, children, domesticity, and gift giving. Jewish children might find "Hanukkah presents" under the family "Hanukkah tree" or around the menorah, and after memorizing and reciting a poem or singing "Maoz Tzur," the "Hanukkah song," they would receive presents and play games with cards or dreidels.[31] Advertisements for holiday gifts in the Jewish press show the tight connections between Christian and Jewish holidays: a Singer sewing machine could be offered as a "Christmas gift" or a more ecumenical "holiday gift"; a pitch for a "grand Christmas sale" in a Jewish department store might appear next to advertisements for "Hanukkah candles" to put on the menorah.[32] The emotional mood of Hanukkah also recalled that of Christmas, as suggested in a poem by German Zionist Hugo Zuckermann, who died in World War I:

> You light the candles for the children today
> And find joy in the quiet glow of the holiday.
> Through the window falls a soft evening light—
> Today you will reveal our miracle to them;
> Today brings the night, when all the enchanted
> Dreams of our childhood rise again,
> With light steps go through the room,
> Today brings the fairy tales of our twilight hours.[33]

Debates about the meaning of Hanukkah and the candles on the menorah likewise paralleled debates about the meaning of Christmas. Orthodox leaders clung to the religious aspects of the holiday and fought to preserve the deep spiritual meaning of the miracle of the temple oil.[34] Zionist Ernst Müller's remarks on the holiday were more typical of the way politics set the terms of public discussion. For Müller, Hanukkah certainly evoked an "indefinite longing for a world of inwardness and childishness," but only in the context of the Jewish nation at large. "The Hanukkah lights," Müller wrote, "which illuminate the individual Jewish home, lead the way to the individual, more holy light of the entire Volk."[35] The menorah, according to another commenter, symbolized "the victory of the spirit of our heroes and the holy peace of family life . . . respect and humility before the most holy, but also authentic pride and authentic inner rejoicing in our perseverance despite thousands of years of pressure."[36] Ideas about family, faith, and the Jewish nation were all ritually evoked when families lit the candles on the menorah and sang Maoz Tzur. With medieval lyrics set to the melody of a popular German folk song (the tune was also used by Luther for a Reformation-era hymn), the six stanzas of this family hymn recount the story of God's redemption of the people of Israel and their victories over the Egyptians, Babylonians, Persians, and Syrian-Greeks.[37] When children memorized this song and performed it with "pride and joy" before getting their presents, they combined a touching family performance with a clear assertion of Jewish victories over persecution and repression.[38]

The rapid growth of Jewish organizational life in the late nineteenth century gave Jews a further means to preserve their identity outside of formal religious services. Each year, Zionist civic groups, charity organizations, and social clubs across Germany held "Maccabee celebrations" that included gifting and singing and speeches about the bold acts of the Jewish ancestors. The 1899 Hanukkah celebration in a Jewish kindergarten in Berlin, organized by the *Israelitische Heimathaus* and funded by charity donations, was typical. Celebrants gathered around long tables laden with presents of toys, sweets, and practical objects. A teacher read a Hanukkah poem out loud "with warm emotion" and admonished the assembled children to please their parents with *Fleiß und Bravheit* (diligence and good behavior). Before opening their gifts, the children had to recite a poem memorized in advance. As the celebrants at the kindergarten sang "the Hanukkah hymn in German translation . . . the faces of the little ones shone with excitement and joy."[39] The opportunity to connect this moment of emotional intensity to Zionist goals was not lost on the organizers, who turned Hanukkah into a celebration of their own ethnically specific family romance that evoked the ties between past and present, family and community, and Volk and nation. Participants in community celebrations invariably listened to speeches about the deeds of "the brave Maccabees" who had promised "to spill all their blood for the inviolability of the inherited holy religion of our fathers." Observers described such celebrations, which imported family rituals into public space and Christmas customs into Jewish tradition, as *recht gemütlich* (really quite cosy).[40] Celebrations of Weihnukka and Hanukkah both provided distinct alternatives to mainstream Christmas celebrations, even as they recycled the sentimentalism of the conventional holiday.

THE JOYFUL TIDINGS OF SOCIALISM

For Adelheid Popp (born 1869), the noted socialist author and feminist agitator who grew up in a working-class family in Vienna, Christmas brought domestic strife and social envy instead of joy and harmony. "I knew nothing of the happy rejoicing brought by dolls, toys, fairy tales, goodies, and the Christmas tree," she wrote on the first page of her autobiography, which charts the growth of her political awareness and her conversion to the SPD. Still, like many working-class Germans, Popp's family wanted a "real" Christmas, with its domestic intimacies intact, even though they could barely afford it. In 1873 her mother pinched pennies until she could buy a tree and some modest gifts. On Christmas Eve, the family waited anxiously for Popp's father to come home from work so they could open their presents. He was very late, and the children went to bed. When he finally arrived, Popp remembered, he had apparently spent most of his Christmas bonus in a tavern, where he "drank more than he could handle." As the sleepy four-year-old looked on tearfully from behind a door, her father grabbed a hatchet and hacked the precious Christmas tree to bits.[41]

This dismal Christmas story would have resonated with German workers who read the socialist press or participated in the festivities sponsored by the worker's associations that flourished in the late nineteenth century. Popp's deconstructed version of the arch celebration of middle-class domesticity tapped into a critical discourse promoted by the SPD, who cast Christmas as a lie that masked working-class poverty and "the moral and spiritual atrophy" of capitalism.[42] Like German Jews, Social Democrats celebrated a different sort of Christmas, which by the end of the century had crystallized into a set of cohesive countertraditions. Though they rejected or redefined the central symbols and practices of the holiday, particularly its Christian aspects, Social Democrats readily appropriated the sentimental mood of bourgeois festivity and the familiar ideals of social harmony—now cast as the promise of revolutionary brotherhood. "Proletarian" Christmas celebrations were alive with the complexities of what historian Vernon Lidtke termed the "alternative culture" of the turn-of-the-century labor milieu. The Social Democratic counterculture offered workers and their families an alternative to dominant middle-class values and activities, even though, as Lidtke concludes, "in substance and style the world of the labor movement drew heavily on the same *bürgerlich* society and culture that Social Democrats also criticized so consistently and bitterly."[43]

After Kaiser Wilhelm II cancelled Bismarck's anti-Socialist laws in 1890–91, Social Democrats energetically worked out the standard features of their counter-Christmas, which would endure to inform socialist celebration in the Weimar era and after World War II. Mainstream, middle-class Christmas stories about family joy and social harmony around the Christmas tree were repetitive and generic; so, too, were the Social Democratic counter narratives. For socialists, the idealized view of social harmony promoted by church and state during the holiday season masked working-class exploitation and the bankruptcy of Western capitalism. An 1892 Christmas Day editorial, published in *Vorwärts*, the SPD's main newspaper, epitomized the bottom line: "And while the glad tidings ring out, what does Christianity offer in reality? The old world clings to its weapons, tens of millions of people armed for mass murder with all the devilish arts that barbarism with its prostituted civilization can prepare, ready in an instant to fall on each other and start a horrific bloodbath. . . . The ruling classes dance in wild turns around the golden calf—work exploited, squeezed dry, repressed like never before. Below misery, above staggering luxury and extensive decadence."[44] Only Marxist revolution could resolve the contradictions in the conventional Christmas message, which spoke of peace and harmony in the next world but endorsed harsh inequality and rampant militarism in this one. As another socialist critic put it, only the "joyful tidings of socialism" would truly bring the masses "Peace on Earth, Good Will to Men."[45]

Social Democratic attacks on Christianity were aggressive and apparently Manichean, but they inevitably revealed that the attempt to remake Christmas relied on dominant narratives. Despite the "priesterly dribble" delivered from the pulpit, *Vorwärts* announced, real-life conditions invariably showed that Christmas Eve was an *entweihte Nacht* (unholy night).[46] Yet the power and appeal of the Christian vision of brotherhood and "Peace on Earth" was undeniable, and socialist writers made every effort to enlist them for the revolution. Even staunch Social Democrats could honor Jesus as a secular being who spoke of freedom from social and political injustice. Jesus was the "first socialist," wrote *Vorwärts*, and though he remained a "child of his time" who could not recognize the materialist-economic bases of oppression, his original demands for mercy, justice, and peace for the poor and humble were noble indeed. If proletarians celebrated Christmas with "deeds of humanity and brotherhood" rather than "empty words of love," they could remain true to "the spirit of the Nazarene."[47] Jesus was first and foremost a political revolutionary, not a spiritual savior; he did not seek to give the "proletarian classes" of ancient Rome "salvation after death" but was resurrected instead to "smash the rule of Rome and erect on its ruins his new empire of peace and prosperity."[48]

Social Democrats took their secular theology most seriously. In efforts to challenge the appeal of Christian observance, propagandists paradoxically clung to the "higher" social truths embedded in the story of Jesus. Year after year, their rhetoric redirected the language and tone of Christianity toward a gospel of revolution, as this passage from an editorial published in *Vorwärts* on Christmas Day 1895 makes clear:

> Hidden in Jesus's own teaching lives . . . the powerful yearning for the "higher, the more pure, the unknown," which might dissolve the pain and need of humanity, the repression and violent acts, the eternal struggle of low and spiteful passions. Jesus, the friend of the poor, honors people in all walks of life, and love of humanity is the core of his teaching. . . . We who preach for and enlist all the passions in the struggle against society joyfully greet the Christian Christmas message with this new meaning, a belief deeply rooted in the earthly world of reality. We too believe that there will be an age of Peace on Earth and Good Will to Men. But no God can give us this peace. Only out of the struggle of earthly powers, ruled by the law of natural development, will freedom for humanity finally be born.[49]

Such language clearly honored the appeal of the spiritual transcendence promised by the church and the humanitarian ethos embodied in Jesus's preaching. Attempts to secularize the notion of Christian "Peace on Earth" furthermore suggest that Social Democratic writers recognized that it would prove difficult to substitute socialist dogma for Christian dogma. The results of their anti-Christianization campaigns indeed appear mixed. Swayed by the rhetoric of the Church Withdrawal Movement (or *Kirchenaustrittsbewegung*), sponsored by the Social Democrats and other freethinking groups, some 20,000 Protestant parishioners per year resigned their church membership in the decades before World War I. In Berlin, for example, about 8,000 Protestants resigned in 1908 and again in 1909, and over 12,000 resigned in 1912 and 1913. Internal church studies showed that most of these were working-class men in their twenties, and *Vorwärts* eagerly claimed success for the antichurch activities of Social Democracy.[50] In a detailed study of popular piety in Imperial Berlin, historian Hugh McLeod writes that such claims may well have been exaggerated. While the SPD drew significant numbers away from the church and "active Socialists" in fact outnumbered "active church-goers," McLeod concludes, "The majority of the [working-class] population had a foot in both camps, and avoided a total commitment to either."[51]

As part of their effort to undermine the popularity of Christianity, Social Democrats championed the winter solstice as a surrogate for the Christian celebration. The use of the solstice had distinct tactical advantages in the struggle to remake the holiday. For proletarians and bourgeoisie alike, the connections between Christmas and the pagan winter solstice inspired pride in the deep history of the Germany community. Like their middle-class counterparts, Social Democrats argued that contemporary festivities had organic links to the rituals of pre-Christian "Germanic" tribes, who recognized that the season marked the "beginning of new life . . . and new being" after the "freezing winter night."[52] The solstice thus offered a compelling metaphor for political renewal and revolution, a lesson not lost on future Nazi propagandists. Class-conscious workers could celebrate Christmas "not as a religious holiday, but as a winter solstice holiday, full of the exalted and joyful belief that this age of social winter night will be followed by a better, sunnier future: the kingdom of socialism."[53] Most crucially, recognition of this seasonal transformation retained the profound emotional impact of Christmas without resorting to Christianity. Solstice celebrations reveled in the uncanny and sublime flow of natural time that marked the "new beginnings" of late December. Light conquered darkness in the immutable cycles of nature, just as the proletariat would conquer their class enemy according to the natural laws of dialectical materialism. Poetic language best expressed the depths of this political/emotional nexus. It was a rare holiday issue of *Vorwärts* that did not include a solstice poem—no doubt meant to be read aloud—that opened with images of snow, cold rooms, and huddled masses, moved through an exposé of clerical deception, and closed with a rousing call to "help freedom's light to victory . . . [and] set the day of changes free."[54]

Solstice poems were only one example of a vast socialist counterliterature that drew on and challenged the sentimentalism of the bourgeois holiday. Scores of proletarian Christmas stories, as generic as their mainstream counterparts, offered socialist readers a different way to imagine class relations during the holiday season. Stock characters like aging widows, honest workingwomen, and begging street children reappeared in socialist fairy tales that reversed the familiar happy endings of middle-class stories. In the typical bourgeois fable, set in a nostalgic and timeless past, a simple gift of a golden coin or Christmas tree could bring joy to an entire family of poor but honest and orderly handworkers. Socialist stories on the contrary were staged in contemporary settings, in gritty urban street scenes or modern factories. They played out themes of abuse, exploitation, and grinding poverty. In "The Game Was Won," published in the Christmas issue of *Vorwärts* in 1891, a "young sweet girl" working in a factory is fired from her job on Christmas Day. Unemployed, she will not be able to pay rent or buy medicine for her sick mother, much less celebrate the holiday. After a visit to the "private office" of her employer, where, the writer implies, the girl is forced to provide sexual favors, she returns home to celebrate with a pocketful of gold coins and a promotion to assistant director.[55] Another story tells of a shabby street urchin who meets a bourgeois mother and her young daughter in a bakery. The daughter gives the boy a penny in what seems, at first, a classic moment of holiday charity. But the boy is accused of stealing and taken off by the police. The daughter begins to weep—such is the innocence of youth. The mother cynically assures her that the police "will only beat him a little bit for his own good" and instructs her to ask God to forgive the little thief in her nightly prayer.[56] Proletarian Christmas stories attacked the hypocrisy of the middle-class stories, yet they only went so far. The real problem with Christmas was poverty, not the holiday itself. Socialist writers pandered to the sentimentalism associated with Christmas in terms as maudlin as those used by the most bourgeois writer.

Social Democrats matched critical rhetoric with an alternative set of practices that appropriated bourgeois celebrations in both private and public spheres. Despite punishing economic conditions, workers wanted to celebrate a "good Christmas," and socialist publishers tried to meet demand. Children's Christmas books like *The Book of Fairy Tales for Proletarian Children* (1893) and *King Mammon* (1905), gifts for committed proletarians, reframed domestic celebration around progressive themes.[57] *The Christmas Book of Equality* (1906), edited by socialist women's leader Klara Zetkin, exemplifies the way socialists rewrote family Christmas books. "Defend against capitalism's werewolf hunger for cheap child flesh," Zetkin wrote to parents in her introduction. "Let us raise our children to struggle for socialism, so they can grasp the banner of victory with clear eyes and powerful hands, when death wrests it from our hands."[58] Such rhetoric hardly made it into the children's Christmas stories in the rest of the book. Meant to be read aloud around the Christmas tree, they promoted ideas about the winter solstice and the revolutionary nature of Jesus familiar from the socialist press. The revolutionary moral was present but underplayed—for example, in a story about talking Christmas tree ornaments that praise the poor handworker who made them and criticize the "snobby" apple from an aristocrat's manor.[59]

The familiar lyrics and melodies of family Christmas carols provided ample material for socialist intervention. Revised carols, such as the popular *Weihnachtsmarseillaise* (Christmas-Marseillaise), dated from the last third of the nineteenth century and had deep roots in working-class culture.[60] It is hard to know whether these modified songs were sung at home or reserved for public performances. It could have been both: *The Worker's Christmas in Song*, published in Dortmund before the First World War, contained standards like "Oh Christmas Tree" and "Kling Glöckchen klingelingeling" (Ring Little Bells Ring-a-Ding-a-Ding) but also religious hymns with rewritten lyrics that evoked visions of the postrevolutionary socialist future instead of the Baby Jesus.[61] The most famous example of this sort of revisionism is undoubtedly the "Worker's Silent Night" by Boleslaw Strzelewicz, a Polish writer and performer who performed across Germany with a socialist theater group named Gesellschaft Vorwärts (Society Forward). The revised lyrics were reprinted numerous times in worker's literature in the Wilhelmine era and the Weimar Republic. The song describes the plight of the impoverished working class, from the hungry child who asks his father for bread and miners who labor to find gold for the rich to the *mutige Kämpferschar* (stalwart battalions), who sit chained in jail because of their revolutionary activities. It exemplifies an entire genre of revised proletarian carols:

> Silent night, sorrowful night,
> All around, splendid light.
> In the hovels just torment and need,
> Cold and waste, no light and no bread.
> The poor are sleeping on straw. (Repeat)

> Silent Night, sorrowful night,
> The hungry babe cries out his plight,
> Did you bring us home some bread?
> Sighing the father shakes his head,
> "I'm still unemployed." (Repeat)

Silent night, sorrowful night,
Working folk, arise and fight!
Pledge to struggle in all holiness
Until humanity's Christmas exists
Until peace is here. (Repeat)[62]

The "Worker's Silent Night" captures the paradoxes of what might be called revolutionary sentimentalism: it mocked the solemnity and hypocrisy of bourgeois celebration even as the evocative tune and lyrics gave lower-class Germans a way to experience the bathos of the holiday. German authorities took the threat seriously; the song was banned as a "danger to the state" during the Imperial era.[63]

The SPD sponsored a range of public holiday festivities that brought workers together in celebrations of socialism and sociability, but they were not alone. Advertisements for proletarian Christmas parties sponsored by a variety of working-class groups surfaced in the socialist press in the late 1870s in urban areas such as Hannover, Kiel, and Flensburg.[64] After the revocation of the antisocialist laws in 1891, a working class segmented by class, trade, and political allegiance could find any number of holiday attractions. In December 1892 in Berlin, for example, workers could go to Christmas parties sponsored by various SPD voting-district leaders, the Ethical Society, the Free Religion Community, the "Tumbling League Fichte," and numerous trade-union associations. Such events featured all the trappings of a middle-class holiday, including concerts, group singing, living pictures, humorous speeches, dance balls, dramatic performances, and gifts for children, typically framed with a propagandistic "holiday speech." The "Grand Christmas Amusements" sponsored by "the men and women tailors of Berlin" was typical. Doors opened at 4:00 P.M. on 27 December. For a small entrance fee, attendees could hear a concert led by the house band and participate in a "grand opening of Christmas presents for children." During a coffee break, the partiers would hear speeches organized by the "agitation committee." Afterward, all were invited to a dance ball—though men paid an extra fifty pennies to attend.[65]

Socialist charity festivities appropriated the notion of "good works" as practiced by the bourgeoisie and the churches in the name of "true brotherhood." The official call for "peace, love and charity!" was "a pretty promise," according to one angry editorialist, but "the love of Christmas Eve is like a drop on a hot stone."[66] The charity party for waiters in Berlin, sponsored by the Christian League for Young Men, was a case in point. The 800 waiters in attendance were reportedly dismayed with the meager dinner and even more disgruntled by the "spiritual nourishment" offered by the attending pastor, who lectured the company about the rewards that awaited the poor in heaven.[67] Socialist rhetoric consistently attacked the notion that charity in the holiday season brought grace to the giver, contentment to the receiver, and overall social harmony. Yet the SPD was compelled by need to undertake charity "actions" of its own for workers on strike or shut out of their jobs. Donations from local SPD offices, trade associations, tavern and theater owners, and individuals subsidized charity parties and showed that workers could establish their own alternative socialist support networks. In Berlin in 1904, for example, over 5,500 children of striking metalworkers, carpenters, upholsterers, and machine workers attended a free party that featured large Christmas trees with electric lights, a concert, puppet shows, and gifts. This "beautiful act of solidarity," wrote a reporter for *Vorwärts*, turned the "class conscious workers, as it were, into a single great family. . . . [T]he mood that animated this great family of struggling proletarians was so joyful, so unforced, that it could not have been better at a Christmas celebration in one's own home." Socialist charity drives that replaced "false humanity" with "true solidarity" obviously borrowed much from standard practices, and the point was similar: Christmas turned disparate individuals into a "great family" and brought the community together around the Christmas tree.[68]

The proletarian holiday did not take place in a cozy family parlor or a fantasy idyll of bourgeois nostalgia but occurred very much in public and in the present. Year after year, Christmas lent poignancy to contemporary struggles for social justice. Reports in the Christmas issues of the socialist press reminded readers about the Berlin beer boycott of 1894, demonstrated solidarity with the revolutionary proletariat in Russia, or attacked the hypocrisy of celebrating Christmas in the atmosphere of increasing militarism before World War I. When 8,000 textile workers went out on strike for a ten-hour working day in Crimmitschau, a mill town in Saxony, in the winter of 1903–1904, the holiday season brought an unprecedented opportunity for pointed agitation. In response to campaigns organized by the SPD, holiday donations for the strikers poured in from Berlin, Leipzig, and other towns. Entire depots full of holiday sweets, toys, and more-practical gifts reportedly stood ready for the workers, but the local authorities cancelled all public Christmas parties. According to an angry SPD editorialist, the "capitalist power elite" of Crimmitschau thus revealed that it well understood the "revolutionary character of the festival of Christ." Mustering familiar outrage and sarcasm, the author ridiculed the idea that Christmas was a Christian celebration for the "little ones and the downtrodden, the defenseless children." Instead, "police officers entered the church with drawn sabers and cocked revolvers, and broke up the meeting of the festival of Christ because of community-threatening intrigues, because of the unsurpassed terrorism of brotherly love."[69] Some 600 workers and their wives withdrew from the local Protestant church in response, and, under pressure, the police relented and allowed workers and their families to meet in small groups of six or seven people to collect their gifts. The textile workers were proud that they had observed Christmas despite state oppression. Still, there was "no peace in Crimmitschau." Revolution had to come first.[70]

SHARED SENTIMENTS

Social Democrats constructed a distinct alternative to the mainstream holiday, and no doubt many workers—especially union members and highly skilled urban residents—participated in some sort of proletarian festivity. Yet the SPD counter-Christmas hardly dominated working-class celebration. German workers enjoyed a lively holiday culture that cut across the goals of the SPD and bourgeois proprieties alike. Working-class festivity was shaped by rowdy popular tradition, the expansion of commercial leisure opportunities, and changing attitudes toward family and private life. Though there are relatively few descriptions of celebration in workers' households from the Wilhelmine period, by the 1890s it appears that most urban working families gathered around a Christmas tree in rituals of gifting, feasting, and family performance that looked a lot like the middle-class version of the holiday. In part public bacchanalia, in part sentimental family festival, the workers' Christmas shaped and was shaped by social tensions in Imperial Germany. The holiday helped build a national culture shared tentatively across social strata, with common familial values that could transcend politics or class allegiance.

There was no "typical" worker's holiday, though firsthand accounts, sumptuary laws read against the grain, and advertisements for holiday activities reveal the outlines of popular celebration. The appeal of Christmas was milieu dependent. Working-class lifestyles varied widely around 1900, when pockets of industrialized, high-density urbanization coexisted with rural areas far less touched by industrial development. Family size and structure and standards of living were diverse, and, as Mary Nolan notes, around 1900 the urban proletariat was "divided by occupation and skill, culture and religion, age and sex, birthplace and commitment to urban life and industrial work."[71] The working class was never homogeneous, but representative experiences at work and at home worked against centrifugal tendencies, particularly in larger cities. Poorer Germans had similar interactions with employers, landlords, and the state. Their lives, according to historian Alfred Kelly, were typically marked by "unemployment, high job turnover, long hours, low wages, grinding drudgery, child labor, crowded housing, alcoholism, sexual abuse, illegitimacy, home work for women, and so on."[72] Attempts by Social Democrats and trade unionists to build an "alternative culture" offered skilled workers and their families a further source of common experience that countered hegemonic middle-class values.[73] Finally, as new commercialized leisure pursuits merged with and replaced more traditional forms of popular entertainment, workers and their families increasingly participated in standardized forms of recreation, particularly during holidays. For those who could afford them, local taverns, Tingel-Tangel (cabaret-style entertainment that featured music, skits, and recitations), dance halls, associational clubs, and public theater constructed a workers' culture stitched together by consumerism rather than a strictly defined class or Social Democratic identity.

Christmas connected in many ways to the world of labor. Perhaps most importantly for workers themselves, the holiday meant time off and a possible *Weihnachtsgratifikation*, or Christmas bonus. Both were valuable commodities around 1900, when the typical factory worker worked six days a week for eleven hours a day and spent most of his or her pay on basic necessities. By the 1850s in Prussia, the largest German state, sumptuary law generally forbade work on Christmas Eve, Christmas Day, and sometimes 26 December, the so-called second day of Christmas. Yet employers only sporadically followed the exacting regulations that mandated free time on religious and other annual holidays, and numerous codified exceptions kept workers on the job in the holiday season.[74] Christmas in fact meant extra work and longer hours for those employed in department and retail stores, domestic service, food industries, and toy and decoration factories, and holiday speedups engendered bitter complaints in the socialist press.[75]

The promise of a Christmas bonus, the extra wage or gift in kind most employers gave their workers to mark the holiday season, offered some compensation. Such "gifts," commented one workingwoman in 1909, were meant to encourage productivity and were "pretty much a part of wages" for both agricultural and factory workers.[76] On a symbolic level, the

Weihnachtsgratifikation, given "voluntarily" by the boss, turned workers into "children" of the company and surrounded labor relations with the paternalism of the bourgeois family holiday. Workers, for their part, viewed the annual bonus not as a gift but as a right, and struggles over its amount and terms of payment could lead to friction between employers and employees. In any case, this moment of ritualized exchange reinforced the symbolic and official contracts that defined working conditions and social status. The size of the bonus depended on position, length of service, and place of employment. Less-skilled workers in temporary or insecure jobs usually got some sort of token bonus or a raise on Christmas Eve—in the early 1900s, for example, a factory worker might receive a two-penny raise on a salary of twenty-five pennies an hour—but this benefit did indeed depend on the "generosity" of the employer.[77] For professionals and skilled workers, Christmas could bring handsome rewards. After 1858, employees at Siemens, the global chemical concern based in Munich, received an *Inventurprämie* (inventory premium) tied to annual profits on Christmas Eve. In 1900 the company formally renamed this annual payment a "Christmas bonus." Salaried employees at the turn of the century received a holiday bonus equal to one month's salary— the so-called thirteenth-month wage—while, after five years of service, blue-collar workers were entitled to a bonus determined by their rate of annual productivity.[78]

The ritualized aspects of employee-employer contact that surrounded the Weihnachtsgratifikation had special resonance for the many women who worked as live-in servants for bourgeois families. For members of the elite bourgeoisie as well as the growing middle class, the employment of at least one *Dienstmädchen* (serving girl, or live-in domestic servant) was an essential way to demonstrate that one maintained a "proper" bourgeois lifestyle.[79] Around the turn of the century, women in domestic service were the largest group of women working outside of the home and represented about one-third of all workingwomen in Germany; their terms of employment typically included some sort of holiday bonus. Bourgeois employers gave annual "gifts" to their servants on or around Christmas Eve in rituals modeled on family celebration but generally kept strictly separated from those of the family circle itself. The Christmas bonuses given to domestic servants varied greatly and depended in large part on the status of the family offering employment. According to economist and social reformer Oskar Stillich, servants in the best Berlin households usually negotiated a holiday bonus as part of their working contract. The bonus averaged 15 percent of wages and could be as high as 25 percent—clearly a significant part of an annual salary that ranged between 600 and 1,200 marks (two-thirds of which was generally paid in room and board). Domestic servants who worked for less-prominent families might get some money, but more likely they received a "gift" of drink, food, clothing, or perhaps a *bunte Teller*, a sort of party plate laden with holiday treats: nuts, apples, sweets, and sometimes a bottle of wine.[80]

The holiday season intensified contact between employers and servants, with high expectations on both sides. For the middle-class "mistress" in a well-managed household, the Christmas season required a conspicuous display of bourgeois luxury to circles of family and friends, embodied in a fine Christmas tree, shopping excursions, and balls and parties. For the domestic servant who did most of the work, the holidays meant special demands, longer hours, and little time for visiting their own families. An article titled "The Servant's Christmas" in a 1909 December issue of a Kiel daily newspaper offered suggestions for ways the "experienced housewife" could successfully manage the emotional and financial conflicts exacerbated by this cross-class exchange. Most of all, the considerate housewife should remember that "Christmas is a celebration of love" and that servants needed the same "loving care" as one's own family. "Search deeply in the soul of your serving girl" the anonymous writer recommended. "Think about the way you would want your Herrschaft [masters] to treat you on Christmas Eve, and act accordingly!" When possible, servants should be given time off for a visit with their own kin, since "it is good for every girl, if the masters take an interest in her family." Servants should never be left alone in a cold kitchen, where they might be a reluctant witness to the "fun and delight" taking place in the master's rooms. As for the "gift" itself, a bonus for one's "girl" was of course a necessity. But the bonus should not consist solely of cash, since that was "functional and cold." Presents should be thoughtful, not cheap, and oriented toward the servants' needs; "worthless fripperies" were particularly bad, since they reinforced "vanity and the desire to have a fling."[81] Beyond revealing the condescension held by the "mistress" toward her servant, this sort of prescriptive language exposes the ideological work implicit in holiday rituals. The caring emotions that putatively surrounded the "serving girl's" Christmas naturalized the notion that young women servants had close, quasi-familial ties to their bourgeois "masters" and thus were not entitled to the rights of an employee. The basic facts clearly contradicted this notion of interclass harmony: domestic labor was notorious for its low wages, long hours, and fast turnover.[82]

Despite economic exploitation, the "matriarchal" structure of employer-employee relationships in domestic service encouraged identification as well as distance. Urban, middle-class mothers acted as "missionaries of 'Bürgerlichkeit'" to their female servants, mostly young women from the countryside who moved to the city to find work.[83] During the Christmas season, the dialectic of control, cultural transmission, and self-assertion played out with particular tenacity, as the memoirs of Doris Vierbeck, a domestic servant in Hamburg in the late 1880s and 1890s, make clear. When Vierbeck worked for a harsh and demanding "mistress" named Frau Sparr, the holiday was a nightmare of petty demands, bickering, and close surveillance. The household spent weeks in 1889 preparing for a large Christmas Day "social," and Vierbeck got up early in the morning that day to begin cooking for the party. She received abundant "gifts" but read this as a cynical act of conspicuous benevolence. Her employer displayed the presents where invited guests could see them so that her friends and acquaintances "would be amazed at how the 'good' Frau Sparr showered her servants with gifts." For weeks thereafter, Frau Sparr admonished Vierbeck for small work-related problems by calling attention to her "ingratitude" for this holiday generosity.

Vierbeck makes it clear that if employers kept to their side of the bargain—offered the right gifts and showed at least some concern for the well-being of their servants—the social contract was acceptable. For Christmas 1892, working in a different household, Vierbeck received clothes, linens, and an expensive watch and chain. When she expressed surprise at such generosity, her "mistress" whispered, "'You know you have a busy working time ahead of you, and to make sure you don't falter, I have prepared this joy for you.'"[84] In this case, both parties recognized the business nature of the employee-employer relationship, even as they drew on holiday sentimentalism to smooth the terms of the deal. The Kiel editorialist, one feels, would find this an appropriate exchange.

Doris Vierbeck may have resented having to prepare Christmas for someone else, but she shared the sentimental feelings that made the holiday an appealing celebration of wholesome family life. "I thought about my heimatlichen [hometown] Christmases," she wrote as she described her labor for the demanding Frau Sparr. "How beautiful, how wonderfully beautiful they were in the circle of my dear, good parents and brothers and sisters! How many joyful Christmas songs we sang, and how great and true was the joy with the modest presents under the glowing Tannenbaum!" Such memories only highlighted what Vierbeck called "the banality" of preparing a luxurious holiday table for her ungracious employer, "whose heart and soul went hungry and thirsty."[85] Like their bourgeois employers, when workers spoke of Christmas they used the rhetoric of family intimacy. Both groups were apparently compelled by what was almost a moral imperative to celebrate the sentimental ties of domesticity during the holiday season. "Christmas is a Freudenfeiertag" (holiday of rejoicing), as one working mother put it around 1910, "the most wonderful celebration for grown-ups and children."[86]

Despite shared sentiments, German workers celebrated on the margins. They saved or sometimes borrowed money so they could afford holiday food, decorations, and gifts. Factory worker Mortiz Bromme fondly recalled Christmas in the early 1880s because on 25 and 26 December he and his family "could eat to our heart's content," an offhand but revealing comment that underscores the rarity of such indulgence. In other years, Bromme's parents could not afford the flour necessary to bake cookies or Christmas fruitcake.[87]

The gifts exchanged among workers reflected a culture of economic scarcity as well as celebration; the seasonal splurge outfitted the domestic space for the rest of the year. Advertisements in working-class newspapers like *Vorwärts* suggest that most presents were practical: year after year, "exceptional Christmas offers" on items like shoes, men's suits and winter coats, women's dresses, bed linens, and dishware shared advertising space with more-luxurious items like tobacco, liquor, and the odd toy. "Practical Christmas gifts" could even include everyday items like spices, dried soup mixes, and bouillon cubes.[88] Homemade gifts were also common. Families of limited means tried to capture what one schoolteacher called the "special magic woven by the wonderful smells and bright glow of Christmas" by forgoing expensive, commercially produced goods and instead making gifts and decorations by hand.[89] These gifts confirmed the intimacy of the handmade, just as they did for wealthier Germans, but most workers were simply too poor to afford to buy many presents. Well into the twentieth century, numerous German children received presents fashioned from cigar boxes, kindling, and scraps of cloth.[90]

A tradition of rowdy popular celebration rooted in Early Modern artisan culture persisted in Germany's streets and taverns alongside the domestic festivities borrowed from the middle classes. By 1900 mumming parades and the visits of proto–Father Christmases such as Knecht Ruprecht were for the most part a play-acted remnant of a once-vibrant artisan culture. Nonetheless, workers often used the free time of the Christmas holidays to engage in rounds of heavy drinking, indulging in the "lubricant of leisure" that was basic to the working-class subculture.[91] During the Christmas season in late nineteenth-century Westphalia, according to one contemporary, "the men were often in Katerstimmung [like tomcats—in other words, in a rowdy mood]. Christmas Eve was a Sauftag [a day for a drunk] par excellence."[92] Railway excavator Carl Fischer captured this alternative Christmas mood in his account of Christmas Eve in 1867: "Then came the last day before Christmas, Christmas Eve," he remembered. "The weather was beautiful, quiet, with a mild frost; I got in a holiday mood and wanted a drink of schnapps, so around 10:00 [A.M.] I went to the pub and bought a bottle of schnapps for two and one-half groschen, and then went back to work." After drinking all day on the job with coworkers and employers, Fischer passed out on the railroad tracks at his construction site and was almost killed by a train. He recovered from his hangover three days later.[93]

Middle-class outrage with those who drank away the holiday, "occupying taverns before Christmas mass, and often during the same," as neo-Romantic author Adalbert Stifter put it, expressed tensions over the use of holiday time that went to the core of the relationship between church, state, and society.[94] Christmas drew close scrutiny from nineteenth-century bureaucrats concerned with public discipline, as the rule of law increasingly cast bourgeois norms as the foundation of the social order.[95] Drunks and rowdies challenged notions of bourgeois propriety in the holiday season in ways that threatened to spill over into more-organized forms of political resistance, particularly with the emergence of organized political opposition and the rapid growth of the SPD toward the end of the century. To counter such threats, government officials and merchants, teachers, and clergy used Christmas to promote the virtues of middle-class, Christian morality: obedience, sobriety, and order. Municipal authorities worked closely with the highest administrative authority in the Prussian Protestant church, the Evangelischer Oberkirchenrat (Protestant Upper Consistory), which for decades monitored the "misuse and disruption" of Sundays and Christian holidays and interceded with government authorities in attempts to control the observance of public festivities.[96] By the mid-1850s, sumptuary laws limiting "all publicly noticeable work" and "public dance entertainments and similar noisy amusements" during Christmas and other church holidays were in force in a number of Prussian cities, including Aachen, Berlin, Coblenz, Düsseldorf, Cologne, Trier, and Frankfurt on the Oder.[97] The regulations banned work in retail, factory, agricultural, and government sectors as well as the loading and unloading of vehicles in public streets and labor in artisan and handicraft shops. Emergency exceptions were allowed by application to the police authorities.[98]

Sumptuary law codified the priorities of church leaders and state bureaucrats, but reading regulations against the grain also reveals the persistent ways that popular festive forms challenged class-based holiday observances. Continued debates over Christmas sumptuary laws—which persisted well into the 1920s—suggest that popular celebration consistently evaded state control. Significant numbers of Germans apparently recognized the birth of Jesus with raucous parties, fireworks, and the discharge of weapons, since Prussian law explicitly forbade target practice with firearms and "all loud amusements in private apartments or private gardens" on Christmas Eve and on the evenings of 25 and 26 December.[99] Official attempts to do away with the noise of popular celebration and instead define the "aural landscape" of Christmas according to the domestic pleasantries of soft chimes and family carols underscore the role of the senses in the construction of modern social hierarchies.[100]

Sumptuary laws grew ever more extensive with the passing years, as state regulations increasingly targeted the parties and entertainments offered for profit by any number of commercial sponsors. In 1911 Berlin officials ordered local police to "determine if religious services require protection" from any number of potential "disturbances," including "public dance entertainment and balls, choral and declamatory readings, plays with actors and all musical performances, in the case that they do not maintain a serious character; speeches, plays, and musical performances in cafés chantants (Tingel-Tangel)." Those who engaged in any form of work, public entertainment, or private "amusements" that threatened "public respect" for the holiness of Christmas, Sundays, and other religious holidays were subject to a minimum fine of sixty marks.[101] Such laws were ostensibly promulgated to protect church services from disruption, but it seems that the authorities also hoped to repress the "proletarian" Christmas celebrations organized by the Social Democrats. In any case, by the turn of the century, it seems safe to assume that statutes outlawing popular entertainment were rarely enforced. New commercial forms of holiday observance had appropriated, merged with, and begun to replace more traditional customs, whether religious, bourgeois, or working-class.

Prussian officials used sumptuary law in attempts to meet church demands for time off during the holiday so workers would attend holiday mass. The effect of regulation may have been somewhat counterproductive, however, since more time off created more time for rowdy behavior. Church and state leaders struggled to encourage religious involvement in what historian Hugh McLeod calls a "half-secular society" in which the working classes, particularly in large cities like Berlin, had begun to move away from the church.[102] Beyond the influence of socialism, there were a number of structural reasons for low church attendance: the mobility of the working-class population kept them from establishing ties with a single parish; poverty created what one contemporary observer, a pastor in Berlin, called "a frightening degree of indifference to anything that is not directly concerned with the business of making a living"; and the social distance between the clergy and working Germans alienated potential worshipers.[103] Still, the great majority of German workers were registered church members, and despite a certain disregard for regular religious observance, Christmas, Easter, and Pentecost services continued to draw crowds. Günther Dehn, a pastor at the Reformation Church in Moabit, a working-class district in Berlin, explained what would be an observable trend throughout the century in the years before World War I. He divided his parishioners into two types: those "loyal to the church" and those "strongly church-minded." The first group, according to Dehn, attended church for the most part only on important festival days, while members of the second were more likely to participate in weekly religious services. His church was full on Christmas and New Year's Eve; the "sentimental character" of these services, Dehn noted, attracted even flagging believers.[104]

Though dominant Christmas narratives championed German unity, the holiday opened social and symbolic space for the assertion of difference. Weihnukka, Hanukkah, proletarian counterholidays, and the diverse celebratory practices of the lower classes reveal that Christmas could absorb and mediate conflicting interests. There were sharp differences between celebrations observed by Germans on the margins and those in the mainstream, yet German Jews, Social Democrats, and workers all found the sentimental mood at the core of the bourgeois holiday indispensable. In short, by 1900, German Christmas anchored a shared national culture while simultaneously revealing the fractures in that culture. The political resonance of this dialectic would appear in full illumination when the nation went to war and Christmas became a celebration of Germans united against a common enemy.

3

Christmas in Enemy Territory

"Jesus needs *us* now, we feel it, so he can fulfill his world purpose with our swords."

—⋄ Christmas sermon of Chaplain D. G. Goens, delivered at
   Kaiser Wilhelm II's General Headquarters in occupied Belgium,
   24 December 1914

ON THE CLEAR, STARLIT NIGHT OF 24 December 1914, British rifleman Graham Williams looked over the top of his trench on the front in Flanders and saw that "lights began to appear along the German parapet." Startled, he looked more closely and determined that these "were evidently make-shift Christmas trees, adorned with lighted candles, which burnt steadily in the still frosty air!" During the night, no shots were fired; instead, German and British soldiers in opposing trenches traded carols, and Williams heard the strains of "Silent Night, Holy Night" for the first time. On the following Christmas Day, several hundred or perhaps a thousand soldiers fraternized in small, individual groups in no-man's-land along a fifteen-mile stretch of the Flanders front. They shook hands, buried their dead, played soccer, and exchanged token gifts of tobacco, chocolate, schnapps, and unit badges.[1] The military authorities on both sides quickly forbade such acts of fraternization as high treason. Yet for one brief moment, in the words of the official historian of the German 133rd Saxons, the war took "the tranquil form of a singing match."[2]

The ironies of the famous "Christmas truce" continue to exert a hold on the popular and historical imagination. The History Channel's DVD *The Christmas Truce* (2007) includes voluminous firsthand accounts of "a remarkable story of the Christmas spirit . . . that symbolized the change from [the] Nineteenth to the Twentieth century."[3] German journalist Michael Jürgs's sentimental book *Der kleine Frieden im großen Krieg* (The Little Peace in the Great War), again based primarily on eyewitness reports, has been through

FIGURE 3.1
The Christmas tree as "Golden Bridge" between front and Heimat.
(*Der Schützengraben* [The Trench], December 1915)

five editions since its initial publication in 2003. The *New York Times* reports that in 2006 an Irish pop star paid $27,000 for an original, handwritten five-page letter describing the events, and the cloying French feature film *Merry Christmas* (2005) turns the truce into a saccharine melodrama of opera, love, and fraternization.[4] Stanley Weintraub's *Silent Night: The Story of the World War I Christmas Truce* (2002) is only the latest English-language attempt to provide a detailed account of events.[5] Historian George Mosse concluded that the fellow feeling shown in the trenches captured the "real" Christmas spirit. According to Paul Fussell, the truce signaled "the last twitch of the nineteenth century" and the opening of the modern era.[6] German historians, for their part, have suggested that the truce shows that ordinary soldiers readily challenged their officers and disobeyed orders from above, calling into question the myth of the trench community propagated by nationalists during and after the war.[7]

This almost obsessive focus on the Christmas truce obscures the history of a much more typical and ordinary wartime Christmas. Indeed the observance of what Germans called War Christmas (*Kriegsweihnachten*) would become all too familiar in the first half of the twentieth century. Between 1910 and 1950, Germans celebrated one out of every five Christmases while the nation was at war. War Christmas forced soldiers and civilians to endure experiences that were hardly Christmaslike. As Catholic chaplain Fridolin Mayer, stationed on the West Front, wrote in his diary on 24 December 1914: "In the field hospital lie wounded from the 111th, the company had formed up in Souchez in order to receive Christmas packages. Bang, a shell, a few men dead, a number of wounded. For a Christmas present, a burial with music."[8] Violence, death, and separation from home during what was supposed to be a celebration of Christian peace and family love led to the emergence of paradoxical forms of ritual practice. War Christmas reshaped long-standing customs in tenuous attempts to resolve the tensions between war and peace, home and front, public duties and private observances. However fragile the results, the contradictions apparently made soldiers' celebrations uniquely moving: whether in 1870, 1914, or 1940, they commented repeatedly on the "unforgettable" nature of their wartime holiday.

War Christmas was a hybrid holiday, an unstable amalgam of official and vernacular practices. The dominant institutions of German society drew on memories of the chauvinist holiday celebrated during the Franco-Prussian War (1870–71) and the militarism and Prussian-Protestant nationalism that already defined the late nineteenth-century middle-class holiday to cast War

Christmas as a celebration of seamless national harmony, appropriate for a Christian nation at war with its enemies. Civic leaders and propagandists claimed that the sentimental bonds of the Christmas mood, fraught with heightened emotion during the crisis of war, dissolved the class, confessional, and regional differences that ordinarily divided Germans from one another. Reports from the front described battle-hardened but pious frontline soldiers celebrating with comrades at boisterous parties "in enemy territory." Thoughts of home and family softened the mood; during the holiday season, authorities claimed, an imaginary "golden bridge" linked front and Heimat and inspired soldiers to defend the nation from Germany's enemies.

Protestant and Catholic clergymen adapted the rhetoric of war theology to the nation's favorite holiday. Sensing renewed interest in God as a response to the crisis of war, Germany's religious leaders called for national solidarity in attempts to bolster flagging church attendance. Their sermons compared soldiers to the "rough herdsmen" who witnessed the birth of Jesus and encouraged the troops to emulate Christ's example of self-sacrifice. Protestant court chaplain D. G. Goens struck what would become familiar notes at the kaiser's own 1914 Christmas party in occupied Belgium, when he reminded the soldiers gathered around a row of thirty-foot-tall decorated Christmas trees that God was on their side: "We draw our swords and lower our flags before Jesus, so he will bless them in a holy battle for our threatened fatherland."[9] Catholic clergy expressed similar ideas, praising the "steel-hard will" of the heroic "warriors" who protected the "Germany of their Fathers" from the enemy.[10] The high-flown rhetoric of Germany's spiritual leaders echoed in the sermons of frontline military chaplains. They spread the dogma of war theology to soldiers during Christmas services, aided by instructional booklets that included nationalistic prayers, songs, and instructions for services—intended, as a prayer titled "War Prayer for Christmas Time" put it, to offer hope in the "sea of blood and bitter tears" unloosed by the war.[11]

Christmas in World War I was in many ways a public exercise, controlled from the chancellery and the pulpit. Celebration nonetheless made room for private needs in practical and symbolic ways. Germans gravitated to familiar holiday traditions in attempts to come to terms with the dislocation and trauma of the war. Social clubs, local parishes, and women's groups organized charity drives and letter-writing campaigns for the soldiers at the front; the resulting exchange of *Feldpost* (army mail) and packages exercised the institutional networks of social belonging that linked individual soldiers to those at home. Just as the celebrations organized by military authorities and civic elites evoked and appropriated family rituals and individual feelings, so the more private rituals of soldiers in the ranks incorporated official discourse. When they participated in military celebrations, rooted in the homosocial barracks culture of army life, soldiers enlisted themselves in a *Leidensgemeinschaft*, a "community of suffering" based on comradeship, forbearance, and shared concern for those at home.[12] Celebrations of War Christmas hardly overcame the deep divisions in German society. Nonetheless, Germans at home and at the front joined leading institutions to construct a self-mobilizing myth of national solidarity centered on the holiday.

CELEBRATE LIKE GERMAN WARRIORS!

The history of German War Christmas really starts with the Siege of Paris in December 1870, when German troops reportedly celebrated a particularly chauvinist holiday in occupied France. This first War Christmas did more than nationalize the holiday or popularize the Christmas tree, as historian Ingeborg Weber-Kellermann argues in an often-cited passage from her social history of German Christmas.[13] Celebration "before the gates of Paris" established the deepest layer of a national myth that would fascinate and trouble Germany's collective imagination for the next century. The myth of War Christmas had its origins in reports about the bombastic celebrations of soldiers at the front during the war itself; it was further codified in the war-memoir literature written in the last decades of the nineteenth century. Memoirs, published diaries, and fanciful stories recalled a difficult but ultimately fulfilling and even joyful soldiers' holiday. An idealized version of War Christmas, exemplified in "true-to-life" accounts by veterans like J. W. Emonts and Carl Tanera, dominated public discourse. Recollections of Christmas in 1870 conveyed a utopian vision of German integration at a time when the affective bonds of national community were taking shape. According to the stories, soldiers proudly celebrated confessional and regional particularities at military Christmas parties. But they also cherished traditional German Christmas customs that evoked a common cultural heritage, which presumably made other social differences intangible or inconsequential.

The jarring juxtaposition of Christmas and modern war encouraged instant mystification, and it is difficult to parse the "real" experience of December 1870 from its idealized representations. The clichés of War Christmas spread quickly. Bourgeois family magazines featured drawings of soldiers outside Paris celebrating around a Christmas tree, sometimes with caricatures of the enemy hanging from its branches, and newspaper reports included glowing descriptions of the wartime holiday. Calls for Christmas charity spoke of a common purpose in the new language of national solidarity. According to the family magazine *Gartenlaube*, a charitable donation expressed communal responsibility for poor and fatherless families at home as well as for "our new comrades in the Fatherland beyond the Rhein"; it further showed that shared "German custom" and "Germanic blood" united the nation, despite the political borders that separated the German states.[14] German civic leaders thus legitimized Prussian war aims with the sentimentalism of the familiar Christmas mood.

For soldiers at the front, Christmas was hardly as joyous as the sanitized accounts in the press at home reported. Grinding work, bad food, and violence continued during the holiday season. "On the 25th and 26th, during the Christmas holidays, we dug bombproof shelters day and night," wrote a soldier in the Fifth Infantry Regiment.[15] In a letter to his father, a lieutenant groused about his "miserable quarters" and complained that he ate only pea soup and slept in straw on Christmas Eve.[16] On the day before Christmas, Ludwig Richter, an infantryman from Bochum in the 77th Infantry Division, hid from enemy shelling in a pile of manure. On Christmas Day, his regiment had to storm several towns to hold off the French and suffered sixty casualties. "Of course there was no talk of the 'Christmas mood,'" Richter remembered.[17] "On Christmas Day no church service, no festive dress," sulked another Bavarian soldier. "Anyone who did not feel Christmas on the inside had nothing else of the celebration, since the French never stopped sending us their holiday greetings, at the usual hour, in the form of bombs and grenades."[18] Even among the highest ranks, where officer-aristocrats could celebrate at luxurious staff parties, the mood turned sour. Friedrich Graf von Frankenberg, an adjutant with the German Third Army assigned to the Voluntary Hospital Corps at Versailles, attended a party with the military elite. Despite the fine presents distributed by lottery and the presence of Prussian Crown Prince Friedrich Wilhelm, who put on a show of merriment, Frankenberg noted in his diary that none of the participants were truly happy. A celebration for wounded soldiers in the Versailles field hospital was particularly distasteful—Frankenberg recorded his irritation over the Christmas sermon delivered by the hospital chaplain, who manipulated the soldiers' feelings until they wept.[19]

In letters and diaries, soldiers expressed their longings for home and family and so lent legitimacy to official claims that a "golden bridge" linked Heimat and front with special intensity during the holiday season. The burdens of war made recollections of childhood celebrations particularly poignant. "Never did our thoughts, never did our wishes fly more warmly to the beloved Heimat," remembered infantryman Florian Kühnhauser, a Bavarian soldier active in his local veterans group after the war. "Memories of past years, yes of childhood were awoken [by this] painful suffering and deprivation."[20] Religious services, according to court chaplain Bernhard Rogge, made soldiers "whole" by reminding them of home.[21] According to the authorities, such feelings were universal. As a Catholic chaplain noted in a typical comment, attempts to celebrate this "holy family celebration" led to common desires: "Who among our soldiers, whether sick or healthy, married or single, does not think of Heimat on this night?"[22] In numerous accounts, the sight of a Christmas tree in occupied France elicited feelings of Germanness and memories of home and childhood. In a letter to his wife in December 1870, General Hans von Kretschmann described the effects of the tree during a religious service: "To the right and left of the altar stood candle-lit Christmas trees, surrounded by our good chaps, with long beards and serious faces; here one felt something akin to: Heimat."[23] When he saw the decorated trees set up by soldiers quartered in a French town, Chaplain Rogge noted, "One could think one walked through a German village."[24] Taking advantage of its symbolic associations, military and religious leaders asked soldiers to swear allegiance to the nation under arms around the Christmas tree in frontline celebrations.[25] The selective use of the tree at the front, however, also revealed its class roots. When one Bavarian rifleman went to his brigade headquarters to pick up his company's orders, he was "allowed" to see the major's "most beautiful illuminated Christmas tree" as the orders were read out loud. The vision helped him forget he was stationed in "inhospitable France." Back in his company quarters, there was no sign of such luxury.[26]

Rowdy barracks parties compensated to some degree for the lack of a conventional family holiday. Soldiers repeatedly described wartime celebration as an unforgettable experience, one in which the intensified desire for wholeness and comfort inspired feelings of close comradeship and national fraternity. Such stories were idealized and often had propagandistic overtones; the jocular soldier's Christmas "in enemy territory" is one of the most enduring aspects of the War Christmas myth. Firsthand accounts, however idealized, nonetheless reveal the existence of a rich celebratory culture within the lower ranks of the German army. As the memoirs of Bavarian rifleman J. W. Emonts show, the war (and the postwar cult of war memory) lent a distinct military cast to the celebration of Christmas peace. Emonts's book on "the sorrows and joys" of military life, which went through several editions in the 1880s, included a detailed description of his unit's party in the French town of Fontenay just behind the front lines. As the holiday approached, Emonts wrote, the soldiers were overcome with waves of nostalgia. "Memories of the sweet, bygone days of youth, that time when one snuggled up with heart's delight in childish love to one's dear parents" reminded the men that they fought on behalf of those at home, and they decided to celebrate Christmas "like German warriors."[27]

As Emonts's accounts suggests, military celebrations drew on the conventions of bourgeois sentimentalism but retained a place for the drinking bouts and displays of rowdy excess typical of homosocial, working-class celebrations. According to Emonts, the excitement began weeks before 25 December, as the soldiers in his unit organized the necessary food, drink, and decorations. Much of this was makeshift and expressed the manliness of military life: the tree, for example, was decorated with shell splinters, and the food was modest, but there was plenty of liquor to lubricate the festivities. During the celebration itself, Christmas was militarized and masculinized, with patriotic speeches, "joyful soldiers' songs," and a torch parade. Enacting familiar family rituals, the soldiers waited outside the decorated mess hall (an ersatz Christmas room) until they were "ordered" inside. After listening to a patriotic speech that extolled national unity—"Bavarian blood," the speaker intoned, flowed in tandem with "German strength and unbreakable loyalty"—the men received the order to "fire." They simultaneously popped the corks on sixty champagne bottles and raised a toast to the Bavarian king Ludwig II, the commander-in-chief of the Bavarian army.

As the evening (and drinking) progressed and the soldiers got drunk, the mood became increasingly boisterous, leading to "the most ridiculous deeds and tomfoolery." The company sang "joyful soldiers' songs" and honored the cook with a torch parade. Two artillerymen jumped on the table and enacted a scene between a king and the suitor of a princess, which ended in great bursts of laughter when the suitor's "flames of love" were doused with a bucket of water. The unit band struck up a military march, and the men, singing, paraded back and forth across the hall. Barracks rituals turned the traditional Christmas *Vortrag*, recited by children eagerly waiting for presents, to racist and militarist purposes. A soldier dressed like a "Turkish" soldier (an apparent reference to the colonial troops in the French ranks) read a lengthy, original poem aloud. The poet promised that the Germans would "whip, whip, whip the Turks," who were compared to devils, apes, and wild beasts. The poet received an excited round of applause and was hugged and kissed by his compatriots. Around midnight, a group of dancers appeared—soldiers who hid their beards and boots underneath women's dresses and shawls made from window curtains. The party lasted until dawn. "As morning broke," Emonts concluded, the soldiers reveled in the knowledge that they "had experienced a Christmas celebration, a sweet celebration of youth, as never before, in an authentic comrade-like brotherly togetherness, which all participants will remember forever."[28]

Such sentimental Christmas scenes apparently piqued the interest of the reservists, armchair generals, and German patriots who had not actually engaged in combat and so saw the war as a missed opportunity.[29] The popularity of stories about War Christmas in the decades after the Franco-Prussian War is, in fact, remarkable. Perhaps no other single event claimed as much space in the collections of letters, published diaries, memoirs, and embellished stories that replayed the events of the war for a generation that embraced growing popular nationalism as war with the French "hereditary enemy" again loomed on the horizon. Firsthand accounts, often edited and published by veterans' organizations, spoke with the voice of authenticity since their authors "were there." Even so, their narratives expressed the biased nationalist proclivities of their middle-class authors, who were typically officers or clergymen. A classic example is Carl Tanera's *Serious and Humorous Memories of an Ordnance Officer in 1870/71*, which went through five editions from 1887 to 1896. Readers of this large, handsome book imagined the glories of war with the aid of color plates and numerous pen-and-ink sketches. Tanera's chapter titled "Christmas Time in 1870" romanticized the national appeal of the holiday and the good time had by the soldiers in France, who cheerfully and willingly performed their duties but still had the time and inclination to celebrate a tender yet manly wartime holiday.[30] More troubled descriptions of War Christmas, which expressed the memories of veterans whose nationalist pride was tempered by the horror of their wartime experience, surfaced alongside such rosy accounts. For Ludwig Richter, the soldier from Bochum whose regiment suffered heavy losses on Christmas Day in 1870, each subsequent holiday reawakened sorrowful memories of "that comfortless Christmas." His comments were nonetheless included in a sumptuous collection of veterans' statements published in 1913 and dedicated to Kaiser Wilhelm II.[31]

After the war, the German armed forces continued to hold Christmas

celebrations, burnishing the appeal of the wartime holiday for a nation saturated with militarist values. On ships in the kaiser's growing navy, in officer
training schools and enlisted men's barracks, soldiers' parties included an
evening of amateur performance, biting satire, and lots of drinking. Simple
commemorative pamphlets or Christmas issues of the *Bier Zeitungen* (beer
newspapers), written by enlisted men and printed in short runs on military
or local presses, commemorated unit celebrations. Their contents typically
included hand-drawn caricatures of favorite comrades and original stories,
poems, and jokes about Christmas in the military; they provided servicemen and their families a lasting token of an unusual event.[32] Articles in the
middle-class press on "Christmas in the barracks" kept military customs in
the public eye. Such reports—along with the voluminous war-memoir literature—guaranteed that the unique care devoted by the military authorities to
Christmas and the special nature of manly soldiers' celebrations remained
a staple of military life, at least in the eyes of interested civilians.[33] While
some saw through Christmas stories that idealized the war experience and
the "honor" of military service, the memoir literature was for the most part
dominated by embellished accounts of the holiday, written for a postwar
generation eager to bask in the reflected glory of German victory.[34]

Around 1900, the marketing of War Christmas nostalgia reached its
height, demonstrated by its ubiquity in the melodramatic Christmas plays
that enlivened public entertainment in the holiday season. The action in
genre dramas like *Christmas Eve in the Captain's Kitchen* (1899), *On Christmas Eve; or, At the Main Watchpost* (1904), *Peace on Earth; or, The Old Soldier's Christmas Angel* (1908), *The Warrior's Christmas* (1909), *The Major's
Christmas Surprises* (1912), and *The Old Soldier's Christmas Eve* (1913) took
place at the front in the Franco-Prussian War, or in family living rooms as
fictional veterans relived memories of 1870–71.[35] Such dramas manipulated
the sentimental connections between front and Heimat and linked standard
melodramatic themes of domestic crisis and resolution to German patriotism and wartime memories. In *Christmas under Kaiser Wilhelm II*, a typical middle-class family drama by nationalist playwright Martin Böhm that
played at Berlin's Concordia Theater in 1910, the conflict between private
need and public duty provokes a crisis of love.[36] Set on Christmas Eve in 1889,
in a "rather elegant room" decorated with a Christmas tree and a portrait of
Wilhelm II, the plot tells of the domestic struggles between widower and
family patriarch Hardtwig, a veteran of 1870–71, and his daughter Selma.
The bombastic nationalism and patriotic Protestantism typical of the genre

are most obvious in Hardtwig's long, patriotic monologue, which includes a holiday toast to Wilhelm II, "the pride of the mighty German Empire."[37]

Military melodrama included a place for women in the national community. The disagreement between Selma and her father over her beloved suitor, Fritz, is a battle between intimate desire and national duty, fought on the terrain of gender and generation. Hardtwig had hoped that Fritz, the son of a comrade who had died in the war, would become a soldier; instead, Fritz studied law, alienating himself from Hardtwig's good graces and the possibility of a marriage to Selma. Acting out clearly defined gender roles, Selma finds her feminine need for love overruled by her father, who places the needs of the state above domestic concerns. Hardtwig's stubbornness, which the audience is meant to understand as unreasonable but excused by his tragic wartime experiences, creates real problems for Selma. Yet she hardly resists. The loyalties of woman to man, daughter to father, and family to nation are never in doubt, and they are rewarded in the end. In the play's final scene, as Hardtwig and his daughter open their Christmas presents, Fritz enters the parlor in the uniform of a sergeant second class (*Vize-Feldwebel*); the rank testifies to Fritz's lower-middle-class origins and suggests the appeal that "moving up" in the military had for Böhm's audience. Standing at attention in the doorway, Fritz calls out greetings to Hardtwig, his "benefactor"; today, he announces, "on holy Christmas Eve," the kaiser has awarded him a commission. After bedecking the kaiser's picture with a Christmas wreath, Hardtwig calls on the characters in the play, as well as the audience, to join in a cheer for "the patron of German might and German Greatness—Kaiser Wilhelm the Second!"—and the curtain falls.[38]

The tidy resolution of the tensions between national duty and family love taught audiences that family and state were strongest when united, and the militarization of Christmas brought the lesson home. Such works must have contributed to popular mobilization for Christmas during World War I, particularly in December 1914, when many Germans tried to revive the familiar melodramatic myths that made War Christmas a meaningful celebration of German community.

FATHER EBNER'S UNFORGETTABLE CHRISTMAS EVE

In December 1914 Father Jakob Ebner (Figure 3.2), a Catholic chaplain from Karlsruhe, spent Christmas Eve with the First Leib-Grenadier Regiment of Baden along the front line south of Verdun. Father Ebner is a particularly

FIGURE 3.2
Father Jakob Ebner in military uniform. (Courtesy
of Bernhard Huber, private family collection)

good witness for an investigation into War Christmas. A German patriot and an enthusiastic soldier-priest who volunteered to serve as a chaplain and army medic during the opening days of the war in August 1914, Ebner would receive the Iron Cross for his work with the wounded. He was well versed in the central tenets of war theology, the nationalist and militarist dogma promoted by Germany's Christian confessions. Chaplains like Ebner transmitted this dogma to soldiers at the front; they also shared news with their personal and professional contacts at home and so shaped public perceptions about life at the front and the course of the war. Perhaps most importantly, Ebner kept a detailed war diary, now in the Archive of the Archbishop of Freiburg. He wrote page after page of glowing prose on what he called his "Christmas labor" along the Verdun front in December 1914. Ebner in fact described his Christmas experience in two versions—one modest and straightforward, the other embellished with sentimental excess and probably intended for publication in a home-front newspaper (my account below draws on both). The priest may have been a mouthpiece for official versions of War Christmas, but he was well aware of the emotions and private needs of the men in his charge. Ebner repeatedly described the contradictory feelings engendered by "Christmas in enemy territory." His "unforgettable" Christmas Eve reveals the ideological penetration of the wartime holiday. It also illustrates the formal and informal networks and the ritual practices at the front that helped turn Christmas 1914 into a national myth.[39]

Chaplains such as Ebner—whether Catholic, Protestant, or Jewish—undertook their missions with substantial institutional support. Clerical organizations on the home front worked hard to supply chaplains and soldiers alike with what the Catholic journal *Feldpredigten* (Sermons for the Field) called "homiletic ammunition from the Heimat."[40] The main ideas of war theology reached clergymen as well as countless soldiers in the field in the pamphlets, prayer books, songbooks, and parish newsletters published and mailed to the front in droves by church groups large and small. Though clergymen were not official propagandists, Christmas in their hands was an important conduit for ideological indoctrination. Priests, pastors, and "front rabbis" preached that the German military was fulfilling God's plan for the German nation. The social harmony supposedly engendered by the holiday revealed the reality of the German *Burgfrieden*, the "fortress (or civic) peace" announced by the kaiser at the start of the war that supposedly united all citizens above class and confession. Traditional ideals of "good will to all men" thus gave way to expressions of national chauvinism. Holiday sermons compared the German soldier to Christ, who willingly sacrificed himself for the good of Christendom, and contrasted the spiritual and cultural accomplishments of the German Volk with the bestiality and baseness of the enemy. Germany was an innocent victim attacked by envious neighbors, clergymen explained, calling on the pious depths of the Christmas mood to inspire loyalty to family and fatherland.

Since the institutions of the Catholic Church were to some extent less willing to promote historicist or nationalist themes than their Protestant counterparts, the discourse of war theology was potentially more nuanced for Father Ebner. Pope Benedict XV took a neutral stand on the war and ministered to combatants on both sides, though his repeated calls for an end to hostilities—including his plea for a Christmas truce in 1914—were consistently ignored by patriotic Catholic citizens in both France and Germany. On the national level, Catholic clergy and laity could be profoundly patriotic. The Volksverein für das katholische Deutschland (People's League for Catholic Germany)—Germany's largest Catholic organization, with around 800,000 members in 1914—repeated the main lines of German propaganda (even though its publications steered clear of claims that God was German).[41] Popular Catholic literature also joined the war effort. The 1914 holiday issues of *Germania*, the leading Catholic daily, noted the pope's call for a holiday armistice; the paper devoted far more space to stories about the ever-fascinating War Christmas in France in 1870 or heroic celebrations aboard a German U-Boat.[42] Catholic leaders, for their part, turned the Prince of Peace into the Prince of War. The 1916 Christmas Letter sent by Bishop of Limberg Augustinus Kilian to soldiers from his parish concluded with what he called a "beautiful war-prayer" for the "fighters in the field." Kilian prayed that "the newborn savior might soon grant freedom to the world he saved and bring you, my dear soldiers, decorated with victor's laurels, back to the Heimat and the arms of your loved ones."[43] Catholic clergy like Kilian and Ebner saw the civic unity championed by the kaiser as an opportunity to overcome decades of anti-Catholic prejudice, and they perhaps used such exaggerated nationalist rhetoric to show that they, too, were good Germans.

Protestant and Jewish institutions and clergy likewise appropriated the holiday to reach the faithful under arms. The Evangelisches Oberkirchenrat (Protestant Upper Consistory, or EOK) in Berlin, the supreme authority of Prussia's Protestant church, directed local pastors to send personalized Christmas greetings to community members in service, even if they were not acquainted. As the EOK put it, a holiday note or gift with "a distinct local coloring" gave troops "a beautiful and perhaps lasting sign of the grateful and heartfelt love of our church and your community."[44] Parish clergy responded with some enthusiasm. By early summer 1915, for example, the district of Posen in East Prussia, with fourteen separate Protestant dioceses, had sent over 57,000 single copies of various publications to troops at the front.[45] A typical newsletter from the Protestant authorities in Limbach—a "Christmas Feldpost Letter" intended as a "German greeting and handshake"— entertained soldiers with generic descriptions of German holiday customs, stories about Christmas in the Franco-Prussian War, and tales about Christmas in the colonies. It brought more personal greetings as well. A statement written by the parish pastor of this small Saxon village reminded soldiers of their links to home with local news, information about community events and charity drives, and casualty lists.[46] Jewish "front rabbis" also adopted the central tropes of war theology during the holiday season. Militarist celebrations of "War Hanukkah" held for Jewish "warriors" in improvised frontline synagogues expressed the political goals of mainstream Jewish organizations, which saw the war as an opportunity to demonstrate their national loyalty and so increase the potential of winning social and political recognition from Christians.[47]

As this overview of the organizational links between home and front suggests, War Christmas animated the institutional networks that provided extensive backing to chaplains like Father Ebner. Yet communications between front and Heimat flowed in both directions. Army chaplains were crucial sources of war news for home-front audiences, and Ebner (like many others) shared his insights about "front Christmas" with a wide circle of readers. Perhaps most important were his contacts with newspaper editors in the Karlsruhe area. The editor of the *Zoller*, in Hechingen, had read letters by Ebner in the *Neuberger Volksblatt*. Impressed by his "inexhaustibility, selflessness, and enthusiasm for sacrifice on the battle field" (the priest copied these flattering words into his diary), the editor requested for his own newspaper eyewitness letters describing life at the front in December 1914. Ebner happily obliged. He also exchanged letters with a number of other middle-class professionals, including a lawyer, a gymnasium teacher, a veterinarian, other priests, soldiers, and his father.[48] The general mood was not particularly cheerful; Ebner's acquaintances worried about the loneliness of the troops during the holiday season, and one priest wrote that the "wounds and damages" of the war would take many years to heal, even with a German victory.[49] This correspondence nonetheless reveals the way everyday habits of keeping in touch at Christmastime wove Germans into coherent communities and shaped public perceptions about the war. Ebner's correspondence included authoritative, firsthand descriptions of life at the front that gave meaning and emotional depth to the more abstract notions of war theology.

Father Ebner had much to tell his home-front audiences about the resonant qualities of War Christmas. He was stationed in the small town of Thiaucourt, some forty kilometers from Verdun, and by mid-December he wrote in his diary that "it was getting Christmasy" all along the front. On the morning of 24 December, Ebner received his Christmas orders—he would have an exhausting holiday. On 25 December at 2:00 A.M., he was scheduled to hold mass for a Bavarian artillery battery; at 4:30 A.M., he would preach in a village church behind the lines; and at 8:00 A.M. on Christmas morning, he would hold mass for the 54th Battalion from Württemberg, "right at the front."[50] Yet Ebner's unforgettable Christmas Eve began well before the commencement of his official duties. On Christmas Eve he paid an informal visit to a crowded field hospital, where he participated in what he called "a moving Christmas celebration in enemy territory." After the wounded men gathered around a candlelit tree to sing "Silent Night" and a staff doctor handed out small gifts, Ebner gave a short homily. The chaplain spoke about the special strangeness of the soldier's Christmas and the love and gratitude of the Heimat; the men, he noted, warmed to the grace of the Christmas mood and the ministrations of hospital workers.[51] The reality of Christmas in a field hospital could be somewhat different, as the diary of one of Ebner's colleagues suggests. According to Father Fridolin Mayer, another priest from Karlsruhe, Christmas failed to hide the "day-long, indescribable martyrdom" suffered by wounded soldiers and the quickly filling mass graves laid out for convenience' sake in the vicinity of the hospitals.[52] Nonetheless, the image of wounded, bandaged soldiers in a clean hospital room, enjoying the attentions of a nurse or opening charity packages from well-wishers at home, became a War Christmas cliché.

Father Ebner next visited his company's Christmas party, which drew on barracks traditions in place at least since the Franco-Prussian War. The mood was set by a large, well-decorated tree, surrounded by numerous smaller trees sent to Ebner's comrades by well-wishers at home, each decorated with its own burning candle. The party began with a song in four-part harmony, led by a company sergeant, and continued with speeches by a second clergyman and the company's "beloved" first lieutenant. Rounds of "well-deserved beer," trucked in from Metz for the holiday, lightened the mood and paved the way for more songs, the distribution of presents, and the recital of an original Christmas poem by the "company musician." Ebner's description of the party drew on generic descriptions of soldiers' celebrations to cast War Christmas celebrations in the best light, perhaps with potential readers in mind. Gathered around the tree, he wrote, the soldiers became an ersatz family, united by a powerful feeling of community. This "soldier's family celebration in enemy territory on Christmas Eve," he concluded, "will stay in all our memories forever."[53]

At midnight on Christmas Eve, Father Ebner rode in the division automobile to a battery of heavy artillery set up in a copse east of Thiaucourt, where he held mass for troops stationed in the nearby trenches. Here, in the "holy calm" that blanketed the front that night—even the guns at Verdun were silent, apparently in recognition of the holiday—another unforgettable event occurred. As Ebner led the service with the assistance of several unit chaplains, anonymous soldiers crowded around the temporary "Field Church," a makeshift altar set up under a small tent canvas and illuminated with candlelight. Ebner's sermon had, in his own words, an *eigenartige Seelenstimmung*, a "peculiar soulful mood." The German soldiers were like the baby Jesus, he preached, because of their stoicism, forbearance, and inner faith in God. The difficulty of officiating in the open air, so close to the violence of the front, lent the scene an intense emotional charge. For Ebner, the effect was electrifying:

> The bell for transubstantiation rang out, the troops bowed down on their knees and prayed to Jesus. The army chaplain held up the Body of the Lord and spoke: "Look on the Lamb of God, which cleanses the sins of the world!" and repeated the joyful, humble word of that Captain of the gospels three times: "Lord, I am not worthy that you should enter under my roof, but only say the word, and my soul shall be healed." It grew lively right and left in front of the altar. New groups of soldiers pushed continually out of the darkness of the night and into the candlelight of the altar, towards Bethlehem, to the House of Bread, to receive the heavenly Host. After the artillerymen from the nearby guns of the Kohler Battery, the brave troops came out of the trenches. With rifle in one hand and helmet in the other, they kneeled down on the hard, frozen ground in front of the altar, to receive the greatest gift of Christmas; a drama for angels and mankind, a great religious deed in a great and difficult time.[54]

Ebner might have exaggerated the simple faith of the enlisted men and their eagerness to participate in the early-morning service. His vivid evocation nonetheless portrayed the strange atmosphere created by the juxtaposition of familiar religious rituals and the burdens of war. Perhaps with his home-front audience in mind, the priest made the most of it: in his hands, the observance of War Christmas created a community united in a grand and mysterious drama of faith and sacrifice.

After the service, Father Ebner packed up his altar linens and rode to the church in Viéville-en-haye, a nearby village, where he held a mass for a unit of Rhenish artillerymen at four in the morning. Here, he paid close attention to the soldiers' heartfelt participation in the minute observances that made Christmas German. The decorations made by a corporal and a Capuchin monk attached to the unit, Ebner noted approvingly, included a hand-carved birchwood Nativity scene—the central symbol of the Catholic holiday. Stars and silver ribbons hung on the Christmas trees that lined the nave; the largest, behind the altar, was thirty feet high. Donations from enthusiastic soldiers billeted in the area paid for the numerous trees and the 300-plus candles that illuminated the church. During the service, a company of 400 officers and men sang "elegant Christmas songs" with "all their heart," and after Communion, a famous concert singer who had joined the army sang a solo version of "Lo, How a Rose E'er Blooming."[55] As Ebner described it, the overall effect was magical, a transposition of time and space between front and home made possible by familiar ritual acts. "A gentle Christmas mood calmed the entire church," he commented, "our thoughts rushed as if on a golden bridge from here to the Heimat, where they were also getting ready for Christmas in church and family."[56]

After a short nap on some rolled-up carpets in the village church, Ebner returned to the front, where he held mass under the open sky for a company of soldiers from Württemberg. Around 400 troops received Communion, many with weapon in hand, and the results were again overwhelming. "On this [Christmas] morning," Ebner wrote, "I saw no glistening dewdrops, but instead glistening tears in the eyes of many weather-hardened soldiers, who I, as a long-time Baden Priest on the Baden-Württemberg border, addressed as dear countrymen."[57] The image of weeping soldiers was disturbing, and though Ebner tried to see this as a celebration of brotherhood, he was drawn in different directions by his Christmas experience at Verdun. "The people feel the contradiction between war and Christmas," he wrote in his diary in a section not meant for publication. "In between the Christmas carols one hears the questions again and again: Will it soon be peace? When will I go home?"[58] Ebner's own description of the frontline holiday, with all its affecting (and affected) contrasts, packaged the contradictions into a powerful narrative of unified suffering and spirituality.

Later War Christmases would neither reconcile Ebner's conflicted concerns nor recapture the special mood of 1914. The chaplain certainly officiated at many subsequent military services, but as the war dragged on, his Christmas sermons—like other memoirs, letters, and even the public press— increasingly showed less enthusiasm for the heroic aspects of the holiday and indeed the war itself. Ebner's diary reflected this general trend. In 1914, he wrote twenty pages about his holiday activities; in 1917, Christmas received only three terse paragraphs. Though he officiated at five different masses, his "Christmas labors" that year had no special resonance.[59] After three and a half years of war, during which he held 1,032 masses in the field, administered the last rites to 476 dying soldiers, and buried 989 dead, Ebner could no longer romanticize "Christmas in enemy territory" as he had in 1914.[60]

CHRISTMAS AND THE FRONT COMMUNITY

Father Ebner's personal account of War Christmas, recorded in his war diary and probably shared with readers at home, included fundamental tropes common to mainstream or official stories about War Christmas. The rhetoric of church and state returned repeatedly to the unusual mood of the soldier's holiday, made all the more poignant and memorable because of the contradictions between war and the Christian message of Peace on Earth. Like Ebner, official sources described Christmas as a national holiday that unified all Germans, beyond differences of religion, military rank, or class. They cast the holiday as a golden bridge that linked front and Heimat, and soldiers and their families, with unbreakable bonds of loving affection. The propagandists, clergymen, teachers, journalists, writers, and artists who composed the holiday texts that circulated in the public sphere readily took up these themes, as they reached for the stability of tradition in the crisis of total war. At the front, War Christmas was more nuanced and contradictory. In small-scale celebrations with officers and fellow servicemen, soldiers grappled with the ironies of the wartime holiday. Familiar scripts evoked broadly shared emotions but at the same time exposed fractures in the ranks.

FIGURE 3.3
Officers and enlisted men celebrate War Christmas in a photo
circulated for propaganda purposes. (Courtesy of Bibliothek für
Zeitgeschichte, Stuttgart/Fotosammlung Erster Weltkrieg No. 96)

Even before the establishment of the official military propaganda department in January 1917 (the *Bild- und Filmamt*, or Office of Pictures and Film), censors and propagandists ensured that an idealized view of War Christmas reached Germans at home. Visual images of all types, including photos, posters, and drawings, depicted Christmas at the front. They invariably showed smiling, clean, well-cared-for soldiers who joined ranks to decorate trees, welcome the arrival of *Feldpost* (army mail), and trade gifts and friendly greetings with each other and with local populations (often in occupied territories). Published in newspapers, illustrated magazines, and commemorative booklets and collected by soldiers and noncombatants in private photo albums, these sentimental images portrayed a brotherhood of officers and men joined together through the symbols and rituals of the wartime holiday.[61] If there was evidence of war during the holiday season, it was clean and nonthreatening and provided the thrill of incongruity. In one often-reprinted photo series labeled "a German Christmas celebration in the trenches in Poland"—obviously staged and "approved" by the military censorship office—a group of soldiers in "pickle-sticker" helmets decorate a tree, sing songs, and man their weapons in a trench defended by a series of barbed-wire obstructions.[62] In another widely distributed photo (Figure 3.3), company officers stand behind a table covered with presents of liquor and tobacco, while noncommissioned officers and enlisted men surround the table, apparently waiting for their commander's speech and the distribution of gifts.

Photographs taken by ordinary soldiers reveal a different side of military celebration. By 1914 simplified technology and less-expensive film and camera prices had placed photographs and the memories they preserved in the hands of the masses. Christmas brought a notable break in military routine and was the subject of numerous private snapshots, as soldiers sought to create a personal record of their unique wartime experiences. Candid Christmas pictures preserve a limited but revealing record of the really existing "comradely infrastructure" that determined personal relations within the ranks and challenged official poses.[63] In the hands of amateur photographers, War Christmas might appear as an anonymous beer party (Figure 3.4) or a moment of bleak-eyed melancholy (Figure 3.5) but rarely as a festive celebration of cross-rank unity.

War Christmas celebrations were, in fact, deeply segregated according to military hierarchy. Few soldiers could dream of a luxurious Christmas party like that celebrated in 1915 by the staff of General von Linsingen, commander

in chief of the "Bug Army." Stationed east of Warsaw, von Linsingen and
some twenty staff officers (including two princes and assorted barons and
counts) spent Christmas Eve in the central hall of Jablon Castle, a former seat
of the Polish aristocracy. The celebration was essentially an elegant banquet,
with decorations, joke gifts, performances, and sumptuous food and drink.[64]
Far more typical was the 1914 Christmas fest of the 8th Artillery Munitions
Column of the Bavarian Grand Corps, rightly billed as "A Christmas Celebration in Enemy Territory and at the same time a Commemorative Celebration of the Fatherland." The Bavarians, stationed in the village of Frémicourt
close to the Belgian border, gathered on Christmas Eve in a church decorated
with a candlelit tree. After an evening spent listening to patriotic songs and
speeches and singing family Christmas carols, the company swore an "un-
shakeable oath" to defend Germany from foreign conquest and then gathered briefly at the church door to silently honor their fallen comrades. After
a break, they reassembled in the quarters of the company captain, where they
received their *Weihnachtspakete* (Christmas packages), which contained gifts

FIGURE 3.5
Christmas in a dugout on the western front, undated. (Courtesy
of BayHSA Abt. IV Kriegsarchiv/Staudinger Slg. 2551)

from home. The concerns of the officers who organized the celebration were
clear: the evocation of home and family; the commemoration of the dead;
the militarization of sentimental traditions; and, finally, the barracks party—
all repositioned the emotional bonds usually reserved for family celebration
around the need for military duty, even unto death.[65]

Private photographs further expose the stark contrasts between the holiday celebrations of officers and enlisted men. An exemplary snapshot from
1916 portrays a group of officers from Air Force Squadron 292, stationed at
Houplin on the western front, at what seems to be a rather jolly Christmas
party (Figure 3.6). Happy faces, a richly laden table, and, most importantly,
the presence of several women testify to the relative luxury of this elite officers' party. Photographs from the celebrations of enlisted men reveal a
separate world. One shows a group of military railroad workers celebrating
Christmas at Skrybowo in occupied Polish territories. Posed stiffly in ranks,
the soldiers wait to open their modest gift packages, which include shoes and
towels, probably sent by a German Red Cross charity drive (Figure 3.7). In

FIGURE 3.6
A holiday for officers: Air Force Squadron 292
celebrates Christmas on the western front, 1916. (Courtesy
of BayHSA Abt. IV Kriegsarchiv/BS IIIk8a, 112)

his diary, Captain Rudolf Binding, a writer and poet who survived the war,
tried to comprehend the behavior of the soldiers who received such "gifts."

> Those at home make such a fuss about the Christmas feast and
> Christmas gifts for the troops that one would expect a correspond-
> ing effect on those who are most concerned. But when you see the
> soldiers, dressed in their ranks about the Christmas table, for each
> man a knife, a piece of soap, socks, cigars, or cigarettes, heaped in
> neat piles and likewise dressed by the right—it is unfortunate that
> you have not the slightest idea how they are taking it. You do not
> know whether they are glad, whether they appreciate the gifts or not,
> whether they are grateful or not, whether they feel inwardly festive or
> whether Christmas did not matter so long as they got knives, cigars,
> and soap. Most of them seem to take it as though they were entitled
> to the Christmas gifts, and everything else that is done for them in the

FIGURE 3.7
A holiday for enlisted men: military railroad workers
receive Christmas packages on the eastern front. (Courtesy
of BayHSA Abt. IV Kriegsarchiv/BS IIIk5a, 30)

same way as their pay and clothing. Their expressions are exactly the
same as when the Sergeant-Major is issuing pantaloons, cord, and the
"happy crowding round the long Christmas table" is a padre's fable.
Christmas can only be properly celebrated by a few, in their family
and their own home.[66]

Binding's sharp critique of War Christmas as an unpopular "padre's fable" no
doubt captured the reaction of many soldiers; at the same time, his incompre-
hension reveals the unbridgeable social distance that divided this bourgeois
staff officer from the lower-class men in his command. For enlisted men, the
extra rations, the liquor, and the masculine, working-class atmosphere typical
of barracks festivity could at once provide a relief valve for pent-up hostility
or anxiety, an escape from the contradictions of Christmas and war, and an
avenue for male bonding. "I really can't speak of loneliness this time," wrote
one soldier about his Christmas party in 1914. "Quite the opposite; on the

24th, the circle of like-minded comrades—and I'm not just thinking of the officers . . . can be really great."[67]

Some soldiers rejected attempts to turn Christmas into a celebration of war. "First some Christmas songs were sung, then that 'Deutschland Deutschland über alles' and 'We Salute You in Victory Laurels.' What nonsense!" wrote Alsatian rifleman Dominik Richert in his private diary after attending his unit's Christmas party. "Captain Grosse . . . made a speech good enough for war," he continued, "but all the less so for Christmas."[68] Other soldiers worried that the conspicuous display of upper-rank prerogatives during Christmas celebrations contributed to the polarization of German society. Ostentatious partying by officers stirred resentment and encouraged left-wing agitation, as one lance corporal reported after witnessing the excesses of his battalion staff's Christmas party: "Can't the 'Gentlemen' realize how much bad blood they make doing that? *Those* are the best agitators for the most extreme Social Democracy. *My* blood already boils when you have to go on and on seeing and hearing this kind of stuff, and of course the people who already belong to the always discontented working class think it is still far worse."[69]

The experience of Private Seaman Richard Stumpf, an ardent Catholic and a member of a Christian trade union who enlisted in the German navy in 1912 and served in the war on the S.M.S. *Helgoland*, underscores the complexities of the popular response to War Christmas.[70] Stumpf was a committed nationalist who remained true to the fatherland throughout his life, but his three Christmases "on board" show that the initial enthusiasm for War Christmas in 1914 unraveled under heavy-handed discipline, war-related shortages, and general disillusionment. Stumpf clearly had warm feelings for Christmas, evident in his diary entries for December 1914. "Christmas! Good God, today is Christmas!" he wrote. In the spirit, he and his fellow sailors decorated the trees provided by the ship's command "as best we could." On Christmas Eve, after receiving presents of nuts and oranges, the assembled sailors "stood around the lights, bright-eyed like children."[71]

A year later, the Christmas mood on the *Helgoland* had noticeably soured. The ship's captain tried to create a "dignified and pleasant" mood by bringing on board forty small trees, decorations, and sacks of fruit, chocolate, and other treats, but only large rations of alcohol improved morale. Recalcitrant sailors in Stumpf's division at first refused to decorate their quarters but then gave in to pressure from the petty officer in charge; they jeered the enlisted men who accompanied the inspection tour of the first lieutenant.[72] In 1916, at the start of the notorious "turnip winter," widespread disgruntlement overwhelmed the command's attempt to create a holiday atmosphere. War-related scarcity made the holiday even worse. Fewer packages arrived from home, and there was less to eat. The sailors openly mocked the privileges of the ship's officers, and on Christmas Eve, Stumpf wrote, "there was a big feast in the officers' mess. They had roast goose. The Champagne corks kept popping. But I was not jealous. Let the gentlemen drink themselves into a stupor—if only they would leave us alone." Outside of the officers' quarters, gloom pervaded the ship. "The only reason why I am writing," Stumpf noted on Christmas Day, "is to cheer myself out of my sadness and monotony. Nothing special has happened. . . . Nothing matters to me anymore, but whenever I think of home I feel like crying."[73]

Beyond conflicts of class and status, War Christmas provoked interconfessional tension, despite official claims to the contrary. Clergymen liked to assert that the holiday spirit overcame religious difference, at least in official discourse. Reports from the front—from clerics as well as ordinary soldiers—sometimes spoke of the surprising "confessional leveling" witnessed during the holiday season, as many soldiers evidently did not care which Christian services they attended.[74] But confessional conflict at the front undermined this idealized view of religious harmony. According to chaplain Fridolin Mayer, Protestant officers often assigned Catholic servicemen to report for duty when Christmas mass was scheduled, and clergy members competed for limited church space on Christmas Eve and Christmas Day, aggravating conflicts between Protestant and Catholic soldiers. Chaplains knew little about the holiday rituals of their coconfessionalists, which created problems in ceremonies with shared officiation. Disagreements arose over which songs would be sung during services, and some chaplains refused altogether to conduct services that included soldiers of both faiths.[75]

For Jewish soldiers trapped "between Fatherland and Volk," Christmas was a particularly ambiguous event.[76] As in peacetime, Jews could demonstrate their national allegiance by participating in official celebrations. According to Herbert Sulzbach, a Jewish soldier on the western front who was promoted to corporal around Christmas 1914 ("a splendid Christmas present," he noted in his diary), the holiday helped eliminate any difference between Jews and Gentiles. Like his Christian "comrades," Sulzbach identified deeply with the traditional symbols and rituals of German Christmas.[77] Far more Jewish soldiers attended "War Hanukkah" services staged by Jewish "front rabbis." War Hanukkah had much in common with War Christmas, including the propaganda, poetry, and package drives of the Christian holiday. In one typical story from a Jewish newspaper, Corporal Moritz Cohn received gifts from unknown well-wishers, promised loyalty to the nation and those at home, celebrated Hanukkah, and then died a hero's death on this major holiday.[78]

The rhetoric of War Hanukkah was influenced both by Zionism and the political goals of Jewish German organizations. Thus one frontline rabbi spoke in his 1915 Hanukkah greetings of "the might of the few," ostensibly referring to the small numbers of truly brave Jewish soldiers who were leaders of the much larger (Christian) "herd." Read obliquely, however, the rabbi's appeals for heroism implied that Jewish minority status—symbolized by the small number of the original Maccabees—mandated a "nobler bravery" to set an example of loyalty for the Christian majority.[79] Jewish leaders by necessity appropriated the central tropes of national unity, militarism, and sacrifice for Germany. The observance of Jewish rituals at the front nonetheless highlighted the differences between Jewish and Christian soldiers. Reports that the soldiers gathered at a Christmas service were united in "only one belief . . . the German belief" at best included Christians only—the quote here drawn from a letter in Philip Witkop's famously chauvinist *Kriegsbriefe gefallener Studenten* (War Letters of Fallen Students), first published in 1915.[80] The patriotic fantasies of middle-class authors masked the class and confessional frictions exacerbated by the wartime holiday. Their repetitive invocation of Christmas harmony suggests that holiday sentimentalism was a useful cultural weapon for a nation at war, since yearnings for home and family were felt with particular intensity by both leaders and their men during the holiday season.

HEIMAT, GERMAN HEIMAT, FULL OF JOY AND JOCULARITY

When soldiers celebrated War Christmas, visions of what one veteran called the "rainbow of yearning" between front and home stood out in sharp relief.[81] Officers and chaplains, journalists and civic leaders—ever-reliable publicists in Germany's informal propaganda machine—used the holiday to remind soldiers of those at home, always in the name of national duty. A selection from a romanticized fable about a lieutenant's return home for the holidays, published in *Der Schützengraben* (The Trench), a well-established soldiers' newspaper printed on a field press in Bapaume, epitomizes the rhetoric:

Yes, and now he is there. And the proud mother closes her old, tall boy in her arms. Finally at home! At home in his parent's house, for Christmas Eve—German Christ-Night! Soft, full notes of an organ, lights playing in the darkness of an ancient tiny church, the most joyful message of an incomprehensible love, peace on earth. Secret preparations and sweet fulfillment, dream-dark desires of young love, warm, wholesome feelings of parental joy and parental goodness, children's laughter and the green of the pine, winter hunts in forests resplendent with frost, until the red ball of the sun sinks down over the meadow, sleigh bells, spraying snow, and steaming window panes. Heimat, German Heimat, inwardness, full of joy and jocularity, of simple seriousness and strong, joyful work, the heart never feels it all so strongly and purely as on this one, single evening of the year, on German Christmas Eve. Finally at home! And the Christmas tree glows with candlelight, and Mother and Father are around me and Hanneli snuggles up to her older brother.

In its flowing, artful, and almost telegraphic style, this passage rehearses the emotional and sensory constellations that defined German Christmas: songs, decorations, candles, piety, God's love, family affection, winter landscapes, childhood memories, a unique sense of German *Innigkeit* or inwardness. The sugarplum vision was too good to be true. The lieutenant awakes from his "dream" to the sound of raindrops on his dugout floor; only now does he understand that the true meaning of Christmas was defense of those at home. Thus official discourse drafted into the German war effort an imaginary holiday homecoming, a sentimental escape into the *heile Kinderwelt* (wholesome children's world) of youth and Heimat.[82]

Attempts to manipulate the most intimate emotions apparently had popular appeal. A review of sources produced by German soldiers at the lower ranks—letters, memoirs, postcards, and drawings—suggests that the defense of family was one of the most resonant ideals of War Christmas for officers and ordinary soldiers alike. As historian Aribert Reimann concludes, "The stylization [of the soldier] as the faithful guardian of the family idyll corresponded quite exactly to the consensus of soldierly self-understanding at the front."[83] The ideals of Heimat and family were instrumentalized from above and below during malleable and vulnerable moments of celebration.

The golden bridge imagined in official versions of War Christmas was paved by the remarkable holiday letter-writing campaigns and charity drives undertaken by Germany's impressive network of civic institutions, including social clubs, schools and universities, community groups, and religious and charity organizations. On average, German soldiers sent and received over 17 million pieces of Feldpost per day (over one-half were postcards). The holiday season intensified this already-dense traffic. Enlisted men received packages from and traded holiday greetings with family and friends, clergymen and employers, and anonymous donors. Civic and community groups sent soldiers an annual barrage of "Christmas Greetings," testimony to the rich associational life animated by the Christmas spirit. A quick glance through the card catalog of the Deutsche Bücherei in Leipzig (under Kriegsweihnachten) shows that the "beloved fighters in the field" received Christmas greetings in the form of newsletters from, among many others, the National Women's Service of Barmen; the city of Zuffenhausen; the Financial Office of the Julius Klinkhaft Company in Leipzig; the Publisher's Society of the German Consumer Club; the Borussia Silesia Swim Club; the Southern and West-German Old-Wandervogels; the Royal Technical Gymnasium of Nienburg; the University of Jena; the Protestant Communities of Krefeld and Verdingen; and the Catholic Theological Society of Gülfia. This epistolary exchange exercised the networks of communication and civic reciprocity that wove individuals into families and communities. It also opened vernacular forms of expression to penetration by nationalist sentiment. Associational news and patriotic holiday greetings from the typical institution's director shared space with evocations of the golden bridge and exhortations to hold out for the good of the nation. The content of the letters was predictable, but that was the point; one enterprising printing company in Stuttgart even advertised a fill-in-the-blanks Christmas letter ("Christmas Greetings from the Community in —— to ——") for groups who lacked either the inspiration or resources to write their own.[84]

The activities of women's organizations like the Red Cross, the League of German Womens' Organizations (*Bund Deutscher Frauenvereine*, or BDF), and the National Women's Service (*Nationale Frauendienst*, or NFD), with branches across Germany, lent further credence to the idea of a nation of Germans united in sacrifice around the Christmas tree. In 1914 the Red Cross had some 6,300 local groups and over 1.1 million members. After war was declared, an influx of young volunteers strained the organization's capacity to absorb new members. Work in military hospitals and on charity and recruiting drives raised public consciousness of women's national war work and gave Red Cross volunteers the opportunity to participate in the war effort;

they often met the nation's heroes face to face. Christmas "Days of Sacrifice," organized and staffed by women's groups, played on the well-publicized loneliness of frontline soldiers with sentimental patriotism. Brightly colored charity-drive posters called for *Liebesgaben* (charitable gifts, literally "gifts of love") of all kinds for soldiers in hospitals and at the front. The images of tree and trench, Weihnachtsmann and Christkind, and glowing candles that graced the posters were at once deeply personal and emblematic of the nation at large.[85] Soldiers deserved "Christmas joy," according to a poster for a drive in Braunschweig, because their "daily sacrifice of life and limb . . . protects Germany's borders and your hearth!"[86]

Donations flowed to central collecting points in cities and towns across Germany, where they were sorted and boxed as "Christmas packages" for transport to the front. Such gifts perhaps spread holiday cheer. They also helped supply the German army, which was suffering from intractable shortages of equipment and goods. In their anonymous Christmas packages, tied up with a ribbon and perhaps sporting a small pine cutting, soldiers might find clothing, pocket knives, electric flashlights, books, games, and toiletries; comestibles like jerky, lard, and powdered milk; sweets such as chocolate, bonbons, marzipan, honey cakes, and dried fruit; and gifts perhaps better suited to a soldier's taste, including rum, cognac, beer, cigars, cigarettes, and pipes.[87] Jo Milhaly, a schoolgirl in Schneidemühl (now Piła in northwestern Poland) worked with local women from the Women's Fatherland Society, the local arm of the Red Cross, packing Christmas boxes for the front. In her diary, she described the way the small acts of creativity normally undertaken for family and friends at Christmastime—packing pretty gifts, writing short Christmas poems, sending notes and cards—were now done for strangers in the name of national solidarity. "Our packages looked cheerful," wrote Milhaly. "I fastened a fresh pine bough on each bundle." Young girls often included their personal addresses to encourage an unknown soldier's reply. In this way, Milhaly began a correspondence with four separate soldiers. She recorded their polite thank-you notes in her diary, and with one fusilier, the exchange lasted the entire war and involved his family in Hamburg.[88]

Civic elites made the most of this private investment in national networks of sociability. Red Cross officials, local clergymen, and professors accompanied "gift trains" to the front, where they visited troops, handed out packages, and later wrote glowing reports about their activities for audiences at home.[89] Rudolf Binding had a more critical take on the pretensions of NFD and Red Cross bureaucrats and claimed that soldiers cared little for the "thousand packages of bad cigars, indifferent chocolate, and woollies of problematical usefulness" sent to the front. "This Christmas-gift stunt," Binding wrote in December 1914, "organized by novelty-mongering, snobbish busybodies in a glare of publicity, creates such an unsavory impression here [at the front] that it fairly makes one sick."[90]

Charity campaigns may have generated an uncharitable response, but soldiers clearly enjoyed trading correspondence and packages with family members and personal friends. Private letter-writing rituals were arguably a form of "self-mobilization from below," in which individuals adopted the patriotic sentimentalism expressed in official texts.[91] The tearful parties with comrades, the singing, the crudely decorated trees, and the moments of melancholy described in enlisted men's accounts read like propaganda dispatches. This clichéd or simplified language no doubt helped soldiers hide the wretched conditions at the front from those at home and gave them a way to describe the indescribable, as Isa Schikorsky puts it.[92] Even accounts of holiday deprivation were linked to memorable celebrations; the irony of Christmas on the front apparently made relatively minor events stand out. "Now the great day is here, when, more than any other, one's thoughts wander towards home," wrote one soldier to his parents in a typical letter. His letter included a lengthy report on what he called "his first moving Christmas experience" in 1914, when he happened upon a group of infantrymen singing "Silent Night" in the midst of a snow-strewn woods behind the lines; it was all very *heimatlich*, or homelike, he assured his parents.[93] Even Captain Binding, the inveterate critic of War Christmas, was captivated by the Christmas mood, almost despite himself. After complaining that "to give Christmas parties for soldiers is to murder the whole beautiful idea," he went on to describe his company celebration as "quite nice ... it really was so."[94]

In private letters, tender Christmas greetings and words of endearment shared space with expressions of chauvinist aggression that were not particularly Christmasy. Writing to his fiancée from occupied France, twenty-year-old Fritz Meyer reported that "right now at Christmas you could never believe what a great desire I have for you and the Heimat. What I want more than anything ... is to rush to your embrace." He closed the letter with an original "Christmas Poem" titled "Alone on Guard," in which sentimental visions of Christmas at home lead to an oath to "remain on the banks of the Aisne ... until death for our dear Fatherland." Meyer resolved the tension between the roles of soldier and family man, felt particularly keenly at Christmastime, with a willingness to "hold out" in language that clearly mimicked official propaganda.[95]

Supporters of the war quickly realized the potential of such letters for shaping public opinion at home. The personal letters printed in newspapers, magazines, commemorative books, and book-length collections of army mail typically included descriptions of life at the front and bold statements about defending the nation "to the death." Publishers included numerous examples of patriotic War Christmas letters since they portrayed a presumably true-to-life frontline Christmas experience and at the same time testified to the deep emotional bonds that kept soldiers fighting. Perhaps the most famous example is Philip Witkop's collection *War Letters from Fallen Students*, a book known for its exaggeration of the spirit of the trench community. First published in 1915, the book was reprinted in numerous editions in the Weimar and Nazi years. It included no fewer than fifteen Christmas letters written by university students. The nationalist tone of Witkop's letters represents a minority view, yet they were real letters written by real soldiers, the cultural elite of the German military as it were. In any case, patriotic holiday letters became a mainstay of War Christmas memories after the war.[96]

Picture postcards, a favorite medium for soldiers at the front, further reveal the interpenetration of popular and official interests. Postcards with War Christmas themes were printed in occupied France—on presses set up by the military authorities behind the front lines—and by over 250 publishers in Germany. In 1914 in Berlin alone, over fifty separate companies produced postcards. Many had photos or drawings contributed by soldiers who were stationed at the front. The images themselves merged traditional motifs with military and nationalist icons. At their most propagandistic, postcards portrayed bestial caricatures of the enemy hung from the branches of a German Christmas tree, chained to a package, or swallowing an artillery shell—"a nice Christmas surprise!" Others pictured an idealized side of war Christmas, with officers or men celebrating in front of guns or in trenches or joyfully receiving Feldpost.[97] The cards most obviously based on soldier's drawings, which often included greetings from a specific military unit, typically stepped back from overt propaganda. Though some featured jaunty images, hand-drawn cards more typically portrayed the dutiful if sorrowful bearing of the German soldier, called on at Christmas to defend a holiday in which he could not fully participate.

In many picture postcards, the Christmas tree appears as an almost magi-

FIGURE 3.8
Postcard: "Christmas Greetings from the Front,"
1917. (Courtesy of BayHSA Abt. V Nachlässe und
Sammlungen/Postkartenslg-Kriegsgrusskarten)

cal token of safety in the presence of weapons and destruction, a fragile yet
powerful symbol of Heimat in the most violent, extreme conditions. Amateur artists played on the ironies of war, merging military and holiday symbols. In one postcard from 1917, a flare floating across the lines stands in for
the Star of Bethlehem, and frontline soldiers gather around a Christmas tree
in their rough dugout, while their comrade stands watch (Figure 3.8). The
imagery makes palpable the longing for the stability of tradition and family
in the crisis of total war. In a card posted from Galicia in 1916, a soldier stands
in front of a city in flames and imagines a decorated Christmas tree in the

FIGURE 3.9
Postcard from Galicia, Christmas 1916.
(Courtesy of BayHSA Abt. V Nachlässe und
Sammlungen/Postkartenslg-Kriegsgrusskarten)

smoke (Figure 3.9). A scene drawn by a soldier on the eastern front and sent
to his family played variations on this basic theme. Here, the tree bridges the
divide between home and front, and the portrait of soldiers on guard suggests a determined defense of loved ones at home (Figure 3.10).

As such imagery suggests, nowhere were the tensions between private
and public more deeply rooted than in the most visible and most German
symbol of Christmas: the Tannenbaum. Diaries, letters, songs, photos,
drawings, postcards, and countless stories and reports in the official media
reveal a widespread fascination if not obsession with the juxtaposition of

Herzlichste Weihnachtsgrüße von Vater. 1915

FIGURE 3.10
"Best Christmas Wishes, from Father, 1915." This private sketch
recapitulates the tree-and-trench imagery of official propaganda
materials. (Courtesy of Bundesarchiv-Militärarchiv/N 287)

tree and trench. During the holiday season, soldiers reported, Christmas trees were everywhere on the German side of the lines. Trenches, dugouts, barracks, churches, field hospitals, train stations, and public streets in occupied towns—all displayed the *brennenden Lichterbaum* (illuminated tree of light), distributed by the High Command, sent to the front by anonymous home-front patrons, or collected by soldiers who searched local woods for the best specimens. The Christmas tree's physical or imaginary presence called to mind the sundered ties between enlisted men and their families. In letters and diaries, soldiers repeatedly wrote of childhood holidays and family togetherness "around the tree," and such memories only accentuated the vast distance between front and Heimat, duty and desire, and war and peace. "Enemy, Death, and a Christmas-tree—they cannot live so close together," noted Rudolf Binding in his diary.[98] This key symbol of Germanness was multivalent and overdetermined, the subject of multiple and conflicted appropriations that together outlined the contours of the imagined German community.[99] The Christmas tree defined togetherness and set boundaries between friends and enemies. For clergymen, it evoked faith and martyrdom; for nationalists, it represented Volk and fatherland; for propagandists, it was a cherished symbol of home that required defense to the death. In countless images, the tree bridged front and Heimat. The cover of the December issue of the trench newspaper *Der Schützengraben*, for example, shows an illuminated tree juxtaposed between a snow-covered village and a bombed-out church graveyard, complete with freshly dug soldiers' graves (Figure 3.1). The tree promised to soothe the contradictions between life and death, Heimat and front; at the same time, it called attention to the vast distance that separated soldiers from their families.

Nationalist definitions of the Christmas tree dominated public discourse. In numerous reports, the Christmas tree transcended regional, denominational, and class differences. Prussians, Bavarians, Catholics, Protestants, and Jews reportedly celebrated together beneath its decorated boughs. Germany's enemies, on the other hand, did not. According to official and private accounts, the German reverence for the tree impressed and amazed the French, including the prisoner of war whose "eyes bugged out [when] the Christmas tree shone and the Christmas melodies rung in his ear."[100] Military chaplains referred to the tree as a symbol of the Christian nation at war and asked soldiers to swear oaths of fealty at its base. At a Christmas Eve service held in 1914 in the Lens cathedral, a Protestant division chaplain explained that the Christmas tree was at once a symbol of Jesus, his evangelical message, and his crucifixion. The Weihnachtsbaum, he preached, "means the Christ-Tree, and Christ died on the cross . . . and beneath the Christmas tree we make the promise that we will strive for the Christlike ideal of manly self control and follow our faith in the savior to our deaths." Death for the nation, the chaplain intoned, was the highest possible fulfillment of a soldier's life. Most importantly, he concluded, the Christmas tree was a symbol of the German people's indomitable will to achieve victory: "The Christmas tree reminds us . . . of our beloved German fatherland. . . . And in this land lives a Volk as strong and simple as a Black Forest pine, but also so strongly rooted, powerful, and immovable as this."[101]

The numerous War Christmas songs that appeared in the trench press—glosses, for the most part, on familiar carols—likewise expressed the conflicted aspects of the wartime holiday. Revised lyrics spoke eloquently about the loneliness and brutality of Christmas at the front, even as they confirmed the necessity of war in the most patriotic terms. One telling example is a revision of Johannes Falk's "O How Joyfully" (1819), one of the most famous and beloved German carols. Renamed "Fighter's Christmas Song 1914" by the Liebenzeller Mission in Württemberg, the first verse is unchanged, but the remaining verses describe "joyful sacrifice" in "bloody battle," the evil of the enemy, and God's love for the German fatherland. Fortunately for the author of the carol, the words *heilige Nacht, Schlacht,* and *Wacht* (holy night, battle, and watch) were obvious rhymes. The new words to this familiar tune were distributed to enlisted men on a one-page flyer in 1914.[102] Other revised standards combine domestic sentimentalism and patriotic bombast. The first verse of a piece simply called "Christmas Song," which was supposed to be sung to the tune of "Silent Night" while "the Christ-Tree is lit in the trenches," makes the horror of the war vanish in a moment of Christmas harmony:

> It wears on you, bears on you:
> Joy and pain, silent heart!
> A holy glimpse of quiet bliss
> Drowns it all in nothingness
> What in the constant fray
> Pounds down every day.

In a typical twist, this carol, published in a Bavarian regimental trench newspaper, becomes a "battle-song" in the last two verses. It closes with an oath: "To you beloved Fatherland / we pledge again heart and hand."[103] Another example from the trench press, titled "War Christmas Tree Song" and based on the melody of "Oh Christmas Tree," takes a similar turn. The first verse envisions violent, apocalyptic destruction:

> Oh Christmas tree, O Christmas tree,
> I don't recognize you!
> When you glow in lighted rooms,
> Then songs of peace ring out.
> Today in your illumination,
> The whole world's engulfed in flames.
> It thunders, hails, howls, and cracks,
> And the earth breaks apart.

This poignant evocation of the horrific irony of War Christmas concludes, like so many others, with a call to "smash our enemies [and above all] the treacherous British dogs to bits."[104]

Most enlisted men no doubt preferred the unrevised traditional carols sung at official celebrations and in small groups at the front. Here again, however, official forms of German patriotism merged with vernacular practice until the two were virtually inseparable. Inexpensive Christmas songbooks, sent to the front by religious groups, charity organizations, and social clubs, regularly bracketed "our most beloved carols" with patriotic songs like the "Watch on the Rhine," "Deutschland über Alles," and Martin Luther's "A Mighty Fortress Is Our God."[105] Family observances were transplanted into the barracks culture of the lower ranks with memorable if somewhat melancholy results. Army cook Michael Bauer, stationed on the Dolomite front in South Tyrol, rehearsed Christmas carols with the men in his unit on a harmonica and other improvised instruments. On Christmas Eve, after the battalion major gave a Christmas speech in their dugout, he asked for a song. "We climbed like monkeys up into the upper level, where we had our practice space," Bauer wrote, "and we went at it: 'Silent Night, Holy Night!' We received applause." Later, the major asked the band to play in the officers' mess. The performance was broadcast to a second barracks: "They had begged that we would also play something for them, and they went nuts when they heard music again. No wonder in the wretched loneliness."[106] Private seaman Richard Stumpf recorded the "unforgettable" feelings evoked by traditional carols, even in the worst conditions. "It was a clear, star-filled night," Stumpf wrote in his diary on Christmas Eve in the Turnip Winter of 1916. "There was only a slight breeze but it carried the lovely and resounding song of a thousand men's voices singing, 'Silent night, holy night. All is calm;

all is bright. . . .' High above the singing one could distinguish the sounds of a trumpet. I was fascinated and filled with emotion as I listened to its solemn tones. . . . At first I thought it was the music of a choir of heavenly angels. It sounded so solemn and so strange. I shall never forget this hour."[107] Singing or hearing Christmas music engendered feelings of sadness, joy, and mysterious contentment, all "bodily emotions" familiar from childhood holidays.[108] Carols at once expressed the appeal of tradition in the cataclysm of war, the interpenetration of official and vernacular discourses, the rowdy pleasures of barracks culture, and the private mood created by nostalgia and loneliness.

The conflicted emotions submerged in this cluster of competing moods and interests could be overwhelming: soldiers often broke down and wept during Christmas celebrations. Aribert Reimann is right to conclude that our understanding of the "real" experience of soldiers and their families remains hidden behind the "discursive strategies of meaning construction" that dominate the texts they left behind.[109] Following Reimann, the trope of crying soldiers needs to be read, like the Christmas tree, for its multivalent meanings. Descriptions of "glistening tears," like those that Chaplain Ebner saw "in the eyes of many weather-hardened soldiers," found their way into far too many accounts of War Christmas to be simple fabrications; the image clearly fascinated and moved contemporaries.[110] Far from seeming unmanly, scenes of emotional excess were said to be deeply moving, beautiful moments. The letters in Witkop's collection show that even committed "front-fighters" touched by the Christmas mood could cry in public without shame. "Shortly after 3 o'clock we began," wrote Richard Kutzner on Christmas Eve 1914. "It's always dark here anyway . . . the little, tiny Christmas tree was alight [with candles], we did songs on the harmonica. G. read the Christmas story aloud—he could hardly make it, all eight other house guests let our tears fall, but it was beautiful."[111] Weeping demonstrated the forbearance and loyalty of the troops—to home and family, to national traditions, and to each other. Tears also showed that Germans were sympathetic and cultured humanitarians. According to the 1915 Christmas issue of *The Trench*, a "Children's Christmas Party in the Field" brought German soldiers and French children together in a single "great family of humanity." The German troops were "extraordinarily pleased with this unusual children's party in enemy territory. We certainly did not regret having to dry many tears in this way."[112] For Corporal Herbert Sulzbach, crying resulted from memories of home but also from the special atmosphere of military celebration. Sulzbach recorded the moving effect of his company's celebration in his personal diary:

It snows, and the Christmas mood is everywhere. . . . [A] big garage
is transformed into a church. On both sides of the altar [candles are
lit on] two magnificent Christmas trees, palms are set up all around.
Officers sit up front, on the left the choir, to the rear the enlisted men.
It is so festive and uplifting that one sheds tears, even before "Silent
Night" rings out. We are all touched and full of melancholy, each
has his own thoughts of Heimat. Then our battery celebrated in our
courtyard around our own magnificent tree—it is a dignified and
beautiful Christmas Eve.[113]

Family sentiment and national chauvinism permeated celebrations at the
front and repeated descriptions of soldiers' tears reveal the incommensura-
bility of these competing claims. Weeping was patriotic, but it also revealed
the burdens of what one German chaplain called the "homesickness [that]
has infected us all."[114] No matter how bombastic, comradely, or sentimental, celebrations at the front could not hide the fact that War Christmas was
in many ways a failed ritual. Contemporaries claimed that tears bridged the
gaps between war and peace, between front and Heimat, but their dewy persistence suggests that the distance between public duty and private need was
never really resolved.

WAR CHRISTMAS BETWEEN MEMORY AND MYTH

In her annual Christmas report to the members of the League of German
Women's Organizations, Gertrud Bäumer described the muted spirit of
Christmas shoppers in Berlin in 1917, who seemed to suffer from advanced
spiritual exhaustion. There was not much left to celebrate, except for the ability to "hold out" in a time of wretched privation, an observance hardly conducive to the Christmas spirit. Store windows were empty, and holiday traffic
in the train station was far quieter than normal. Berliners simply wanted to
"withdraw from the world for several days," where they could spend their
"saved-up joy" in a few "short silent hours." The NFD charity drives continued,
but now Bäumer paid more attention to government attempts to distribute
much-needed food and heating materials to Berlin residents—not to soldiers at the front—and the nationwide mass strikes of January 1918 were just
over the horizon.[115] Reading news reports on the negotiations over the Russian surrender of Brest-Litovsk, Bäumer wondered if hopes for a new order
promoted by official channels were valid: "The strangeness of it all connects

the eternal meaning of the Christmas message to the question, does this really shape the beginnings of something historically new—the first stones of a new foundation for a *Völkergemeinschaft* [community of peoples]? Will later peoples see this Christmas as a naive episode or as the germ cell of an entirely new world?"[116]

The German government had an answer to Bäumer's question. In December 1917 the newly established War Press Office, under the command of General Ludendorff and supporters of the right-wing Fatherland Party, issued a holiday press release that could be quoted or reprinted without citation. Celebrations this year would be admittedly meager, according to the military Press Office. Germans would have to do without Christmas trees, candles, sweets and cakes, or heating coal. Yet if conditions forced Germans to be "frugal at home," they were "rich in the Fatherland!" Courage came from the love of nation and dedication to the future. This simple, serious Christmas, free from "non-German influences" and "holiday opulence," would be a "milestone" on the way to a "flourishing Germany" for the postwar generation. Though children would receive few presents this year, the government insisted that "the love and the feelings of duty to the Fatherland of the parents will give them something else instead: *the memory of a very great, uplifting, soulful experience!*" Rather than the *Völkergemeinschaft* (community of peoples) at the center of Bäumer's musings, military officials saw the holiday as a precursor of a "Volksgemeinschaft," or people's community—the term later adopted by Nazis to describe German society united under fascism.[117]

The foundations for a postwar mnemonics of War Christmas were thus laid during the war itself, by government communiqués, by civic leaders like Father Ebner and Gertrud Bäumer, and by the intense feelings experienced by countless Germans in wartime celebrations. Saturated with conflicting emotions, War Christmas became a site of memory for the postwar generation.[118] Visions of an authentic Imperial Christmas increasingly out of reach—which seemed to represent an entire world (or Reich) gone missing—were combined with longings for absent or dead family members made particularly acute by the joy of the holiday season.[119] Idealized memories of War Christmas bridged these incommensurate feelings and at the same time encouraged Germans in the interwar period to visualize the beautiful and noble side of war; wartime myths, as historian Eric Leed concludes, "alleviate contradictions by reframing the elements that conflict in reality."[120] For enlisted men, celebrations of War Christmas might have primarily "put the present time out of mind."[121] Postwar public memories, however, were constructed by the very officers and civic leaders who dominated Christmas during the war; they preferred to cast the holiday as a heroic celebration of a trench community that had sacrificed everything for Germany. The fabulistic threads of War Christmas turned into a "true story" that revealed the dramatic manifestation of the sacred on the German side of the lines and the emergence of the Volksgemeinschaft out of the crisis of total war.[122]

The tragedy of death was one of the most jarring aspects of War Christmas, and the fallen rose again to populate the postwar myth. Just as Jesus sacrificed himself and was resurrected for the common good (so the dominant narrative explained), individual sacrifice on the front would find resurrection in a reinvigorated national community. "Christmas is the great, holy celebration of sacrifice," wrote a Bremen newspaper editor back in 1914. "In this way God showed his love for the world. . . . The sacrificial deed that gives everything, the love that renounces all, which in the end voluntarily sheds blood for a holy matter and for a besieged people—that is the idea and the core of Christmas."[123] The wartime notion that death at Christmas was a holy service to God and nation left enduring traces in the postwar imagination. In the postwar decades, the community of the dead served again as a down payment on national renewal. The most famous example is perhaps "The Christmas Legend of the 15th Regiment" by trench poet Walter Flex, who was killed during the war and became a legendary figure in the postwar youth movement. On Christmas Eve 1914, the poet supposedly read the tale aloud to his company in a shell-torn village church on the western front. In the story, an anguished war widow drowns herself and her children in a pond on Christmas Eve; they are brought back to life after meeting the ghosts of German soldiers. After the war, Flex's "Christmas Legend" was often reprinted, and with other chauvinist Christmas stories it became a staple of Nazi Christmas books and later World War II propaganda. The theme of death and rebirth—this time of civilian women—foretold the resurrection of the nation through the sacrifice of war and drew on the interplay of gender common to War Christmas narratives, in which soldiers protect women who symbolized the Heimat at large.[124]

Like other myths, War Christmas had conflicting social geographies. In the 1920s and 1930s, competing political groups sought to define and control its meaning. Social Democrats promoted a myth of War Christmas centered on themes of death and comradeship in the trenches, but they emphasized the poverty of the ordinary soldier, the heartless lies of authoritarian officers, and the tragic ironies of Christmas at the front. Soldiers certainly died contentedly in front of a dugout Christmas tree, but for no grand purpose; their bodies were simply thrown outside to freeze on the "field of death."[125] The victory of German Social Democracy in 1918, such stories concluded, meant the victory of a new, all-inclusive Germany, which justified the Christmas sacrifices at the front.

German Jews remembered War Christmas in ways that paralleled Jewish confrontations with the holiday in the late nineteenth century. In response to increasing anti-Semitism in the 1920s and then the violent oppression of the Nazi era, Jews cast "War Hanukkah" as a sign of a separate Jewish identity that was still very German. As *Der Schild* (The Shield), the Jewish veterans' journal put it in 1937, "12,000 Maccabees from 1914–1918" fought and died for the fatherland.[126] Recollections of Jewish participation in military Christmas celebrations served as evidence that Christians and Jews had served and celebrated together, and that Jews had been willing to sacrifice their own separate religious observance to become "German." The strategic inclusion of a 1914 Christmas letter from Rabbi Alfred Zweig at the end of *Gefallene Deutsche Juden: Frontbriefe 1914–1918* (Fallen German Jews: Front Letters, 1914–1918), published in 1935, testifies to this failed effort. In the letter, Zweig tells of his "right" to participate in no less than two Christmas celebrations because "enemy bullets don't differentiate between individuals." "In the field," Zweig wrote, "there are no Catholics, no Protestants, no Jews, no Center [Party] people and no Social Democrats, no Poles and no Danes or Lothringians; rather there are Germans, as our Kaiser stressed." The letter appeared on the final page of the book—a last-ditch appeal, as it were, to familiar readings of War Christmas as a celebration of national harmony in the year that saw the promulgation of the brutally anti-Semitic Nuremberg Laws.[127]

Alternate readings by Social Democrats or German Jews hardly hid the fact that collective recollections of War Christmas fit best in the mythical universe propagated by National Socialism. "Statistically, myth is on the right," Roland Barthes reminds us in *Mythologies*. "There it is essential. . . . It takes hold of everything."[128] The Nazi version of War Christmas recalled manly comradeship and wartime sacrifice for the "new Germany." The Christmas issues of the Nazi press regularly featured firsthand accounts of hard-faced "storm troopers" who went out killing and then broke down in tears at the sight of a Christmas tree. A typical and once again "unforgettable" account by veteran and early Nazi convert Hans Zöberlein described "Christmas on the Siegfried Line" and a British attack purposefully timed to "disrupt"

German festivities. After a heroic counterattack, described by Zöberlein in bloody detail, "it was 'Silent Night' forever for a good dozen Tommies," and the Germans retired for a solemn but hearty celebration.[129] Myth, as Barthes claimed, transforms "history into nature" and masks social and political power. In the hands of the Nazis, the truth of War Christmas "went without saying."[130] The holiday outlined boundaries between the national enemy and good Germans and collapsed those between Volk and fatherland in ways that were so obvious as to make them universal.

World War I gave a decisive boost to the ongoing nationalization of German Christmas. In the postwar period, Christmas was more than ever a potent national symbol that was open to appropriation by competing groups and interests. Yet a focus on the high drama of war and politics can obscure more-subtle cultural change, which unfolded at a slower tempo. Before moving on to the overt politicization of Christmas in the Weimar and Nazi years, we need to step back and consider broad cultural continuities across the late nineteenth and twentieth centuries. The consolidation of Germany's modern consumer regime during the forty years that bracketed World War I made a profound contribution to the construction of Christmas as a celebration of national belonging. The mass-produced material culture that increasingly defined the holiday linked emotions to things and remade the connections between self and community. At the same time, the commercialization of Christmas inspired serious debates about the effects of modernization on traditional German values, and by the late 1920s, the ability to deliver the goods during the holiday season itself had become a telling measure of political success or failure.

FIGURE 4.1

Crowds outside the "Grand Christmas Sale" at Tietz Department
Store, Alexanderplatz, Berlin, circa 1925. (© bpk Berlin 2009)

4

Under the Sign of *Kauflust*

The daily newspapers expand with such abundance of advertisements
that they become true tomes, giant colorful bulletins cover the poster
kiosks, the show windows display elegant get-ups with fairylike illumination, Christmas trees shine in the windows, electric lights glitter,
flashing crystal mirrors double the pleasures on view, model sets and
automated puppets attract children and adults, carousels and pyramids
swing through their slow, measured rounds, music boxes awaken the
desire to dance in the onlooking crowd.... Everything is tried out at
Christmas time, and anything goes!

—☙ "Christmas," *Die Reklame*, 20 October 1893

IN 1893 IT WAS STILL EASY for the editors of *Die Reklame*, one of Germany's first professional advertising journals, to marvel at the opportunities created by the commercialization of Christmas. An expanding industrial economy had placed an array of mass-produced goods on Germany's store shelves,
and modern marketing techniques incited waves of seasonal *Kauflust*, the
"urge to buy" that moved crowds of Germans into the stores and streets in
search of holiday gifts.[1] Things looked different some thirty-five years later
in the waning years of the Weimar Republic. Germany had barely recovered
from war, revolution, and economic crisis. In November 1928, H. Ahlsmann,
a small shopkeeper in Berlin and self-proclaimed "little man," wrote his local
Protestant church council to complain about hard times in the retail trade.
Ahlsmann reserved special ire for a proposed law that would shorten store
hours on Christmas Eve. Protestant leaders, along with their Catholic coconfessionalists and representatives of the Social Democratic Party (SPD), were
eager to move the closing time for retail stores and most other businesses
from 7:00 P.M. to 5:00 P.M. Two extra hours off from work would give hard-
pressed workers a much-deserved break (according to the SPD) or let them

attend a Christmas service to celebrate the birth of Christ (according to clerical representatives). A regulatory bill named "Store Closings on the Twenty-Fourth of December," considered by the German Reichstag (Parliament) the following year, was only the latest attempt to design sumptuary laws that balanced religious, commercial, and popular use of holiday time. But for small shopkeepers like Ahlsmann, who felt squeezed by the unstoppable rise of large department stores such as Tietz and Wertheim, the legislation had vital economic importance. "You all think only of the big business men and not a single person thinks about *wir Kleinen* [us little guys]," Ahlsmann griped. Closing early on Christmas Eve—even by two hours—would undercut his seasonal profits. "You gentlemen are all in mostly well-paid positions," he continued in expressive if awkward prose. "We little people have to support it all through taxes and not a single person considers that we taxpayers only do business after 5:00, when people from the stores and from work come and only then buy from the small shop keepers. . . . [W]e are grateful when someone supports us, but unfortunately soon everyone will be guilty when even more old people lie out [homeless] in the street."[2]

Ahlsmann's tirade was personal, but, like the Reichstag representatives who argued over sumptuary law, he articulated larger concerns about the effects of consumerism and Kauflust on this most traditional of holidays. Debates on the commercialization of Christmas had serious implications. Labor movements, organized religion, competing business interests, and the state struggled to control the symbolic and monetary capital generated during the holiday season. The contest was entangled with the desires of ordinary people for a holiday with just the right balance of material abundance and emotional depth. Reichstag deputies were no doubt removed from the hardscrabble existence that troubled ordinary voters. They nonetheless brought the interests of their constituents to bear on their discussion of the store-closing bill. Speaking for the committee that wrote the legislation, SPD deputy Wilhelm Sollmann asserted that the "great majority of the people" demanded shortened hours "with rare unanimity." Sollmann argued that retail-store employees in particular deserved a break from the unrelenting overtime required during the Christmas season. Waxing sentimental, he appealed to the domestic intimacies of the holiday and cited the potential joy of wives and mothers if their men made it home from work in time for a proper celebration. Paying lip service to the concerns of his opponents—one hardly wanted small businesses to suffer, especially at Christmastime—Sollmann concluded that the Reichstag, which had so often disappointed voters in the past, should unanimously pass a resolution "that damages no one and burdens no one but spreads a small measure of Christmas joy among numerous *Volksgenossen* [people's comrades]."[3]

Arguments in support of the proposed legislation expressed well-established positions on the use and abuse of popular celebration. Protestant and Catholic deputies, who had insisted for decades that sacred time needed state protection, backed the resolution. Officials of both denominations had become increasingly concerned with the commercialization of Christmas, expressed most dramatically in the transposition of the Advent Sundays preceding the holiday into "Silver" and "Golden" Sundays, special shopping days with relaxed sumptuary laws. As Deputy Thomas Esser, a businessman from Cologne, declared for the Catholic Center Party, "I hardly need to state that the promotion of the observance of the holiness of the evening before Christmas is entirely in the direction that the Center Party has always followed in these questions."[4] A supporter of Protestant interests soberly admitted that it was impossible to "bring the Christmas experience into the soul through a law" but nonetheless supported the bill because a short pause in the "mad rush" of the Christmas season might deepen spiritual thinking.[5] A Communist Party representative grudgingly voiced his own approval. To mocking laughter from the chamber, he called for a forty-two-hour workweek and for the extension of the early-closing law to all Saturdays and other holidays, "as Russian workers already have."[6] The Nazi Party also backed the bill, though none of their deputies spoke during the debate.

Statements against early closing hours by representatives of the conservative German People's Party (DVP) and the Economics Party (WP) voiced the resentments of the *Mittelstand*, the craft workers and small businessmen like Ahlsmann who made up the economically pressured lower middle classes. Dr. Friedrich Pfeffer, deputy for the DVP, contended that the law would demoralize small shopkeepers, who already suffered under the weak economy. Most workers traditionally received their holiday bonuses on Christmas Eve and could only shop for presents late that evening; early closing hours would prevent this money from being spent in smaller stores, which offered the benefits of local convenience and personalized service. The proposed legislation threatened not just livelihoods but also long-existing ties of familiarity and conviviality. "Indeed the entire collapse of the *Mittelstand*," Pfeffer warned, "can be traced to a not insignificant degree to the strict regulation of the working day."[7] In a direct attack on Germany's department stores, Artur Petzold of the WP argued strenuously that the two shopping hours between

5:00 P.M. and 7:00 P.M. were indispensable for *Mittelstand* profits. There was little enough gain for the small shopkeeper in the holiday season, he maintained, because "the large department stores draw the public like sweets attract puppies." Undaunted by catcalls from the Social Democrats, Petzold attacked the SPD's position by mocking the counter-Christmas discourse that dominated socialist rhetoric in the holiday season: "You [Social Democrats] want to achieve a social deed so that all the *Angestellten* [salaried workers] will be drawn close to your social-democratic heart. For you, the sacredness of Christmas is just good enough for that, otherwise you do not take your holiness in too strong a dose."[8] The deputy of the tiny German Peasants Party added his voice to the opposition, asserting that the new law would not be obeyed in the countryside in any case.[9]

The early-closing bill passed the Reichstag on 10 December 1929 by an almost three-to-one margin, supported by an unusual coalition of the anti-clerical SPD and Communist Party of Germany (KPD), the confessional parties, and the National Socialists. Although political bickering delayed final promulgation until 1931 and enforcement remained spotty, the new law confirmed the sanctity of Christmas as well as the power of organized labor and big business.[10] It also showed that consumerism, which promised to democratize German society by making more goods available to more people, worked to divide as much as to unite. During the decades bracketing the First World War, the arrival of mass culture and a new media landscape of daily newspapers and then radio and film altered conventional nineteenth-century consumer practices. Commercialization appropriated popular traditions—like the annual outdoor Christmas markets set up in German towns and cities, or the family rituals practiced around the Christmas tree—and sold them back to the masses in new forms. Access to the goods and practices that inspired the Christmas mood was now more than ever tied to the ability to pay rather than the cultural capital of bourgeois social status.[11]

The commercialization of Christmas furthermore weakened familiar boundaries between public and private life. During the holiday season, marketing campaigns and mass-produced consumer goods unavoidably encroached upon the practices and emotions of family intimacy. Tender expressions of love and feeling were increasingly tied to and expressed through modern consumer culture, transforming the very foundations of the interiorized self. This process of cultural mediation had the potential to create common experiences that leveled class and confessional differences, even as new modes of "getting and spending" and commercialized entertainment gave Germans alternate ways to assert social hierarchies and self-identities.[12] From the marketing professionals who saw Christmas as a time "to try it all" because "anything goes" to critics across the political and confessional spectrum, who condemned the hollowing out of Germany's favorite holiday, contemporaries used Christmas to grapple with the effects of modern consumer practices. In symbolic and practical terms, Christmas exposed the fractures between tradition and change, faith and secularization, money and morality, and public and private life in a society increasingly dominated by mass culture.[13]

THE SIGNATURE OF THE CHRISTMAS SEASON

"The world stands at the present time under the sign of *Kauflust*," wrote a Berlin newspaper in December 1898. "On the streets rushing people loaded with giant packages, in front of the magnificent show window displays a multitude who want to see if not shop, in the stores a jostling, cheerfully excited crowd: this is the signature of the Christmas season."[14] The rampant commercialization of Christmas seemed to take contemporaries by surprise in the late nineteenth century, and reactions varied from delight to dismay. The emergence of a ubiquitous consumer culture, the professionalization of marketing techniques, and the commercialization of leisure time had the potential to create cheerful crowds who simply wanted to buy and see and do things. Kauflust could pull Germans together, since the acquisition and use of new products and the pursuit of new leisure pastimes created social affinities that transcended class or politics.[15] Cultural critics believed, however, that slick advertisements manipulated vulnerable shoppers. The overwhelming desire for goods threatened to replace faith and piety with selfishness and shallow materialism, and the department store—the modern "cathedral of consumption"—was a site of foreign and "Jewish" decadence that awakened consumer desires impossible to fulfill.[16] From the last decades of the Kaiserreich through the Weimar years, commercialization generated conflict as well as solidarity, anxiety as well as satisfaction. When Germans debated the meaning of Christmas, they spoke, by proxy as it were, to the apparently unavoidable but deeply confusing changes in the most basic practices of everyday life.

The commercialization of Christmas accelerated the arrival of a national self-awareness based on the close connections between things, families, and a broadly shared German culture. "Thus does the economy, as the dominant institutional locus, produce not only objects for appropriate subjects, but subjects for appropriate objects," as anthropologist Marshall Sahlins put it.[17] The changing array of items offered for sale as Christmas gifts across the nineteenth century—here drawn from indices of holiday-season print advertisements in Münster-area newspapers—underscores the ways that the economic upturn of the late 1880s, new mass-produced goods, and national markets transformed the holiday and the world of goods that defined family celebration. In 1850, when the German states were still divided and industrial takeoff was just on the horizon, books and baked goods accounted for two-thirds of all advertised presents (44 percent and 22 percent, respectively), followed by textiles such as coats, furs, and carpets (7 percent) and toys, glassware, and flowers (3.5 percent each). In 1886 shoppers could choose from a larger assortment of potential gifts that included a growing number of industrial goods. Books and baked goods remained popular, but the number of advertisements for textiles and glassware—products of the dynamic factory sector—had basically doubled. The expanded gift possibilities included items unmentioned in 1850, such as technical and mechanical appliances, Christmas decorations (including commercially produced nativity scenes), metal wares, musical instruments, paper goods, and clocks, which together accounted for about 20 percent of all advertisements. By 1910 the dominance of manufactured goods was complete. Mass-produced clothing and textiles topped the list of potential gifts (22 percent), followed by modern industrial products like sewing machines and bicycles, as well as decorations and other items made specifically for the holiday (7 percent each).[18] Giving gifts still expressed familial affection but depended increasingly on the rapidly expanding networks of production and distribution that by 1900 had turned the trademark "Made in Germany" into an internationally recognized sign of industrial quality.[19]

The arrival of modern technology, as ethnographer Hermann Bausinger points out, did not so much destroy as standardize and commodify "traditional" folk culture, which took on new national significance.[20] The construction of the southeast Saxon Erzgebirge (Ore Mountains) as the Heimat of German Christmas is an excellent example of the way industrialization transformed and modernized local production and at the same time reified notions of handcrafted authenticity that actually depended on rationalized productive forces. The familiar Christmas nutcracker—"made in the Erzgebirge"—epitomizes the process. Lionized in E. T. A. Hoffmann's fairy tale and sold today around the world as an example of German folk art, the nutcracker retains an aura of genuineness; it remains a requisite item in the extensive retail displays of German Christmas ornaments at the Käthe Wohlfahrt Christmas Shop in "Christmas City" Rothenburg ob der Taube (Bavaria) or at the Yankee Candle Company outside Amherst, Massachusetts.[21] Since the early 1700s, miners in the economically depressed Erzgebirge had been making nutcrackers, toys, and glass and carved-wood decorations to supplement their incomes. During the 1850s, as mass-produced ornaments made of paper, tin, wood, and especially glass began to replace homemade and edible decorations, products from the Erzgebirge gained a national reputation. By the last third of the century, handwork in the region had for the most part been replaced by factory-style production lines; decorations were the end product of a highly technical manufacturing process. Their growing popularity reflected in part the contemporary efforts of local craft and historical-clothing societies, which tried to preserve and promote regional folk cultures with increasing enthusiasm after German unification.[22] Mass-produced decorations like the nutcracker, marketed as German handicrafts, were sold throughout Germany and then the world, and after 1945 they provided East Germany with much-desired foreign currency. The preservation of folk authenticity and notions of Germanness were thus achieved through industrialization, commodification, and the growth of (inter)national markets for regional goods.

Consumer culture theoretically made the material trappings required for the "Christmas mood" available to everyone, though the market for goods like ornaments and Christmas cards was deeply segmented by the ability to pay. Building on advances in glassblowing techniques and transportation networks in the 1870s, the decoration industry expanded rapidly. By the end of the decade, distributors in Nuremberg, Gera, Cologne, and Berlin could deliver via mail order a glittering selection of glass ornaments. Prices for balls, pinecones, stars, pearls, and fruits—available in boxes of twelve—ranged from thirty pfennigs to several marks; simple papier-mâché ornaments cost less. Wealthy Germans could buy angels and Father Christmas dolls, artificial Christmas trees priced according to height, and a mechanical rotating Christmas tree stand that played "Silent Night" as it turned the tree—for a costly twenty-two marks.

Consumption was also segmented by confessional preference. The Peter Feldhaus Company in Catholic Cologne could ship on demand Nativity scenes that included a stable, the Holy Family, the three kings, and an assortment of angels and shepherds. Carved in wood, these sets ranged in price

FIGURE 4.2

Advertisement for mass-produced Christmas decorations: "Glass Christ-Tree Ornaments—Wonderful!—Unsurpassed!" (*Der Wahre Jakob: Illustrirte humoristisch-satirische Zeitschrift*, 27 November 1906)

from thirteen to 300 marks, depending on the size and number of the figures. Nativity scenes made from papier-mâché and wax scenes were significantly less expensive but nonetheless represented a significant outlay in a time when the average weekly wage for workers in industry and handicrafts was about eleven marks and for lawyers and educators about thirty-five marks.[23] Prices fell with economic expansion. In the later years of the German Empire, five marks could buy a vast assortment of ornaments, and advertisements for all manner of decorations filled the pages of the middle- and working-class press alike (Figure 4.2). Germany's booming Christmas-card industry further testifies to market segmentation and the commercialization of the Christmas mood. By the 1880s, the vast majority of the world's Christmas cards were made in Germany. Printers in Berlin and elsewhere worked year-round to manufacture and ship hundreds of thousands of cards and embossed envelopes to the United States; the British reportedly spent between 12 and 15 million marks for German cards each year.[24] Sentimental holiday imagery also graced the commercial "thank-you notes" popular in Germany, and embossed, gilded stationary cost far more than simple printed sheets.[25]

A growing appreciation for the "scientific" nature of salesmanship and advertising accompanied economic expansion in the late nineteenth century, and since Christmas required gifts, marketing professionals were quick to recognize that the holiday was "high season" for retailers. The December issues of professional trade journals—such as *Die Reklame* (The Advertisement), founded in 1890, and *Seidels Reklame*, first published in 1913—invariably featured critical reviews of the latest Christmas advertising posters and store-window displays, as well as practical suggestions for creating "modern and *anständig* [respectable] advertisements" that store owners could use to wring the most profit out of the holiday season.[26] Well aware that the holiday season exacerbated conflicts of interest between *großen Kaufleuten* (large-scale retailers) and *den Kleinen* (small shopkeepers), the magazines spoke to both. If the display windows of the smaller stores lacked creativity and splash, the big stores nonetheless "should make the greatest effort to impart to their customers the belief that the large-scale salesman is not there just to do business, but that he also understands that his task is to give every possible support to his colleague, the small retailer."[27]

The language of respectability and support for the disadvantaged revealed a certain disquiet about the effects of rampant Kauflust on the Christmas spirit, even among advertising experts, who carefully masked commercialization with appeals to sensitivity and tradition. Christmas was nonetheless an appropriate time to experiment with cutting-edge, modern forms of advertising. A lengthy article published in *Die Reklame* in 1894 offered detailed instructions for organizing a full-blown holiday sales campaign, complete with suggestions for limiting the negative impact of overly aggressive marketing. Local merchants, according to the article, should organize a "Collective Exhibition" to display merchandise in a festive, Christmas-marketlike atmosphere. A fancy invitation card might lure potential customers to the exhibition—though it must include the words "No Pressure to Buy!" to be truly successful. Four weeks before Christmas, *Die Reklame* suggested, retailers should encourage newspaper editors to publish articles about "Christmas Sights" or "Christmas Strolls," which introduced readers to the exhibitions and sales organized by local stores. Reporters should, however, include mention of all sights that were noteworthy and not concentrate solely on stores that advertise with the paper, lest readers grow suspicious that they were being misled. *Die Reklame* also recommended group advertisements, in which several stores offered wares under a banner statement such as "Christmas 1894: The firms below guarantee trustworthy, inexpensive prices and will take back inappropriate items until 29 December." Indeed, the journal argued that retailers should institute an easy-return policy—for store credit—during the holiday season, when customers might be disappointed with gifts that did not fit, such as gloves or clothing. This was still a radical idea in the 1890s, but the trade journal assured its readers that the calculation would pay off: a public return policy reassured shoppers at the point of sale, and customers who returned gifts would usually buy something that cost more, since they would not want to give money away by getting a less-expensive item. They might even become regular customers if impressed by the politeness of the merchant.

Recommendations for producing newspaper advertisements—according to *Die Reklame*, the most effective way to reach the customer—were quite explicit. Rather than advertise only in the holiday season, it was better to place small advertisements throughout the year to generate customer recognition and then do something splashy for Christmas. And it was important to advertise early. After 1 to 10 December, "the season reached its highpoint" and potential customers were so worn out that they no longer paid much attention, even to the best advertisements. A rationally planned sales campaign, however, held out the prospect of great success. Around 1 or 2 December, *Die Reklame* suggested, retailers should print an ad in the form of a visitor card—without too much text, just the name and address of the firm. The following week (around 5 or 6 December), they should follow up with a business notice in the form of a modern "telegraphic dispatch" intended to generate excitement about the goods for sale and draw attention to the advertisement itself. Finally, the third ad in the series should take the form of a traditional child's letter to the Christkind, printed in childlike handwriting and asking for the goods offered by the store.[28]

The sentimental family and Christian imagery of the holiday—Weihnachtsmann and Christkind, Christmas trees and snowy landscapes, angels and elves, lit candles and joyous children—were ready-made for advertising purposes. Posters, print ads, and store displays all appropriated this rich iconography. *Die Reklame* publishers even sold what they called *Frei-Clichés*, model advertisements with cloying illustrations that bracketed blank spaces where retailers could insert their own sales pitch (Figure 4.3). At the same time, the journal recommended that because of the "unusually stiff competition" in the holiday season, ads should be "original, eye-appealing, and tasteful"—seemingly contradictory advice given the glut of similar-looking images that dominated the advertising pages each December.[29] The question of taste was important, however. The new advertising professionals evinced real respect

FIGURE 4.3

Your business here: model Christmas advertisements
marketed by *Die Reklame*, 5 December 1896.

for the deep emotional investment of potential customers in an authentic Christmas and tried to strike a balance between hyperbole and tact—nowhere more evident than in "The Ten Most Important Commandments" for "every type of advertising" published by *Seidels Reklame* in December 1914. The title alone testifies to the ongoing commercialization of Christian piety. Yet the content called on marketers to approach the public with sensitivity. Advertisements were supposed to be direct, clear, convincing, and positive, but also "tasteful and sympathetic" because "all that is beautiful, friendly, [and] harmonious attracts and awakens trust."[30]

Stores advertised goods year-round, but at Christmastime goods became gifts, surrounded by the emotional patina of the holiday and the special appeal of an increasingly commercialized Christmas mood. The goal for retailers was clear: "Of course the advertisement, which always adapts flexibly to public trends, makes use of the collective Christmas mood and exhibits during the season, as far as possible, an appropriately atmospheric impression."[31] The ability to sustain the proper "mood" made all the difference between a good and bad advertisement, and correctly placed iconography had unavoidable psychological effects. One simple poster held up as an example by *Seidels Reklame* in 1913 displayed the appropriate "modesty" but nonetheless effectively evoked a "Christmassy mood," since "the black pine bough adorned with burning candles is so skillfully set against the blue background that one involuntarily imagines the entire festive Christmas tree behind it." Capitalizing on the mood was linked directly to generating Kauflust in children as well as adults, and youths were often the central targets of marketing campaigns. A "pretty poster" for a display of toys at Tietz department store exemplified the way the right pitch "certainly produces a joyful Christmas mood among big and little and stimulates the desire to buy toys among them all."[32] Department-store display windows were also important for generating the popular mood. Year after year, the authors of this new prescriptive literature carefully evaluated the displays of moving puppets, village landscapes, and fairy-tale scenes in the ground floor display windows of Germany's major department stores. They criticized composition and its potential effects, ranked the strengths and weaknesses of different types of puppets, and held up the best windows for broad emulation. Sensitivity to mood was, as ever, of greatest importance. As *Seidels Reklame* wrote in 1913, the display of moving village handworkers going about their business, set up in the huge Tietz store on Frankfurter Allee in Berlin, "is really put together with a great understanding, with much taste, and above all with a love that one finds

FIGURE 4.4

"How these puppets greet each other, quarrel, how they work, how they show surprise, this is truly enchanting." Christmas display window, Tietz Department Store, Frankfurter Allee, Berlin. (*Seidels Reklame*, December 1913)

quite rarely. . . . How these puppets greet each other, quarrel, how they work, how they show astonishment, this is truly enchanting" (Figure 4.4).[33]

Professionally designed show windows were only one of the more visible manifestations of the commercialization that brought Germans into city streets in the holiday season. A Weihnachtswanderung, or Christmas Stroll, through the tawdry Christmas market or the new urban theater and retail districts to view the goods, shows, and characters on display was a requisite part of the big-city holiday experience. Prussian patriot and cultural critic Ludwig Rellstab, famous for his descriptions of the "Christmas Strolls" he took each season through Berlin, set the tone early on. Published in the *Vossische Zeitung* from 1826 to 1859, Rellstab's sentimental reports on the moods and curiosities of the holiday—the "unusual visitors" at the outdoor Christmas market, the effects of the weather, the faces of joyous children, and the "grand crush of splendid men and women shoppers"—apparently fascinated readers.[34] By the late nineteenth century, however, newspaper accounts of "Christmas Strolls" were little more than advertising in another guise—precisely as the professional literature recommended. The December issues of the stolid *Vossische Zeitung*, like other big city dailies, still took readers on a "Christmas Stroll through Berlin," but only through the well-established retail stores that stocked the goods made available by modern productive forces. A series of columns from 1893, for example, presented glowing descriptions (with prices) of the great variety of gifts wealthy Germans might place under the tree. The cornucopia included toys of all types—from dolls to electric trains, construction sets, and toy soldiers—and an abundant assortment of items for adults, the products of a booming consumer culture: liquor and spirits, furniture of all kinds, eyeglasses and opera glasses, jewelry, houseplants and fresh-cut flowers (including poinsettias and mistletoe), bicycles, musical instruments and player pianos, and suitcases and travel apparel. Readers of the newspaper apparently shopped only in the best stores with well-established pedigrees, like "the highly elegant 'Cylinder-Distillery' of D. Schlefinger, Leipziger Strasse 90 . . . founded in 1797."[35] Appeals to "tradition" and "elegance" helped mask commercialization and turned mass-produced industrial goods into personalized, quality gifts.

Urban residents had a wide choice of Christmas activities tied to distinct milieu-based attitudes and identities. "The most important question for the holidays for many families, friends, and relatives . . . is the question: 'where to go?'" wrote the *Vossische Zeitung* in 1893. The wealthy could spend the holiday at the elegant Grand Restaurant in Potsdamer Platz, where percussion-orchestra concerts and an extensive menu of beer, wine, and fine foods welcomed revelers; or they might choose "the Etablissement Ronacher, a comfortable rendezvous for the best society." The Restaurant H. Jaeger was more of a middle-class family place, where "an elegant Christmas tree gives the inn special decoration, the gas light bulbs cast a friendly glow in the rooms and salons, and the ventilation is excellent, so that women also feel at their best."[36] Less-refined Berliners could visit the "Grand Christmas Display" at Castan's Panopticon, attend the holiday concert at the Zoological Garden, or quaff a beer beside the "gigantic Christmas trees with fairy-like electric lights" promised by the Germania Pracht-Säle.[37] Workers and the middle classes alike could attend any number of dance balls, concerts, and parties thrown by private taverns and breweries, Tingel-Tangel (vaudeville) music halls, and *Schnapskasinos*; sumptuary laws were enforced sporadically if at all.[38] Civic groups and labor organizations of all kinds organized shows, dinners, and parties for their members. This array of activities was a far cry from the sober descriptions of the typical workers' Christmas mooted in the socialist press. The Social Democrats, in fact, threw their own parties, and beyond the rhetoric there was apparently little difference in the entertainment offered at the "Grand Matinee" organized by the Third Voting District of the Berlin SPD, the "Christmas Attractions" offered by the Confederation of German Woodworkers, or the "Grand Holiday Performance" at the Friedrichshain Brewery.[39]

The new business of leisure was nowhere so evident as in the special Christmas plays performed in Germany's many public theaters in the Christmas season, which further reflected the fractures in commercial festival culture in the Wilhelmine period. Different venues specialized in avant-garde experimental theater, bourgeois classics, middlebrow melodrama, or socialist agitprop—all designed to capitalize on but also spread rather specific versions of the Christmas mood.[40] *Peace on Earth! or: Deportation on Christmas Eve*, a proletarian play about Christmas during the Hamburg dockworkers' strike of 1886, was staged for working-class audiences around 1900. The play portrayed the supposedly true-to-life tribulations of a laborer who agitates to improve workplace conditions and is ordered to leave the city limits on Christmas Eve or face six months in jail, only "because [he] did what the Nazarene taught."[41] In the words of the authorities in Chemnitz, who banned a performance of *Peace on Earth!* at a socialist Christmas party in 1894, "the presentation of [this play] is apparently intended only to . . . involve Christian celebrations and the dramatic arts in the service of hateful, political passions, to use an appealing form to degrade religious activities, to slander persons of the nobility, to evoke class hatred, envy, rowdiness, and discontent among the audience, and by these means to foster inappropriate actions, immorality, and unlawful transgressions."[42] The rule of law thus mandated the appropriate holiday spirit.

The authorities had no problem with the vast majority of Christmas plays, in which familiar narratives dramatized the pleasures of the holiday season. Generic plots with stock themes and stereotypical characters scripted Christmas as a moment of domestic crisis, typically involving lost love, financial hardship, hidden identities, and family misunderstandings. By the last scene—generally set in a modest family room—domestic harmony reigned supreme. All problems had been resolved, often in a melodramatic *Weihnachtsverlobung*, a "betrothal around the Christmas tree." Titles that appeared in the decade before the First World War, such as *The Lost Keys to Heaven*, *Missing and Found Again*, *The Reconciliation*, *Unexpected Christmas Joy*, and *The Good Angel of the House* (about a hospital nurse), suggest the way commercial holiday theater played on the rules of middle-class propriety.[43] The story line of *Love Is the Kingdom of Heaven* (1913), for example, dramatizes the desires and anxieties of a turn-of-the-century middlebrow audience.

After a series of mishaps that revolve around fears of downward mobility and lack of money, a sundered family is made whole again on Christmas Eve. When father, daughter, and suitor are reunited, all agree that "the kingdom of heaven" depends on love, not money, and a marriage engagement ends the show.[44] The basic story of domestic crisis and resolution during the holidays had variations, but the genre portrayed Christmas in the simple family parlor as a realm of piety and tender feeling, a refuge from an increasingly harsh and competitive society. The late nineteenth-century boom in commercial theater was of course a product of this same competitive world, which eagerly sold audiences an entire range of high and low culture. Family melodrama offered reassuring commentary on the very conditions that made its existence possible. When mainstream holiday plays concluded that ordinary people could find "heaven" or happiness in simple family intimacy and that the pursuit of money and material pleasure was ultimately misguided, they suggested that the excesses of consumer capitalism could be ameliorated through the supposedly universal values of middle-class morality and domesticity. This now-familiar yet deeply conflicted Christmas message would be repeated again and again in any number of holiday productions.

Other responses to the commercialization of Christmas were far more critical. Both Protestant and Catholic commentators viewed the rise of modern commerce as a distinct threat to popular piety. As one Catholic critic fumed, giving presents had nothing to do with "the mysteries of belief, the holy miracle of God-given human dignity." For far too many, "the 'celebration of love' has become a celebration of covetousness and greed," and theater shows, concerts, and cabarets were only so many examples of excessive superficiality. The preservation of faith over such attractions required almost heroic exertions, the critic continued, in order "to renew the promise of the celebration of the birth of the Savoir to fight for Him and his realm, until once again a springtime of belief comes to rich fruition everywhere in German and non-German lands."[45] Protestants agreed. The devil had unleashed a "feverish disquiet" to destroy German Christmas, wrote one Pastor Gordes in the *Frankfurter Kirchlichen Anzeiger* in 1900. The satanic "fever" preyed on shopkeepers and retailers with particular venom: "Christmas meant only *business, business, and more business,*" and "the celebration of the purest love became an orgy of naked profit seeking." The devil's plans extended beyond the circle of shopkeepers. "The Christmas fever raged in the streets and homes," wrote Gordes, until mothers, fathers, children, aunts and uncles, and even servants were caught up in its sway; they cared only for presents and parties. "The Christmas message announces: 'See, I bring you tidings of great joy'—but men think about the success of the Christmas business, women about the celebratory roast, and children about their dolls or tin soldiers." What was worse, Gordes concluded, "Now even Jews and atheists celebrate the Birth of Christ." Only small pockets of true faith persisted in the land, and the devil rejoiced in his triumph.[46]

Social Democrats thought differently but no less harshly about the intersections between Christmas and commerce. The socialist press defetishized the central symbols and rituals of the middle-class holiday—such as Father Christmas, the tree and decorations, the mystique of the Thuringian handworker, "Golden Sunday," and even the ideal of childhood—by revealing the class exploitation that determined their origins. The Christmas fantasy of a long-bearded Weihnachtsmann bringing a sack full of toys and sweets from his distant forest was good enough for the pampered children of the bourgeoisie, but according to *Vorwärts*, workers knew that "the skilled hands of uncounted thousands of proletarians made all the colorful necessities and trivialities. The working proletariat, that's the Weihnachtsmann." Tin and lead toy soldiers poisoned their makers, Christmas trees were grown and cut by "poor forestry workers," glass decorations were blown "in the shabby huts of poor mountain villages." The fine holiday clothes worn by rich bourgeois matrons were sewn by poor seamstresses who labored "stitch by stitch until their cheeks fell in and their fingers were bent crooked from eternal sewing." Workers in the booming German toy industry were the worst off. During the Christmas season, their lives were determined by "hunger, care, unemployment, and feverish overwork." At other times of the year they were out of a job.[47] Crowds certainly mobbed the streets on Golden Sunday, but their Kauflust was hardly joyful. Instead, "hundreds of thousands had to see if they could squeeze a few Marks from their last two weekly wages before Christmas, to prepare some paltry joy for their loved ones at home." Commercialization was a mock job, a bourgeois fantasia that had essentially destroyed any true remnant of the German holiday. "Christmas has developed into more of a business than ever," wrote *Vorwärts* in 1909. "If, after one hundred years, it was abolished, that wouldn't be so bad."[48]

THE CHRISTMAS MARKET AS CONTACT ZONE

Christmas, of course, was not abolished. Such vituperative comments nonetheless reveal the tendentious and controversial nature of commercializa-

FIGURE 4.5
Schubert and Halle, *The Berlin Christ Market in Breite Strasse*, 1796.
(© bpk Berlin 2009/Kupferstichkabinett, SMB/Jörg P. Anders)

tion—a process clearly evident in the transformation of Germany's Christmas markets, the outdoor fairs that dominate public space during the month
of December. In 2007 the total number of Christmas markets in towns and
cities across the country topped 2,100. The Berlin area alone hosted at least
forty of these popular street fairs, and each year over 2 million visitors crowd
the beloved Christkindlesmarkt in Nuremberg. The Christmas market combines the charm of tradition with the hustle and bustle of an open-air marketplace. Visitors shop for expensive handcrafted gifts, cheap plastic kitsch, and
all manner of decorations. They munch on grilled bratwurst and gingerbread
(*Lebkuchen*) and drink mulled wine, play games of chance, and put their
children on carnival rides. Travel agents offer seven-day "Christmas Market
Tours" through markets across Germany, with mandatory stops at the most
famous, including the Weihnachtsmarkt in Berlin, the Streizelmarkt in Dresden, the Christkindchesmarkt in Frankfurt, and the Christkindlesmarkt in
Nuremberg. "When you visit them with us," promises the travel agency Atlas
Cruises and Tours, "you will feel a kind of magic in the air and know beyond
doubt that the Christmas enchantment of childhood is once again drawing

FIGURE 4.6
After Karl Rechlin, *Christmas Market in Berlin—An Unwilling Customer*, 1865. (© bpk Berlin 2009)

near."[49] Charmed by these seemingly obvious examples of popular festivity and holiday spirit, historians have described the Christmas market as a space marked by tradition, where rich and poor mingle in an atmosphere of relaxed festivity. The history of the Christmas market belies this nostalgic view of collective holiday harmony. The arrival of industrial consumer society deeply marked these supposedly timeless, indigenous markets, as the bourgeoisie struggled to restrain and reinvent the time and space of popular festivity. Transformed by late nineteenth-century industrialization and urbanization, the turn-of-the-century Christmas market became a contact zone where a diverse range of actors negotiated competing social and economic interests and established positions of inequality and coexistence.[50]

Two images of the Christmas market in Berlin, from 1796 and 1865, respectively, illustrate the transformation of one of the most storied outdoor fairs in Germany. Both show views of the annual Berlin market, on Breitestrasse, leading away from the Lustgarten and the royal palace in the center of the city (Figures 4.5 and 4.6). The print of *Berlin Christ Market in Breitestrasse*, drawn and engraved by academicians J. D. Schubert and J. S. D. Halle, takes us back to the market on Christmas Eve in the 1790s. Well established and renowned for its beautiful goods and public sociability, the Berlin market was invariably included as an attraction in late eighteenth-century Berlin travel guides.[51] Some seventy years later, genre painter Karl Rechlin's *Christmas Market in Berlin—An Unwilling Customer* portrays the same street and market, but, under the impact of urbanization and industrialization, the harmony of 1796 has frayed into disorder.

In Schubert and Halle's print, the market is crowded but clean and decorous; poverty is sanitized; and aristocrats, burghers, and poor vendors mingle freely. To the left of center, a gentleman holds a bolt of luxurious cloth, while his wife beside him examines a box of toys held up by a small boy dressed in shorts or ripped pants, who might be a beggar; just to his left, a saleswoman sorts through a large basket of goods. In the center of the picture, a portly burgher holds a cane, engaged in an animated discussion with his peers. Behind him, to the right, a vendor hawks banners and holds up a Christmas tree. To his right is a late eighteenth-century couple dressed in bourgeois finery. Their son wears a suit and hat and holds a cane, mimicking his father's dress and manners. A carriage moving through the midst of the crowd suggests a possible visit by the Prussian king or members of his court, a common occurrence in the eighteenth century, and the regal buildings surrounding the market frame the entire scene. Fully one-half of the illustration shows the royal palace, and on the right are wealthy urban villas, lending the whole a reassuring sense of stability. In sum, the print presents a Christmas market where the social orders "know their place" and public celebration is festive but orderly.

This genteel vision hides as much as it reveals. Around 1800, the market was still of vital importance for economic exchange among a variety of social groups. On Breitestrasse, the main thoroughfare, wealthy customers certainly examined expensive goods, often fashioned by immigrant Huguenot craftsmen. Gold- and silversmiths, wig makers, wood turners, furriers, toy makers, and clothiers erected stalls alongside professional bakers selling *Nascherei*, traditional holiday sweets like gingerbread cakes. The market served other groups as well. In crowded alleys branching out from the main square, members of the lower estates bought housewares, boots, shoes, and baskets from urban artisans. Local farmers, who made a rare trip to the city center to attend a Christmas service, purchased equipment from potters and barrel makers. Official regulations limited the sale of such prosaic items to side streets, which helped hide the transactions of lower orders and encouraged the idealized view of the market pictured in the Schubert-Halle print.[52]

A chronicle from 1790, which includes a detailed description of the Berlin market, suggests that the mingling of social estates between the stalls was regimented but not entirely harmonious. In the 1790s, the fair was open from 12 December to the end of the month and included some 250 booths. After an initial week of relative quiet, the chronicler notes, the "refined and rich" visited in wagons or on foot in growing numbers, buying holiday gifts from the aggressive salespeople who grew increasingly desperate to sell their wares. On Christmas Eve, the *Volks-Jubel*, or popular jubilation, reached its climax in a veritable parade of the social orders. During the day, *mittlere Bürger* (welloff or middling class citizens) took their turn, emptying market shelves of the best goods. Only in the evening hours did servants, handworkers, and day laborers have time to celebrate their own *Feier-Abend*, or time off, and they came to the market in droves. After 6:00 P.M., the chronicler remarks, such vigorous crowds swarmed through the market that "on occasion one is pleased to get away with honor and without harm," a tongue-in-cheek comment that nonetheless expressed unease with the consuming desires of the masses.[53] The rowdy Christmas Eve spectacle was potentially disruptive but in the end a moment of controlled release, since legal codes and social customs alike regulated interaction among the estates and disciplined the time and space of commercial exchange.

Later generations would remember the fragile social balance of the late eighteenth-century Christmas market with passionate nostalgia. For Ludwig Tieck, one of the most popular Romantic writers in the German states, memories of the market heightened the feelings of loss that circulated through the modern city. In a rags-to-riches urban fairy tale titled "Christmas Eve," first published in 1835 and anthologized many times since, Tieck took his readers back to the Berlin Christmas market of 1791. The generic plot revolves around a destitute mother and daughter, a lost silver taler, and a last-minute reunion that sets up a happy ending for all concerned. This little morality tale no doubt inspired countless emulators; more interesting is the way Tieck framed the story with a look at a lost "Christmas past," already vanished by the 1830s. In this happy age, he asserted, "customs and traditions and festivities" still gave life poetic meaning.[54] As if describing Halle's print, Tieck depicted the turn-of-the-century market as a place where aristocrats, bourgeoisie, and artisans recognized and accepted their social status. Here, the visit of the royal family "doubles the joy" of the onlooking burghers; there, the social classes mingle freely; and the elderly gentleman, the mother and daughter, the well-dressed couple, and the businessman all lose themselves in the "din and confusion" between the booths. Enchanted by the Christmas spirit, even beggars observe without envy the unobtainable treasures on display.[55] In seemingly endless sentences and dizzying strings of short clauses, Tieck tenderly described the human mass that crowded the market, the colorful goods on sale, and the sights, scents, and sounds that dazzled the senses of passersby:

> But most splendid were the evening hours, when this wide street . . . was illuminated by many thousands of lights from the booths. . . . All estates wove happily and noisily in and out. . . . And thousands strolled along, jovial with plans to buy, telling stories, laughing, crying out loud across the sweet aromas of the various sugar and marzipan pastries, those fruits, in alluring imitation, figures of all kinds, animals and people, all shining with bright colors, which smiled out at the eager onlookers; here an exhibition of truly deceptive fruits, apricots, peaches, cherries, pears and apples, all artistically formed out of wax; there in a gigantic booth rattled, rang, and tinkled thousands upon thousands of toys made of wood, in all shapes and sizes, men and women, jesters and priests, kings and beggars, ice-skates and sleds, maidens, women, nuns, horses with bells, entire households, or hunters with stags and hounds, whatever one's thoughts can playfully imagine is here on display, and the children, nursery maids, and parents were called upon, asked to choose and to buy.[56]

The long sentences suggest the enchantment of the eighteenth-century market as well as the timelessness and fragility of the links of memory, as Tieck tried to recover the Romantic poetry of the Early Modern world for an audience who no longer had access to such profound pleasures.

Tieck's description of the harmonious community and sensory delight of the market was a nostalgic vision of loss. By casting his story in the "once-upon-a-time" of childhood (*"Als ich Kind war . . ."*), he intimated that the longed-for space of the market had vanished as irrevocably as youth. Recalling the Christmas market of 1791 in 1835, "when all that is poetic and marvelous is disappearing from life," was both an act of recuperation and a regretful confirmation of the inescapable losses of passing time.[57] "Every celebration and every institution," Tieck wrote, "grows with the years, and reaches the point of completion, from which it again quickly, or unnoticed, sinks away. This is the fate of everything human, small and great alike." For the Romantic, the *Volksfeierlichkeit* (popular festiveness) of the Berlin Christmas market had reached its peak between 1780 and 1793, after which it was undermined by the modest beginnings of modern commerce, represented for Tieck by the establishment of independent retail shops and the seductive displays of local Konditorei or confectionaries. In precursors to the lavish holiday displays that would appear in department-store show windows later in the nineteenth century, the Konditorei attracted customers with elaborate sculptures made of tragant, a hard, colored sugar. Berliners could enjoy miniature, three-dimensional models of contemporary events such as the Battle of Nations at Leipzig or familiar sights like the streets and buildings of Berlin. Tragant sculptures were clearly part of the visual appeal of an urban Christmas, but for Tieck, they embodied the costs of the modern. Commercialization had called forth a depressing transformation of popular attitudes and indeed a new sort of individual, inflected through the dubious pleasures of a nascent consumer culture. "A self-glorifying consciousness, an affected surplus of presumptuous artificial productions has destroyed that childish and childlike naturalness," Tieck concluded, "and at the same time carousing has taken the place of the cheerfulness and jesting" that made the older market a unique celebration of innocence and authentic community.[58]

Writing in 1835, Tieck could only anticipate the economic and social changes that transformed public festivity in the later decades of the century. The dynamics of late industrialization and rapid urbanization, the transformation of a society of estates into one based on class, and the effects of the staggering population growth experienced in Berlin after 1860 are captured in Karl Rechlin's 1865 drawing, *Christmas Market in Berlin: An Unwilling Customer* (Figure 4.6). Here, the sense of stability and community portrayed in Halle's print and Tieck's story has given way to disorder. The market has become kitschy rather than luxurious. It no longer serves any real economic purpose, and the explosive growth of the urban poor has ruptured the social harmony portrayed in the late eighteenth-century print. The royal palace is still evident in the background of Rechlin's print at the top right, but the perspective has shifted, and these diminished regal buildings no longer provide a stable sense of place.

In the cacophonous Breitestrasse of the mid-1860s, the masses rather than the forces of tradition control the market. Between busy booths that display cheap trinkets—dealers no longer sell quality goods—representatives of the new middle classes reveal their distaste for the squalid scene. A portly man dressed in overcoat and top hat—the archsymbol of the nineteenth-century capitalist—walks through the market with his wife, who is dressed in an ostentatious fur jacket, bonnet, and full petticoats. The pair clearly symbolizes the pretensions of new money, and they attract unwanted attention from the salespeople and the crowd. The man looks away with disdain as a youthful beggar boy tries to sell him a Hampelman, a holiday noisemaker sold at the Berlin market. The boy is clearly a *fliegender Händler*, or flying dealer—contemporary slang for those who tried to sell whatever they could at the market but could not afford the fee necessary for an official license. On the left, a more modest couple examines mass-produced dolls; the man is dressed in a soldier's uniform, and he watches the disgruntlement of the wealthy pair with apparent amusement. On the right, a policeman disciplines a mischievous urchin, also a flying dealer, as evidenced by the Hampelmen tied to his belt. A pair of dogs scuffling in the right foreground, fighting over yet another Hampelman, captures the general atmosphere of social discord. Rechlin, better known for the paintings of battle scenes he sold to the upper middle classes, clearly exaggerated the scene for comic effect; his satiric vision nonetheless illustrates upper-class frustration with the raucous atmosphere of popular festivity on the eve of German unification.

The Christmas market was losing its charm, and urban reformers, retail business interests, and city authorities viewed with alarm the growing urban underclass that crowded into the city center during the holiday season. By the 1870s, civic elites no longer welcomed the carnivalesque atmosphere of the market. The number of flying dealers had increased; unlike the regular salespeople, who honestly paid their vendor fees, hundreds of unlicensed beggars, war invalids, street urchins, and unemployed people aggressively accosted market visitors. Official vendors also contributed to the seedy atmosphere of the market, offering attractions like Tingel-Tangel and setting up *Rummelplätze*, or midways, with rides and games of chance. Unruly crowds upended class hierarchies, undermined the sentimental spectacle of the Christmas market, and threatened the profits of the urban middle classes. Rudolph Hertzog, owner of one of Berlin's first department stores on Breitestrasse, repeatedly complained to authorities about the "tumultuous character" of the Christmas market, which, he asserted, prevented well-heeled customers from shopping in his store during the holiday season. In 1873, as the bottom fell out of the German economy, city authorities responded. They closed off

Breitestrasse, which had long been the center of the Berlin market, and limited festivities to the nearby Lustgarten.[59]

In contrast to other popular markets and street fairs, many of which disappeared altogether in the late nineteenth century, the Christmas market survived. Yet its "historic rights" and popular festive character did little to dampen criticism. The conflicts of interest climaxed around 1890, just as the department store emerged as an alternative site for shopping and sociability. In 1889 the Berlin chief of police reopened the campaign against the public market, complaining that the "nuisance-makers" in the Christmas market sold poor-quality "rummage." The "inconsiderate pushiness of the poor"— just outside the Royal Palace at the head of the showcase avenue Unter den Linden—threatened the "good reputation" of the Reich's capital city. The Berlin city magistrate's office, to the contrary, took a sympathetic view of the street fair. The magistrate argued that the market's "joyful mercantilism" gave the lower classes a chance to shop without the financial and social constraints imposed in exclusive department stores. A visit to the market in the city center gave working-class children a chance to at least see delightful displays of toys, "almost their only Christmas joy." The chief of police replied that department-store show windows could provide the same solace. Social Democrats complained bitterly that impoverished city dwellers made a substantial portion of their annual income at the fair, and plans for relocation to other downtown districts faltered when wealthy local residents complained about potential disturbances. Finally, in 1893 the chief of police moved the market to Akrona Platz, located in the midst of a working-class district on what was then the northeastern edge of the city. There, it languished for the next forty years. "Only the meager remnants of the Christmas market in the east of the capital city still tempt the desires and the hopes of children," wrote journalist Hans Ostwald in 1924.[60]

The Christmas market's return to Breitestrasse and the Lustgarten in the Nazi years provides something of an uncomfortable coda to its nineteenth-century decline. In December 1934 the city administration, in collaboration with the Arbeitsgemeinschaft zur Belebung der Berliner Innenstadt (Working Group for the Reinvigoration of Berlin's Inner-City), moved the market back to the city center. Led by Karl Protze, a Berlin senator and National Socialist Party member, the Working Group convincingly asserted that "this wonderful German custom" breathed life into the Nazi slogan "Gemeinnutz geht vor Eigennutz" (Collective Need before Individual Greed). "For fifteen years," the group noted in reference to socialist street demonstrations, "the Berlin Lustgarten has been a showplace for fanatical popular instigation and political strife." Now the return of the Christmas market would turn this prominent public square into "a place of peaceful and friendly events."[61] The history of the famous Christkindlesmarkt in Nuremberg had a similar trajectory. Commercial interests had forced the market out of the central market square around the Church of Our Lady in 1898. In 1933 Nazi mayor Willy Liebel brought it back—a way to erase what he called the "un-German and race-alien influences" that had inspired the market's relocation—and established a new opening ceremony. This festive "Prologue," a sentimental speech delivered by a *Rauschgoldenengel* (golden Christmas-tree fairy) on 4 December, St. Barbara's Day, is still delivered today to popular acclaim.[62]

In Berlin, a grand and festive ceremony commemorated the 1934 reopening of the downtown market. Berliners lined the streets to watch a parade of Father Christmases march down Unter den Linden from the Brandenburg Gate to the Lustgarten, led by circus-artist-turned-film-star Cilly Feindt, who rode a white stallion. Reichministers Goebbels, Göring, and Hjalmar Schacht delivered speeches from the steps of the Berlin Cathedral adjacent to the market. The crowd joined in with collective renditions of "Silent Night," "O How Joyfully," the German national anthem, the "Horst Wessel Song," and countless "Sieg Heils."[63] At the gates to the "reinvigorated" market stood an eight-meter Christmas tree, decorated with advertisements for specifically "German" gifts, and an SA-Brown Shirt band played songs in front of the Altes Museum from 5:00 to 10:00 P.M. Volunteers stood by, handing out copies of a *Christmas Primer for the German House*, complete with instructions for celebrating "a most beautiful *German* Christmas."[64] The attempt to capitalize on "honorable traditions" and *bodengebundene Volksfeste* (Volk holidays tied to the soil) apparently resonated with locals and tourists alike. Record-breaking numbers went to the market in 1934 and again in 1936; official counts recorded 1.5 million and 2 million visitors, respectively.[65]

A trip to the Christmas market brought various pleasures. It could evoke the romantic Christmas past described so succinctly by Ludwig Tieck, reinforce the notions of racial community championed by National Socialists, and provide an evening of distraction. Germans went to the Christmas market to find beer and snacks and holiday handicrafts, but by 1900 the most important product was the experience of the visit itself. The real commercial action now took place in big-city department stores like Tietz and Wertheim, where customers shopped for all the goods and services modern industry could offer.

GOLDEN SUNDAYS

"There was a time when the Christmas trade took place almost entirely in the outdoor booths set up for this purpose, from which it later moved for the most part to the increasingly numerous retail stores," wrote a Berliner in 1889. "Now it seems that the critical hour [for these small businesses] is not far off. The so-called 'department stores' and giant outlets, which can buy large quantities of goods and sell them at cheap prices, increase their numbers from year to year, and are putting an end to the way shopping is done in the Christmas season, along with so many other traditional customs."[66] The comment was prescient. The department store emerged relatively slowly in Germany but underwent a veritable boom in the 1890s. In comparison with other countries, this was indeed late—Marshall Field's in Chicago, for instance, opened in 1865, while the cornerstone for the new and expanded but already well-established Bon Marché in Paris was laid in 1869.[67] Germany soon caught up. In 1901 there were approximately 109 department stores nationwide. Five years later, despite discouraging taxation policies, the number had doubled. Wertheim and Tietz, two of the largest chains, had stores across the nation. By 1892 in Berlin alone, Wertheim had stores on Oranienstrasse, Rosentalerstrasse, and Leipzigerstrasse, and Tietz had a flagship store on Leipziger Platz as well as large branches in Alexander Platz and Frankfurter Allee. The Kaufhaus des Westens—the "uncrowned emperor of Berlin"—opened in 1907.[68] Christmas shopping would never be the same.

As a generation of boosters saw it, "the department store is the most modern form of retail business and the most strongly influenced by modern capitalism."[69] Though in 1900 spending in department stores accounted for a relatively modest percentage of retail expenditures, the stores had high symbolic value. The conglomerates exemplified progressive commerce, supporters claimed. Modern methods of retail marketing, improved quality of goods, and easy credit increased customer satisfaction. For cultural critics, on the contrary, the stores embodied the pathologies of modernity. Manipulative advertising awakened Kauflust that was impossible to satisfy, victimizing vulnerable women, who went on uncontrolled spending sprees or engaged in illicit acts of shoplifting. The "Jewish parasites" who owned the main stores supposedly preyed on employees and customers alike and stole profits from good German shopkeepers.[70]

The department store certainly offered enticing new forms of consumer gratification. The fifty departments in a typical store sold an exhaustive variety of gifts and goods, including clothes, housewares, foods, and spirits. By 1910 major stores boasted travel bureaus, theaters (and later movie houses), picture galleries, refreshment stands, lending libraries, and reading rooms.[71] Customers did not even have to leave their homes to peruse the goods on sale; they could order from catalogs, and deliveries to Berlin and its suburbs were especially heavy during the holiday season.[72] Aggressive advertising campaigns with newspaper promotions, flyers, and posters introduced as wide a circle of customers as possible to comparison-price shopping and the wonders of mass-produced goods. Advertising changed the way Germans bought things; it also transformed the way they thought about and used city space. Elaborate displays both inside the stores and in the large plate-glass windows on the ground floor—exciting, modern architectural features in themselves—attracted passersby. Retail districts became destinations for both locals and visitors, who used advertisements in the daily press to plot their own "Christmas strolls" through the city.[73]

During the holiday season, spectacular window displays—with Christmas trees, moving puppets, neon lights, and of course stacks and stacks of retail goods—drew swarms of shoppers and onlookers. In Berlin, famous across Germany for its luxurious holiday shopping, storefront displays on Potsdamer Platz (with Leipzigerstrasse), Friedrichstrasse, Rosenthalerstrasse, the Spittelmarkt, and Alexander Platz turned urban space into a sparkling consumer spectacle during the Christmas season.[74] The crowds were particularly dense on "Silver" and "Golden Sunday," the two Advent Sundays directly preceding the holiday, when authorities relaxed usually strict sumptuary laws prohibiting Sunday shopping. "Despite the disagreeable weather, yesterday's 'Golden Sunday'—the popular name for the last Sunday before Christmas—lured hundreds of thousands into the streets, where in the afternoon and evening a life of great festivity and illumination developed," reported Berlin's *Vossische Zeitung* in 1887.[75] By 1900, to meet popular demand, the authorities let stores open on the third Sunday before Christmas as well, and even this "Copper Sunday" drew "a truly colossal assault of the general public" into Berlin's streets.[76] The consumer spectacle had a dark side. The Berlin police sent mounted officers to Leipzigerstrasse to control the unruly crowds in front of the stores, and undercover detectives waited inside to catch shoplifters and the gangs of pickpockets who preyed upon inattentive shoppers; in the days before Christmas 1907, they arrested ninety-six shoplifters in Berlin-area stores.[77] Social Democrats, for their part, took a dim view of the "Christmas lollygagging" that took place in front of the department stores. *Vorwärts* observed that pitiful child-beggars worked the crowds, and the sensitive observer searched "the bustling streets" in vain for some sign of the "true Christmas poesy [of the outdoor Christmas Market], which once made our hearts so joyous."[78]

The department stores were temples of commerce and middle-class respectability, and a large part of their appeal lay in the myriad ways they supposedly improved upon older forms of exchange, thereby raising working-class living standards and lifestyles.[79] As Paul Göhre, a theologian turned social-democratic reformer, wrote in what he called a "scientific" study of the new stores, "cleanliness in the store, politeness in the treatment of the shopper, [and] tasteful, friendly packing of the wares purchased" defined this new space; the old newspapers used for packing material in other shops were after all "so dangerous to the health."[80] The customer could exalt in the brightness and beauty of the goods for sale and in the sense of the modern engendered by the vast architectural space. "When one paces through these soaring, rich rooms," Göhre exclaimed, "when one looks over all the wares laid out in their newness and unblemished shine, or climbs up and down the wide stairs, everywhere light, shine, beauty flows over one . . . and a visit in such a house, yes, even buying itself, becomes a joyful act, a pleasure, a celebration, just as shopping at seasonal markets and fairs . . . has been a celebration for the Volk for years." Yet the pleasures of the department store far exceeded those offered by the outdoor markets. Indoors, the "celebratory spirit" was "higher," "cleared up," and protected from poor weather. "No smell of bratwurst or beer," Göhre continued in poetic tones, "no clouds of tobacco or cigar smoke, none of the mass confusion created by the use of loud musical instruments, but instead a regular sound that fades away, talking and calls, here and there a clock chimes, the shine of light and the delicate scent of perfume, of fruit, of fresh lacquer, of flowers, chocolate, coffee, tea, and soap. Happy movement all around, cleanliness." Shoppers could look forward to attractive floor personnel as well: "the youth of most of the saleswomen and men: this creates a real desire to buy."[81]

Göhre's evocative prose no doubt expressed his heartfelt enthusiasm for the refined atmosphere of the department store and its potentially healthful effects on working-class consumers (how different from Tieck's appreciation for the "din and confusion" of the outdoor market); it also shows that industrial consumer goods could be thoroughly fetishized by proponents of modernity. In the department store, Göhre enthused, "the goods of modern culture in all their wealth and beauty surround us"; walled off from the common stink of the sausage stand, the purchaser bought not only goods but also the values of cleanliness, respectability, and even youth so valued by the new middle classes. The act of purchase itself was pleasurable and festive, an almost sensuous act of participation in a modern consumer economy. If we trust Göhre's description, a visit to one of the new stores exposed diverse groups to a consumerist spectacle that transmitted bourgeois values to the lower orders. The large and magnificent stores embodied the expansive strength of the newly industrialized nation, and everyday acts of shopping helped turn both workers and middle-class burghers into consumer citizens.[82]

Such transformative splendors were not available to all in equal measure. Despite the democratic appearance of the crowds that mobbed the decorated streets and aisles in the holiday season, department stores were sites that crystallized social difference for shoppers and employees alike. Contemporaries understood quite clearly that the choice of store was a sign of status. Class and even individual identities were increasingly determined by the ability to consume rather than by family status or participation in productive processes. Members of "so-called good society" shopped at Wertheim, wrote Göhre. The "comfortable middle-classes" preferred Tietz, while "'better-off' Berlin workers" and the "little man" looked for bargains at Kaufhaus Jandorf.[83] Such divisions were always permeable. Buying a Christmas present at a better store offered a transitory moment of class transcendence and self-transformation that marked the gift, the giver, and the recipient as something special. Even the exclusive Wertheim advertised in *Vorwärts*, the main newspaper of the SPD. But many Germans could simply not afford to shop at the big stores. Reduced social status was tangible in the charitable Christmas vouchers handed out by Wertheim, Tietz, and Jandorf (among others) at celebrations "for the children of the unemployed" in working-class districts across Berlin, redeemable at any of the major stores for any goods.[84] An advertising ploy to be sure, such campaigns nonetheless spoke to the very real need of the poor. And for those who could not afford the department store at all, an alternative version of modern shopping could be found in the dozens of *Konsumgenossenschaften* (Consumer Collectives) that dotted big German cities, selling food and drink "for Christmas celebrations" at cut-rate prices.[85]

The most active working-class participation in the department-store

Christmas probably took place behind the counter: the frantic pace of the holiday season meant that temporary help swelled the ranks of the men and women *Angestellten* (white-collar employees) who staffed the stores. From 20 November to Christmas Eve, the number of department-store workers mushroomed. Managers eagerly hired *Aushilfskräfte* (temporary workers) to deal with the holiday rush since seasonal sales accounted for a significant proportion of annual net profits. Class and gender stratified workers as well as customers. At Wertheim on Potsdamer Platz, the 3,500 regular employees were joined by over 1,000 part-time workers, including saleswomen, "women packers," "cashier girls," and "kitchen girls" as well as salesmen, male customer-service representatives, and carpenters.[86] The job titles alone reveal the gendered division of the work force. Most of the temporary holiday workers, who reportedly returned to work every December, were women; many were former salesgirls, now married and so "unsuited" for full-time employment. The 2,000 regular "cashier girls" at Wertheim typically began working when they were fourteen years old; when they reached sixteen, they were retired to make room for younger help.[87]

For booster Paul Göhre, always of good cheer, the massive numbers of temporary saleswomen who worked the holiday rush brought to mind "the reserve- and local militia exercises of our national citizens doing their military duty."[88] This was a particularly apt metaphor, since sales staff worked under militarylike discipline. Rigid workplace rules mandated fines for a long list of illicit behaviors, including arriving late to work, loud talking or laughing, private conversation in the presence of customers, eating or drinking on the shop floor, and *jeder nicht geschäftliche Verkehr* (all nonbusiness contact) between the sexes.[89] Sales staff had to work overtime during the holiday season, when regular hours were extended and constant holiday traffic strained exhausted personnel (and store heating systems).[90] Annual Christmas bonuses, an expected part of a normal pay package, were another source of contention between employers and *Angestellten*. Forced to work until 6:00 or 7:00 P.M. on Christmas Eve, when managers distributed these "Christmas gifts," sales staff scurried into the streets looking for last-minute bargain gifts.

Popular Kauflust brought handsome profits to department stores but also significant dislocation, real and imagined, to small shopkeepers. The arguments of boosters like Göhre, who insisted that small merchants would enjoy "excellent business" from the crowds of Christmas shoppers as they walked through major retail districts, found little favor among the champions of the Mittelstand, or lower middle classes.[91] Independent shopkeepers and family-business owners felt squeezed by the department store's hegemony. The Christmas season, with its profit potential and symbolic resonance, brought sustained bouts of annual discontent. Year after year, the anti-Semitic Berlin newspaper *Staatsbürger Zeitung* summed up the concerns of the "little store owners and small businessmen." In racially coded language, the editors warned about "the big bazaars, whose owners for the most part hardly understand the Christian meaning of Christmas."[92] The good German would "energetically and clearly warn [his] wives and daughters that it is forbidden to meet their Christmas needs in department stores, shopping warehouses, or junk bazaars!" they admonished. "In your own interest, give the hand worker, the Christian and German small craftsman something to earn." Those who violated this advice "desacralize the holy Christmas holidays and despite all protests to the contrary can not justly call himself a friend of the Volk and the fatherland, a German, or a Christian!"[93] Historian Paul Lerner has identified the term translated here as "junk bazaars"—*Ramschbasaren*—as an orientalized label for Jewish-owned stores, often used by the anti-Semitic press.

The racist rhetoric was just one part of larger campaigns against Jewish stores.[94] An outdoor "Anti-Semitic Christmas Market" set up in Berlin in 1891 offered shoppers a way to avoid "Jewish" department stores altogether, but it apparently met with little success.[95] In the years around 1900 in Berlin, members of the anti-Semitic German National Party passed out "Christmas flyers" in front of Jewish-owned department stores. One flyer warned shoppers that the Talmud encouraged Jewish merchants to cheat and steal from Christians. Another, distributed in 1903, held forth in threatening, pseudo-biblical tones: "Cursed is every item and unlucky for the home, every item under the Christmas tree bought from Jews. But honor to those who do not abandon their own, their brothers; even the smallest gift that you buy from them brings blessings!" In the German Empire, such overt acts of prejudice could be prosecuted under state laws intended to protect the sanctity of religious belief and ensure the free traffic of commercial interests. In the 1903 case, the chief editor of the newspaper *Deutsche Hochwacht* was penalized in court for paying for and distributing the flyer.[96]

The department store remained a flash point for issues of commercialization, class frustration, and German identity in the Weimar years. On the surface, things looked good. Annual holiday newsreels on "preparations for Christmas" showed huge illuminated advertisements on department stores, crowds in the streets, and fanciful animated decorations in store windows.[97] Even in the final years of the Weimar Republic, at the height of the global depression, Berlin newspapers reported that Silver and Golden Sundays drew such numbers that "the crowds eager for a view advanced only slowly, step by step, up the stairs and through the doors of the department stores."[98] According to economist Claudius Langwadt, whose dissertation, "The Christmas Business in the Department Store," appeared in 1932, holiday sales accounted for a large proportion of profits for all retailers. The annual bump allowed retailers and manufacturers alike to smooth out inevitable downturns in the economic cycle. Yet the depression of 1929 had cut average department-store sales and profits by about 10 percent, despite tax breaks and wage cuts.[99] Contemporaries held out vague hopes that the *Kauffreudigkeit des Publikums* (the public's enthusiastic joy for shopping) would yield a "good Christmas business" and so ease the worst aspects of the depression, at least for a while.[100]

Rising levels of unemployment and meager gifts under the tree testified to the steep costs of the economic crisis. Shoppers waited for postholiday inventory sales to spend their Christmas savings, skewing annual sales charts. As Langwadt concluded, "This example shows that even an ancient custom can be influenced by economic factors."[101] Competition for holiday profits increased, and the small shopkeepers of the Mittelstand—who were hardest hit by the crises of Weimar—turned Christmas shopping into a political issue, exemplified in attempts to regulate store closing hours on Christmas Eve in the late 1920s. To picture the doldrums faced by downwardly mobile Germans, one need only recall the fate of the often-unemployed department-store clerk Johannes Pinneberg, the antihero of Hans Fallada's consummate Weimar-era novel, *Little Man—What Now?* Employees like Pinneberg, whose holiday overtime turned his store into a shimmering vision of Christmas plenty, could hardly afford to shop where they worked. Pinneberg's own holiday was defined by the ineradicable stink of the cat feces in the pot of his live Christmas tree.[102] Contemporary drawings and photos of ragged children gazing with longing through the windows of big-city department stores were cute enough, but they also revealed the unrequited desire of Christmas in the Weimar years. As an urchin in a cartoon by Berlin illustrator Heinrich Zille swooned: "At night I dream—it's all mine!"[103] The image captured the new calculus of celebration and consumption that transformed Christmas in the 1920s, as Germans increasingly organized their activities and identities around the ever-elusive products of an industrialized consumer society. Changing forms of private celebration reflected the familiar features of a full-blown mass-consumer society but also its fractures and dislocations—the pathologies of modernity described by historian Detlev Peukert as the leit-motif of the Weimar years.[104]

A NEW CALCULUS OF CELEBRATION

On the night of 23 December 1918 in Berlin, a group of radical sailors occu-pied the royal palace, and on Christmas Eve they began a shooting battle with government troops that left thirty-four dead and sixty wounded. According to a contemporary news report, this "Red Christmas" would remain a "sor-rowful day of memory for all time."[105] Christmas 1918 was indeed a troubled celebration. The lost war, the revolution and founding of the German Re-public, and violent civil conflict weighed heavily on the holiday mood. It was no surprise that nostalgia for the Christmas past expanded beyond fond recollections of childhood innocence or longings for home and Heimat. The vision of a harmonious and prosperous German nation united around the Tannenbaum, familiar from the final decades of the German Empire, evoked a comforting sense of continuity with the past but also hope for the future. These years saw a wave of nostalgia that arguably turned an idealized version of the late nineteenth-century holiday into the "real" German Christmas. "The golden twilight with the deeply familiar shadow play of the branches," observed feminist Helene Lange on Christmas Eve 1918, "the Christmas songs, the music of Handel's variations, and then outside the pure, star-clear winter sky after dark days. All that brought belief and strength out of the collective treasure of numerous similar experiences."[106] The "poetic magic" of the family holiday, the eternal return to light of the winter solstice, and the birth of Jesus offered convenient ways to think about rebuilding Germany after the "night of war," wrote philosopher-theologian Theodor Kappstein. Christmas in 1918, he continued, was "the light beaming in the darkness," and faith in the evangelical message of the holiday—life, light, and love—would aid Germans in their struggle to "transfigure harsh reality."[107] Philosopher and Nobel Prize winner Rudolf Eucken expressed similar ideas in 1924. The "characteristic value" of Christmas, he believed, will "serve us as a path finder and advance guard" on the way to spiritual and national recovery.[108]

Eucken and others clearly recognized that the domestic bliss associated with Christmas could be a powerful symbol of postwar reconstruction. In the context of the massive demobilization of November and December 1918, stories about soldiers coming home just in time for Christmas idealized the process of reintegration. The intimate joy of the family Christmas offered compensation for the soldier's sacrifice at the front—the reward, as it were, for soldiers who returned to private life after years of military service. Kapp-stein caught the simple appeal of a holiday homecoming. "After four years of war Christmases," he wrote, "the soldiers have the right a thousand times over to want to be with their families around the glowing Christmas tree."[109] The standard of domestic bliss pictured in family magazines like the *Leipziger Illustrirte Zeitung* was no doubt difficult to achieve in a time when declining birthrates raised widespread anxiety and the wartime deaths of millions of young and middle-aged men had created what contemporaries viewed as an alarming "surplus" of women. Visions of the "Christmas candle's shining light" and the "quiet peace of the home" nonetheless reaffirmed the normative family structures and bourgeois values that defined conventional notions of private happiness.[110] As ever, motherhood was central to these narratives. "Certainly one can celebrate this holiday with one's beloved or with comrades," wrote one newspaper editor, "but that is not the true Christmas; only the mother can create that."[111] Protestant pastor Rudolf Mühlhausen believed that the "joys of motherhood" engendered by domestic celebration would encourage women to return to their "customary duties" in the home, as they made way for demobilized soldiers in the public world of work.[112] Repeated pronouncements about family, love, and motherhood in the Christmas season apparently worked to some extent. Annual "marriage waves" took place during the holiday season, and even in the crisis year of 1932, more than 20,000 German couples *haben ihr Jawort gegeben*, or "said 'yes'" on Christmas Eve. The popularity of a holiday engagement drew on sentimental notions of holiday romance familiar from countless popular Christmas stories. It was also practical. With stagnant wages and the ever-present possibility of unemployment, couples could use Christmas bonuses to pay for wedding parties and holiday vacations as honeymoons.[113]

Women's Christmas activities sustained the imagined historical trajectories that linked the family to the cultural heritage of the German Volk. Household rituals were increasingly associated with the invented traditions of German nationalism, reflecting ongoing interest in the holiday's "pagan remnants" as described by scholars in the late nineteenth century. The observance of "ancient national Christmas customs," explained Leipzig ethnographer Paul Zinck in 1923 in a typical comment, "lead us back to the age of the *heidnischen Urväter*," the primordial pagan fathers.[114] Even as National Socialists began to employ these ideas as the basis for their own politicized celebrations of *Volksweihnachten* (People's Christmas), housewives learned from disparate sources that gifting, decorating, and cooking directly recovered venerable German traditions. The supposedly "Germanic" elements of Christmas nurtured the national community with matriarchal affection. According to the Association for Women's Apparel and Women's Culture in Hannover, the recipes handed down by "our mothers" for traditional Christmas cookies were "a part of a never-vanishing Germany" and "a symbol of German motherly love."[115] Thus the manly and militarist nationalism that dominated in the Weimar period, described by numerous historians, had a private and feminine "loving" side that was as fully patriotic as its public, masculine counterpart.[116]

Germans used Christmas to reconstruct private life after World War I but also to transform it. After the economic crises and hyperinflation of the early 1920s, enticing visions of material abundance "under the Christmas tree" symbolized the return of economic stability and private prosperity in a new key. Christmas presents conveyed the excitement and promise of mass culture and likewise anchored the rich emotional field of the holiday in consumer goods. Many of the typical appliances of modern society—radios, electric irons and hair dryers, toasters, vacuum cleaners, even smoke removers and electric Christmas-tree lights—were widely marketed as Christmas gifts in the Weimar period, symbolic and practical inducements to domestic modernization. Families like the Wagners in Berlin-Charlottenburg proudly displayed increasing numbers of such gifts in annual photos of their Christmas Eve celebration.[117] Judging from contemporary advertisements, things became important signs of well-being, tokens of a Christmas mood well realized. Advertising copy openly if not crassly colonized the personal nostalgia associated with the holiday. A typical print ad for Kupferberg champagne inquired, "Do you still think about it? Ahh, yes—the parents gave us champagne that time as well, and how happy it made us!" Another advertisement for body creams—a banal but revealing example—enthusiastically linked holiday emotions to the pleasures of consumption when it promised "exquisite Christmas gifts for an everlasting memory. These magnificent hand-care gift cases, containing the world-famous Cutex products, spread radiant joy and boundless delight."[118]

In conscious attempts to profit from the Christmas mood, advertising professionals now combined "American methods of marketing research" with insights into "psychological factors" in order to commercialize the emotions of the holiday.[119] While they looked back to and built on their experience in the Wilhelmine years, the campaigns proposed by Weimar-era advertising experts paid less attention to anxieties caused by transgressing boundaries of taste and authenticity; they were far more open about the need to manipulate consumers. Given the harsh realities of the day, professionals like Bertold Ert believed that appeals to feelings would be particularly effective. As Ert noted confidently in 1926, "There is no doubt that the more the times follow the path of coldness, sobriety, and mechanization, the greater the effect released by the evocation of a simple *Stimmungsmoment* [moment of feeling]."[120] In the department store, wrote another expert, indoor decorations and bright lighting not only put products "in 'the best light'"; decorations and displays were also "capable of influencing the subconscious stimuli, which we call moods and which to a certain extent superimpose themselves on our conscious psychic functions of thought and will and so effect them productively." Department-store windows, light displays, newspaper ads, and posters could "reawaken memories of childhood and its joys" and so contribute to "the elevation of the Christmas mood and thereby the *Kauflust* of the public."[121] The Christmas mood itself was thus thoroughly rationalized and commercialized.

Sales staff and marketing experts paid close attention to gender roles as they designed holiday advertising campaigns. Statistics showed that though women typically did 80 percent of all daily shopping, during the Christmas season, men and women shopped in equal numbers.[122] As primary household consumers, women still deserved special attention. Advertisements were supposed to excite "the psyche of the woman [who] thinks differently from the man." After all, wrote one expert in 1920, the ability to awaken and satisfy "the Kauflust of the world of women" meant a steady stream of loyal female customers throughout the year and "happiness for retail and advertising specialists."[123] Upbeat ads and proconsumption prescriptive literature repeatedly described the special joys of shopping that women supposedly experienced in November and December. "The appeal of shopping combines with the magic of the Christmas weeks in a pleasure that women zealously pursue," asserted the caption to a photo of well-dressed women looking at a window display of perfume.[124] Another writer joked that "days of great battle" typified the holiday season, as women mobbed city department stores.[125] By contrast, "a man buys quickly, because he depends less on pretty words than on his own judgment." Men, it seemed, were less willing to spend time in the store and preferred to purchase gifts already in their wrapping.[126]

The materialist fantasies promised by Christmas advertising in the Weimar years required planning and deferral rather than carefree participation.

The creation of the all-important Christmas mood meant that women had to adopt sober models of consumer rationality even as they cloaked their activities in an aura of joy and sentimentalism. Frugality and calculation were period buzzwords, and advertisements and "how-to" articles repeatedly advised those searching for presents to combine economy and practicality with desirability. The right gift spread "true joy"; finding it was a difficult task in which "heart and reason should correspond."[127] Practical giving often meant that families saved for months in order to purchase expensive household items they needed anyway. Rational holiday shopping could also bolster the national economy. A slogan that ran in numerous newspapers in 1931 encouraged gifting despite the crisis: "Whoever requires necessities should go shopping, he can use [his purchases] himself, and he creates work and bread for others."[128] To be sure, the manager-housewife labored under heavy expectations during the holiday season. She revitalized the "Germanic" roots of Christmas; decorated the home; bought, wrapped, and presented gifts; planned, cooked, and served "modern" meals; and hosted family, friends, and acquaintances at holiday parties. Cultural critic Greta Daeglau openly acknowledged the emotional pretense that accompanied the intensive work of celebration. "For the goal-conscious housewife" in a "technologized household," she wrote in an article on strategies for domestic celebration, "advance preparations for Christmas can't be taken too seriously." The "protectress of the hearth fire" perforce hid her efforts behind a veil of depth and emotion, Daeglau confided. "It is the developed life-style artifice of knowledgeable women that makes it still possible to create the appearance of deep inwardness and secrecy, despite all the work and cares, all the calculation and planning, all undertaken with the greatest thriftiness."[129] The feelings once spontaneously generated by holiday rituals had become a matter of feigned appearances, burnished by rationalized domestic strategies and the world of mass consumer goods.

Even under conditions of deferred gratification, the holiday season opened private life to the blandishments of mass consumer culture in particularly effective ways. The arrival of radio, for example, clearly restructured private life around new forms of mass media.[130] At Christmastime, the new broadcast medium served up an appealing blend of tradition and modernity. According to radio reporter Alfred Braun, the first Christmas Eve broadcast in Berlin in 1924 included carols by a local children's choir, a reading of the Christmas story from the Gospel of Luke, and even the sound of candles on a Christmas tree—the sharp noise of matches, struck close to the microphone, were carried out over the airwaves to hundreds of listeners. The response was widespread and enthusiastic. Letters and telephone calls of appreciation reached the station from all over the city, and Braun was charmed. His comment that the disparate residents of Berlin "became one great family" as they listened to the holiday broadcast combined the usual fantasies of holiday universalism with the imagined effects of the mass media, which indeed worked to standardize the holiday experience.[131] In the early 1920s, however, when owning or even listening to the radio still required wealth and status, this remained an idealized view of radio's potential. A drawing in the *Leipziger Illustrirte* titled "Radio Christmas 1923," which shows a group of obviously wealthy men and women dressed in evening wear as they listen to a holiday broadcast in a richly appointed living room, was hardly an exaggeration.[132] Though radio had become a mass medium by 1930, when there were over 3 million registered sets in Germany, the vast majority of households did without this modern appliance. Even the cheapest radio receivers were quite expensive. For the Wagners in Berlin, who spent a total of seventy-nine reichsmarks on Christmas presents in 1931, a new radio would have been a major expense. In the early 1930s, a low-end set cost about 120 reichsmarks, compared to sixty reichsmarks for a relatively inexpensive vacuum cleaner, fifty reichsmarks for a suit jacket, or twenty reichsmarks for a home movie projector. Only for Christmas in 1937 could the Wagners afford to spend eighty-seven reichsmarks to replace their old set with a Volksempfänger VE-301, the infamous People's Receiver promoted by the Nazi propaganda ministry.[133]

Despite its expense, radio began to organize private celebration and popular piety around commercial forms of entertainment. A radio console itself was a special gift, "the most beautiful Christmas surprise" and the focus of much attention in the popular press.[134] The new medium reportedly intensified holiday emotions; according to an advertisement from 1928, a Siemens radio set "brings Gemütlichkeit and a happy holiday mood into the home."[135] Perhaps such claims revealed an element of truth. Already in 1924, holiday specials began two to three weeks before Christmas Day, gained momentum as the holiday approached, and dominated the airwaves on 24, 25, and 26 December. Broadcasters quite consciously designed Christmas specials to dovetail with family and religious observances. At 4:00 P.M. on Christmas Eve in 1925, radio listeners in the Munich-Nuremberg area could hear a show called *Vorfreude* (Before the Joy) that opened with Martin Luther's "From Heaven Above to Earth I Come" because, as the program notes explained, "what child's heart does not beat faster to this joyful message!" To pass the unbearable wait before "the beautiful moment, when the brightly lit Christmas tree appears," the station broadcast classic Christmas music for choir and orchestra. Finally, to the strains of "that beloved 'Silent Night, Holy Night,'" the family was supposed to open their presents. The night ended with *A German Christmas Play*, which was about the birth of Christ and presumably brought listeners sated with material pleasures back to the reason for the season.[136]

Radio structured the popular observance of Christmas Day with similar pleasures. For the religiously divided community serviced by the Cologne-Münster-Aachen network, holiday broadcasts were consciously ecumenical. Christmas Day specials in 1928 began at 6:00 A.M. with the live broadcast of a holiday mass from the famous Protestant Mother Church in Unterbarmen-Wuppertal. At 9:00 A.M., five minutes of ringing church bells from St. Jerome's in Cologne introduced a Catholic morning service that featured a sermon and religious carols. The rest of the broadcast day included a program titled *Christmas in the Plastic Arts*, fairly tales for children, a *Christmas Legend in Bavarian Dialect*, and hours and hours of Christmas music. An evening *Christmas Concert* began at 8:00 P.M., when the Orchestra and Choir of the West German Broadcast Company performed a selection of holiday standards. An "Hour for the Betrothed" followed, with wedding music by famous composers—an appropriate background for the thousands who had or were about to plight their troths around the Christmas tree. The orchestra then played dance music—waltzes, fox-trot, slow fox, and one-step—until 1:00 A.M., a nod to the popular revelry that still animated the holiday.[137] The schedule paralleled conventional Christmas Day rituals. Listeners hardly had to leave their homes to enjoy all the traditional activities: a religious service, a family party, a Christmas concert, and an evening of ballroom dancing.

To be sure, radio helped establish a "national audiovisual space" that encouraged Germans to develop "an awareness of the nation as an audiovisual unity." The new mass medium also segmented audiences across gender, class, age, religion, and region.[138] As ever, Christmas was defined by a wealth of musical texts, now available to anyone who could afford a radio set. Radio thus spread and democratized access to a common German cultural heritage. Ubiquitous solo, choral, and symphonic renditions of sacred carols and family songs, combined with repeated broadcasts of classics like Bach's *Christmas Oratorio*, the *Christmas Cycle* by Peter Cornelius, or the operetta *Bübchen's Christmas Dream*, all reinforced the notion that Germans had a unique identity as "the people of music."[139] Broadcasts about the cultural-historical origins of Germanic customs reminded listeners of the holiday's national pedigree; Christmas stories, poems, and plays by famous authors like Fontane, Storm, and Stifter underscored Germany's distinct literary heritage. But holiday broadcasts also spoke to diverse interests and audiences. Housewives could listen to the *Woman's Hour*, which offered tips for recipes, shopping, and homemade decorations. Workers had their own holiday shows, clubs, and journals, which offered criticism (and sometimes approval) of mainstream broadcasts. Children certainly received extra attention during the holiday season, with "Fairy Tale Hours" that broadcast familiar stories like Hansel and Gretel or fanciful anecdotes about radio staff visiting the Weihnachtsmann. Reports on Christmas traditions in Silesia or Alsace or readings of local stories in Plattdeutsch (Low German dialect) underscored the ethnic diversity of the German Volk. The morning services broadcast on Christmas Day could be targeted for Catholic audiences in Münster, Protestant congregations in Leipzig, or in rotation in the ethnically diverse city of Breslau. German Jews, however, had to do without any ethnically based entertainment. No radio play list that I examined included a Hanukkah broadcast of any kind.[140]

The goods and attractions of a mass consumer culture no doubt enhanced the celebrations and indeed the everyday lives of many Germans, but by the mid-1920s, the rampant commercialization of the holiday generated notes of bitter resignation. Neo-romantic composer Richard Wetz, whose *Christmas Oratorio on Old German Poems* was featured in Christmas radio specials, spoke with some dismay about the costs of modernity. "I am aware that my 'Christmas Oratorio' appears in an age that pursues entirely different goals," Wetz wrote. "Nonetheless I believe that even in the religious and artistic ruins of the present there still exist people whose hearts are not desacralized: I wrote for them."[141] At a conference on religious folk customs held in Munich, a Catholic priest expressed the dilemma in similarly resigned tones: "In the age of hasty machines and electric light it seems that there is no time left for religious poesy or for the dreams of pious customs and sayings."[142] Even the aging Robert Hösel, cofounder and editor in chief of *Seidels Reklame*, the journal for marketing professionals, decried the glut of commercialization that undermined authentic holiday feelings. "Christmas was once a celebration of joy, a celebration of inner feeling, a celebration for young and old, especially in Germany," he wrote in 1926. In the past, Hösel reminded his audience of professional businessmen, Christmas was not just about presents; "it was much more inward." When the only "true joy" of the holiday was felt by business owners as they counted their profits, "inwardness is such a luxury that today we no longer even search for it." Certainly the Christmas displays in show windows had a "true Christmas character," but the majority of posters and print advertisements were transparent ploys: "a sketch of a pine bough, when necessary Saint Nicholas or a couple of dripping candles, and then the four words: 'the most precious gift.'" Anything could be a Christmas gift—automobiles, vacuum cleaners, aluminum pots—and even stores that once had nothing to do with Christmas now depended on the holiday for a hefty share of annual profits. There was no longer time or place for the loving, homemade gifts of young boys and girls. Though poorly crafted, such intimate presents had once "evoked such great joy." Artificial Christmas bells rang out of radio receivers, making home recitals superfluous. *"Put money in your purse,"* Hösel wrote in English, no doubt referring to the Americanization of the holiday, "and then Christmas joy really arrives, for the businessman and the public alike."[143]

In late November 1929, Berlin resident Emil Frauenhof wrote to the Protestant Consistory of Charlottenburg-Berlin to urge church leaders to protect the holiday from overcommercialization. Like Richard Wetz and Robert Hösel, Frauenhof believed that the irrepressible growth of advertising and "Christmas business" over the previous decades had had profound and debilitating effects on the spiritual qualities of the holiday. Things would probably get worse, Frauenhof predicted. The "sharpness and embitterment" of ongoing political struggle would no doubt *"disturb the peace of Christmas"* in the coming month. Frauenhof's lament expressed broad concerns with the "postsentimental" Christmas of the late 1920s. He also spoke to the deep investment in the national harmony that supposedly brought Germans together in the holiday season. "The traditional character of Christmas as a celebration of peace and as the greatest celebration of German Christendom must not be broken by far-reaching political struggle," Frauenhof warned. "This would threaten the unity of the German people, already so difficult to maintain." His words were prescient. The waning years of Weimar witnessed a determined fight over Christmas, as Germans struggled to control the use and meaning of the holiday.[144]

THE BATTLE FOR CHRISTMAS IN THE WEIMAR REPUBLIC

In his rather woeful Christmas Address of 1931, Chancellor Heinrich Brüning asserted that the spirit of Christmas could unite Germans despite economic and political crises. "At hardly any other time have people hoped more urgently for the fulfillment of the joyful [holiday] message," he admitted regretfully. Germany's "painful sacrifice" would ultimately lead to national recovery, the chancellor promised, but first, he wished, "the inner meanings of the Christmas season—belief, love and hope—must find their way back into the hearts of the people."[145] Faced with stubborn economic decline and social unrest, Weimar's elected officials tried to preserve the holiday spirit, calling for patience and calm and ordering police into the streets to preserve public order. The symbolic face of official attempts to provide some measure of Christmas cheer to the growing ranks of the unemployed was visible in the hundreds of "Christmas Trees for All" set up by local authorities in public squares throughout Germany in the late 1920s and early 1930s. More-practical measures included renewed government attempts to organize Winter Relief charity drives during the holiday season. The official emphasis on faith, charity, and the symbol of the tree invoked the familiar terms of the middle-class holiday. But as unemployment reached record levels, Dickensian appeals to sentimental values hardly masked the deteriorating conditions that placed out of reach the consumer abundance at the heart of the holiday. Political rhetoric filled the void left by the failed promise of prosperity. Communists and Nazis appropriated Christmas as a symbol of the nation's decline but also its potential, at times mocking sentimental, mainstream observances and at times decrying the collapse of the "German" holiday. At no time was the "battle for Christmas" in modern Germany more public and vicious than in the closing years of the Weimar Republic.[146]

The left had already subjected the holiday to radical deconstruction in the Wilhelmine years, and the avant-garde continued to mock bourgeois celebration; think only of John Heartfield's swinelike *Prussian Angel*, installed at the First International Dada Fair in 1920 and bedecked with a banner featuring lines from Luther's well-known carol "From Heaven on High," or his *German Yule Tree*, with branches twisted into the shape of a swastika. Communist intellectuals and fellow travelers attacked the key values and symbols of the holiday to demonstrate their disrespect for modern consumer culture, organized religion, and general bourgeois values. Hard-edged Christmas poems and stories by Kurt Tucholsky, Bertolt Brecht, Erich Mühsam, Erich Weinert, and Erich Kästner called attention to the impoverishment, unemployment, and chauvinist politics masked by middle-class sentimentalism.[147] Anonymous parodies of church carols such as "Silent Night," "O How Joyfully," "From Heaven on High," and many others updated the Social

Democratic alternative culture of the Imperial period. Weimar-era lyrics had a hard edge. Erich Kästner's anti-Christmas song from the late 1920s, a typical example, satirized the consumerist fantasies of a popular carol with lines such as "tomorrow Father Christmas comes, but only to the neighbors" and "tomorrow children you'll get nothing."[148]

The KPD mounted a vituperative critique of Christmas in the waning years of Weimar. In marked contrast to their Social Democratic competitors, who walked a delicate line between the rejection of capitalist abuse and appropriation of the conventional holiday, Communists avoided "proletarian" alternatives and indeed called for the abolition of the holiday altogether. Communist propagandists attacked the "preacherly opium" spread by church and state during the holidays, demanding that a call to arms replace the hypocritical sound of the church bells rung by the "class enemy."[149] "No, no peace with this class responsible for all this holiday squawking," wrote Paul Körner, the editor of *Die Rote Fahne* (The Red Banner) in 1928. Körner evinced a special distaste for the mainstream holiday. "Fight them, hate them!" he raved. "First must come a 'celebration' of revenge that will lead the ruling society to the scaffold. And only then: 'Peace on Earth and Good Will to Men.'"[150] Exhortations to leave the church were particularly loud during the Christmas season; the Central League of Proletarian Freethinkers in Berlin (founded in 1881 and centralized in 1922), for example, warned the authorities that an "army of millions" would "present the bourgeoisie and the priests with the bill for their 'Christmas gift' when ten thousands of working men and women mobilize for a mass resignation from the church."[151] A terse cartoon in *Die Rote Fahne* (Figure 4.7) pictured a worker's muscular hands destroying religious symbols and tearing apart a Christmas tree decorated with soldiers, shells, and gas bombs. The caption admonished committed readers to "Abolish this Gift-Giving of the Ruling Classes!"

KPD cadres sponsored public anti-Christmas protests that aroused the ire of churchmen, government officials, and National Socialists alike. Demonstrators regularly broke storefront windows and "plundered" (or looted) grocery stores during Christmas Hunger Marches—acts that expressed the desperation of the working-class marchers, brought food to the table, and ultimately underscored the connections between politics and consumer scarcity. To the dismay of observers, left-wing demonstrators repeatedly attacked the Christmas tree, the most venerable of Christmas symbols. After a street battle with police in Wuppertal, south of the Ruhr area, protesters doused the town's Christmas Tree for All with gasoline and set it on fire. In another

Weg mit dieser Bescherung der herrschenden Klasse!

FIGURE 4.7
"Abolish This Gift-Giving of the Ruling Classes." Anti-
Christmas cartoon. (*Rote Fahne*, 25 December 1926)

town, rumors spread that the Communists intended to break every store
window displaying a Christmas tree.[152] "Proletarians, the bourgeoisie and
their clerics celebrate the 'festival of love' at the same time that millions in
Germany are dying of starvation," announced a flyer that summoned workers to an anti-Christmas demonstration in 1930 in so-called Red Bernau,
a town close to Berlin. "'Peace on Earth,'" the flyer continued in mocking
tones. "The capitalist world is thick with weapons. Germany pays one and
one-half billions for its militarism. No money for the starving jobless. Fight
this system." The protesters formed ranks at 8:00 P.M. in Bernau's central
marketplace, as did Nazi Sturmabteilung (SA) storm troopers. According to
one Pastor Schulz, who witnessed the demonstration, it was impossible to
tell Nazis from Communists in the resulting fracas. Only the intercession of
the police, wielding billy clubs, restored order.[153]

A horrified pastor from Driesen, a small East Prussian town of some 5,500
inhabitants (now Drezdenko in western Poland), witnessed the results of
a similar demonstration. In a long letter to the Evangelische Konsistorium

(Protestant Consistory, or EK) in Berlin, the upset pastor described the events, all intended to "desacralize the Holy Eve." At 6:00 P.M. on Christmas Eve, a group of about fifty workers, with a brass band and two large red flags, marched through the town. After singing the "International" in the central square, they paraded past the Protestant church, where "their band played the shrill revolution song. This suddenly broke off as the procession went by the vicarage. Here the demonstrators chanted 'down' three times. The ugly, shrieking music and the deafening drumbeats started up again, and for a long time these disturbers of the peace continued on through the city streets." Though "shouts of indignation and resentment at this vulgar kind of disturbance rang out from most houses," the pastor was amazed that the local authorities were either unable or unwilling to halt the protest. "Immediately after the beginning of the disturbance of the celebration," he reported, "I telephoned the police guard. No one answered!" Later, the pastor discovered that such demonstrations were legal in Driesen; nonetheless, he asked the EK to intervene with the local authorities to ensure that such events would not recur.[154]

In contrast to the Brüning government, which promoted an orthodox Christmas message of hopeful palliatives, or the Communists, who condemned Christmas outright, National Socialists defended the holiday with vociferous rhetoric and violent street action. Party ideologues drew on long-familiar notions about the pagan rites of pre-Christian German tribes to cast the holiday as an arch symbol of the Volksgemeinschaft, the "people's community" promised in Nazi propaganda. Christmas, they repeatedly explained, had roots in the primordial "blood and soil" of the German ethnic nation, and the outrages perpetrated by the KPD only helped legitimize Nazi calls to protect the holiday from the nation's internal enemies—Communists, Jews, and government bureaucrats. Nazi propagandists took the rhetoric of resentment to new heights during the economic crisis of the late 1920s, as this excerpt from a poem attacking the 1929 Young Plan (for rescheduling Germany's war reparations) suggests:

> We hate forth under the Christmas lights
> With heated breasts and burning hearts
> In the exalted holy Christmas night
> All those responsible for Germany's plight.
> We hate the red and the black rapscallions
> Wilson's blind-eyed stab-in-the-back diviners

> Who croak for freedom and scream for peace,
> As they dunk their pens in pasteurized ink.[155]

National Socialists also attacked German Jews during the Christmas season. In the "Yule speeches" delivered at Nazi-sponsored celebrations, party leaders accused Jews of "seizing and corrupting . . . the most honorable German holiday." These "oppressors" would have to be "smashed" before Christmas could again be truly German.[156] Drawing on late-nineteenth-century precedents, Nazi propaganda portrayed "Jewish" department stores as examples of decadence and big-city commercialism that enslaved honest workers, exploited German shoppers, and threatened German businesses and holiday values alike. Ugly caricatures of Jewish-owned stores and physical assaults on the stores themselves exemplified Nazi willingness to use Christmas—long associated with "good will to all"—to exacerbate racial divisions.[157] In the early 1930s, members of the Nazi SA—the brown-shirted "storm troops" at the vanguard of the Nazi movement—set up picket lines around Jewish-owned department stores across Germany, and in several cases they encouraged customers to "buy German" by throwing tear gas bombs in stores crowded with Christmas shoppers. According to the liberal press, however, Nazi boycotts had little effect.[158] They were nonetheless rehearsals for fascism, which in historian Andrew Bergerson's words transformed "friends and neighbors into Jews and Aryans" and encouraged Germans to accept the subsequent Aryanization of Jewish-owned department stores with little protest.[159]

The Christmas celebrations of the SA perhaps best exemplify the connections between ideology, sentimentalism, and violence that typified the Nazi holiday in the late Weimar period. Organized into local paramilitary units with a nationwide infrastructure and complete with ranks and uniforms, SA troops saw themselves as ascetic and dedicated fighters for German renewal, the avant-garde of the "brown revolution."[160] For the SA, Christmas was a key ritual in the secular religion of national aspiration. Celebration provided an ideological myth and a moment of communal solidarity that shaped the identity of individual members. Entertainment at the annual celebrations held in the SA "locals," the combination barracks–tavern–social club headquarters of district units, typically included a Christmas speech from a *Sturmbannführer* (Storm Unit Leader); a concert performed by the local SA band; a traditional Christmas play performed by the League of German Girls or the Hitler Youth; and the presentation of a living picture, in which live actors froze in position, playing out a scene from German history or the Bible. During the festivities, held around a Christmas tree decorated with swastikas, the poorest SA men received free coffee, cake, liquor, and other small gifts. The men sang the inevitable "Silent Night," as well as the marching anthem "The Horst Wessel Song" and other nationalist hymns. Visiting dignitaries, invited to recite a "fatherlandish speech," might include local clergymen, sympathetic aristocrats, and local Nazi Party leaders.[161]

SA celebrations generated group solidarity and helped raise the level of "Christmas hatred" to a fever pitch. Undercover police observers in Munich, ordered by city officials to monitor their festivities, commented repeatedly on the "festive mood" of the participants and their approval of ideological Christmas speeches.[162] SA members themselves described an almost spiritual celebration of community and determination. "One felt the communal heartbeat of all the old fighters in brown-shirts gathered here," wrote an SA man about his troop's Christmas celebration in 1931. "All eyes expressed the timeless manly German faith in the Führer and the belief, as well as the ardent desire, that the birth of a more pure, better age for our Fatherland might arrive after this Christmas."[163] The emphasis on manliness, comradeship, and fatherland, fervently expressed in Christmas rituals focused on national rebirth, helped establish the us-against-them mentality that both inspired and legitimized aggressive holiday activities. Exhortations to revenge and action reached their climax on Christmas Eve, when solemn groups of SA men swore oaths to the national cause around the Tannenbaum: "We promise again, in this holy Yule Night, that we will fight tirelessly against all the low, cowardly, and vulgar forces within us and without us [in the] holy struggle for our folk."[164]

Heavily charged with calls to struggle in the name of national redemption, SA Christmas celebrations could lead to open acts of violence. In the waning years of Weimar, the holiday season inspired numerous street fights between the SA and opposing groups of Communists, police, members of the Reichsbanner (the Social-Democrat paramilitary group), and even the Stahlhelm, the World War I veterans organization hardly known for its leftist views. "Red-murder haunts the Christmas season," movement poet Heinrich Anacker warned in the poem "SA Christmas 1930."[165] Such ideas apparently resonated with the rank and file. In Berlin on Christmas Eve 1932, SA men drove through the streets, firing shots into taverns frequented by Communists; and during hand-to-hand fighting in the worker's district of Moabit, a twenty-three-year-old SA man was knifed in the belly.[166] The SA interpreted its attacks against the "red terror" as acts of self-defense, undertaken to protect German Christmas from the nation's enemies. "The red terror moved against us," SA leader Gerhard Pantel reminded Berlin SA men just before Christmas in 1929. "Comrades, we saw the result! Blood where we stand and fight. Blood wherever we look. The holy blood of our comrades! It was shed for Germany." Nazis blamed holiday disturbances on Communists and complained bitterly about the shooting and knifing of innocent SA men. As Pantel wrote, "In the shadows of the night, the SA man was butchered with cowardice and treachery and in the morning we found him, cut to bits and trampled in the gutter."[167] According to the Nazi press, SA men preferred to spend Christmas peacefully, in rapt contemplation of Germany and "true comradeship." Only national betrayal forced them into action.[168] The veracity of such stories is doubtful; reports in mainstream newspapers show that at the very least, Christmas was a time of "heightened activity" for the SA as well as Communists.[169]

Government officials relied on police powers to end the political violence that increasingly disrupted the Christmas peace, but to little avail. In both 1931 and 1932, emergency decrees outlawed political meetings and public demonstrations during the holiday season. Reports of police using rubber truncheons on Communists at anti-Christmas demonstrations, and less frequently on rowdy SA men, met with approval in the pages of the liberal press. In December 1932, the last month before the Nazi takeover, the "Civic Peace" announced by the government in the Christmas weeks included frantic suggestions for ending unemployment and increasing winter charity aid. The German parliament, increasingly desperate, announced a Christmas amnesty that shortened or annulled prison terms for about 15,000 political prisoners. Mocking the Weimar government's weakness, Nazis observed the holiday with hundreds of *Volksgenossen* (peoples' comrades) newly released from jail.[170]

The violent conflicts on Christmas Eve testify to the overall brutalization of Weimar society in the early 1930s; they also show that German Christmas had become an emotionally laden and politically contested symbol of national prosperity. In the end, the National Socialist version of Christmas ironically appeared to resolve the tensions the Nazis themselves did so much to provoke. Unlike Communist anti-Christmas protests or bourgeois platitudes, the Nazi Christmas envisioned a proud national future based on an invented ethnic past. Its rhetoric and rituals promised to heal the national community with "blood and soil" mythologies, economic recovery, and racial exclusion. After gaining power in 1933, the rhetoric of resentment popular in the "years of struggle" no longer met the needs of a party in power. Instead, National Socialists would use all the resources of an avowedly totalitarian state to promote a harmonious People's Christmas, which celebrated the values and goals of the Nazi racial state.

Christmas in the Third Reich

But Christmas is miraculous and filled with the finest streams of German being, not as a celebration of universal happiness, thankfulness, or joyfulness, but rather as a day of quiet, of love. And just as it is impossible to imagine a German holiday without the setting of its home-like natural surroundings, so the quiet beauty of the German forest in winter, with its glittering snow, scent of pine, and shining starlight has filled the celebration of human love. Ages old is the demand and desire of the German to bring the experience of nature and God into his house, to sanctify festivity and life. Thus the tree of light made its way into every German home, as the fairy tale and reality of the winter night, with its burning candles that announce the myth of the rebirth of the light, which triumphs over death and ossification. And equally ancient and at one with the tree in our Volk is the myth of blood, the holy belief in the God-willed order of eternal procreation, of the being and rebirth of the child.

—⟡ Auguste Reber-Gruber, "German Christmas," *National Socialist Education for Girls*, December 1936

NATIONAL SOCIALIST IDEOLOGUES like Frau Dr. Auguste Reber-Gruber, director of the women's division of the National Socialist Teachers' Union, were well aware that the familiar imagery of candle-lit trees, snowy landscapes, and regeneration made Christmas a powerful vehicle for naturalizing a radical political culture rooted in a mythic national past. Just as French Jacobins and Russian Bolsheviks transformed their festival cultures in attempts to shape new revolutionary citizens, so National Socialists redesigned Germany's holidays to conform to the state's racial and ideological agendas.[1] The Nazi intelligentsia clearly believed that the family rituals performed around the Christmas tree engendered an emotional surplus, which could be manipulated to construct and sustain a sense of national feeling and

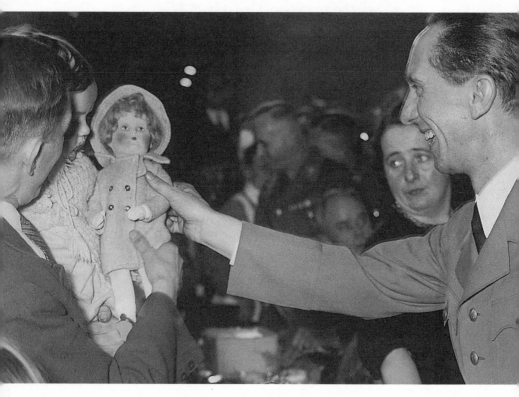

FIGURE 5.1
Propaganda Minister Joseph Goebbels gives a girl a doll at a
Winter Relief celebration, 1936. (© bpk Berlin 2009)

a "fascist self."[2] "The significance of holidays and rituals—from the political standpoint—lies in the spiritual or emotional deepening of the experience of community," wrote Hannes Kremer, poet, propagandist, and by 1941 director of the Propaganda Ministry's *Amtsleitung Kultur* (Directorate of Culture). "The [Christmas] ceremony should appeal not to the knowledge of the few, but to the spirit, the life feeling, of the many. . . . We do not want simply to touch the emotions (a movie with a 'happy ending' usually can do that much better!), but rather to make people aware of their responsibility for the nation's fate."[3]

Kremer's confidence in the power of performance drew on a history of celebration that went back to the founding of the National Socialist German Workers Party (NSDAP) in 1920. From the start, Christian liturgy, symbols, and sentiments enticed Nazis who sought to appropriate religious and family rituals. Reber-Gruber's own version of a de-Christianized Christmas based on "the myth of blood and the God-willed order of eternal procreation"— her attempt, in short, to supplant the birth of Christ with the birth of an archetypal "Aryan" child—revealed the constant slippage between piety and politics, race and religion, and Christian ritual and pagan rite that defined Nazi celebration.[4] Borrowing from their Social Democratic adversaries, Nazi propagandists cast Christmas and the winter solstice as a metaphor for the rebirth of the German nation. Family celebration, according to Nazi authors, preserved the ethos of the pagans, when "the feeling of unity with native soil and nature was still alive, the desire for light and strength had strong roots, [and] Yule festivities remained a sacred manifestation of God."[5] The recovery of mythic Nordic rites hardly ruled out appeals to the Christian aspects of the holiday. Parroting the conclusions of late nineteenth-century ethnographers, Nazi loyalists asserted that the "merging of national characteristics and Christianity" exemplified in Christmas revealed the origins of "the German character."[6] "Christ on the cross, and Odin on the World-Ash . . . there is something equally divine in both images," claimed one Frodi Ingolfson Wehrmann, a member of the occult group Svastika-Zirkel, in 1925; imitation of the sacrifice of both Gods could bring the "turn of fate" required for Germany's contemporary salvation.[7]

After the National Socialists took power in 1933, the parties and celebrations organized by local party offices (*Ortsgruppen*), the SA storm troopers, the National Socialist League of Women, and the *Hitlerjugend* (Hitler Youth, or HJ) all deemphasized Christian and pagan observance and instead played up the supposedly universal German aspects of the holiday. The so-called People's Christmas (*Volksweihnachten*) was an inescapable part of the orchestration of everyday life in Nazi Germany. Like other Nazi policies and programs—such as the workers' vacations sponsored by the Strength through Joy (KdF) organization, the racially inspired anticancer campaigns, or the ever-popular radio "request concerts"—the Nazification of Christmas generated support for the regime, and not just among party members or loyalists. With its incessant focus on national unity and "eternal-racial" customs, the Nazi holiday, however twisted, reminded Germans of their common cultural heritage. Rituals that rehearsed sentimental allegiance to German blood and soil, according to Nazi texts, brought satisfactions that were more authentic than the decadent distractions of modern consumer culture. Annual celebrations held by party leaders, Nazified workplace parties, and *Winterhilfswerk* (Winter Relief, or WHW) charity campaigns linked neighbors and friends into tangible networks of sociability and civic self-help (Figure 5.1). The emphasis on traditional gender roles gave families and particularly women renewed pride in the accomplishments of domesticity, always in the context of the racial state. The observance of everyday forms of Nazified celebration—making winter solstice cookies, for example, or singing National Socialist Christmas carols—constructed fascist identities in the private space of the home.[8]

The People's Christmas lent "racially acceptable" Germans a sense of moral certainty and "ethnic virtue," even as the practices of celebration segregated "Aryans" from others and normalized racism, terror, and ultimately mass murder.[9] Adolf Hitler's "Yule Speech," delivered in 1921 at the National Socialist German Christmas Celebration in the Munich Hofbräuhaus, set the tone early on. According to undercover police agents on hand to monitor the party, a festive crowd of some 4,000 supporters cheered "der Führer" as he attacked "mammonistic-materialism," Jews, and government politicians.[10] Once in power, the party backed away from Christmas propaganda that openly attacked German Jews or working-class leftists. Nazi celebration nonetheless worked to exclude those deemed unfit by the regime. Open anti-Semitism surfaced at Christmastime in boycotts of Jewish-owned department stores and criticism about displays of the "German" Christmas tree in Jewish store windows.[11] And though official holiday discourse rarely mentioned Jews, countless images of the invariably blond-haired, blue-eyed German families gathered around the Christmas tree promoted ideologies of racial purity, as did repeated exhortations to buy German gifts or observe what propagandists called a "racially correct" (*arteigene*) holiday.

Party cadres had the power to shape and control holiday rituals, but attempts to radically revise a much-beloved family and Christian holiday exposed the fault lines in the "revolutionary" culture of National Socialism. Since Nazi celebration challenged Germany's clergymen with a set of remade rituals that traded allegiance to Christian faith for belief in the Volksgemeinschaft—the "People's Community" promised by the regime—the holiday became a hot point in the struggle between church and state. Christmas refracted divisions among at least three factions of Nazi supporters: radical neopaganists, more "moderate" Nazis who sought to overcome confessional divisions, and the so-called German Christians, the Protestant splinter group of Nazi sympathizers who wanted to build a unified *Volkskirche*, or National church, based on blood and race. Mainstream Protestant and Catholic leaders, for their part, used the popular investment in conventional religious observances to shelter popular piety from Nazi de-Christianization campaigns. The history of Christmas in the Third Reich complicates assumptions that all National Socialists were avowed anti-Christians even as it reveals the opportunism of mid-level functionaries like Reber-Gruber, who relished the opportunity to de-Christianize the celebration of the birth of Jesus in their search for a national "new order." Ordinary Germans, who were generally on the receiving end of these highly conceived political projects, expressed dismay with the turmoil: Christmas was not fascist enough for Nazi Party loyalists but too politicized for Christian believers.[12]

The People's Christmas faltered on confessional, class, and political differences, as well as on the increasingly difficult conditions of daily life, particularly during the crises of World War II. Yet the Nazi holiday's all-too-obvious successes suggest that Nazification made remarkably deep inroads into the fabric of everyday life during the twelve years of Nazi rule. This was not simply a result of top-down manipulation; nor was Nazi political culture a "beautiful illusion" that lacked popular legitimacy. Seemingly minor acts of popular observance became self-constructing signs of engagement with National Socialism. As Germans participated in Nazified public rituals and private celebrations, they built the racial state in degrees, from the bottom up.[13]

INVENTING TRADITIONS IN NAZI GERMANY

Perhaps the most striking feature of Christmas in the Third Reich was its reinvention as a neopagan holiday that celebrated the supposedly Nordic roots of the "Aryan race." Recent scholarship has underscored the speciousness and manipulative function of the pseudoracial ethnographies devised by Nazi scholars and popular writers.[14] This hardly means that the fire-and-light rituals promoted by state functionaries lacked popular appeal or legitimacy. Nazi propagandists drew on the nationalist holiday literature written by late nineteenth-century scholars and family authors, and Social Democrats had already adapted the winter solstice to political purposes. Interest in the "Germanic" aspects of Christmas grew exponentially after World War I, when a marked increase in popular and scholarly articles on the ancient German heritage of the holiday and the tight connections between pagan and Christian observance reached an apparently eager readership. In the 1930s, intellectuals interested in interpreting Christmas as a "living example" of blood-and-soil ideologies found institutional support in institutes like the Lehr- und Forschungsstätte für indogermanische Glaubensgeschichte (Teaching and Research Post for the History of Indo-Germanic Faith), the SS-sponsored Deutsches Ahnenerbe (Society for the Study of German Ancestral Heritage), and the Arbeitsgemeinschaft für deutsche Volkskunde (Working Group for German Folklore).[15] Ideas about the pagan aspects of the holiday percolated down to a mass audience in articles, books, and documentary films in the 1920s and 1930s, continuing a process of popularization evident since the 1880s. The key terms of Nazi Christmas were hardly new inventions created by crackpot propagandists. Germans had embraced völkish ideas about the Germanic roots of Christmas long before the Nazis adopted them.

The Nazi reconstruction of pagan ritual—with appropriate "guidelines for celebration in the home"—helped reenchant Germany's political discourse and served multiple ideological goals. National Socialists eagerly politicized the links between private celebration, leisure time, and the mass media in attempts to construct a specifically fascist self at home with fellow "people's comrades" in the reconstructed racial state. Ambitious plans for reinventing holidays and festivals filled the pages of the journal *Die neue Gemeinschaft: Das Parteiarchiv für nationalsozialistische Feier- und Freizeitgestaltung* (The New Community: The Party Archive for the Organization of National Socialist Celebrations and Leisure Time), published by the Reich Ministry for Popular Enlightenment and Propaganda (RMVP).[16] This publication, distributed to party organizations "for internal use only," was just one part of an extensive media apparatus of magazines, journals, newspapers, newsreels, radio broadcasts, Christmas books, and holiday ephemera; all brought the invented traditions promulgated by the RMVP to millions of German citizens.

By 1937 National Socialist propagandists had divided the holiday season into a series of distinct celebrations, each with its own political relevance. The list included *Vorweihnachten*, or "Pre-Christmas" celebrations, meant to replace Christian Advent traditions with "racially correct" observances; People's Christmas charity parties, organized for the poor and especially their children by the National Socialist People's Welfare Office; "Winter Solstice" and "National Socialist Christmas Celebrations," held for the many members of the party's mass organizations; and "German Christmas," observed by individual families in the privacy of their own homes.[17]

Nazi guidelines for celebrating Christmas trod a thin line between tradition and invention, pleasure and politics, and Christian observance and pagan rites. Festivities sponsored by party organizations, wrote *Die neue Gemeinschaft* in a special issue on "German Christmas" in 1937, should be sober, serious, and openly political, without presents, raucous partying, or dancing. In rooms adorned with swastikas, torches, and modestly decorated Christmas trees, Christian customs and cultlike pagan practices were all taboo. The Ministry of Propaganda informed cadres that "a National Socialist Christmas celebration does not give Christmas a churchlike Christian expression but rather a German and völkisch sense and purpose." At the same time, the holiday was not a "field of activity for the prophets of a new religion" who wished to promote a "Yule-night cult." Instead, official celebrations "should make visible the position above the confessions held by the Party. . . . A National Socialist Christmas celebration has to place *meaningfully* the ancient traditions of the German Christmas festival at the center of our own epoch, in order to make the participant feel that beyond all questions of confession the old Christmas symbols of fire and tree still have a living and deep meaning for *our* time."[18] Party officials repeatedly promoted a national holiday intended to unite Germans above long-standing confessional differences. Ongoing attempts to establish definitive guidelines in the language of orderly control nonetheless suggests that the boundaries between pagan, völkisch, and Christian observances were not easy to define or police.

Sociability, celebration, and ideology merged, however uneasily, in factory canteens, local meeting halls, town squares, and school classrooms, where Germans participated in a dense network of holiday festivities organized by National Socialist mass organizations. At such events, historian Alf Lüdtke suggests, "the capacity for submission as well as the pleasure of being involved were stimulated simultaneously."[19] Across Germany, the Nazi Party District Offices, the HJ, the National Socialist Women's League (NSF), and

FIGURE 5.2
A German Labor Front Christmas party at the Mercedes-
Benz plant in Berlin, 1938. (© bpk Berlin 2009)

the German Workers Front sponsored Christmas celebrations tailored to the needs of their members. The public orchestration of Nazi Christmas was not just a big-city product, as shown by local historian Fritz Markmiller's careful reconstruction of everyday Nazism in Dingolfing, a small town north of Munich; Nazi mass organizations reached deeply into the fabric of German society in both rural and urban areas.[20] Each December, teenagers gathered for the "home evenings" of the HJ and handcrafted small presents to raise money for the Winter Relief campaign. Groups of workers joined the "pre-Christmas celebrations" sponsored by KdF (Figure 5.2), where they sang carols and participated in performances of music and theater that expressed "faith in the victory of light in the time of greatest darkness." Teachers received a Nazified Christmas curriculum for schoolchildren of all ages in the journals of the National Socialist Teachers' Union, which taught that school celebrations should embody "the experience of the community of life, struggle, and fate of the German people." Texts for advanced students again emphasized

"Aryan-Germanic" culture as the source of Christmas traditions. An extreme version of "blood and soil" ideology found expression in the highly ritualized celebrations of the SS, who swore "light oaths" to Hitler, the German family, and the national community while lighting candles on the "Yule Tree."[21]

Conventional Christmas imagery—decorated trees, happy families, snowy landscapes, Father Christmas—and a wealth of instantly recognizable carols made the holiday a powerful vehicle for inventing a national culture rooted in sight and sound. By the late 1920s, radio and newsreel reports on Christmas (portrayals of decorated city streets, famous German churches, Christmas markets, geese ready for table, choirs singing holiday carols) greeted Germans each holiday season.[22] Enjoying some form of centralized mass entertainment was in and of itself a holiday ritual. Even before the arrival of the National Socialist "media dictatorship," Christmas encouraged a growing audience to envision Germany as a "national audiovisual space."[23] In the 1930s, the mass media became increasingly important for the popularization of national self-identities refracted through leisure and holiday time, and a strikingly similar process was at work across Western societies. For Americans and other Europeans as well as Germans, this "most dramatic era of sound and sight" created novel sources of common experience for huge audiences.[24]

If the annual lighting of the "National Community Christmas Tree" in Washington, D.C., described in dramatic radio broadcasts in the 1920s and 1930s, embodied the democratic impulse behind Progressive-era reforms, in Nazi Germany the new media Christmas was shot through with fascist ideology.[25] Christmas radio shows, by the 1930s a familiar aspect of private festivity, seamlessly blended propaganda and family entertainment. *Father Christmas's Radio Program*, broadcast on Christmas Eve in 1937 (when all major German radio stations carried the official program), typified the genre. Those who tuned in at 8:00 P.M. that night heard a "Christmas message" from Rudolph Hess (the "Führer's Deputy"); carols sung by a children's choir; a show on Christmas festivities in the army, navy, and air force; and the sound of ringing bells broadcast from Germany's most famous cathedrals.[26] The audiovisualization of the German Volksgemeinschaft was repeatedly realized in radio broadcasts and newsreel shots of Christmas bells ringing in famous churches throughout Germany. Unlike Russian Bolsheviks, who, during the "Great Turn" (1928 to 1932) saw church bells as symbols of the "Old Way of Life" they wished to destroy, Nazi propagandists used modern media to colonize and exalt sacred practices.[27] Rapid cuts between snow-covered church towers and chiming bells in famous cathedrals in Munich, Danzig, Cologne, and Berlin provided visual evidence of the regionalism that anchored German national identity.[28] Such scenes capitalized on the broad appeal of sacred symbolism yet were a historicist pastiche, emptied of any real religious content. At the same time, they reveal a determined attempt to appropriate and remake the Christian foundations of German identity.

Cinema was very well suited for nationalizing and Nazifying the holiday. Annual Christmas newsreels featured glowing reports on Christmas markets, special concerts, holiday speeches by political leaders, WHW collections, and other party-sponsored activities. Newsreel reports on People's Christmas envisioned a resurrected national community, free from the political fractures and social dislocations of the Weimar years. Scenes of NSDAP ministers Joseph Goebbels, Hermann Göring, and Hess collecting donations for the WHW in the streets of Berlin, or of Göring handing out presents to Berlin street urchins in the reception hall of the Air Force Ministry building, showed that Germans were "one Volk" under the paternal guidance of their political leaders.[29] A typical Christmas newsreel from 1934 featured Propaganda Minister Goebbels officiating at a carefully choreographed celebration with a group of children in the traditionally left-wing Berlin district of Friedrichshain. There, Goebbels praised government efforts to provide the needy with Christmas joy. "Today throughout Germany," he exclaimed, "we have called together 5,200,000 children with their parents, in order to give them a joyful Christmas Eve. They sit in the brightly illuminated rooms of the big city, in the lonely school rooms and inns on the Friesian islands, in wide Masuria, in snowy Black Forest villages, or in the Bavarian countryside." As Goebbels evoked the different regions of the German nation, the newsreel cut to scenes of snow-covered terrain, visualizing the distinct spaces that together comprised the national community. The propaganda minister closed his speech with an "inward plea that fate will further receive Führer, Volk, and Nation in its merciful protection, and will above all bring the German people the immeasurable good already pronounced to mankind in the Christmas message, Peace on Earth."[30]

This single example of a newsreel Christmas spectacle—there are many others—brings together the diverse strands of official Nazi celebration: the ideal of class unity based on acceptance of National Socialism; the paternal appropriation of holiday charity by the Nazi state; the charismatic celebrity of leadership; the appealing sentimentalism of mother and child; and above all, the carefully translated Christian language that lacked any overt reference

FIGURE 5.3

Propaganda Minister Joseph Goebbels speaking at an SA street celebration
in a working-class district in Berlin on 23 December 1933; note the torchlight
parade and brass SA band at the bottom left. (© bpk Berlin 2009)

to God or the birth of Jesus—all packaged in a mass-media presentation that
reached an audience of millions in movie theaters filled with seasonal crowds,
in radio broadcasts, and in press reports. Of course, real people participated
in such events as well. Hand picked or not, the shadowy workers in the background who received WHW "gifts" took part in what must have been a memorable occasion. The Nazi press took care to explain the political conversion
supposedly inspired by such events. The popular enthusiasm for "People's
Christmas in the Street" showed that Germans of all political persuasions
(former Social Democrats and even Communists) had come together in the
national community. "Two or three years ago, the [Communist] commune
still exercised its terror [in Friedrichshain]," noted one reporter. During the
celebration with the propaganda minister, however, "former agitators looked
bashfully at the ground when they witnessed the joy and happiness brought
here by the once so-hated Nazis" (Figure 5.3).[31] While some Germans no
doubt saw through such cynical attempts to sanitize the public image of the
SA and NSDAP, and indeed to bastardize socialism, others were drawn to

the appeal of Nazi celebrities and their apparent largesse. When one young girl's parents were invited to a Christmas celebration with Göring in a villa in Hannover, they returned home laden with "wonderful presents." The mother was thrilled by the party and "entirely taken by Hermann Göring, because he was such a charming and handsome man."[32]

The success of the Nazification of Christmas depended not only on party leaders and mass organizations; it also required the committed efforts of a number of enthusiastic and relatively independent midlevel "inventors," who worked in the interstices of the Nazi cultural community to adapt established practices and symbols to National Socialist ideology. The impact of such relatively anonymous figures is exemplified in the work of three telling cases: schoolteacher Florentine Gebhardt, who wrote scripts for a variety of national celebrations and encouraged teachers to celebrate Nazism in their own classrooms; youth-group leader, poet, and children's book author Hans Baumann, who revised the carols and poems performed during family celebrations on Christmas Eve; and movie star and film director Luis Trenker, who used the audiovisual power of film to burnish the appeal of the solstice rituals favored by Nazi believers. Working along with but outside of formal party organizations, these disparate actors Nazified Christmas and introduced Germans to new syncretic ritual practices that blurred Christian traditions and fascist inventions.

The story of Florentine Gebhardt suggests that the invention of Nazi tradition depended on the avid participation of informal enthusiasts at all levels of society. Born in the mid-1860s to a lower-middle-class family, Gebhardt was a devout Protestant and German nationalist; shortly before her death in 1941, she proudly wrote that she had spent her entire life in "service to the Volk."[33] From 1896 to 1924, Gebhardt taught high school in Berlin, and around 1900 she began a writing career that would span the next forty years. Her teaching, built around the annual school calendar with its festivals and holidays, encouraged an enduring interest in celebration and performance. Gebhardt became an accomplished author of plays and programs for local and national festivals. She composed songs, poems, and speeches for church holidays, veterans' meetings, Heimat-club celebrations, monument commemorations, and other patriotic occasions and published her work in newspapers, magazines, school readers, and small booklets. From 1926 to 1930, Gebhardt edited and wrote about two-thirds of the content of a magazine called *Feierstunden der Schule* (Ceremonies for School), often using male pseudonyms.[34]

Both Gebhardt's holiday scripts and autobiography express a passion for the Volk and "soil" of the German nation.[35] In her hands, Christmas was a celebration of faith, patriotism, and social integration. She wrote extensively about the decoration of home and classroom, and her intricate scripts for group celebrations instructed parents or teachers to lead children in the memorization and performance of plays, speeches, songs, games, and dances. Her programs typically mimicked the course of a religious service: participants recited prescripted dialogues and delivered solo and group choral performances. Though Gebhardt's Weimar-era Christmas scripts recognized confessional difference—she conveniently included material suitable for Catholics as well as Protestants—they invariably called attention to the special German aspects of the holiday that were shared by both denominations.[36] While not as overtly chauvinist as her other works (for example, her directions for a celebration of the return of the Rhineland to Germany), Gebhardt's Christmas scripts expressed the nationalist assumptions that underlay all of her work.

The continuities between Gebhardt's work in the Weimar years and the Third Reich highlight the connections between National Socialist celebratory culture and preexisting, popular forms of festivity. Gebhardt welcomed the Nazi "revolution" that "pulled Germany back from the precipice" of Bolshevism; she supported Nazi foreign policy and their respectable sexual morality.[37] She also was a convinced anti-Semite. After the Nazi "seizure of power," she admitted, she began to base her prejudice on racial rather than theological grounds.[38] Gebhardt wrote for the Nazis with some enthusiasm, despite her age. At the request of her publisher, himself a longtime SA man, or "old fighter," she authored a series of instructions for National Socialist holidays, including "mother's evenings," the harvest festival, the "day of youth," and solstice celebrations. In 1933 she quickly reworked and Nazified a collection of holiday material first published in 1922. Gebhardt added several pro-Nazi poems to the collection and addressed the main Christmas speech in the collection to the *Volksgenossen* (people's comrades); her publisher put a swastika on the cover. Little else was changed.[39] Both the form and content of Nazi celebration readily appropriated festive customs already that were well established in the Weimar period and familiar from school, social club, and family celebrations. The close links between Christian, nationalist, and National Socialist liturgies revealed in Gebhardt's work would be a hallmark of Nazi festivity.

The career of Hans Baumann, the "house poet of the Hitler Youth," shows how the blood-and-soil traditions popular in the interwar youth movement informed Nazi inventions.[40] Born the son of a professional soldier in 1914, Baumann joined the HJ in the late 1920s and quickly earned a reputation as a talented and politically committed National Socialist poet. His lyrics and poetry expressed the radicalism, romanticism, and mysticism of the German youth movement. In 1932, when he was eighteen years old, Baumann wrote the infamous Nazi marching song *Es zittern die morschen Knochen* (The Rotten Bones Are Trembling), which included the notorious lines "today Germany belongs to us/and tomorrow the entire world." During the war, he served as an officer in the Wehrmacht. Baumann's literary talents could apparently shine in any political context. After 1945 he became a successful children's book author and in 1962 won the Gerhart Hauptmann Prize (sponsored by the Freie Volksbühne in Berlin) for his drama *Under the Sign of Pisces*, published anonymously. Baumann was forced to return the prize because of complaints about his National Socialist past.[41]

Baumann and other sympathetic intellectuals wrote numerous poems, songs, and stories for the winter-solstice and Christmas celebrations favored by the Nazis during the 1930s. Their work was featured in Nazified Christmas books, collections of carols and poetry, magazines, journals, and Propaganda Ministry directives.[42] Baumann stands out, however, because he composed the most famous and popular Nazi carol, "Hohe Nacht der klaren Sterne" (Glorious Night of Shining Stars). The song was reprinted repeatedly in Nazi texts, broadcast in radio programs and newsreels, and performed at Nazi Party celebrations. The melody, which copies that of a traditional carol, was readily adaptable to harmonic choral arrangements. The lyrics draw on folklore and nature worship and merge conventional themes with the mystical imagery of fire and light. References to world redemption, shining stars, and a newborn child replay familiar Christian motifs. But here, and in dozens of similar, less-famous songs and poems by writers like Propaganda Ministry functionary Thilo Scheller and teacher-turned-Gauleiter Hans Schemm, Christian themes are couched in terms of the winter solstice.

> Glorious night of shining stars,
> like broad bridges do appear
> spanning distance from afar
> o'er which our hearts draw near.
>
> Glorious night with splendid fires
> on all mountains mile by mile,

today the earth seeks its renewal
like a newborn radiant child.

Mothers, all the stars and fires,
are for you alone unfurled;
Mothers, deep within your own heart
Beats the heart of the wide world.[43]

Contemporaries admired Baumann's work, noting its usefulness for ideological indoctrination. Nazi musicologist Walter Pudelko wrote in 1938 that
Baumann's lyricism was not "disturbed" by overt political messages, yet his
verse "rang with the recuperated and liberated life-rules of our type."[44] In
an extensive review of Baumann's career that appeared in 1939, professor of
pedagogy Hermann Bertlein wrote that his songs "embody in the same measure tradition and the future." Baumann was "the awakener and prophet of
the musical powers of the young generation," and his work with youth would
"revitalize for the entire German folk the important life values of musical
power." As Bertlein suggested, Baumann's lyrics "spoke of mother with great
honor, love, and gratitude" and evoked the "deep inwardness" associated
with "mother love" and Heimat.[45] Recitation of "Glorious Night of Shining
Stars" in public or private celebration certainly drew on the sentimentalism
of a traditional family Christmas. The lyrics, however, encouraged celebrants
to entertain sublime visions of a place out of time, which hardly depended
on the birth of Jesus or on the provision of abundant gifts and toys by the
Weihnachtsmann, as described in so many nineteenth-century family carols.
Rather, Baumann's song evokes a vague primordial landscape populated by a
Volk close to the splendors of nature, who welcome the rebirth of the winter
solstice with torches and solemn images of a cosmic earth mother.

The connections between Christmas, the winter solstice, and ideologies of
blood and soil were portrayed as a stunning cinematic spectacle in the feature
film *Der verlorene Sohn* (*The Prodigal Son*), which premiered in Germany in
November 1934, just in time for the Christmas season.[46] Directed, written
by, and starring mountain film veteran Luis Trenker, whose earlier movies
had already made him a favorite of the Nazi leadership, the climax of *Prodigal Son* features a primeval winter-solstice scene based loosely on a Tyrolean
Rauhnacht (Demon Night) festival (the threads of invention and actual ethnography in the film are difficult to unravel). The film tells the story of Tonio
Feuersinger, the hero of a mountain village forced to choose between the organic cycles of village life and the decadence of city life in the contemporary

United States. Contemporaries lauded the film's dark portrayal of New York City and its loyalty to an authentic vision of nature. When the film opened in Berlin, admiring crowds mobbed Trenker and the producer when they left the theater. Nazi officials sent the movie to the 1935 Venice Film Festival, where it won a prize; one critic declared it the best film of the year. A review in the trade journal *Film-Kurier* declared that "every German wishes and hopes that Trenker's vision of divine creation and its liberating grandeur will be shared by all German filmmakers and that out of the film of the past will arise the art work of the future, a film shaped by a world view rooted in nature, an authentic German folk."[47]

Prodigal Son opens with a portrayal of the purity and simplicity of Tonio's life in his German-speaking Tyrolean village. He is a community leader, a manly forester who wins the affection of Barbl, the local beauty. Driven by wanderlust and entranced by a wealthy American tourist named Lilian, Tonio decides to visit New York City. His failure to find Lilian or permanent work leaves him homeless and at the mercy of policemen and charity handouts; Tonio wanders through the dark streets of the city, populated with beggars and thieves. After a chance reunion with the wealthy Lilian, Tonio joins her in her father's luxurious townhouse. They are about to kiss when Tonio sees the hand-carved mask of the Rauhnacht god that Lilian's father had brought home from the Tyrol. The pleasant background music is broken by the sound of a loud gong, and Tonio decides to leave New York and Lilian for home and Barbl.

The third and final part of this "enactment of . . . national homecoming" features the return of the prodigal son during the Rauhnacht festival, a twenty-minute filmic frenzy replete with bonfires and fireworks, glittering masks, pagan rites, and Dionysian revelry—contained, in the final scene, by a Catholic midnight mass.[48] The ceremonies begin with the awakening of the spirits of the woods, the wild meadow, the sown field, and fire, who lead a wild parade through the narrow village streets. Tonio arrives just in time to take his ordained place as Rauhnacht King and choose a bride from twelve virgins dressed in glittering masks and shiny gowns. He recognizes and selects Barbl from the twelve and leads her from the hall to the bawdy chortling of the onlooking villagers. The scene cuts to Tonio and Barbl running through the woods outside the village, where they remove their masks and exchange a chaste kiss. Meanwhile, the solstice celebration reaches a fever pitch, visualized in trick photography: wild dancers are double exposed against flames, pyres, and masks, while shadowy figures run between the flaming pyres holding torches. The kiss signals an end to this rowdy excess, which is tamed by the powers of order — represented by the appropriate coupling of Tonio and Barbl and the transfer of festivities from the streets to the Catholic church. One by one, the villagers remove their masks and enter the chapel, signifying the victory of Christian piety over the raw passions of pagan carnival. The film ends as Tonio and Barbl walk through dense clouds of incense up the main aisle to the altar. With pious expressions, they bow their heads in reverent prayer before an immense statue of the Virgin Mary, backlit with candles. The camera zooms in on the altar and the Virgin, and the shot dissolves in a vision of heavenly clouds.

The happy ending that turns pagan rite into Catholic ritual recapitulates the supposed historical evolution of German Christmas from solstice worship to Christian celebration. From Tonio's spiritual awakening in New York, sparked by the sight of a mask and the sound of a gong, to the final kiss of the village couple — all has been accomplished through the mystical powers of the holiday. In contrast to decadent New York, the pristine Tyrolean village provides spiritual and material sustenance for its members, as blood-and soil-rituals revitalize the Volk community. Tonio's kiss with Barbl, set in the snowy forest during the winter-solstice festival, evokes a native passion that is quite unlike the kiss given by the modern Lilian in her wealthy father's New York mansion. By rejecting Lilian, Tonio's sexual energy is transformed into a spiritual force that serves the Volksgemeinschaft; he rejects the seductive but wasted pleasures of modern capitalism. In the end, the film portrayed a tantalizing vision of the organic ground of Christmas in the Third Reich, in which the false pleasures of modernity and immodest sensuality are erased by the authenticity of primitive celebration.[49]

WINTER RELIEF

The vision of Nazi national community was realized in a more practical way in the annual "actions" of the National Socialist WHW (Winter Relief) campaign, which kicked into high gear in the holiday season. Touted by "Reich Bishop" Ludwig Müller as "living proof of the new spirit of a new era," the WHW was a quotidian and, for many, welcome aspect of People's Christmas in Nazi Germany.[50] By the mid-1930s, the WHW was the only officially sanctioned charity agency (with the exception of the German Red Cross), and the pressures applied on religious and other aid organizations exemplified the Nazi strategy of Gleichschaltung, or "coordination" — the restructuring of existing groups and institutions to conform to the dictates of National Socialism. Gleichschaltung transformed social policy as well as institutional structures. The ideas behind Winter Relief explicitly challenged Christian, liberal, or socialist philosophies of charity, which held that a common sense of humanity should inspire aid to the needy. Nazi welfare, to the contrary, was meant only for those deemed capable of making a positive contribution to the "biological legacy" of the German Volk. The public face of the WHW campaign focused on volunteerism and inclusion in ways that implicitly reinforced this racial ideology, and the refusal to extend WHW benefits to Jews after 1935 clearly revealed the intent behind Nazi narratives of belonging.[51] The campaign nonetheless brought an attractive set of symbolic and material rewards to broad strata of the population, as long as they were "Aryan." Campaign publicity like the one-page photo essay from the *Leipziger Illustrirte* published in December 1936 (Figure 5.4) lent radicalized Nazi welfare policy the sentimental appeal of conventional Christmas charity.

A nationwide network of district branches, overseen by the *National-sozialistische Volkswohlfahrt* (National Socialist People's Welfare, or NSV) in Berlin, made Winter Relief an unavoidable part of public life during the holiday season. Local NSV and WHW block captains and volunteer assistants organized aggressive publicity campaigns and collected and distributed donations in cash and kind. Official statistics put the number of volunteer staff between 1.1 and 1.4 million, while scores more donated and received "gifts" of food, heating supplies, clothes, money, and Christmas trees. Members of the Nazi women's organizations, the HJ, and the League of German Girls staffed collection points at outdoor festivals and street corners. HJ *Pimpfe* ("lads") stood at busy intersections shaking WHW collection cans, which themselves became icons of the Christmas season. They waved banners, sang songs, and acted out short skits that praised contributors and ridiculed "petit-bourgeois *Spießer*," the "philistines" who hid their pocketbooks as they walked past.[52] According to internal NSV documents, street collections raised anywhere from 9 to 19 percent of the agency's annual budget, but the symbolic value of the public drives, especially the Christmas collection, was far greater.[53] Christmas was the most important and highly publicized "action" in the annual Winter Relief schedule, when the vision of mutual responsibility included all members of the national community, from party leaders to the most anonymous Volksgenossen. Newsreels showed women handing out WHW badges in sidewalk collecting campaigns and HJ and uniformed SA men delivering Christmas trees and WHW packages to grateful recipients.[54]

WEIHNACHTEN
IM WINTERHILFSWERK

Die Geschenke des Weihnachtsmanns
werden den freudestrahlenden Kindern von NSV.-Schwestern
während der Christbescherung übergeben. (Phot. Bittner.)

Die Weihnachts-
päckchen des
Winterhilfswerks
werden gefüllt und ver-
sandfertig gemacht. Hier-
für leisteten die Ange-
stellten der NSV.-Ver-
teilungsstelle wöchentlich
an zwei Tagen zwei Stun-
den freiwillige Mehr-
arbeit. (Phot. Scherl.)

Links:
Auch die
traditionellen
Christstollen
gehören zu den Weih-
nachtsgaben der Winter-
hilfe. (Phot. Bittner.)

Rechts:
Aber das ist eine
Überraschung!
Eine freiwillige Helferin
bringt den Weihnachts-
baum und die Gaben-
pakete ins Haus.
(Phot. Scherl.)

Glückliche Kinder mit ihren Geschenktüten,
die ihnen bei der Weihnachtsbescherung einer SA-Standarte überreicht wurden. (Presse-Bild-Zentrale.)

Die unbekannten Helfer,
die in ihren Sammelbüchsen die
Scherflein für die Winterhilfe zu-
sammentragen. (Phot. Bachmann.)

Denke an die weniger bemittelten Volksgenossen,
gib, damit auch sie ein frohes Weihnachtsfest feiern können!

FIGURE 5.4

The many faces of the WHW. "Christmas and the Winter Relief," *Leipziger Illustrirte
Zeitung*, 10 December 1936. (Courtesy of the collections of the Rare Book and
Manuscript Library of the University of Illinois at Urbana-Champaign)

Press reports claimed that the WHW ensured that "no German will freeze or go hungry"—the central slogan of the 1933 campaign—and showed that "the entire German people have become one great family."[55]

Despite the unavoidable door-to-door collections, forced payroll deductions, surveillance by NSDAP block wardens, and the threat of imprisonment for failure to contribute, propagandists could claim with some justification that they had "improved" on the Weimar-era welfare state by energizing the collective spirit of the masses. Internal reports showed that national Winter Relief campaigns enjoyed high levels of participation and effected an impressive redistribution of goods and personal resources. The WHW of 1933–34 collected over 358 million reichsmarks, three times more than the emergency drives in the final years of Weimar (also called "Winter Relief"), which totaled 97 and 91 million reichsmarks in 1931–32 and 1932–33, respectively.[56] Those who donated to the holiday campaigns received a small paste or wooden badge in the shape of a Christmas decoration, and campaign workers passed out millions of them. For the Christmas campaign of 1936 alone, WHW district leaders ordered 18 million badges from the NSV central office (the total population of Germany was about 67 million).[57] Even the numbers of free Christmas trees distributed nationwide was proudly listed in Winter Relief annual reports (741,436 in 1934–35 and 695,681 in 1935–36).[58] As one reporter enthused, the "inner emptiness and hopelessness" of Weimar-era Christmas charity had been replaced by a "beautiful, wonderful feeling" of collective concern for the humble "people's comrade."[59] Propagandists clearly exaggerated the success of Winter Relief, but poor Germans benefited from the campaigns. Even the underground agents of the Social Democratic Party in exile (the Sopade), who complied and published reports on popular opinion in Nazi Germany that were highly critical of state-sponsored activities, recognized the way the WHW generated support for the regime. Sopade agents regularly acknowledged that the annual WHW Christmas campaign was not only a publicity stunt. According to an extensive Sopade report from 1934, Germans in some districts expressed satisfaction and praised the efforts of the Nazis. For many, a WHW "gift" was a vital source of sustenance. In one Bavarian town, the free WHW Christmas trees delivered by Nazi storm troopers made an especially good impression when given "without prejudice" to former Marxists, confirming the general thrust of Nazi propaganda claims.[60]

In other districts, reactions to Winter Relief were decidedly mixed; popular approval depended on the competence of local organization. Workers complained bitterly about the failures of the charity drive, joking that the acronym WHW stood for *Wir Hungern Weiter!*, or "we're still starving!"[61] Disgruntled "people's comrades" revised the campaign's central slogan. The official line promised "no one will starve, no one will freeze"; vernacular voices joked "no one will starve without freezing."[62] Strong-arm collection tactics, corruption, and the ad hoc distribution and quality of WHW benefits undermined the drive's appeal. Rumors circulated that donations paid for NSDAP parties, such as Hitler's Christmas celebrations with his favorite SA troop in Munich. The authorities discouraged outspoken criticism. After asking recipients about the quality of their Christmas handouts, a policeman in Essen reported that "because of their answers . . . most of those who received gifts are ripe for the concentration camp"—a blunt reminder of the repressive apparatus that ensured public compliance with WHW campaigns and People's Christmas celebrations.[63] Jokes and rumors, informal complaints, and irritation with the uniformed SA men who solicited door-to-door for donations illustrate the disappointments of the WHW campaign and, at least for some, the scramble for material well-being masked by upbeat National Socialist propaganda. Complaints also suggest that numerous citizens depended on state provision of the material goods necessary to enjoy the "Christmas spirit."

Through the auspices of Winter Relief, Germans experienced firsthand the "really existing Volksgemeinschaft," with its dubious opportunism and incomplete social leveling.[64] Yet even when the WHW made promises it could not fulfill, the vision of a community of German "Aryans" engaged in providing "self-help" for the disadvantaged was partially realized in the Christmas campaign. Participation in a WHW campaign, either as benefactor or recipient, involved a public performance of consent to regime agendas that blurred racial ideology, familiar forms of holiday charity, and community spirit. Despite complaints and problems, the campaigns generated enthusiasm, mass participation, and general gratitude.[65] Attempts to remake private festivity and colonize the domestic "spirit" of the holiday season met with more ambiguous results.

THE SPIRIT OF THE GERMAN HOME

In his response to an ethnographic survey on Christmas traditions undertaken in 1956, an unusually frank school administrator from Westphalia explained that "in the beginning National Socialism made a halting attempt" to preserve the traditions of the family Christmas, but because of their defeat, "it wasn't carried out." Since then, he complained, "family celebration has been degraded into the simple giving of presents and the mother has been dethroned."[66] Such remarks are as revealing as they are rare: Germans seldom expressed open admiration for the values explicit in Nazi celebration in the postwar years. Yet the Nazi Christmas had much to offer. As the administrator recognized, the remade holiday promised a return to middle-class respectability and family values and symbolized "the emancipation of women from the women's emancipation movement," as Nazi ideologue Alfred Rosenberg famously put it.[67] The family festivities promoted by the Nazi intelligentsia valorized the public life of the Volksgemeinschaft over individual privacy and handmade goods over mass-produced commercial kitsch. They were relentlessly Nordic (despite official attempts to limit the holiday's cultlike aspects) and tacitly—when not avowedly—anti-Semitic. Though Nazi celebration at times clashed with Christian observance, Christmas was an effective example of what historian Adelheid von Saldern calls the "apparently productive synthesis between the 'public' and the 'private'" that typified everyday life in Nazi Germany.[68] In short, the choice to observe features of a "brown" Christmas let Germans celebrate the dictates of the racial community in the privacy of their own homes.

The Nazification of the family Christmas was primarily women's work. As pedagogy expert Auguste Reber-Gruber put it, the German mother was the "priestess" and "protector of house and hearth," and under her moral and physical direction, traditional family holidays would "bring the spirit of the German home back to life."[69] Another expert on "women and tradition" suggested that women naturally understood the importance of the "new Christmas" because they were "anchored more deeply than the man in the native soil of authentic national character."[70] Women's holiday preparations, which required feminine creativity and a talent for *Bastelei* (handicrafts), had "eternally German" meanings that resonated with the cult of sentimental Nordic nationalism. Lighting candles on the Christmas tree, according to folklorist and women's writer Dora Hansmann, created an atmosphere of "pagan-demon magic" in the home, inseparable from deep feelings of "Germanness." Mothers and children could help revitalize German culture by making homemade decorations like "Odin's Sun Wheel," or by baking holiday cookies shaped like a loop (a fertility symbol) or a "Sig-rune: the sign of struggle and victory."[71] "Take care of the old Christmas traditions," one holiday pamphlet admonished. "They belong to you like the air you breathe, like the water you drink, like the song you sing. With them you honor the entire Volk!"[72] Professor and propaganda ministry functionary Wolfgang Schultz declared that everyday objects had profound historical/racial meaning, and one could recognize a National Socialist by the way he (or more likely she) decorated the home: "Instead of hanging junk on the tree, we hang shaped cookies, the forms of which are still preserved in our customs. They are cut from dough and sprinkled with sugar, taking the form of deer, swans, eagles, squirrels, horses, fish, branches, etc." Even an item as banal as the Christmas-tree stand took on heightened connotations. Schultz reminded his readers that the proper stand was handmade, not store bought, a "beautifully carved . . . family heirloom" shaped like a "Yule wheel," with decorative Germanic runes that "symbolize[d] the closed circle of our lives and of time, the year and the months." It went without saying that these organic traditions were reserved for "racially pure" Germans.[73]

Committed National Socialists took a dim view of the wasteful nature of mass consumption and consciously reshaped consumer practices—always contested in the holiday season—to conform to the ideology of the racial state. Propagandists laid claim to the emotional charge of holiday giving and redefined the Christmas gift to express a distinctly fascist mode of consumption. "In the last years the custom of gifting has become an anti-custom," explained one Nazi tract. "[I]t has made the hearts of humanity more empty." The best gifts were handmade, crafted by members of the family circle gathered at home on cold December nights. Friends and family could yet find a real "kingdom of riches" if they remembered the "old-new myth of trust in nature and human community."[74] If one did have to purchase gifts, according to the "Ten Christmas Commandments for the German Housewife" from 1934, shopping should provide joy not just for the recipient, but also for the Volksgenossen "who earn their bread from producing Christmas presents." The careful purchase of toys made in Germany and decorations handcrafted by suffering artisans in the Erzgebirge and the Thuringian Forest would "give out streams of joy and love, and you and yours will be happy in the holy consciousness of your solidarity with the Volk." Autarky was wrapped in all the sentimentalism holiday discourse could muster, though attacks on the "foreign goods that were swamping the German market," such as "foreign powders, perfumes, and so on," were quite explicit.[75] By 1935 the mail-order Christmas catalog of a large department store could feature a sticker assuring customers that "the *Kaufhof* has been taken over by an Aryan!," pasted over the cover drawing of a fair-haired mother wrapping Christmas presents. In effect, the profits generated by holiday shopping were meant to help build a specifically "German capitalism" as an alternative to the class bias of socialist leveling or the free-market economics of liberal mass consumption equated with Jewish "decadence," Americanism, and feminism. Private, individualized acts of holiday shopping thus naturalized the exclusions of the racial state and reinforced the social death of German Jews.[76]

Shopping at "brown" Christmas markets and trade fairs let Germans spend their holiday budgets in an appropriate environment that supposedly supported the small shopkeeper or handworker victimized by Germany's flagging economy. Nazified craft fairs around the nation promoted "German" handicrafts, such as handmade ornaments, Nativity scenes, and baked goods. This "native" holiday trivia had the appeal of authenticity; better yet, its purchase supported needy "people's comrades," not Jewish commercial interests. At the "Brown Christmas Trade Fair" in Lübeck in 1933, one of many sponsored by the Ministry of Propaganda in the first years of Nazi rule, local shop owners and artisans rented stands to promote their holiday wares in an atmosphere that mixed festivity, commercialization, and redemptive nationalism. Long lists of participating vendors, from ironsmiths to electronic appliance stores, show that such attempts to boost the economy—to sell "German goods to create a strong and healthy German Folk in an independent German state," as one Nazi Party bureaucrat put it at the opening ceremony—met with broad participation.[77] This direct appeal to economic as well as ideological interests was typical of the new Christmas spirit championed by the party. Access to consumer goods and to their practical and symbolic benefits, as Victoria de Grazia concludes, was limited to those deemed able to contribute to the "health and dignity of the racial body."[78] Full faith in Nazi racial ideology was hardly necessary to enjoy the festive mood at the Christmas market or purchase gifts at "brown" Christmas trade fairs. Participation nonetheless supported the "German capitalism" promoted by the regime.

We will never know how many Germans baked rune-shaped Christmas cookies or bought Christmas gifts at "racially correct" Christmas fairs, but these everyday activities are worthy of serious consideration. Contrary to assertions that Germans celebrated Christmas in a domestic niche impervious to Nazification, family celebration opened private life to ideological penetration. The Christmas memories of Hermann Glaser—part of the "uncanny idyll" of his childhood under National Socialism—reveal the subtle way Christmas merged ideology and consumption in the private sphere. At

Glaser's friend's house, the presents under a large tree included Winter Relief badges, the receipt for a payment on the family Volkswagen, and an anti-Semitic tract by Julius Streicher, the notorious Nazi bigot.[79] To the consternation of religious leaders, Germans sang a number of Nazified carols, which combined the pathos, and often the words and melodies, of older songs with ideologies of blood and soil; Baumann's "Glorious Night of Shining Stars" was so popular that it could still be sung in the 1950s as part of an ordinary family holiday.[80] The kitschy commercial trivia of domestic celebration likewise merged with fascist symbols. Home decorations featured Nazi insignia, including swastika-shaped Christmas tree lights or chocolate SA or SS men.[81] The popularity of sentimental National Socialist knickknacks is revealed by party efforts to enforce a "law for the protection of national symbols" after 1933, which banned the "misuse" of Nazi symbols, including various forms of Nazified Christmas kitsch.[82]

Internal reports on public opinion compiled by the Nazi Security Service (*Sicherheitsdienst*, or SD) and circulated at the highest levels of the Nazi government tend to confirm the popularity, or at least the acceptability, of the Nazi holiday. At times, the SD noted, people worried about shortages of essential goods, despite government attempts to get extra rations on the market in time for Christmas.[83] But more often, according to the SD, Germans approved of official holiday entertainment and greeted annual holiday speeches from Hitler and Goebbels with particular enthusiasm.[84] Reports on popular opinion in Nazi Germany compiled by underground agents of the Sopade concurred. Agents repeatedly expressed surprise at the effectiveness of Christmas propaganda and wondered why discontent with shortages, so deeply felt in a time of celebration, did not translate into direct political action.[85]

The surviving "activity and mood reports" of the National Socialist Women's League (NSF) offer further insight into the permeable boundaries of private celebration. The remarkable number of female volunteers in the NSF and its satellite organizations in the mid 1930s—about 11 million, or one-third of Germany's 35 million women—gives some indication of the potential for the adoption of remade domestic rituals.[86] The NSF was organized according to the top-down "leadership principle" used by Nazi administrative organs, and directives from Reich women's leader Gertrud Scholtz-Klink in the central office in Berlin instructed NSF leaders across the nation to expend extra effort during the holiday season. In part, Christmas was the time for National Socialist women to think of others: the arrival of winter "closed the great ring of the community of fate," and Scholtz-Klink urged women to "take up the struggle against need."[87] NSF volunteers readily answered the call. They staffed Winter Relief drives for their neighbors and organized special collections of books, household goods, and cash for needy *Auslandsdeutsche* (ethnic Germans in foreign territories). NSF women sponsored exhibitions with holiday themes, put on school plays, organized Christmas markets, and held "pre-Christmas" holiday celebrations for youth and women's groups; they also ensured that the holiday issues of the national press regularly featured articles on German Christmas customs, "simple and inexpensive" holiday preparations, and "practical suggestions for handicrafts."[88] Christmas was clearly a peak moment for symbolic and practical action in the "special female public sphere," described by von Saldern as "a relatively autonomous field of activity within the general framework of National Socialist values and norms."[89]

In line with Nazi assumptions about gendered separate spheres, NSF members remained primarily responsible for Nazifying Christmas at home. In November 1936, Scholtz-Klink sent district leaders across the nation instructions about the "special task" that faced women during the holiday season. She warned NSF members against undertaking too much public activity at Christmastime: "So-called Christmas celebrations of the most varied groups and clubs" propagated "kitschy festive forms," while *Reklamemacherei* (advertising swindles) had turned the holiday into "a pure business." Good Nazi mothers should instead concentrate on their families. If mothers helped children make presents and decorations at home, told stories, and sung songs, Scholtz-Klink concluded, "the celebration will create an authentic community of experience (*eine rechte Erlebnisgemeinschaft*)." A lengthy list of appropriate story- and songbooks—and other prescriptive texts for games, family celebrations, and homemade gifts and decorations—followed. The list drew on traditional as well as Nazified holiday texts; all were meant to contribute to the larger goal of "turning all love and energy towards the family celebration."[90]

The instructions were clear, but the collapsing boundaries between Christian customs and Nazi inventions troubled German women. Scholtz-Klink had to remind NSF women that, though Christmas had important religious aspects, it was in the end a "German celebration . . . rooted deeply in German nationality and customs."[91] Shaping a "racially correct" celebration was nonetheless a difficult task. Heavy-handed holiday propaganda clearly alienated potential supporters. As an underground Sopade agent wrote in an extensive report on Christmas in 1938, "the more extensive the official celebration, the greater the people's self-awareness."[92] Divided allegiances cut both ways. In 1936 a letter from one NSF district office noted that loyal cadres experienced "much doubt and discontent" when confronted with the question of whether "convinced National Socialists" could observe the holiday with Nativity plays and Christian carols. Committed NSF members had difficulty finding Nazi Christmas books and other holiday articles in stores that still primarily sold conventional Christmas goods.[93] Yet district NSF leaders reported that attempts to avoid traditional carols or sing "very tasteless revisions" at party festivities angered women who still held Christian beliefs, and clergy of both denominations took advantage of the confusion. Christmas observances organized by the *Herrn Pfarrer* (the gentleman pastor) gave mothers strong incentive to send their children to church, where they were swayed by religious "propaganda." To counteract this influence, Scholtz-Klink ordered all local women's leaders to closely monitor youthgroup activities in the holiday season.[94] In some cases, local NSF leaders had forced members to either resign from the church or quit the women's group, and Scholtz-Klink warned that Protestants—particularly members of the Confessing Church, the breakaway group that resisted the German Christians and asserted the church's autonomy from the Nazi state—could use the harshness of such tactics to undermine support for National Socialism. An NSF group leader in Düsseldorf-Benrath complained that both confessions had used Christmas to promote their respective women's groups, and that Catholic clergy had threatened to excommunicate women who joined the NSF. For fear of evoking "intense conflicts and resistance" among local women, she had not distributed NSF guidelines for Advent celebrations and Nativity plays. Another local leader reported that confessional conflicts had led women to join opposing camps, boycott NSF meetings, and ignore WHW collection campaigns. The Volksgemeinschaft, she noted sharply, was "falling out over the religious struggle."[95]

CHRISTMAS BETWEEN CHURCH AND STATE

While Nazi propagandists successfully encroached upon domestic celebration, their efforts to use Christmas to blur the boundaries between religious and national identities exposed the awkward juxtapositions at the core of National Socialist political culture. Reich minister of church affairs Hans Kerrl captured the contradictions in his 1936 Christmas address when he asserted: "'in these days' Adolf Hitler will be everything for the Germans that

Christ was for humanity 'in the old days.'"[96] German Christmas had long been open to collaborating and often competing religious, political, and national impulses, revealed in the affinities between modern Protestant piety and Prussian-German nationalism, the popular recognition of the links between pagan and Christian observances, and the quick turn to war theology in the First World War. All foreshadowed Nazi attempts to use Christmas to construct a *Volkskirche*, or "people's church," in the Third Reich.[97] Nazi believers, however, exceeded these precedents, and the resulting tensions turned the holiday into an open site of negotiation and contest. Christmas celebrations became the focus of a complex, multilevel debate centered on the relationship between church, state, and society, and the debate was productive, insofar as it produced different and competing versions of the holiday. Party cadres, neopaganists, Catholic and Protestant churchmen, and German Christians—the anti-Semitic, pro-Nazi Protestant splinter community founded in 1932—worked to mold Christmas to their own agendas. The results took the holiday to radical, but in some ways predictable, extremes.

The revised holiday promoted by the German Christians epitomizes the religious and political conflict at the core of Christmas in the Nazi years. Their attempts to invent a "racially correct" holiday, as historian Doris Bergen suggests, expressed a determined yet paradoxical and often noxious effort to synthesize Christianity and National Socialism.[98] German Christian doctrine combined Nazi ideology with reformed and de-Judaized Christian traditions that cast nation, Volk, and race as gifts of God. In July 1933 the group won two-thirds of all votes cast in Protestant church elections across Germany and took control of all but three of Germany's regional bishop's seats. Their ascendancy was short-lived. That same autumn, the Nazi regime declared its official neutrality in religious matters and withdrew its support. In November a scandal ensued after a German Christian leader crudely attacked the Jewish influence on Christianity and the Old Testament at a mass rally in Berlin. The movement faltered, and by 1937, the Nazis had essentially abandoned its initial efforts to build a unified "Protestant Reich Church" around the German Christians. The movement's 600,000 members nonetheless continued to agitate for a Nazified Protestantism.

As Bergen shows, the Nazi-Christian liturgies propagated by German Christians "transformed the meaning of Christianity from a religion built around an act of atonement to a ritual empowerment of Nazi ideology."[99] Theologians like Wilhelm Bauer believed that revised Christian ritual, "cleansed" of its Jewish roots, could forge the bonds of a new Volksgemein-schaft. Rituals reached into the "dreamlike and imaginative" recesses of the unconscious, wrote Bauer in *Feierstunden Deutscher Christen* (Celebrations for German Christians, 1935), an extended instruction manual for the move-ment's doctrine and liturgy. "The spoken and sung word, music and read-ings come together," he asserted, "then the visual image that is awakened in us through the word and reading moves us further, and rhythm and sound opens the soul to the reception of God's truth."[100] For Bauer and other Ger-man Christians, "God's truth" meant the "Germanization of Christianity," a process supposedly begun by Luther. To continue this work, the church should purge Judaic influences from Christian theology and texts, excise "Jewish" psalms from the Bible, and replace "Jewish" names and terms in prayers and hymns with German-Nordic equivalents. "The people of Is-rael," Bauer suggested, should be renamed "the people of God"; Jerusalem and the biblical cedar of Lebanon could be called "the heavenly abode" and "the pines of the German woods."[101] The script for Bauer's "Advent Celebra-tion" revealed the results of this doctrinal revisionism. The "Germanized" liturgy included a vaguely rendered version of the Bible story of the birth of Jesus that omitted all reference to Bethlehem and the names Joseph, Mary, and Jesus; the text instead concentrated on a "morning star" arising out of darkness.[102] As such revisions suggest, German Christians struggled uneasily to remake familiar religious observances, and Christmas in particular was a consistent sticking point. The editor of *Das Volkstestament* (The People's Testament), a set of Gospels revised to meet German Christian criteria, felt compelled to explain his expurgated version of the birth of Jesus. "Legends were excluded," he wrote in an afterword. "Only the Christmas poetry of the Holy Night and the Wise Men from the East could not be left out because these stories have penetrated so deeply into the people's sensibilities. We have simply freed them of Jewish-Christian accretions."[103]

In practice, German Christian liturgy engendered a heterogeneous mix-ture of political and religious observances. The official Christmas celebration of the National Railway Authority (*Reichsbahndirektion*) in 1933, just as the group's influence began to wane, exemplified early attempts to shape a "posi-tive Christianity" that would conform to fascist ideology.[104] An enthusiastic crowd of railway workers, officials, and their families gathered in the Berlin Sportpalast around a thirty-foot-tall Christmas tree crowned with a gigan-tic swastika outlined in electric lights. They listened to railroad executives and NSDAP functionaries extol "Our Führer Adolf Hitler . . . the ruler of the people's fate" and watched a Christmas play entitled *Under the Sign of the Cross*. The play—written, directed, and narrated by the accomplished dramaturge Hans Batteux and performed at the end of the rally—further burnished Hitler's messianic cult and revealed the odd historicist fantasies of German Christian doctrine. The scenes moved from the manger in Bethlehem, the crusades, and the rise of Lutheranism to World War I and the Weimar years, when, according to Batteux's narration, the "gold devil" forced Germany to the brink of destruction. National Socialism saved the day, Batteux continued: "In dire need, God sent us the Savior, our Führer! Our glorious SA!" The play's final scene culminated in a "living picture" of a rather unconventional Nativity scene. Under an iconic photo of Hitler, Mary and Joseph gaze down on the baby Jesus, surrounded by the three Wise Men, peasants and Teutonic crusaders, and a ring of storm troopers in full uniform holding a swastika banner. A collective rendition of "Silent Night" and the sound of ringing church bells brought the rally to a close.[105]

Though nominally Protestant, German Christian adherence to racist ideologies of blood and soil led to ritual practices that differed only in degree from those advocated by neopaganists. Wilhelm Bauer's liturgies for summer-solstice celebrations or his "Forest Prayer for a Spring Morning," for example, focused on nature, race, and nation and hardly mentioned God.[106] National-racial ideology also penetrated more conventional liturgies. A German Christian Advent service held in Berlin-Tegel in 1935 brought together traditional holiday observances such as candles, Advent wreaths, and Christian carols with songs that evoked blood-and-soil motifs. The officiating pastor confirmed the connections between piety and politics when he asked celebrants to place a lit candle in their windows to show that "in this home, we pray for Führer and Volk!" A German Christian Christmas "Cantata," held in 1940 in the district of Westphalia, blended traditional carols, New Testament readings, Nordic myth, and Nazi propaganda and included liturgical incantations about "a race in German lands, a strong, upright, and blue-eyed clan."[107] Even the material culture of Christmas expressed the admixture of ideology and Christmas. An enterprising pastor in Marienberg-Saxony (in the Erzgebirge) advertised decorations made especially for Germany Christians, including a "Volksgemeinschaft" Christmas lantern that featured Nativity figures, workers, farmers, and soldiers that was designed to turn the holiday into a "celebration of enlightenment and Volk solidarity in Christ."[108]

The German Christians who had taken over the leadership of the Protestant Upper Consistory, or EOK, in Berlin in the church elections of 1933 at times found themselves in an ambiguous position in the church-state struggle over Christmas. Though they supported the agendas of the racial state, they also worked to protect the Christian aspects of Christmas from radical Nazification and de-Christianization campaigns. The EOK used its connections to parish clergy to monitor holiday observances on the local level and interceded with state authorities when Nazification went too far. Such negotiations had clear limits: EOK administrators did not so much dissent from Nazi policies as try to convince regime authorities that it was in their own interest to preserve at least some of the holiday's Christian aspects. In December 1936, in a typical exchange, Superintendent von Scheven of the Protestant Church District of Pomerania wrote to the district gauleiter's office to complain about the de-Christianized carols sung at official Nazi celebrations. Von Scheven cited several revised carols, including "Silent Night" and "From Heaven Above," which he claimed only began to represent the numerous examples sent to his office by concerned parishioners. The enclosed lyrics were not overtly political, but, as von Scheven carefully explained, they "discarded the original Christian content." References to candlelight, the winter solstice, and victory over darkness—without any mention of Jesus or God—caused "irritation among *christlich empfindenden Volksgenossen*" (people's comrades sympathetic to Christianity).[109] In this case, the gauleiter's office acceded to von Scheven's request. "I am in agreement with you," replied a district official, "that the revision of old church songs through the rewriting of the text must be stopped, if only for reasons of taste and stylistic sensitivity, and I have issued appropriate instructions for the District of Pomerania."[110] Similar concerns with the Germanization of kindergarten and grade-school Christmas celebrations circulated through EOK offices in 1938, reflecting the deep and conflicted investment in the holiday on the part of Nazi leaders and Protestant-German Christians alike.[111]

The church-state struggle over Christmas also brought Catholic and more independent Protestants into conflict with National Socialist authorities. The Nazi Security Service (SD) and Gestapo observed clerical activities and harassed clergy during the Christmas season, and Catholic and Protestant clergy alike used the popular investment in religious observance to resist state-sponsored de-Christianization campaigns.[112] According to SD surveillance reports, Christmas encouraged "intensified activity" on the parish level. Church attendance was "especially strong" during the holiday season, and priests and pastors used sermons, fliers, booklets, films, illegal charity campaigns, group meetings, and choir rehearsals to lure Germans away from NSDAP-sponsored celebrations. As one Nazi observer succinctly recommended, "We have to find a way to take on and castigate the behavior of the church and many of its clergy, without at the same time suggesting that the simple, Christian convictions of individual people's comrades are something contemptuous or anti–National Socialist."[113] Catholic church-men in particular worked against Nazi attempts to "paganize" the holiday. In his Christmas address of 1934, Pope Pius XI attacked the paganization of the holiday, and in 1936 he again spoke out against Nazi de-Christianization campaigns.[114] Leading German Catholics also challenged the connections between Nordic rite and Christmas ritual—as they had since the late nine-teenth century—though that hardly meant they rejected other aspects of National Socialism. While Cardinal Faulhaber's Advent sermons delivered in Munich in 1933 famously protested Nazi paganism, his remarks included anti-Semitic undercurrents; and Faulhaber readily turned to militarist rheto-ric and solstice symbolism in his Christmas sermons after the war started.[115] Leading members of the Confessing Church also remained committed to a traditional Christmas theology. Mainstream Protestant clergy struggled, however, with conflicted loyalties to church and state and the intersections between Christian and pagan rites—long recognized by Protestant theolo-gians as an important component of the German holiday.[116]

The tensions between tradition and invention, and between church and state, played out with particular force in carols and choral singing, central to both the Christian liturgy and the ideological dramaturgy of National Socialism. Lyrics and melodies were mutable and adaptable to the purpose at hand, and Nazi meetings and celebrations large and small invariably fea-tured collective singing—punctuated by the requisite "Sieg Heils" instead of "Amens."[117] The general intent of the Nazi intelligentsia regarding holiday music was clear. Carols were not simply Christian but *urdeutsch*, or "primor-dially German," wrote *Die Spielschar*, a Hitler Youth journal devoted to cel-ebration and leisure time. "This gives us the right to set them free from all that is not German.... Who would get excited if we changed some words to this or that Christmas song... so that it conformed to the understandings of our time?"[118] *Der Allemanne*, an anti-Semitic paper published in Freiburg im Breisgau, put it more bluntly: "Hardly anyone would miss our old, beloved Christmas carols, but the same applies to many other time-honored customs:

we want to fill the beloved form with new contents, in accord with our Welt-anschauung."[119] Authors such as Hans Baumann, Karola Wilke, Franz Biebl, and Gottfried Wolters wrote dozens of revised or entirely new songs to meet the requirements of "our time." Their compositions filled the pages of Nazi Christmas literature, such as youth-movement musician Ernst Moritz-Henning's 1937 collection *Nun brennen viele Kerzen: Neue Lieder um die Weihnacht* (Many Candles Are Now Alight: New Songs for Christmas).[120]

German Christians, for their part, found it difficult to entirely eliminate "Jewish" and Old Testament references in popular family carols. They none-theless "Germanized" familiar hymns and songs with alacrity. The Christmas songs in Bauer's *Feierstunden Deutscher Christen* included traditional hymns with new lyrics, such as a rendition of Friedrich Spee's muscular "Oh Sav-ior, Tear Open the Heavens," with the reference to "Jacob's house" omitted. Bauer's unabashed revision of the words to Luther's "From Heaven Above to Earth I Come" described (an unnamed) Jesus as a combat-ready "victorious hero" instead of—in Luther's words—"a tender child of lowly birth."[121] It was no doubt easier for dedicated German Christian composers such as the prolific Paul Schwadtke to write new songs, which could seamlessly merge national-racial, blood-and-soil images of fecundity with an evangelical mes-sage that owed more to nature worship than to Christianity. The lyrics to Schwadtke's hymn "Weihenacht" or "Sacred Night" included the verse:

> Christmas! Christmas! Blood and soil awake!
> Above you God's stars shine;
> Below you sing the seeds in the fields;
> Volk, from God's light and power; your honor
>   and heroism come.[122]

The title of the carol itself was an intentional misspelling or respelling (*Weihenacht*) of the normal German word for Christmas (*Weihnacht*), a common practice in neopagan circles intended to underscore the holiday's "Germanic" roots.

Attempts to revise lyrics to traditional carols met with stiff resistance from Christian clergy. "For some contemporaries, even the good old Ger-man Christmas songs are no longer German enough," wrote an anonymous critic in the *Katholisches Wochenblatt* (Catholic Weekly) in 1937. The author cited a number of insulting new lyrics for classic carols such as "Silent Night" and "From Heaven Above to Earth I Come." "Of course they do not expect us to dispense with the intimate, wonderful, old melodies," he continued, "but they expect us to substitute *other lyrics* for these melodies. This is in fact an outrage!" The work of Mathilde Ludendorff was especially insulting. The wife of the World War I general and cofounder of the neopagan Verein für Deutsche Gotterkenntnis (Society for German God Consciousness) had the gall to "Germanize" the opening lines of Johannes Falk's "O How Joyfully," so they read:

> Oh you joyful, oh you solemn, trusted
>   German Christmas time!
> Honoring elders, proud proliferation
> Rejoice, rejoice to be the German type.

The Ludendorffs' book *Weihnachten im Lichte der Rassenerkenntnis* (Christmas in the Light of Racial Knowledge), published in 1933, summarized the neopagan version of the holiday.[123] Such revisions were not the work of "mainstream" Nazis, however, and when revised lyrics strayed too far from the favorite standards, even committed party members rejected them. An editorialist writing for *Die HJ*, the newspaper of the Hitler Youth, expressed dismay with East Prussian nationalist Erika Thomy's version of "Oh Christmas Tree," which opened with the lines:

> Oh Christmas tree, oh Christmas tree
> how do you greet us Hitlerites?
> Do you affirm our German valor?
> Do you feel our German blood?

This went too far, even for Nazi stalwarts; according to the *Die HJ*, the lyrics slandered the "inviolable values of the folk."[124]

The Second World War exacerbated the church-state struggle over Christmas. United in the belief that Bolshevism and materialism presented a greater threat to popular faith than Nazism, clergymen used the familiar holiday rhetoric of nation, Volk, and family to encourage all Christians to support the war effort—even as they continued to challenge overt acts of de-Christianization through back channels. Few church leaders were as "brown" as the Catholic military bishop Josef Rarkowski, an avowed Hitler supporter, but his Christmas sermon to Catholic soldiers in 1939 shows how clergy of both denominations adapted the emotional and spiritual qualities of the holiday to sustain what he called the nation's "mission."

Christmas is a festival of the German soul. In every language there are words which work a special magic upon us in their very sound. To these blessed words belongs the word *Weihnacht*. . . . What do the French know—or the English—of our German Christmas? We are German and, as such, a Volk of particularly deep spirituality. Others will never understand this in us. Nevertheless, we are proud of it, and it is precisely at Christmas that we are made properly aware that, as Germans, we have a mission which the Lord God, the Ruler of societies and peoples, has given us. No one understands these thoughts better than the German soldier. He wields the weapons to defend the Vaterland, to keep the shield of honor of our German nation shining and unsmirched; and he will be especially conscious of this, his great responsibility, precisely at Christmas time when all the depths of the German soul are made manifest."[125]

Even prominent Catholic critics of National Socialism, such as Archbishop Faulhaber of Munich, used Christmas to rally laypersons for the war effort. As Nazi War Christmas newsreels showed bells ringing at well-known cathedrals throughout Germany, Faulhaber used his 1941 Christmas message to justify the confiscation of church bells in Munich as a sacrifice for "the precious Fatherland," necessary to assure "a happy conclusion to the war and the defeat of Bolshevism." Faulhaber's "fervent Christmas prayer" sanctified the war effort and "our brave soldiers" alongside calls "to remain ever loyal to your Almighty God, your Savior, and your Church!"[126] Protestant rhetoric likewise emphasized the connections between faith and war. As the Christmas "message" sent by the EOK to local parishes in December 1943 concluded, "Christmas speaks to us thus: *God is with us and we are with God; we will achieve victory!*"[127] As late as 1944, the EOK's "Christmas Greetings" proclaimed "the enemy . . . can never destroy the soul of our people, as long as belief in Christmas is anchored deeply in our hearts and holy duty drives us towards the mission of love, the love that today binds home and front in an incomparable readiness to sacrifice for the victory and life of the Volk."[128]

Though church leaders colluded publicly in the war effort, behind the scenes they sought to use the deep popular faith associated with the holiday as a safeguard against Nazification and secularization. Catholic clergymen at all levels of the church voiced opposition to the de-Christianization of Christmas and used holiday sermons, pastoral letters, and church group activities to reinforce popular piety. Catholics reserved particular venom for neopaganism and for Nazi ideologue Alfred Rosenberg, author of the radically anti-Christian *Myth of the Twentieth Century*. This "false prophet," warned the Catholic dean of the Cathedral of Münster in his Christmas sermon of 1940, "wrapped himself in the cloak of erudition which he before long had to lay aside, because his proofs revealed themselves to be untrue."[129] In his 1939 booklet *Christmas Pastoral Message for Children*, Conrad Gröber, the Catholic archbishop of Freiburg from 1932 to 1948 and an early supporter of National Socialism, reminded the faithful that the holiday celebrated the birth of Jesus, not the winter solstice; like other Catholic leaders, Gröber nonetheless walked a narrow line between loyalty to church and state. Despite the "pressing need for the Volk's unity" in times of war, he warned the faithful, "there are still people . . . who want to use a different message to encroach upon and spoil the joy of Christmas, as we Christians and Catholics celebrate it."[130] Catholic bishops used Christmas to speak out against de-Christianization campaigns, but they rarely critiqued the genocidal policies of the Nazi regime. As historian Guenter Lewy notes, when it came to protests against the Final Solution, churchmen "played it safe."[131]

Carols and hymns were again central to Catholic opposition to wartime de-Christianization campaigns. Leading clergy placed great hopes in what the bishop of Würzburg called the "beauty and power of attraction" inherent in religious music. Guidelines from the Fulda bishops' conference directed parish priests to use hymns and choral performance not just in religious services, but also to create a Christian "Volk culture" that would inform the everyday life of the laity, especially in rural areas. The spirituality embedded in sacred hymns, the bishops felt, was shared by all German Catholics. Church music could preserve faith and community spirit when military service separated individuals from their local congregation, and parish priests held music lessons and "singing hours" for church choirs and organized singing societies that performed during Advent and Christmas masses. To the dismay of Nazi observers, "vigorous singing work" thrived in Catholic communities.[132] And despite official harassment, Christmas Eve continued to record the highest levels of church attendance in the year.[133]

Like their Catholic counterparts, the German Christians in the EOK used Christmas to resist heavy-handed Nazi de-Christianization campaigns. Pastor and publicist Hermann Sauer laid out the rationale in his *Evaluation of the Church's Responsibilities and Possibilities during War Christmas*, written at the behest of the EOK in October 1939. According to Sauer's brief, *das alte Gut*, or "the ancient customs," of Christmas comprised "both the line of *least resistance* and *the greatest possibilities*" for the preservation of popular piety in a time of relative powerlessness. Christmas customs and songs expressed the "*popular spiritual dynamic* of the Protestant message," and Sauer argued that the struggle for Christmas had to be "*the order of the day.*" The proper presentation of the holiday could save the German Volk from a spiritual crisis, provoked by "anti-Christian propagandists," wartime atheism, and the general secularizing tendencies of modernization. Above all, Sauer saw potential in the "the personal character" of a Christian holiday service, in crucial contrast to the coldness of state-sponsored celebrations. "It is exactly the soulful connection between Volk and Church that needs to be confirmed, maintained, and in this serious hour of trial protected," he emphasized. "Without that personal moment, it will be annihilated instead of stimulated."[134]

Clearly influenced by Sauer's report, the EOK opened its campaign for Christmas in November 1939 when Friedrich Werner, president of the EOK and a staunch anti-Semite and German Christian, wrote to Hans Kerrl, the Reich minister for church affairs. Werner warned Kerrl that attempts to de-Christianize holiday rituals and carols in party-sponsored celebrations alienated many otherwise supportive Germans. "The systematic avoidance of the Christian content of Christmas," he asserted, was a "violation of the people's sensitivities" and an example of "artistic iconoclasm [that] shakes the spiritual confidence of our Volk." At the same time, Werner recognized that the party had a right to its own version of the holiday and proposed to Kerrl that 21 December (the winter solstice) be set aside as a "political celebration." Because "the displacement of Christmas by the Yulefest" divided rather than united the German people, Werner suggested that Christmas Day itself be reserved for religious and private family celebrations, tacitly sacrificing Christmas Eve, the holiday's peak moment, to the party.[135] Kerrl forwarded copies of Werner's letter to the NSDAP chancellery and to the Reich ministers of education, propaganda, and the interior, who apparently agreed with, or at least condoned, the EOK's proposal.[136] On 6 December 1939, army chief of staff Wilhelm Keitel issued detailed instructions for Christmas celebrations in the military. Balancing the needs of church and state, Keitel warned, required "the greatest tact" on the part of military officers. The order outlined a dual structure that closely followed Werner's suggestions. All soldiers would celebrate a National Socialist "German Christmas" centered on the Christmas tree, which Keitel termed "a primordial Germanic symbol of the tree of life." A special two-hour radio broadcast on 24 December, produced specifically for the army, would accompany this celebration. But troops could also participate in separate holiday services performed by a Catholic or Protestant chaplain on 25 or 26 December.[137]

The EOK took further steps to sustain popular Protestant faith through the *alte Gut* of Christmas. In accordance with Sauer's recommendations, the EOK issued directives to all member churches asking pastors, deacons, and lay assistants to undertake letter-writing campaigns for soldiers in the field. The EOK asked pastors to ensure that every parish member in service received a handwritten Christmas note and suggested that children, youth, and women's groups—and especially community choirs—make special visits to hospitals and military hospitals to sing Christian carols.[138] Clergymen mailed newly pressed phonograph records of Christmas music to chaplains at the front and paid "tactful" holiday visits to parents and families of soldiers killed in action.[139] The general intent, according to the EOK, was to "make evident particularly at Christmas time the connections between the Church and its members with an authentic and natural warmth."[140] In December 1940 the EOK also asked local communities to adopt a version of the *Quempas Songbook*, a collection of traditional Protestant Christmas songs that, according to Quempas promotional material, had "authentic and deep roots" in German folk tradition.[141] While the ultimate success of this plan is difficult to judge, reports on the local use of the songbook in church services and meetings during Advent and Christmas in 1943 show that most communities had adopted the text as instructed—though Allied bombing attacks, particularly in the western parts of Germany, made undertaking as well as reporting on collective church activities increasingly difficult.[142]

Committed Nazis complained about the influence of the Christian clergy at home and in the military. As one soldier reported to an SD informant, both churches flooded the troops with printed Christmas sermons and flyers meant to appeal to the psyche of the frontline soldier. "The blows against our world view are undertaken with all force and will doubtless be met with success," he griped. "What is the Party doing against it?"[143] Women in the NSF likewise worried about the persistence of Christian observance. They praised the Christmas issues of the *Frauenwarte*, the Nazi Party women's journal, and appreciated the journal's instructions for "arming" the household with homemade decorations and presents that evoked "the great meaning of the celebration." Not all interested families received the journal, however, or had time to make their own decorations. "People's comrades" in Berlin, Vienna, Stuttgart, Hamburg, Dresden, and Freiburg worried about the limited availability of Christmas materials suitable for Nazi forms of celebration. The stores were full of advent calendars, candleholders, decorations, and picture books, all of which displayed Christian symbols like angels, the three kings, and the Christ child; loyal Nazi mothers worried that their children would "for practical purposes experience Christmas in its Christian form."[144]

Competing claims on ritual practice between church and state over Christmas upset Christians as well. The files of the EOK include numerous letters from pastors and soldiers who condemned de-Christianized celebrations or praised church attempts to protect the religiosity of the holiday. First Lieutenant Eberhard Eilers wrote from Italy in 1944, and again from Brüggen in 1945, to assure the Protestant Council that his company Christmas celebrations included religious music. In 1945, Eilers wrote, carols were a "miracle" that preserved "the word of God."[145] Not all army celebrations were so pious. A wounded corporal recuperating in a military hospital in Züllichau reported that although authorities allowed patients to sing traditional carols, "none of the nine Christmas celebrations was Christian" and "the magic of the winter solstice was the sole feeble content of the celebration." Only a "handful" of his comrades professed a strong Christian faith, the corporal wrote; "most soldiers act passively" in the face of Nazification.[146] The EOK at times investigated such reports. Hospital authorities in Posen, they confirmed, had refused to allow a Christian service because they worried that SS men in the hospital might take offense.[147] After an investigation of military celebrations in Silesia, the EOK informed a local pastor that religious observance had been denied in a hospital because of Keitel's order, which prohibited clergy from making speeches during official military celebrations.[148]

The church-state struggle over Christmas had complex and paradoxical results. Christian observance offered ordinary Germans a real alternative to participation in Nazi ritual, at least when it was allowed. Singing a Christmas hymn, for example, could be an act of political dissent that expressed allegiance to the institutions of the church rather than the party, and to a set of German traditions that contradicted the NSDAP's claims to exclusive control over national belonging. At the same time, the fact that Christmas could be partially Nazified despite resistance suggests that Nazi ideological transformations effectively colonized at least some realms of popular religious practice. Even when the regime's ideological and institutional superstructures lay in ruins, the sparring continued: in April 1945 EOK councilor Friedrich Weineke wrote to Hans Fritsche at the Propaganda Ministry to complain about state censorship of an Easter radio address.[149]

"Germany arms itself again for People's Christmas, which will bring together all Germans on the front and in the Heimat on Christmas Eve," intoned the authoritative voiceover in a War Christmas newsreel from late December 1940. Scenes of boys from the Hitler Youth collecting toys for the WHW in a private home and a group from the League of German Girls making dolls for holiday charity followed, a visual testament to the sentimental links between home and front. The newsreel closed with footage from a flak position on the English Channel: a lone soldier standing watch greets the delivery of Christmas mail; descends into his bunker; opens presents of books, liquor, and tobacco; and celebrates lustily with fellow soldiers—a generic sequence in which individual duty is well-rewarded with gifts from home and comradeship at the front.[150]

Newsreels like "Christmas at the Front," "War Christmas," and "Christmas Preparations at the Front and in the Heimat" brought similar sights and sounds to the millions of Germans who went to the movies during the holiday season in the war years.[151] Soothing views of the German countryside, where peasants carried Christmas trees across mountain meadows covered with snow, or of domestic interiors, in which happy children smiled at beautiful mothers in the glow of the Tannenbaum, completed the picture of national celebration.[152] Yet the most fascinating action was at the front. Even in the most "barbaric" situations—in the tundra or taiga, in the desert or on board a submarine in the North Atlantic—a soldier found time to celebrate German Christmas. Newsreel images condensed these ideals in a repetitive sign system that reached an apparently receptive audience: from 1939 to 1945, the internal reports of the Nazi Security Service repeatedly recorded the positive response of ordinary Germans to War Christmas newsreels.[153] The *Innigkeit*, or inwardness, displayed in the pensive face of the lonely soldier standing guard, the feeling of community evoked by a manly celebration with comrades, all the various connections between home and front implied by the Christmas tree—these symbols of German "kultur" observed in an empty, war-torn landscape legitimated the colonial aspirations of the "master race" and testified to the sentimental links that bound Germans into a national and cultural community.

Newsreels were only one product of a vast propaganda machine that provisioned soldiers at the front and citizens at home with books and pamphlets, radio broadcasts, special journals, and countless press articles lauding the special qualities of German War Christmas.[154] The public face of the holiday returned to the myths and realities familiar from celebrations of War Christmas during World War I. Barracks parties demonstrated unity among the ranks but generated sadness behind the scenes. Touching examples of soldiers' longing and forbearance testified to the "golden bridge" that War Christmas established between front and Heimat. The willingness to celebrate joyfully under the worst conditions showed that "people's comrades" at home and soldiers at the front all stoically but cheerfully observed a wartime holiday.

The reality at home contradicted such upbeat images. A remarkably thorough SD report on Christmas on the home front in 1941 described a disgruntled population, worried about the availability of gifts, food, and coal. According to SD agents stationed across the Reich, Germans shopped earlier and much more quickly than in peacetime to avoid the shortages generated by the last-minute rush. Widespread fears about the limited availability and poor quality of gift items encouraged excessive and thoughtless spending. Shoppers reportedly cared little about price and spent freely and even recklessly on toiletries, household items, wine and spirits, and other practical gifts. Storekeepers used the opportunity to unload poor-quality stock. Books— not subject to rationing—were extremely popular, and in the rush to find presents of any kind, people bought books because of their weight or the appeal of their cover appearance, not because of the title or contents. Shoppers complained about rude sales staff and suspected that the best goods went to regular customers with close connections to shopkeepers. In big cities, retail staff overwhelmed by the crush of desperate shoppers had to close salesrooms or receive customers in small groups; in several cases, the police had to intervene to keep order, predominantly in tobacco and toy stores. Because of shortages, German newspapers ran pages of private ads offering used gift items for sale or exchange. Despite problems with shopping, reports from across Germany agreed that the special distribution of "emergency holiday rations" of coal and food met with "great contentment," though complaints from more than one housewife about receiving two eggs instead of the promised five testified to home-front deprivation.[155]

The response to holiday celebrations sponsored by mass organizations like the League of Nazi Women, the Hitler Youth, and the German Labor Front, which continued to promote a de-Christianized holiday, was likewise mixed. SD agents reported that "non-confessional" Christmas celebrations organized by the party had achieved their goal of "strengthening inner composure and the feeling of unity between home and front." Yet they often failed to purvey a "unified meaning . . . and a corresponding use of the standpoints and materials" provided by the propaganda ministry. While some Nazi festivities drew such oversized crowds that organizers had to turn away eager participants, others, particularly in rural areas, found little popular resonance. Ordinary Germans complained about the party's failure to choose a specific day for its Christmas celebrations and voiced confusion about the changing names given to the holiday—"People's Christmas, German Christmas, Third War Christmas, Yule Festival, etc." The SD concluded that such inconsistencies made it difficult to give official celebrations a truly festive character: "Party-organized celebrations could not become central for the population, but rather in most places still stood in the shadow of religious Christmas celebrations."[156] Radio propaganda—potentially broadcast to 15 million households with registered radio receivers—had similarly mixed results. Observations from all parts of Germany in December 1941 agreed that, though listeners enjoyed the Christmas *Ringsendung* (ring broadcast) and appreciated the serious tone of Goebbels's Christmas address, they still complained that the musical programs were not "Christmasy" enough. The SD recommended that in order to create an "authentic Christmas mood," future broadcasts should include Christian carols like "Silent Night" and "Lo, How a Rose E'er Blooming."[157]

The emergency winter-clothing drive for German troops on the east front, undertaken during the holiday season in 1941, further challenged the legitimacy of state-sponsored versions of War Christmas. Propaganda Minister Goebbels's claims that the donation of over 67 million articles proved "our certainty in victory" were exaggerated, but his conclusion that the drive was a great "collective deed" was not. The participation of millions of Germans, above all women and children, showed that party organizations could still mobilize the Volksgemeinschaft around themes of social solidarity, mutual help, and Christmas charity (Figure 5.5).[158] Yet the success of the clothing campaign masked undercurrents of dissatisfaction that would become increasingly apparent as the war progressed. The SD pointed out that doubts and questions had shaken popular confidence in the government. Germans wondered why it had taken the authorities so long to act on the army's clothing-supply problem, and the drive led some to question the veracity of propaganda newsreels that showed comfortably dressed German troops. Others wondered if donations would reach soldiers in a timely manner, safe from theft or misappropriation. Repeated radio ads calling for donations

FIGURE 5.5
Berlin schoolgirls pack Christmas "Gifts from the Führer" for
soldiers at the front, circa 1942. (© bpk Berlin 2009)

irritated some listeners, who believed that reports supposedly broadcast from
the front were staged. Later SD reports made it clear that many Germans
gave to the drive because of a sense of charity and personal duty. They cared
little for propaganda about the deeds of the national community and complained that "'way too much has been said about it.'"[159] Indeed, the SD concluded, the population's "unlimited faith in the organizational talents of the
Germans has for the first time received a decisive blow." For many "people's
comrades," the clothing drive was "almost shockingly sobering, though in a
positive sense," as they now realized the war was a "battle for life or death."[160]
It was clearly a mixed blessing for the regime that some Germans, in particular the "elder generation" who remembered the First World War, asserted
"with visible satisfaction that the third War Christmas presented a decisively
better situation than in e.g. 1916."[161]

The conjuncture of Christmas 1942 and defeat at the Battle of Stalingrad
left deep traces in the popular psyche. According to SD reports, as the holiday approached, the "people's comrades" waited "on the hour" for special
radio bulletins from the Volga front. Rumors about the possible encirclement of the German Sixth Army surfaced in the weeks before Christmas, as

doubts increased about the veracity of official news reports that described heroic fighting and the repulsion of Soviet attacks.[162] Goebbels's normally upbeat Christmas speech, broadcast each year on Christmas Eve, emphasized current difficulties and coming hardships. The propaganda minister had special words of consolation for German mothers. Over time, he asserted, "the hurtful wounds of today [will] become the honorable scars of tomorrow." War Christmas, as ever, epitomized the links between home and front. "How happy is the soldier out there, that his family lives in quiet security. That is what he fought for. He places his life on the line, so the lives of his Volk remains protected." In a rare concession to popular needs for spiritual guidance during the troubled holiday season, Goebbels concluded with a call on "the all-mighty" to protect Volk and führer and to ensure victory and a "better peace" for "tortured mankind."[163]

The infamous Stalingrad "ring broadcast" that followed the minister's speech provided listeners with a more gripping version of War Christmas. As in previous years, the 1942 holiday show lasted over an hour and featured a radio operator who purportedly exchanged holiday greetings with German soldiers on a variety of fronts. Troops from Stalingrad, Lapland, southern France, the Gulf of Biscayne, Leningrad, the English Channel, Zakopane, Crete, and other posts supposedly answered the call of the central station. Though the connections were faked on a sound stage in Berlin, the dramatic call-and-response format, complete with echoes, feedback, and fading signals, lent the show an aura of authenticity. For anxious listeners, the broadcast embodied Goebbels's metaphors about a "golden bridge" that linked home and front. The linkup with Stalingrad included the classic tropes of War Christmas, all presented with the drama of a "live" wartime broadcast. After five minutes of similar reports and greetings, the central station, responding to the "spontaneous wish of the comrades" stationed in the Crimea, led all posts in a rendition of "Silent Night" and signed off. According to the *Völkischer Beobachter*, the special holiday broadcast showed that "the miracle of technology has once again triumphed over space and time."[164]

The popular response to the dramatization of Christmas at Stalingrad and all the rest of the sentimental kitsch of the official War Christmas, SD agents reported, was fairly positive. As in previous years, the people's interest in political and military events decreased during the holiday season, as families tried to enjoy Christmas free from the burdens of war.[165] For Nazi leaders privy to the confidential SD reports, however, the news was decidedly mixed. Goebbels's Christmas speech may have "struck the right tone and spoke to

FIGURE 5.6

Workers at the Moabit Hospital in Berlin observe Christmas
in an air-raid bunker, 1944. (© bpk Berlin 2009)

the heart," but the warning of the struggle to come confirmed public suspicions that victory had been spoken of too easily in the years before.[166] As the minister intended, women were especially touched by the speech, though a housewife from Düsseldorf, a city bombed by Allied aircraft on a regular basis, expressed doubts about the "security of the homeland" cited repeatedly in the Christmas Eve address.[167] The voices of the soldiers from Stalingrad had merely shown listeners that, while rumors about the encirclement of the Sixth Army might be true, the troops in the city had not yet surrendered. The daily worries already noted in 1941 grew as the holiday neared, especially for women; confusion and complaints about the distribution of rations, including meat coupons and Christmas candles, dominated the reports. At the very best, the "numerous contributions" in radio and press, like Goebbels's Christmas Eve address, had succeeded in turning people's vision inward by "calling on a speechless, dignified, way to appeal to behavior and spiritual values."[168] Couching its impressions carefully but bluntly, the SD concluded that the crisis had prevented "the otherwise normal Christmas mood from appearing in the same measure as in previous years."[169]

In the last years of the war, constant shortages and attacks from Allied bombers made attempts to observe Christmas increasingly difficult (Figure 5.6). Some Germans in the greater Reich gave up the holiday altogether.

Others, like Frau E. L. from Innsbruck, found it impossible to celebrate despite their best attempts.

> The Christmas tree could only be lit for a maximum of five minutes because we were afraid, that if the alarm came, the lit tree would be in the room. So there was no real Christmas mood. On Thursday we had to go repeatedly into the air-raid shelter and were afraid of the same last night [Christmas Eve]. We ate our Christmas cake and other trifles very quickly. We were all eyes and ears for the anticipated alarm. We stayed awake until 11:30 in the kitchen, and then Erich slept in the only usable room. After 9:00 today, Christmas Day, we were on pins and needles all over again. About 10:30 the alarm. We sweated for two hours in the cellar. After an hour, another one and one-half hours of alarm. It was very warm, nine degrees above zero and anything but a Christmas mood.[170]

Though enthusiasm for celebration waned during the last years of the war, functionaries in the Propaganda Ministry stepped up efforts to promote increasingly radical ceremonial forms, which became more dogmatic and even bizarre as the war went on.[171] Official attempts to observe Christmas smacked of desperation. On 26 December 1942, for example, perhaps in response to complaints about missing Christmas mail, the German air force delivered 680 *Weihnachtspakete des Führers* (Christmas packages from the Führer) to soldiers at Stalingrad.[172] As late as 1944, Martin Bormann, the "Führer's deputy," ordered Gau and Kreis Leaders to make a special effort to give all families with children a Christmas tree because of its "powerful symbolic meaning" and its effect on the popular mood; shortages and problems with the rail system, however, meant that families without children and single Germans would have to make do with a single pine branch.[173] The party chancellery ordered local functionaries to ensure that servicemen refrained from expressing dissent at public Christmas celebrations; instead, they were supposed to set an example by proclaiming "Sieg Heil," singing the "songs of the nation," and raising their arms in the "German greeting."[174]

According to propaganda ministry directives, celebrations of what was now officially titled "German War Christmas" should focus on the "constant interchange between life and death, the great 'death and becoming'" supposedly exemplified by the laws of nature.[175] Attempts to popularize a new Christmas ritual based on the "cult of death" associated with World War I was promoted in any number of stories, songs, poems, and images, including a chilling drawing of a Christmas tree surrounded by soldiers' graves in the shape of the Iron Cross from the official German War Christmas book (*Deutsche Kriegsweihnachten*) published in 1944 (Figure 5.7). Author and poet Thilo Scheller, Reich Labor Service functionary and winner of the 1943 Hermann Löns Prize for literature, fleshed out a set of rites for German War Christmas in a number of propaganda texts.[176] In his poem "The Dead Soldiers' Homecoming," a classic example of the genre, soldiers return from the grave on Christmas Eve to visit the loved ones they left behind. While the poem tacitly acknowledges the suffering of bereaved German families, its dominant mood is one of forbearance and pride. The dead soldiers find satisfaction in the knowledge that they died for the fatherland and remain dedicated to the "eternal watch" they keep for the nation.

> One time a year, in the holy night,
> the dead soldiers abandon their watch,
> that they keep for Germany's future.
> They come home, to ensure that all is well.
> Silently they enter the festive room—
> one can hardly hear the tread of their hobnailed boots—
> they present themselves quietly to father, mother, and child,
> but they can tell, they are expected guests:
> A red candle burns for them on the Christmas tree,
> a chair stands for them at the dinner table,
> a glass glows for them with dark red wine.
> And with a joyful heart, faithful and gay,
> They join in the Christmas songs,
> On top of the picture with the steel helmet there on the wall
> is a pine cutting with a silver star.
> A scent of pine and apples and almonds fills the air.
> And when the Christmas tree candles burn to the end
> the dead soldier places his earth-encrusted hand
> Lightly on each of the children's young heads:
> We died for you, because we believed in Germany.
> Once a year, after holy night,
> the dead soldiers return to their eternal watch.[177]

Shortly before Christmas in 1943, "The Dead Soldiers' Homecoming" was reprinted in a Christmas propaganda booklet called *Light Must Return*, and Propaganda Ministry directives ordered party officials to distribute the

FIGURE 5.7

"They sacrificed themselves so that we can stand in the light." The War Christmas cult of death. (*Deutsche Kriegsweihnachten*, 1944)

booklet to the wives and mothers of fallen soldiers in personal visits. The poem also appeared in other publications, which encouraged mothers or widows who wanted to observe this revamped War Christmas ritual were encouraged to follow Scheller's suggestions and decorate a picture of the fallen soldier with a pine bough, set a place for him at the table, and light a single red candle on the Christmas tree.[178]

The effectiveness and popularity of these reworked wartime rituals, which linked deeply felt emotional vulnerabilities to the glorification of death, is difficult to gauge. Perhaps most Germans dismissed them as irrelevant, the callous products of desperate propagandists. Yet at least some contemporaries responded to such efforts. Placing candles on the graves of loved ones on Christmas Eve—particularly fallen soldiers—was a long-standing popular tradition, and these expropriated rituals thus dovetailed with familiar customs.[179] An SD report on the distribution of Christmas candles suggests that the commemorative rituals promoted by Scheller and others had some resonance. According to the SD, older single people and "war widows" felt the lack of candles particularly harshly, because private Christmas Eve "memory celebrations" to honor dead or "fallen" relatives required candlelight; without a candle, their Christmas "loses all its meaning."[180] Myths about the return of the dead on Christmas Eve reached back to Walter Flex's First World War Christmas poems and to sentimental nineteenth-century stories that had originally inspired a holiday cult of death, such as Hans Christian Andersen's *The Little Match Seller* (1846). Internal Propaganda Ministry reports from the last holiday of the war maintained that radio broadcasts of Goebbels's Christmas speech and the subsequent holiday "ring broadcast" continued to have a "most powerful moral effect" and helped wives and mothers come to terms with their "heavy sacrifices" and strengthened belief in "the struggle for the victorious end."[181] For their part, the clergy at the EOK remained confident that Nazification had little resonance: "With *these* means our opposition won't be able to cancel out the Christian message of Christmas," commented an administrator on a de-Christianized Christmas booklet in 1943. "This is demonstrated once again by the events of this year's celebration."[182] Another possible response to the regime's last-ditch attempt to promote a War Christmas cult of death survives in a Christmas joke that made the rounds in Berlin in the last years of the war: *Praktisch denken, Särge schenken* (Think practically, give coffins).[183]

Such witticisms were a far cry indeed from the Christmas address delivered by Goebbels in December 1933. The new "People's Christmas," the propaganda minister had then proclaimed, was "the most beautiful day of the nation [and] a bridge to a new community."[184] During the Third Reich, Nazi intellectuals and functionaries reworked familiar customs to invent a holiday that celebrated the ideologies of the racial state. From the militaristic campaigns of the Winter Relief to the most intimate family rituals, countless Germans had participated in Nazified celebrations. Capitulation, destruction, and occupation after 1945 exposed the criminal nature of the National Socialist "new order" and its holidays. Defeat called attention to the ambiguities of popular festivity in Nazi Germany, when singing a Christian carol, decorating the tree with solstice cookies, or shopping at a brown Christmas market became political acts. Yet the holiday's long-standing associations with social harmony, middle-class respectability, and material abundance survived the war and indeed proved quite useful in the decades that followed. After 1945, Germans replaced Nazi Christmas with other versions of Germany's favorite holiday, fabricating sanitized versions of the personal and collective past as an appealing foundation for new national solidarities.

Ghosts of Christmas Past

The birth of the Savior—throughout all the centuries for us Germans it is the most beloved celebration, the celebration that moves everyone deeply: young and old, men and women. No matter where in the world a German finds himself on Holy Eve—his thoughts make their way back to the homeland, to childhood, to his perhaps long-lost parents and brothers and sisters. This celebration awakens sensations, touches on values, on feelings, which have been shaken by the bustle and haste of our day and appear to have died out. But they are not dead, they are only masked by the pressure to work for ourselves and for those close to us. They are masked as well by the restlessness and the pleasure seeking of our time. When Christmas approaches, when Holy Eve is upon us, then these feelings, these values come back to life in us all.

—◦ Annual Christmas address, Chancellor Konrad Adenauer, 1955

"BUT IT'S CHRISTMAS, PEACE CHRISTMAS!" cries war criminal Ferdinand Brückner at the end of Wolfgang Staudte's *The Murderers Are Among Us*, the first feature film released in Germany after the Second World War. Produced in 1946 by the East German studio DEFA, this exemplary rubble film tells the story of Dr. Hans Mertens, a traumatized veteran who at the start of the film believes that "mankind is no longer worth saving." As he moves through the ruins of postwar Berlin, Mertens slowly recovers his sense of self-worth. He proposes marriage to his companion Susannah and begins to lead a normal life. First, however, he has to overcome the mental anguish caused by memories of the atrocities he witnessed in a small village in occupied Poland on Christmas Eve 1942. It was no coincidence that director/writer Wolfgang Staudte used Christmas to frame his protagonist's confrontation with the Nazi past. As Chancellor Adenauer asserted repeatedly in his annual holiday addresses, celebrations of "Holy Eve" awakened emotionally

FIGURE 6.1
Christmas miracle on the Ku'damm: gift-wrapped
Opel Kadett. (*Der Spiegel*, 22 December 1965)

loaded memories of lost loved ones and fragile spiritual values. The holiday encompassed a vision of wholeness for Germans coming to grips with their shattered past and present, determined to remake their history in whatever way they could. *Murderers* offered postwar audiences a prescient, almost uncanny reading of the main themes that would circulate through German Christmas in the postwar decades. Like Mertens, Susannah, and Brückner, Germans on both sides of the Iron Curtain used the holiday to regain a sense of stability in the crisis of the immediate postwar years, to manage memories of National Socialism, and to rebuild family lives after the brutalities of war. Politicians, leading clergymen, and ordinary citizens alike remade Christmas to deal with the exigencies of a Cold War world.[1]

The climax of *Murderers* uses War Christmas as a freighted backdrop for the requisite confrontation with the Nazi past. As Susannah and Mertens prepare a modest celebration on Christmas Eve 1945, a flashback reveals the cause of Mertens's distress. Three years earlier, his army unit had massacred over 120 Polish civilians on Christmas Eve, including women and children. Commanding officer Brückner had ordered the massacre, and, despite his best efforts, Mertens was unable to prevent the slaughter. In a scene clearly meant to shock contemporary viewers, the film shows Captain Brückner and his uniformed staff officers singing "O How Joyfully" around the candlelit tree—an image all too familiar from Nazi holiday newsreels—and then cuts to the bodies of the innocent victims felled by the firing squad. Christmas is the setting for atrocity, but also atonement. By chance, Mertens has met Brückner in Berlin after the war. The former captain is now a prosperous factory owner, an opportunistic "murderer among us" who has successfully hidden his criminal past. Now, overcome by a need to remake his own history, Mertens decides to take revenge in the "name of humanity." He abruptly leaves Susannah over Christmas dinner, takes his revolver, and walks through the Berlin rubble to Brückner's factory. Mertens observes Brückner presiding over his company Christmas party and draws his pistol to take revenge, but he hesitates as a frightened Brückner professes his innocence and invokes the spirit of Peace Christmas. Before Mertens can shoot, his fiancée, who followed him to the factory, pulls down his arm. In this final act of mercy, Mertens masters the Nazi past and recovers his humanity. The film ends with Brückner in jail, framed by a vision of a snow-covered graveyard, cross after cross recalling the victims of Nazism at the same time as Christ's birth and resurrection. "Peace Christmas," the film suggests, offers consolation and redemption, based on the human and Christian values at the core of the traditional holiday. Like many other films, novels, and memoirs from the 1950s and 1960s, *The Murderers Are Among Us* also used Christmas to portray the ironies of War Christmas under the Nazis. Mertens indeed prefigured a stock character in 1950s West German "war stories": the good soldier who sought to do his duty but was misled and betrayed by fanatical National Socialists.[2]

The ramifications of *The Murderers Are Among Us* went beyond calls to forgive the past and renew the social contract. The film was a *Lehrstück*, a didactic morality tale with socialist overtones, and the plotline gave audiences an early view of the way Christmas would play in Cold War socialist propaganda. The bourgeois pieties of the German holiday, *Murderers* suggested, lent a false sense of legitimacy to postwar opportunists and unreconstructed Nazis like Brückner, who stood in for other (West) German war criminals who had returned to the commanding heights of power. Contemporaries recognized the film's political ramifications. American and French occupation authorities refused to license the script, and its production under Soviet auspices hinted at its potential value as a propaganda piece. Upon its release in November 1946, a reviewer in the Western press was "annoyed" that the film "hung the liquidation of a village on the Christmas tree." A writer for the socialist *Berliner Zeitung* argued to the contrary: "This blood-soaked Christmas from 1942 somewhere in Poland was reality—and it still is!" The *Spandauer Volksblatt*, published under British license in the Berlin suburb, noted more soberly, and perhaps more realistically, that the audience measured the movie's success "less in loud applause than in the quiet and reflective emotions it evoked."[3] This range of views played out in the propaganda battles that dominated political appropriations of Christmas over the next fifteen years. In the Federal Republic (FRG), West Germans rebuilt Christmas to reflect the "traditional" values of liberal Christian democracy: faith, family, and free-market economics. East German socialists, for their part, looked back to the alternative holiday traditions shaped in the social-democratic culture of the German Empire and the Weimar years. Official celebrations organized by the Socialist Unity Party (SED) turned Christmas into a "socialist peace celebration" designed to evoke the egalitarian ethos of the Communist state and remind citizens of socialism's victory over fascism.[4]

The penultimate scene of *Murderers*, in which Mertens and Susannah celebrate Christmas together in the privacy of their rebuilt but still modest apartment, pointed to the everyday pleasures and material abundance that would drive national reconstruction in both East and West Germany in the postwar decades. Again, it was no mistake that Christmas framed the film's final scene. Christmas 1945 brought a still tenuous moment of joy, but the vision of the nuclear family made whole and enjoying some degree of material comfort pointed toward a better future. Across the 1950s and 1960s, the holiday measured personal and national prosperity in both Germanys, as each nation shaped a consumer regime appropriate for competing capitalist and socialist economies.[5] West Germans grappled with the effects of rampant consumerism on this cherished symbol of traditional Christian and family values, and East German efforts to channel the individualist material pleasures associated with the holiday into socialist agendas met with mixed success. In the 1950s, Cold War realities still framed a politicized and relatively modest holiday. By the 1960s, the consolidation of a society of consumer abundance on both sides of the Berlin Wall had undermined the appeal of politics and faith alike, as ever-broader groups found the joys of a "good German Christmas" in the private pleasures of mass consumption.

PEACE CHRISTMAS

On Christmas Eve 1945, "the church was overcrowded . . . as it had not been for a long time," remembered West German politician Josef Ertl. Refugees, displaced persons, and evacuees from former East Prussia helped fill to capacity the chapel in his Bavarian village. The crowd's mood was hushed but hopeful. "During the evening mass," Ertl wrote, "one became suddenly conscious of how the people felt. Here was a place where everything that had so torn this Volk apart on the inside—guilt, sin, but also human failure and human weakness—could all of a sudden be seen differently . . . that despite it all one found oneself together again in church, and that perhaps hope could again be recreated and faith not lost."[6] The first postwar holiday brought a moment of respite and reflection, as Germans searched for missing family members, "organized" holiday necessities on the black market, and made gifts from used matchboxes and empty thread spools.[7] Nostalgia for this unusual moment has grown in the subsequent decades. Museum exhibitions, television and radio specials, and memoirs return repeatedly to what contemporaries called *Friedensweihnachten*, or Peace Christmas. As the telling cover blurb of a collection of firsthand accounts titled *Christmas 1945: A Book of Memory* reads, "Germany lay in ashes, but despite everything, Christmas 1945 was again a celebration of peace, a celebration of hope. . . . The horror of the war belonged to the past, an unjust regime had lost its power, and the first halting attempts to create a democratic new order had become visible."[8] Recollections that focus on postwar deprivations, spiritual yearnings, and hopes for a better future no doubt capture the experience of many Germans in the first years after the war. They also tend to overlook the ongoing political appropriation of Christmas and the determined attempt to remake the holiday to suit the needs of reconstruction by religious authorities, West German politicians, and Allied occupiers.

The notes of forgiveness and redemption struck by Ertl echoed in the official discourse of West Germany's religious leaders. Leading clergymen re-Christianized Christmas in efforts to elide the Nazi past, reaffirm conservative values, and bring wayward parishioners into the fold. Despite all-too-common examples of accommodation and collaboration, Germany's Christian churches had survived the war with a reputation for resistance to National Socialism more or less intact, and they were well positioned to administer to West Germany's moral reconstruction. As the church reasserted its control over the holiday, clerics abandoned the militarist and pro-Nazi language of folk and fatherland that littered Christmas rhetoric during the Third Reich. By 1946 the Protestant bishop of Berlin had prepared new Christmas materials for distribution to local schools and parishes that were designed to overcome any remnants of Nazi "falsification" and "emphasize the true Christian character of Christmas."[9] Instructions for Advent sermons issued in 1945 by the Protestant leadership in Stuttgart maintained that the Christmas message embodied God's forgiveness and revealed the "mercilessness" of oversimplified judgments of guilt and innocence (that is, Allied accusations of collective guilt).[10] A similar missive, sent to parish clergy by the conservative bishop of Hannover August Marahrens, argued that Christmas was a celebration of God's promise of rejuvenation but failed to mention National Socialism or the bishop's own support for Hitler. "In other years," wrote Marahrens, "it seemed as if one could survive winter without the Christmas message. Today we know and we feel, that we—are dependent on the miracle of God's mercy!"[11] Here it seems that Marahrens spoke for both the German people and the Protestant clergy, whose complicity with National Socialism had been addressed but hardly resolved by the Stuttgart Declaration of Guilt issued by Protestant leaders in October 1945. Open engagement with the church's support for Nazi policies was in fact quite rare. As historian Matthew Hockenos explains, ordinary clergymen and conservative bishops, including Marahrens, Otto Dibelius, and Theophil Wurm, all "regularly employed empty exercises that did not require a serious working through of the Nazi past. Instead they drew on the crucifixion, suffering, and resurrection of Jesus Christ—images undeniably central to Christian teaching and thought."[12] Pleas for Christmas "mercy," issued from the chancellery and the pulpit, washed out sins of omission and commission alike in waves of pious amnesia.

In the Manichean atmosphere of the early Cold War, the re-Christianized Christmas became a prominent weapon in West German propaganda, a symbol of belief in God and Christian morals as a bulwark against the secular evils of Communism. Historian Dianne Kirby rightly asserts that the Cold War was "one of history's great religious wars." For embattled West German churchmen seeking to erase their own dubious political pasts, anticommunism quickly gained "doctrinal status."[13] Pope Pius XII set the tone in his 1945 Christmas sermon, which demanded the "abolition of totalitarian states across the world." "How long will it take to heal the wounds dealt by this terrible war?" the Pope asked. "Humanity is awakening to the consciousness of just how much wisdom and patience and good will it will take to bring the world true peace, justice, and order."[14] Protestant leaders likewise worried that a new enemy to the east was manipulating Christmas in "totalitarian" de-Christianization campaigns, similar to those undertaken by National Socialists. The Protestant chancellery in West Berlin now targeted its parish-level surveillance efforts, honed in the Nazi period, on celebrations in the Soviet Zone. In 1946 the chancellery sent a letter to East German parish pastors asking for information about the "curtailment" of Christian observances. The response suggested that "only in a very few cases" was the "Christian sense" of the holiday ignored.[15] A decade later, Protestant administrators reported that observances of "People's Democratic Christmas" in the German Democratic Republic (GDR) included a range of dubious and decidedly anti-Christian observances: workplace recitations of poems and songs about peace and friendship and the democratic unity of Germany under socialism; children's celebrations that praised the peaceful use of atomic energy and space exploration; speeches from the Weihnachtsmann on the "industriousness of the working population"; and visits from members of the Volkspolizei and the Volksarmee, which taught children that these representatives of the state were their "true friends." The Protestant chancellery continued to monitor East Block de-Christianization campaigns into the early 1960s, when overt politicization faded from view.[16]

Christmas symbols and rituals became ideological props that portrayed the material and spiritual benefits of capitalism and the lack of democracy and tolerance "over there." "There is no freedom in the Soviet Zone," intoned West German chancellor Konrad Adenauer in his 1950 Christmas address. "They try to steal away the holiday's redemptive meaning." This abuse, the chancellor was sure, would "only strengthen the inner power of the Christian festival of Christmas."[17] According to the mainstream West German media, the limits on freedom of expression in the GDR were shocking. Communists callously redefined religious customs, explained Gerhard Jacobi, the dean of the Protestant church in Berlin. Advent wreaths in the Soviet Zone, for example, were decorated with five candles instead of the normal four, a symbol of the five continents slated for Communist takeover.[18] The West German media adopted the angle of a Protestant Press Service release from 1958 titled "Advent in the Zone/Old Symbols Disappear." "They avoid everything that points to . . . the Christian origins of the celebration. In the face of this transformation the church communities unite even more closely, to observe Christmas as a celebration of Christ."[19] According to the Western daily *Die Welt*, the Christkind had "died out" in East Germany, a victim of the "state party." To celebrate at all was an act of opposition that united those "over there" in a conspiracy of ritual observance: "The Weihnachtsmann has become more secret, and for many the Christmas tree has become a kind of contraband. . . . The comrade hides his Christmas holidays behind a fine veil. They sing the Christmas carols more quietly in the Soviet Zone, but probably not with less inwardness."[20] The Communist state reportedly viewed Christian observance as a punishable offense. The West German news magazine *Der Spiegel* gleefully reported that SED propaganda "functionary" Herbert Prauss, a practicing Catholic, had been demoted after the secret police found a forbidden Nativity scene alongside his Christmas tree; Prauss subsequently fled to the West.[21] Remember those in the "divided part of Germany," Adenauer reminded West Germans in 1959, "where those who live in slavery are not allowed to celebrate Holy Eve as we do." The desecration of this most Christian holiday, according to the chancellor, led to "naked atheism . . . with all of its desolate consequences, just as the sacralization of the state leads to the destruction of one's own thought, one's own feeling, one's own personality."[22]

To show concern for their disenfranchised conationalists and reinforce calls for unification under Western auspices, the West German authorities installed large illuminated Christmas trees along the border with East Germany on the Elbe River and in Berlin. Such activities may appear trivial, but they had deep symbolic resonance. As Adenauer explained in his 1956 holiday speech, "The dismemberment of our fatherland becomes especially painful to our consciousness during the Christmas holidays. Indeed in these days hundreds of Christ-trees light up the Iron Curtain. They offer greetings to the Zone, where people know only a dreary glow of the Christmas lights."[23] The image of illuminated trees along the Berlin Wall, with its attendant ironies, remains a Cold War icon. West German propagandists also dusted off the venerable tradition of lighting a candle at home for absent friends or family members—last used to some effect by the Nazis in the final years of World War II. Starting in 1958, the *Kuratorium Unteilbares Deutschland* (Trustees for an Undivided Germany), a conservative citizens group that organized a variety of pro-unification activities, called on West Germans to place a lit candle in their windows for the Germans "over there." For some, politics and private ritual merged easily if somewhat uncomfortably. "Of course my family placed candles in the window during the Christmas season [in the 1960s], which were supposed to remind us of our brother and sisters in the East," noted one West Berliner. "Was it arrogance? I thought it was a beautiful custom, even if at first I did not recognize its political ramifications."[24]

The idea of a "German" Christmas rooted in faith, popular customs, and a timeless sense of homeland and family lent an aura of sentimentalism to the hard-edged problems of the postwar world. Official Christmas scripts sanitized American occupiers and cast a pleasant glow around reconstruction efforts in the western zone of occupation and then in the Federal Republic of Germany. This narrative of progress under Western auspices dominates the newsreels that portrayed holiday activities in the first years after the war. One early newsreel, issued on 11 December 1945 under American authorization, included a segment on orphaned children from the Belsen concentration camp, who were flown to London by the Allies as a "Christmas present" for "the littlest victims of National Socialism." From 1946 on, however, holiday newsreels in the FRG resolutely ignored politics or the horrors of the past and instead focused on familiar Christmas scenes. Reports on the history of Knecht Ruprecht, the Hamburg toy exhibition, the Christmas market in Nuremberg, and cutaway shots of ringing church bells, snowy rural landscapes, children in front of store windows: these seemingly static symbols of German Christmas, once readily appropriated by Nazi propagandists, now reminded viewers of the innocent national past embodied in the holiday. Images of American GIS collecting donations to give chocolates to poor German children or singing Christmas carols sentimentalized the occupation, and descriptions of holiday customs around the (Western) world subtly drew the boundaries of German community to exclude the East Block. In a particularly telling episode from 1950, a group of German children presented a local Marshall Plan administrator with a Nativity scene as an appreciative gift.[25]

Traditional customs remade national allegiances but also highlighted absence, personal loss, and the costs of war-related dislocation. The popular press repeatedly featured stories about the father missing from the cozy Christmas room or the good German family forced by war and "totalitarianism" to observe the holiday in strange and foreign lands. The postwar Christmas thus contributed to what Robert Moeller has called the "integrative myth" of German suffering, which used the plight of POWs and expellees from East Prussia to shape a "usable past" for a remade national identity.[26] The need of displaced persons and expellees in the postwar years was real enough, as the charity actions organized by the U.S. occupation authorities, the Bavarian state government, and the West German Red Cross make clear. A holiday "Plea to the Bavarian People" from December 1946, for example, called on the population to donate clothes, blankets, shoes, beds, and other household wares for refugees, expellees, returning POWs, and homeless victims of Allied bombing campaigns. A generous donation would show that "we have fulfilled the deep Christian sense of this holiday in the best way"; similar campaigns continued into the early 1950s.[27] As Moeller has shown, however, narratives of German victimization for the most part ignored victims of Germans and were instrumentalized by a variety of actors. Adenauer, for his part, made the connections between Christmas, German victims, and Cold War politics quite clear. His 1950 holiday address offered "Christmas joy" to "thousands of German prisoners of war and forced laborers [who] still suffer in inhuman slavery," to the "millions" who had been forced out of their Heimat in the East by the peace accords, and finally, and somewhat vaguely, to the "victims of a totalitarian power-state [who] lost their property as well as their freedom and health"—a comment that could encompass Nazi Germany but was more easily read as a reference to East German socialism.[28]

Public presentations of West German Christmas in the early 1950s inevitably called attention to the ongoing suffering of POWs and refugees. The "Picture of the Times" in the December 1952 issue of the *Frankfurter Rundschau* depicted a mother with two children around a Christmas tree; her husband, in uniform and trapped behind barbed wire, appeared in a haze above her head. "99,000 mothers and wives are lost in their thoughts on Christmas Eve," the text explained, "where the barbed wire imprisons the forgotten ones of this war." A drawing called "Camp Christmas" in the 1953 Christmas issue of the *Reform Rundschau* likewise showed a group of POWs laboring in a camp on a snowy night with an imaginary Christmas tree above their heads. A three-page photo spread with accompanying poem in *Heute* from December 1951 pictured the fate of a homeless couple, fleeing an unnamed territory in the east with their belongings in a wagon. In a riff on Mary and Joseph's journey to Bethlehem, the woman is pregnant, and in the end she gives birth in a refugee camp.[29]

For expellees from former East Prussia, who either fled their homes before the Soviet advance in the winter of 1944 or moved west after the Potsdam peace accords, the holiday aroused feelings of estrangement but also offered the opportunity to celebrate the lost customs of the Heimat. In the early 1950s, special Christmas parties for expellees featured regional customs and were attended by local dignitaries. At one celebration in the southern Bavarian district of Miesbach, "refugee ombudsman Zarusky" reported that the 250 guests included East Prussians, Pomeranians, Silesians, and Swabians, who were moved to tears by the "rousing words of chaplain Polzer" as he paid tribute to "the old Heimat." At a similar celebration of "Silesian Christmas in Tegernsee," the chairman of the Silesian refugee community spoke of "the longings and endeavors to finally once again possess the inherited soil of the Heimat and finally once again have one's own home."[30] The Bavarian government monitored these festivities and commented approvingly when expellees and locals worked together to hold combined celebrations—in part, no doubt, because these were resolutely Protestant celebrations in Catholic territory.[31] Yet, as the suggestions for organizing Christmas celebrations in an internal "working letter" from the Bund der Vertriebenen (League of Expellees) make clear, the deep feelings evoked by memories of Christmas in former German territories had political valence. "Heimat politics is good and necessary, today more than ever" wrote a league supporter in the early 1960s. Yet preserving the faith required tact. "The memory that suddenly arises, awoken by a song or a poem, a star made of straw, or Christmas cookies is far more valuable than an awkward 'Heimat letter.'"[32] Peace Christmas in postwar West Germany served contradictory agendas, and the celebrations of individual families clearly evoked very real feelings of loss, suffering, and hope. If "the West German emotional regime manifested itself in a proliferating discourse on fear and anxiety throughout the first postwar decade," as Frank Biess has argued, then the tender Christmas mood gave Germans a way to salve postwar angst and gain a sense of emotional stability.[33] Public authorities ranging from Chancellor Adenauer to church leaders and East

Prussian revanchists eagerly tapped into such emotions to serve the political goals of postwar reconstruction, shaping a reformed national identity based on Christian values and a hazy past made palatable by memories of innocent family celebration.

LIGHT, LIFE, AND LOVE:

THE *MADONNA OF STALINGRAD*

The connections between re-Christianization, reconstruction, and German suffering circulate with telling effect around one of the more unusual products of the Nazi War Christmas: the *Madonna of Stalingrad*, a large sketch of the Mother Mary cradling Jesus in her arms (Figure 6.2). Drawn in a German bunker on the Stalingrad front in December 1942 by Lieutenant Kurt Reuber, the *Madonna* anchored a postwar cult of memory centered on the victimization and redemption of the "ordinary" German soldier. Reuber, a staff physician and Protestant pastor with the German Sixth Army, was taken prisoner in January 1943 and died in a Russian prisoner of war camp two years later. His *Madonna* was flown out of Stalingrad on the last transport plane to leave the surrounded German Sixth Army. The three-by-four-foot sketch depicts Mary wrapped in a large shawl, holding the infant Jesus close to her cheek, echoing iconic versions of Madonna and Child. On the right border, Reuber penciled in the words "Light, Life, Love" from the Gospel of St. John, a quote that expressed his training as a pastor as well as longings for home and family. By the time Reuber's heirs donated the drawing to the Kaiser Wilhelm Memorial Church in 1983, the *Madonna* had a well-established history that stretched back at least to 1945. In novels, memoirs, and reportage published in the twenty years following the war, Reuber came to represent the "ordinary" German soldier as a Christian caught up in a war he neither wanted nor believed in. Despite his disagreements with National Socialism, however, this faithful soldier never abandoned his post and was taken prisoner by the Red Army. Reuber's death in a Soviet POW camp underscored his status as victim—not only of the Nazis, but of the Communists as well, a conflation that well suited the Cold War politics of the postwar decades as well as the 1980s.[34]

Hanging in the blue-tinged light of the Memorial Church chapel, the war memorial and tourist site in the heart of West Berlin, the *Madonna* is open to multivalent readings. At the 1983 dedication ceremony, church officials positioned the *Madonna* as "an expression of hope found in the depths of

FIGURE 6.2

Kurt Reuber, *Madonna of Stalingrad*, charcoal on paper,
1942. (© Lutherisches Verlagshaus, Hannover)

[Reuber's] own passion," a symbol of peace and *Geborgenheit*—that familiar (German) Christmas feeling of comfort and security.[35] The symbolic space framing the *Madonna* is redolent with the Protestant church's own attempts to atone for its role in the war. The preserved ruins of the Memorial Church tower, built in the late nineteenth century and destroyed by Allied bombing raids, are one of West Berlin's central landmarks, meant to remind viewers of the cost of war; the church itself is formally dedicated to "the will to peace in this city and in the entire world."[36] The drawing hangs next to the "Martyr's Tablet" donated by Berlin bishop Otto Dibelius, a member of the Confessing Church and general superintendent of the Protestant Church Council during and after the war, to commemorate the Protestant victims of the Nazis. A placard accompanying the *Madonna* recounts the circumstances of its creation and explains that the three words that grace the sketch—light, life, love—"became a symbol of the will to life for hundreds of thousands. With this hope in their hearts began the indescribable suffering of a dying army as Russian prisoners of war."[37] By picturing the German soldiers who invaded Russia as martyrs "with hope in their hearts," the drawing suggests that German soldiers at Stalingrad, like Reuber, were innocent victims of the Nazis and Communists alike. The publication in 1992 of a collection of Reuber's drawings and letters, and various recollections about the *Madonna* and its theological meanings on the battle's fiftieth anniversary, testifies to the Protestant church's ongoing presentation of the drawing as a sign of "atonement," a way to "honor the legacy of this talented Christian who met a premature end."[38]

The story of the *Madonna* impressed observers at the 1983 dedication ceremony, who wrote to the *Berliner Morgenpost*, a popular city daily, to describe the "deep sentiments" felt in the presence of the drawing and the "deeply distressing" memories of Stalingrad it recalled. Just as the United States was stationing nuclear missiles on West German territory, one woman from Berlin drew connections between the (re)escalation of the Cold War and the trauma of World War II: "When I think back full of horror on the terrible years of the war, I wish that all the ruling statesmen in the world, who stand again on the edge of the abyss, would have to stand in front of the Stalingrad *Madonna* and memorize the words 'light, life, love,' so that the insane arms race would end and the world would get true peace and liberty." Even after the official dedication ceremony, the *Madonna* continued to prompt expressions of memory and remorse. According to an attendant at the souvenir stand in the anteroom of the church, some visitors returned repeatedly to view the *Madonna*, including "visibly moved women," one of whom whispered "my husband also fell at Stalingrad."[39]

The legend surrounding the *Madonna of Stalingrad* was based on a famous "true" story told in Reuber's personal letters about Christmas, written in the Stalingrad "cauldron" and flown out with the drawing. The letters were reprinted time after time in books, collections of letters, and newspaper articles. "I went to all the bunkers, brought my drawing to the men, and chatted with them," Reuber wrote. "How they sat there! Like being in their dear homes with mother for the celebration." Later, Reuber hung the drawing in his candlelit bunker for his unit celebration. "When according to ancient custom I opened the Christmas door, the slatted door of our bunker, and the comrades went in, they stood as if entranced, devout and too moved to speak in front of the picture on the clay wall. . . . The entire celebration took place under the influence of the picture, and they thoughtfully read the words: light, life, love. . . . Whether commander or simple soldier, the Madonna was always an object of outward and inward contemplation." The drawing, wrote Reuber, "became a symbol of the desire for all that which is outwardly so lacking and which in the end can only be discovered in our most inner depths. I wanted to represent these three things [light, life, love] in the earthly-eternal recurrence of the solace of mother and child. This earthly object became for me a symbol of the eternal all—and then in the end it was Christmas and the Madonna appeared before us."[40]

As one prominent military historian put it, Reuber's letters are "a vivid description of Christmas celebrations in the bunkers of the city of Stalingrad."[41] No doubt. Such comments also reveal how easily history, myth, and memory wash together in the sentimentalism of Germany's favorite holiday. The postwar image of the *Madonna of Stalingrad* owes much to clichéd versions of War Christmas stretching back to the Franco-Prussian War and World War I. The Nazis themselves were quite willing to promote similar stories about Christmas among the troops at Stalingrad, as a "Comprehensive Report on Opinion" drafted by the Stalingrad mail censor makes clear. This report, probably written after the defeat of the German army, exaggerates the heroism of the German troops for propaganda purposes, but it is precisely this exaggeration that contributed to a War Christmas myth that proved surprisingly durable over the following decades. In the Nazi report, Christmas is a prime example of how much deprivation the soldiers could bear and still fight on. Christmas Eve at Stalingrad exemplified the "golden comradeship of the soldiers" because they happily shared what little they had as makeshift gifts. At the same time, the report noted that soldiers felt the "inner conviction" of the "heroic German spirit of battle" with equal fervor.[42] The fortitude and persistent loyalty of the German soldier, despite abject conditions, was symbolized in attempts to celebrate a "real" German holiday at any cost.

The early texts that established the Stalingrad Christmas as a postwar legend show how Reuber and his *Madonna*, icons of popular memory, elided the differences between Nazism and the postwar Protestant revisionism favored by church officials and the Christian Democratic Union (CDU). Navy chaplain Arno Pötzsch's *The Madonna of Stalingrad*, a book of poetry complete with reprints of the *Madonna* and Reuber's sketches of his fellow officers and still sold in the museum shop at Berlin's Memorial Church, had already turned Reuber into a Protestant martyr by 1946. Pötzsch, who delivered the eulogy at Reuber's memorial service in the Hessen village of Wichmannshausen, sounds very much like a writer for a Nazi radio broadcast when he describes the bearing of the soldiers at Stalingrad.

> Our gaze was steadfastly focused on the East
> where true to their honor at lost positions
> they fought to the death for the Reich.

Yet in Pötzsch's revisionist poetry cycle, the German Reich is Christian; Reuber's *Madonna* becomes a symbol for the Christian faith of the German soldiers, victims described as "the poorest of the poor" who turn to God for comfort."[43]

The *Madonna* surfaced again in Heinz Schröter's full-length book, *Stalingrad—"To the Last Round"* (1953). Schröter, a lieutenant in a propaganda company at Stalingrad, authored an "eye-witness" account of the battle, and his chapter on Christmas is the longest in the book. His report includes long quotes from Reuber's letters and an unusual and moving series of vignettes that supposedly took place on Christmas Eve. Schröter tells of mystical Christmas trees with candles set up in open spaces, quickly blown up by enemy fire; of a Russian POW who sings a German carol in "a beautiful, strong voice"; and of Christmas Eve conversions to and reaffirmations of the Christian faith. In one presumably true story, a company of 150 men march for four hours along the Stalingrad front late on Christmas Eve. After midnight, the company reaches "hill 426.5," where about twenty-five wounded stragglers have set up a ragged Christmas tree. The men remove their helmets "without any need of a word of command" for an informal benediction. The leader of the wounded men, who wanted to be a priest in civilian life, makes a moving speech that turns on the innocence of the German soldier: "We do not know these men against whom we fight, nor would it occur to us to shoot at them, had it not been for the war. We are told where to go, and what to do." The ecumenical soldier/priest recites the "Latin prayer" and then the Lord's Prayer, "for the benefit of those who were not of his faith." The men answer "Amen" and together sing "Silent Night." "Never has this carol been sung in a lonelier place than this Christmas Eve," Schröter concludes.[44] Descriptions of the activities of supposedly pacifist and even dissident chaplains would play a key role in the sanitation of Stalingrad in the postwar imagination, but there is little evidence to suggest that chaplains like Reuber organized any real resistance to Nazi ideology.[45]

By 1952, critics recognized that the popularity of the "literature of the private first-class" was beyond question, and a reconstituted myth of War Christmas was recounted time after time in firsthand and fictional accounts of Christmas at the Battle of Stalingrad.[46] Books such as Theodor Plivier's *Stalingrad* (1945), Panzer officer Heinrich Gerlach's *The Forsaken Army* (1957), communications officer Fritz Wöss's *Dogs, Do You Want to Live Forever?* (1958; filmed in 1959), and war correspondent Heinz Konsalik's *The Doctor of Stalingrad* (1956; filmed in 1958) were published in dozens of editions and sold hundreds of thousands of copies; Konsalik's second novel, *The Heart of the Sixth Army*, alone went through thirty-three editions between 1964 and 1991. As literary historian Jörg Bernig convincingly shows, these popular novels and films were "anti-Nazi" insofar as they criticized the German political leadership and High Command. Nonetheless, most contain distinct racist, militarist, and even National Socialist language and themes.[47] Even a cursory examination of the Stalingrad reportage, novels, and films of the 1950s shows that Christmas has its place in this postwar literature alongside other generic scenes of the battle (including wounded soldiers fighting for a place on an out-going transport plane, starving troops eating soup made from horse bones, the insanity of Hitler's commands, the "cadaver obedience" of the weak-willed General Paulus). Scenes of soldiers gathered around the Christmas tree in a freezing dugout underscored the cheerful comradeship but also the victimization of "simple soldiers" forced into an unjust war, while an emphasis on the Christian traditions of the holiday created a space for a battle between ideologies, where National Socialism always lost out to simple Christian piety.

Heinrich Gerlach's chapter titled "Black Christmas" in *The Forsaken Army* best exemplifies the postwar fictional deployment of the Stalingrad

Christmas and the lingering power of War Christmas themes that stretched back to the Franco-Prussian War and World War I. In the novel, groups of ordinary soldiers improvise "comradely" celebrations despite horrific deprivations. They decorate their bunker and fashion gifts for each other with the materials at hand, and so create the atmosphere for a moving celebration in which the "miraculous sound" of holiday carols cements the bonds of comradeship and turns grown soldiers into children. Christmas evokes a community based on piety, not politics; open bibles and praying soldiers suggest allegiance to Christianity, not National Socialism. In one scene, Lieutenant Breuer, the main character who supports Nazism out of opportunism rather than conviction, gives an impromptu Christmas speech during his company Christmas party. Using terms familiar from countless War Christmas stories, Breuer evokes the "inner peace, which we can only find in our own hearts" and maintains that Christmas at Stalingrad will be an "unforgettable" holiday. Later that night, Breuer is confronted by First Lieutenant Wiese, who compliments Breuer's "beautiful" Christmas speech but flatly accuses him of self-deception: "Whoever still understands the celebration of Christmas . . . he can't really be a Nazi, can he?"[48] In the course of a lengthy conversation, Wiese insists that National Socialism and Communism are "as similar as two apples on the same tree" and that Breuer's opportunism, representative of millions of his fellow Germans, is the worst sort of duplicity. Yet there was hope for such fellow travelers, because in the end they were innocent of the worst abuses perpetrated by "real" Nazis.

Like other war memoirs, Gerlach's "Black Christmas" is a self-conscious passion play, complete with visions of resurrection that sanctify the sacrifices of the ordinary soldier. What Gerlach called "the invisible cross of Stalingrad, which hundreds of thousands bore on their shoulders and died on," would be justified by the postwar emergence of a reborn Christian Germany. As one soldier on watch confesses to a sympathetic priest, "I can't listen to any more Christmas songs. For me, God died at Stalingrad." The priest answers that "Yes, God died at Stalingrad, a thousand times. He fell alongside each of our dead—and at Stalingrad he will rise again!"[49] As such reputedly firsthand accounts suggest, West Germans used War Christmas stories to "work through the brown past" in ways that differentiated between a small number of evil Nazis and a large majority of good, Christian Germans.[50] Reworked War Christmas scenes thus legitimized contemporary political choices in 1950s West Germany, including faith in Christian democracy as a bulwark against the totalitarian threat to the east and the necessity of rapid rearmament. In this atmosphere of Cold War anxiety, East Germans responded with their own version of Christmas "under the red star of Bethlehem." Drawing on long-standing countercultural traditions, state functionaries in the GDR mounted a determined critique of the myth of West German War Christmas and engaged in a de-Christianization campaign intended to remake the foundations of the holiday.[51]

RED STAR OVER BETHLEHEM

The 1957 Christmas market in Communist East Berlin was a "complete success in political and economic terms," according to an extensive report by the Berlin Exhibition and Commerce People-Owned Enterprise.[52] The 2 million visitors who went to the market from 11 November to 22 December in Marx-Engels Platz included citizens from the "democratic sector" of Berlin and outlying districts, as well as West Berliners who crossed the still-open border. Approaching the market from the Kurfürsten Bridge, they walked past a giant Christmas tree and could then choose several paths, each designed to entertain and educate. In the "trade division," comestibles and other goods offered in booths sponsored by the state-run retail chains HO and Konsum vied for attention with products from a much smaller number of private vendors. Children and adults alike could marvel at the mechanical puppets in the fairy-tale forest and the displays in the exhibition pavilion, where rows of stalls featured handicrafts from different parts of Germany, including the famous nutcracker, made in the Erzgebirge. The crowd found other pleasures across the street, in the *Rummelplatz*, or amusement park, placed sacrilegiously in front of the main doors of Berlin's Protestant cathedral. Here, adults could try their luck at dice, games of chance, and shooting galleries, while children rode Ferris wheels, mechanical swings, and live ponies. The committee of administrators in charge of the annual market took the political content behind these simple and familiar pleasures most seriously. The Christmas market, the committee concluded, offered "lessons" to SED officials whose main job was building a socialist society. The annual East Berlin Christmas market was in many ways a microcosm of what the party called "Peace Christmas." Its history is a fitting introduction to the East German holiday and indeed to the contradictions of everyday life in East Germany. The market's successes and failures reveal the fissures between Christian observances and ideological appropriations, between popular desires for "joy" and prosperity and the more sober moral demands of the socialist consumer regime.[53]

The market meant holiday fun and distraction to be sure, and a set of three goals issued by the Berlin magistrate guaranteed that its appeal would not go to waste. First, the magistrate directed that the market's various attractions should teach visitors that "Christmas is a celebration of Peace." Under progressive socialism, this was no longer a "dream wish," as in the capitalist West. Good East Germans should also understand that "Peace on Earth" resulted from a determined struggle in the here and now—it was "no gift from heaven." Second, visitors should learn that they had to work to build the future; they should leave the market aware that "everyone should do a good deed for freedom and socialism." Finally, the magistrate asked organizers to call attention to the social welfare provided by the state. "Christmas is a celebration of children and the family," he noted, but also a symbol of the "great love" for children expressed by "Volk and government." Visitors should see that the Communist state provided "generous material support for the spiritual and bodily development of our offspring." These goals were all achieved, the organizing committee reported. The political speeches; the banners, posters, and advertising; the "central slogan" of the market, *Frieden—das ist Sozialismus* (Peace—that is Socialism)—all "helped rouse the people for the struggle for freedom and socialism, even during the Christmas season."[54]

Yet there was room for improvement. For one, the quality and availability of goods for sale at the market in East Berlin gave cause for concern. After the June 1953 uprising, the SED clearly realized that the failure to supply the population with adequate consumer goods had "*systemsprengende Kraft*"—the power to destroy the system—and competition with the West clearly troubled the market organizers.[55] The high quality of the goods on sale by a handful of private Western vendors hardly "shamed our worker's and peasant's state," the committee noted proudly, but the lackluster appeal of some East German goods and amusements nonetheless left visitors disgruntled. The number of visitors from West Berlin had declined from previous years, in part because of the lack of quality goods. Centralized planning also created problems. The mass organizations and numerous cultural institutions that participated in the market needed proper coordination to correct mistakes in layout and ensure a better balance between political and traditional decorations; the abundance of model Sputniks, the committee concluded, annoyed visitors who expected a more festive atmosphere.[56]

Uncontrolled activities in the amusement park posed a more trouble-some challenge. Gangs of youths gathered in front of certain booths in the *Rummelplatz* to listen to loud, unseemly music, and only "certain measures" undertaken by the "political and security organs" kept things under control. The previous year had been worse, the administrators noted, because "youths influenced by antagonistic attitudes" had then rampaged through the fair. A more visible police presence had prevented attempts by "western wire-pullers" (*Drahtziehern*) to again disrupt the public order. Though the rowdy pleasures and carnivalesque mood encouraged improper behavior and sat uneasily with the larger project of building socialism, the authorities argued that the amusement park was a necessary evil. "Doubtless young people are the main contingent of visitors to the Christmas market and their behavior and social actions do not always correspond with our wishes and ideals," the committee wrote, yet "boredom and passivity represent the powerful allies of our enemies." "An authentic, appropriate level of people's amusement does not contradict the principles of socialist culture," they concluded; indeed, improved attractions would keep youth occupied and "vitiate the influence of our enemies."[57]

As this excursion through the East Berlin Christmas market suggests, the East German holiday combined the familiar and the new. Socialist celebra-tion retained the pleasures of domestic celebration with its sentimental *Ge-mütlichkeit*, or "coziness." The iconography of happy families and innocent children gathered around Christmas trees decorated with lit candles contin-ued to grace holiday imagery of all kinds. To be sure, public festivities fea-tured the *Jolka-Tanne* (Jolka-Tree) and *Großvater Frost* (Grandfather Frost), both derived from the atheist *Jolkafest* promulgated in the Soviet Union after the 1920s; yet these obviously politicized customs hardly replaced the Ger-man Tannenbaum and Weihnachtsmann. The East German state clearly ex-pected its citizens to enjoy and celebrate the holiday season, and in this they broke with the Weimar-era Communist Party, which called for the abolition of the holiday altogether. Nor did GDR socialists follow Nazi attempts to root the holiday to a pre-Christian "Germanic" past. Where Nazis had devel-oped a holiday vocabulary revolving around supposedly ancient racial-folk traditions and pagan solstice rites, the numerous carols and Christmas poems penned by socialist writers in the 1950s focused on peace, freedom, and the arrival of a New Age. In the GDR, Peace Christmas looked to the future, not the past, for the realization of a secularized Christian-Christmas mes-sage. The harmonious language of this socialist evangelism, as Doris Foitzik suggests, masked the profane content of the socialist holiday message behind pseudospiritual language.[58]

The collapse of the Nazi state, the tragedies of loss and separation, and the burden of guilt—all cycled through memories of War Christmas—loomed large in the postwar imagination on both sides of the East/West divide.[59] "The faster we can deal with the causes of and the remnants of the disastrous German past—that is, Nazism, racial insanity, and hatred of others, the sooner we can overcome the results of the war," claimed a 1946 Christmas editorial in *Neues Deutschland*, the main party newspaper.[60] Yet where West Germans used the holiday to spin war stories that evoked the religiosity and victimization of the ordinary soldier trapped in a war he never wanted, East Germans called attention to the hypocrisy of the Nazi Christmas. Stories about War Christmas under National Socialism meshed well with the general antifascist propaganda line promoted by the SED, and the film *Murderers Are Among Us* was only one early attempt to recall the horrors perpetrated by the Nazis. News reports in the 1950s returned repeatedly to the brutalities of the Nazi Christmas past, not only in accounts about the surviving victims of the war, who deserved special consideration during the holiday season, but also in repeated stories about the gruesome brutalities practiced in the concentration camps during the Christmas holidays (for example, "The Gallows under the Christmas Tree" or "Christmas 1938 in the Buchenwald Concentration Camp"). Drawing attention to the perversion of fascist claims on the true German Christmas, GDR discourse underscored the continuities between fascism and capitalism and reminded East Germans of a none-too-distant past in which the state had used the holiday for criminal ends.[61]

Regime rhetoric and practice laid claim to a secular-socialist version of the biblical message that ignored traditional Christian motifs of the birth of the redeemer and the Nativity scene. In his 1947 Christmas address, "Peace on Earth," SED party cochair Otto Grotewohl set the tone that would dominate socialist celebration until East Germany's implosion in 1989. After a nod to Stalin's peaceful intentions and a call to remember the tragic wartime losses perpetrated by "the Führer" and his Nazis, Grotewohl struck a note of holiday optimism for Germans living under Soviet occupation: "In our practical political struggle for peace, we take the Christian message of salvation out of its two-thousand year sphere of patient faith, and place it in the midst of the people here on earth. If the star of Bethlehem shines for Christian socialists in the Christmas night, for us Marxist socialists it shines today and for ever as the glowing star of solidarity."[62] Year after year, public celebrations of

"Peace Christmas" revealed the SED's attempts to appropriate the traditional Christian values of peace, unity, and social justice without open reference to Christianity. East Germans had supposedly stopped believing in such superstitions. "The religious veil has lost its meaning for the majority of our population," wrote SED politician and cultural worker Herbert Gute in 1959 in a book on Germany's major holidays. "We need no 'merciful promises' but rather build the bases of socialism with scientifically grounded methods."[63]

In 1950s East Germany, the (Soviet) red star rose on Christmas Eve. The many East Germans who attended holiday festivities sponsored by state mass organizations—especially the Free German Youth (FDJ) and the Free German Trade Unions (FDGB)—celebrated socialism, not the birth of Jesus. Official celebrations often included a declamation of Erich Weinert's Weimar-era agitprop poem "The New Star," with its typical adaptations of Christian language and imagery.

> Above the courtyard, in the icy night,
> An awakened star is shining bright.
> It stands over the window of the poor
> With blood red brilliance;
> And its five points stream wide and far
> In misery, hunger and darkness.
> It shines everywhere on earth,
> Where poor children are given birth.
> Not just one Savior among us stands,
> But millions of Saviors in all the lands.[64]

As we have seen, West German Protestants shuddered at the thought of these remade rituals, which promised that millions of working-class revolutionaries would rise up to replace the one true Christ. The East German authorities for their part refuted Western claims about the state suppression of religious expression. Christian symbols and rituals had in fact hardly vanished in East Germany, even in state-sponsored festivities. Parties held by the mass organizations and radio and television holiday specials routinely included traditional carols and church music. In 1961, for example, East German television proudly broadcast Bach's *Christmas Oratorio* from the Thomas Church in Leipzig and bragged that "unlike West German television, our broadcasts on Christmas Eve hardly need to search for choirs and songs in Denmark, Holland, England, or Finland." [65] Yet the state clearly wished to take the Christ out of Christmas. In the early 1950s, functionaries observed religious services and compiled lists of pastors who used their holiday sermons to engage in political discussion or champion belief in Christianity rather than materialism.[66] A decade later, overt repression no longer seemed necessary. "Certainly few of our readers celebrate Christmas as a religious holiday," observed an editorial in *Neues Deutschland* in 1963. Another noted that the state generously recognized seven Christian holidays. In the socialist state, however, Christmas was mostly a time for presents, though "of course entirely progressive people . . . get tears in their eyes when they gather around the Christmas tree to sing [Luther's famous carol] 'From Heaven Above to Earth I Come.'"[67] SED officials liked to argue that the expression of religious feeling was a sentimental holdout, an emotional response to familiar ritual frames but hardly a sign of true inner faith. Plummeting levels of church membership—resignations peaked in the late 1950s—suggest they may have been correct.[68]

The history of Christmas in Stalinstadt (Stalin City), the model socialist steel town founded on the border with Poland in 1950 and renamed Eisenhüttenstadt, or Iron Works City, in 1958, reveals the way Christian and socialist celebration clashed at the grass roots of GDR society. Official celebration in the steel town adopted the standard model. Following the directives of the city commissariat, the FDGB and FDJ organized festivities for families and children with "new forms and methods with new content" that expressed "the socialist relations of production in Stalinstadt." State-sponsored celebrations focused on "the child in the circle of his parents and siblings" (instead of communities of faith) and were meant to purvey "thoughts of Peace."[69] Decorations at the Stalinstadt Christmas market included familiar Christmas trees and fairy-tale puppets, and schoolchildren "spread joy" by making handicrafts and being polite and kind to one another. At parties for youths, Young Pioneer members sang and danced and put on performances such as the play *The Dove of Freedom*.[70] Workplace "brigade" parties were divided into "serious" and "sociable" components: first, workers listened to official speeches, after which the Weihnachtsmann appeared, bearing food, gag gifts, and schnapps.[71]

For Pastor Heinz Bräuer, head of the Stalinstadt/Eisenhüttenstadt Evangelical "Peace Congregation" from the early 1950s to 1983, Christmas was an important and recurring moment in the ongoing attempt to preserve popular piety from SED pressure and, indeed, from more general processes of secularization. Bräuer's recollections capture the tensions in SED-church relations and at the same time suggest that the real drama of the state-church conflict in Stalinstadt played out in numerous small interactions and incidents over a long period of time. Throughout Bräuer's tenure, Christmas remained a compelling if at times embattled sign of community faith and solidarity. In the mid-1950s, he held informal "so-called Christmas celebrations" in the workers' barracks, with singing, prayers, and modest gifts, but he faced competition. "The company celebrated with their employees," he noted. "The brigades gave parties, and each collective no matter how small also celebrated." Bräuer denigrated these "collective 'prescribed' celebratory rites . . . at which the true Christmas played no role at all." Yet many workers went from party to party—including Bräuer's Christian ceremonies—to take advantage of the free food and gifts, and the pastor soon halted efforts to use the holiday to reach the workers in their barracks.[72] Celebration remained an important moment for the demonstration of faith. Bräuer was especially proud of his ecumenical holiday choir, established in 1967, which included one Baptist and two Catholic members and performed at Christmas services throughout the region. The separate faiths undertook few common activities, but the practice sessions of the Christmas choir, which began in September, encouraged friendships across confessions in an at least tacitly hostile environment. "Now you knew," Bräuer wrote, "that 'the one over there' was also a Christian."[73]

The 1953 Christmas Eve visit of Berlin-Brandenburg bishop Otto Dibelius, chairman of the Evangelical Council and a sharp critic of SED policies, marked a high point in the tense encounters between faith and politics in the early years of Stalinstadt. Bräuer devoted several pages of his memoir to the events. Though the numbers drawn by the bishop's visit would surely overwhelm the modest capacity of the small trailer where services were usually held, the Stalinstadt works director refused to let Bräuer hold services in the Hall of Culture, citing scheduling conflicts and ongoing renovations. Instead, Dibelius was forced to give two separate sermons, to standing-room-only crowds, in two local taverns; for many in the audience, who had recently moved to the growing city, this was their first Christmas in unfamiliar territory. In his sermon, Dibelius struck familiar Protestant chords, reminding listeners that the birth of Jesus was God's gift to the world, a sign of his mysterious but all-encompassing love. The bishop blended politics into his text. He expressed pleasure at his invitation to the city but challenged the authorities to proceed with building a church for the community. Citing the Bible, Dibelius spoke of the church's love for "the workers of Stalinstadt," preaching that they should know that "the church has a heart for workers—whether this friendly feeling is returned or not." Immediately after the bishop concluded, Bräuer noted grimly, a state security agent phoned in a report on the service. Later the same evening, agents confiscated photos of the assembled crowd in an apparent attempt to censor knowledge that "many hundreds of Christians" lived in "the new city."[74] A report in the *New Day*, a regional party newspaper, later criticized the "American-patsy Bishop" (*amerikahöriger Bischof*), declaring that his hypocritical "heart for the German worker" and his "words of Christian love [and] love of neighbor" hardly squared with his support for the atom bomb as "a guarantor of peace."[75]

Such open antagonism was exceptional, and according to Bräuer did relatively little to undermine the allegiance of the faithful. His statistics, complied over twenty years, show that despite SED pressure and a rather steep decline in members, the small Eisenhüttenstadt congregation tenaciously preserved its existence. In 1957, with the city's population at 13,000, the Peace Congregation counted some 8,000 members, or about 61 percent of the total population (though Bräuer states this figure may be exaggerated). In 1967, ten years later, the city had grown to 35,000, and the number of parishioners had fallen to 3,800. In 1977 the city had some 41,000 inhabitants, and the congregation had fallen further to only 1,990 souls, a little less than 5 percent of the total population. At weekly Sunday and Christmas services alike, women attended in numbers two or three times that of men, underscoring the persistent "feminization" of faith in the socialist state. Statistics showing that these numbers paralleled trends in Berlin-Brandenburg as a whole hardly made them more palatable, and Bräuer blamed the decline at least in part on the "'atmosphere' of Stalinstadt," which encouraged formerly faithful immigrants to the city to leave the church. Yet the de-Christianization campaigns of the SED were not solely or even primarily to blame. They offered only "the *opportunity*" for a decline in faith, Bräuer emphasized; the greater problem lay with the church's failure to offer "new ways" of observance appropriate to changing times. There was cause for hope as well. Head counts for attendance at all formal services had slipped (from 6,614 in 1957 to 5,639 in 1967 and 4,321 in 1977—a decline of about 35 percent) yet these numbers (relative to total membership) meant that the remaining congregants were attending service more often. Individual rates of charitable giving also grew precipitously, from an average of forty-seven GDR-marks in 1957 to 171 GDR-marks in 1977.[76]

Bräuer's story ends in the early 1980s, and he says little about the role of religion in the collapse of the East German state. His account of his time in Stalinstadt confirms that the East German Protestant Church, still a "people's church" in the 1950s, had become a "minority church" by the 1980s.[77] Yet throughout this period, religious groups struggled against state-sponsored secularization campaigns. East German Protestants campaigned publicly against rearmament, the abolition of religious instruction in the schools, and the introduction of the *Jugendweihe*, the ersatz, de-Christianized confirmation ritual introduced by the SED in 1955. Christmas offered a less confrontational but nonetheless meaningful way to engage in nonconformist behavior. Christmas Eve services were the best attended of the year, with numbers far above normal services and other holidays; the formal ritual of an evening Christmas sermon held its appeal despite state pressure and declining church membership. Everyday forms of celebration, especially on church holidays, used the well-established institutional structures of the Protestant church and the long-standing ritual practices of a confessional milieu to exert independence despite "systematic discrimination against anyone with strong religious ties."[78]

While East German Communists consistently suppressed the Christian aspects of Christmas, they were quite attracted to the domestic sentimentalism, family togetherness, and social harmony and order associated with this historically "German" tradition. Indeed, the notion of a Christmas miracle, which might resolve the various tensions that undermined belief in socialism, had real appeal. The film *Ach du fröhliche* (roughly "Ugh How Joyfully," a play on the popular Christmas carol), which premiered in 1962, the year after the erection of the Berlin Wall, revealed as much.[79] The film preserves a remarkably upbeat vision of an ordinary "Peace Christmas" in early 1960s Berlin. From the family Christmas tree decorated with animated model Sputniks to the well-stocked department stores bustling with shoppers, it suggests that everyday life in the GDR was stable and prosperous. Yet "Ugh How Joyfully" also poses a moral dilemma that transposes the familiar "happy end" of family Christmas melodrama into a socialist setting. In the beginning of the film, a factory director who returns home after the Christmas Eve celebration of his work brigade to discover that his daughter wants to marry Thomas, a young man whose natural intelligence and ability is undermined by his "unpositive attitude to the workers'-and-farmers' state."[80] The upset father then wanders the streets of Dresden on Christmas Eve, trying to understand the upsetting behavior of his future son-in-law. In a series of encounters, he witnesses the insincere opportunism that some East Germans use to advance in the system. When he realizes that Thomas's father was one such opportunist, and that the son is simply struggling with the legacies of his unfortunate upbringing, the family is reunited around the Christmas tree. The moral is clear.

The spectacular front page of the Christmas issue of 1962's *Neues Deutschland* reinforced the idea of socialist miracles. The holiday, pronounced the editors, promised that "a new age has begun in the history of the German Volk: the age of socialism." The illustration of a young girl entranced by a candle on a pine bough, in front of a new housing site on Stalinallee in Berlin, connected private satisfaction to the paternal state and suggested that the good life was just over the horizon (Figure 6.3). Though the SED did not directly say so, the text suggested that the erection of the Berlin Wall had created new opportunities to leave behind the trappings of the bourgeois, Western celebration and by extension the abuses of capitalism. "Neither the Christian legend nor the Germanic nature-myth nor the mood of Christmas customs have the power to create the steady confidence of the message that our age announces to the people: the program of socialism," the editors wrote. "Let us turn our faces entirely to the New Age, which we will build with our hands and our minds. Let us do what it demands of us: close ranks, to achieve the great deed." "Hard tasks" faced the population, the editors acknowledged, but "work is more joyful and life is happier in the air of socialism."[81] The establishment of the socialist New Age indeed faced stiff competition on one of the classic grounds of the modern Christmas: prosperity for all, embodied on the other side of the Berlin Wall in the flashy and increasingly unavoidable consumer culture of the West German Economic Miracle.

MIRACLE ON THE KU'DAMM

The annual arrival of Christmas turned the Kurfürstendamm, West Berlin's famed shopping corridor, into a consumer wonderland. High-end department stores, flashy nightclubs, and well-stocked Christmas markets lured West Berliners into the city center. The holiday glitz on the Ku'damm, mirrored in the pedestrian malls built on the bombed-out rubble in the center of West German cities large and small, epitomized the success of West Germany's Economic Miracle. The ability to purchase more—and more-expensive—gifts testified to the rapid, consumer-led economic recovery that reshaped the holiday and German society alike. The miracle on the Ku'damm was a West German phenomenon, yet its effects are inexplicable without an account of its competitor and doppelganger in East Germany. Citizens in

Proletarier aller Länder, vereinigt euch!

NEUES DEUTSCHLAND

ORGAN DES ZENTRALKOMITEES DER SOZIALISTISCHEN EINHEITSPARTEI DEUTSCHLANDS

17. Jahrgang / Nr. 353   Berlin, Montag/Dienstag, 24./25. Dezember 1962   Berliner Ausgabe / Einzelpreis 15 Pf

Ein neues Zeitalter hat begonnen

Der Zeitpunkt, auf den die Weihnachtssage fixiert wurde, ist gleichzeitig der Nullpunkt unserer Zeitrechnung. Die christliche Weltbetrachtung sah offenbar in jener Geburt im Stall den Wendepunkt, den Beginn einer neuen, ganz anderen Zeit.

War die folgende Zeit wirklich so ganz neu? Wir wissen, daß auch damals schon die Menschen sich nach dauerhaftem Frieden sehnten. In der Weihnachtslegende selbst fand jener Sehnsucht Worte, die sogar mit himmlischer Autorität ausgestattet waren: Friede auf Erden! Doch die fast 2000 Jahre, die seitdem vergangen sind, waren durchtobt von Kriegen, die immer mörderischer wurden. Wir wissen auch, daß damals ein großer Teil der Menschheit in Sklaverei, unter dem Druck furchtbarer Ausbeutung lebte. Seitdem wechselte die Ausbeutung zwar ihre Formen, aber sie prägte die Volksmassen durch die Jahrhunderte. So ganz anders war die Zeit also nicht geworden.

Wir aber, die Menschen des zwanzigsten Jahrhunderts, sind wahrhaftig Zeugen für die Geburt einer neuen Zeit. In der Weltgeschichte ist eine Kraft eingetreten, die der Ausbeutung und der Ausrottung der Menschen durch den Menschen ein Ende zu machen berufen ist: der Sozialismus. Das Kapitel Zwei der Weltgeschichte beginnt nicht mit dem Jahre Null, sondern mit dem Jahre 1917.

Auch in Deutschland hat der Sozialismus Einzug gehalten. Noch nie hat das deutsche Volk eine so glücklichere, so glückverheißende Weihnachtsbotschaft vernommen wie in diesem Jahre mit dem Programmentwurf unserer Partei. In lauten die ersten Sätze dieser Botschaft: „Ein neues Zeitalter in der Geschichte des deutschen Volkes hat begonnen: das Zeitalter des Sozialismus. Es ist das Zeitalter des Friedens und der sozialen Sicherheit, der Freiheit und Gerechtigkeit, der Menschlichkeit und Lebensfreude."

Noch nicht in ganz Deutschland ist die neue Zeit angezogen. Aber bei uns in der Deutschen Demokratischen Republik hat sie schon festen Fuß gefaßt. Es gibt ein sozialistisches Deutschland, Hort des Friedens und Bild der Zukunft für die ganze Nation. Die Wende, die damit vollzogen wurde, ist viel wunderbarer und realer als ein erzunschlostes Dinge, die über die Geburt im Stall erzählt werden.

Blicken wir nicht zweitausend, sondern nur zwanzig Jahre zurück. Weihnachten 1942: In Stalingrad und an allen Fronten starben Menschen, gemordet durch den Wahnsinn des deutschen Imperialismus. Über Deutschland lag tiefste Nacht. Und heute schützt ein sozialistischer Staat in Deutschland den Frieden, in engster Freundschaftsbunde mit der Sowjetunion und den anderen sozialistischen Bruderländern. Die größte Revolution in der deutschen Geschichte hat statt in unserer Republik vollzogen. Die Arbeitermacht hat die Macht in ihre starken Hände genommen. Die großen Reichtümer, die Fabriken, Werke und Eisenbahnen, die Bodenschätze, die Felder, Gewässer und Wälder gehören dem Volk, das sie erschließt und mit ihnen arbeitet.

Die Ausbeuter, die Militaristen haben hier für immer ausgespielt. Der König Herodes in der Weihnachtslegende hörte etwa läuten, daß da in Bethlehem so etwas wie eine neue Zeit geboren sei. Er bekam Angst um seinen Thron und fuß vorsichtshalber alle kleinen Kinder in Bethlehem und Umgebung umbringen, um die alte Zeit zu retten. Aber er verfehlte bekanntlich sein Ziel. Der deutsche Imperialismus steht ihm weder an Bestialität noch an Angst vor der neuen Zeit nach. Doch er reißt vergeblich mit dem Kopf gegen die Mauer. Man kann den Sozialismus nicht mehr in der Wiege töten. Dazu ist er schon zu groß und stark. Herodes Adenauer ist machtlos gegen die neue Zeit.

Ja, das Fundament steht fest, die sozialistischen Produktionsverhältnisse haben gesiegt. Unsere Botschaft, unser Programm, ist nicht nur Verehrung, Hoffnung, Anweisung auf ein Glück in fernerer Zukunft. Hier ist auf solider Grundlage die Aufgabe gestellt, jetzt den Sozialismus umfassend aufzubauen und zu vollenden. Hier wird nicht auf einen Segen vertrauen, den von oben kommt. Hier werden die Schöpferkräfte der Menschen aufgerufen. Unzählige neue Gedanken und

gute Taten für den Sozialismus werden nötig sein, bis wir das Ziel erreicht haben.

Die Geburt der neuen Zeit kann nicht ohne Geburtswehen vonstatten gehen. In unserem Programm ist aufgezeichnet, wie der Aufbau des Sozialismus vollendet wird. Aber nirgends steht geschrieben, daß das von selbst geschehe oder daß es leicht wäre. Das erfordert Arbeit und Findigkeit, Ausdauer und Standhaftigkeit. Aber ist das denn ein Unglück? In früheren Generationen gab es viele werktätige Menschen mit tüchtigen Anlagen, die jedoch ihre Kräfte nicht entfalten konnten. Der Zugang zur Wissenschaft war ihnen versperrt. Sie schufen Kulturgüter und große Reichtümer, aber andere eigneten sie sich an und bestimmten darüber, oft zum Verderben der Arbeitenden. Die einst gefesselten Kräfte der Ausgebeuteten sind heute durch den Sozialismus befreit. Sie können frei zu aller Nutzen wirken und damit zugleich zum eigenen.

Wir haben schwere Aufgaben vor uns, aber in der Luft des Sozialismus arbeitet es sich froher und lebt es sich glücklicher. Das Menschen Glück ist kein Fernziel, es wächst mit und in unserer Arbeiter-und-Bauern-Macht. Sozialismus, das laß nach den Worten unseres Programms je auch dieses: „Die Beziehungen der Menschen zueinander sind gekennzeichnet durch kameradschaftliche Zusammenarbeit und gegenseitige Hilfe. Mit dem Sozialismus beginnt die menschenwürdige Gesellschaft freier Menschen Wirklichkeit zu werden, die durch gemeinsame freie und erhoipherische Arbeit verbunden sind." So gewinnt der Gedanke der Brüderlichkeit, der Freundschaft zwischen den Menschen, der seit je mit dem Weihnachtsfest verknüpft war, nun durch den Sozialismus eine feste Grundlage in der wirklichen Welt.

Ebenso ist es mit dem alten Weihnachtswunsch nach Frieden zwischen den Völkern. „Friede auf Erden" – das war einst ein frommer Wunsch und eine bange Frage, und das USA wahre. Unsere Botschaft weiß auf diese Frage eine Antwort: „Der Sozialismus ist die sichere Grundlage für die Freundschaft der Völker und die friedlichen Zusammenleben. Sozialismus, das ist der Friede."

Ein Schweizer Gelehrter hat ausgerechnet, daß die Menschheit in ihrer bewegten Geschichte 14 000 große und kleine Kriege erlebt hat. Damit soll und wird es nun ein Ende nehmen. Zum ersten Male ist die Möglichkeit gegeben, die Welt von der Geißel des Krieges zu befreien. Das ist wahrhaft eine Zeitenwende.

Erst vor wenigen Wochen haben wir erlebt, wie die Sowjetunion den Frieden gerettet hat. Die amerikanischen Imperialisten standen im Begriff, das sozialistische Kuba zu überfallen. Aber die Kraft, über die Sache des Friedens heute schon verfügt, nötigte der USA zum Rückzug, zum Kompromiß. Der Überfall auf Kuba wurde verhindert und die Gefahr des atomaren Weltkrieges abgewendet. Chruschtschow konnte vor dem Obersten Sowjet feststellen: „Die Sowjetunion, die Kräfte des Friedens und die Sozialisten greifen nicht den Menschen wird an, sind aber, wenn die Kriegstreiber den Frieden aufzwingen." Heute stehen hier dem Frieden auf Erden die stärkeren Kräfte, mehr als nur das Wort: der Engel.

Weihnachten war stets vor Optimismus überplant. Das gilt von der christlichen Weihnachtstradition, der Legende von der Geburt, mit der die Menschen unbestimmte Hoffnung verknüpften. Das gilt ebenso von den älteren germanischen Tradition der Weihnachtsfeiern, der Sonnenwende, die die wachsenden Tage schon einen neuen Sommer entgegenhieb. Das gilt auch von den weihnachtlichen Volksbrauch des Weihnachtsbaums, unter dem man sich gegenseitig beschenkt und Freude macht. Doch weder die christliche Legende noch die germanische Naturmythos noch die Stimmung der Weihnachtsbräuche vermochten eine so feste Zuversicht zu begründen wie die Botschaft, die unsere Zeit den Volke verkündet: das Programm des Sozialismus. Wodehn wir unser Antlitz ganz unserer neuen Zeit zu, die wir mit unseren Händen und unseren Hirnen gestalten wollen. Tun wir, was sie von uns fordert: die Reihen fest zu schließen, um das große Werk zu vollbringen.

Fotomontage: ND/Raschke/Schönfeld

Das Reich der Gleichheit, der Brüderlichkeit, des Friedens und der Freiheit

Ein neues Zeitalter in der Geschichte des deutschen Volkes hat begonnen: Das Zeitalter des Sozialismus. Es ist das Zeitalter des Friedens und der sozialen Sicherheit, der Menschenwürde und Brüderlichkeit, der Freiheit und Gerechtigkeit, der Menschlichkeit und Lebensfreude. Die jahrhundertealte Ausbeutung des Menschen durch den Menschen wird beseitigt. Das Volk, das alle Werte schafft, genießt sein Schicksal, das Geschick der Nation. In der neuen Gesellschaft gilt der Grundsatz: Alles mit dem Volk, alles durch das Volk, alles für das Volk.

Die Deutsche Demokratische Republik ist in dieses neue, das sozialistische Zeitalter ein Deutschland bereits eingetreten. Hier hat die Arbeiterklasse im Bündnis mit den Werktätigen der Stadt und Land die Staatsmacht erobert und gemeistert. Sie wurde dazu befähigt durch die Überwindung der jahrzehntelangen Spaltung der Arbeiterklasse, durch die Vereinigung der Kommunistischen Partei und der Sozialdemokratischen Partei zur Sozialistischen Einheitspartei Deutschlands.

Seit über hundert Jahren ist die sozialistische Gesellschaft das Kampfziel der revo-

lutionären deutschen Arbeiterbewegung. Ihrem heroischen und opferreichen Kampf ist es zu verdanken, daß heute der Sozialismus in der Deutschen Demokratischen Republik Wirklichkeit wird.

Der Sozialismus ist die Zukunft des ganzen deutschen Volkes.

Er wird die nationale Gemeinschaft auf eine höhere Stufe heben. Durch den Aufbau des Sozialismus und die Beseitigung des Klassenantagonismus wird die deutsche Nation zur neuen sozialen Grundlage erhalten. Nur als sozialistische Nation wird sie eine stabile Einheit erlangen, die sichere Perspektive einer friedlichen Entwicklung und einen geachteten Platz unter den Nationen der Welt. Der Sozialismus wird die deutsche Nation durch friedliche Arbeit zur Blüte und Größe führen.

Er ist das Ergebnis unzähliger guter Taten von Millionen Menschen. Er ist die bewußte und planvolle Verwirklichung aller freiheitlichen Ideale und fortschrittlichen Bestrebungen der deutschen Werktätigen. Er ist der Übergang in das Reich wahrer Menschlichkeit, der Gleichheit und Brüderlichkeit, des Friedens und der Freiheit.

(Aus dem Programmentwurf der Sozialistischen Einheitspartei Deutschlands)

the "Workers' and Peasants' State" found their own Christmas miracle in the spacious walkways and department stores that lined East Berlin's Stalinallee—"Uncle Joe's miracle mile in Red Berlin" (*Life* magazine, 1952). West Germans remained unimpressed. Press photos of empty department-store windows in East Berlin revealed the supposed spiritual and economic poverty of everyday life "in the zone" and burnished the glamour of consumerism in the West. The competition over holiday prosperity was more than a propaganda exercise; these cultural clashes injected Cold War politics into simple, everyday acts of spending, giving, and getting.[82]

Given its associations with material abundance, Christmas was an obvious time to showcase the connections between personal and national recovery in the postwar decades. West German government ministers and marketing experts eagerly promoted the virtues of private enterprise and an economy driven by consumer demand in the holiday season. In the West German "social-market economy," social equality would be achieved through rising wages and ever-greater access to consumer goods, not through compulsory and "totalitarian" class leveling. Christmas in this context was about individual choice. "Personal" holiday messages from Economics Minister Ludwig Erhard reminded West German citizens that shopping was the reason for the season, that the free market meant consumer choice, and that price controls would lead to a "socialist-style command economy." Economic indices released during the holiday season testified to the success of postwar reconstruction.[83] For "ordinary" West Germans, the annual Christmas splurge lent what historian Michael Wildt calls the "uncanny dynamic of consumption," an aura of pleasure and progress.[84] As the household budgets of "Family Z" from Kiel show, shortages and low incomes in the postwar decade forced West Germans to expend much effort procuring basic goods and services, and even a modest Christmas splurge could bring the "first moment of joy" after years of forbearance. In December 1949 Family Z tapped their bank account to buy toys, special foods, a Christmas tree, and, for the first time since the end of the war, "real bean coffee." The ability to spend on such relative luxuries marked a real step toward recovery. When in 1953 the family could finally afford a Christmas goose, they recognized that they had enjoyed a *ganz tolles Weihnachten* (a really great Christmas). The holiday marked time on the path from crisis and deprivation to normality and prosperity.[85]

The ability to acquire things was central to a sense of recovery, and advertisements for Christmas presents showed the way. In the early 1950s, ads hawked conventional gifts like books and liquor, but as the Economic Miracle took off, they increasingly encouraged West German shoppers to buy the televisions, refrigerators, and other big-ticket "modern" appliances that drove economic recovery and helped put individual acquisitiveness at the core of a reformed West German identity. As ever, domestic bliss was central to the pitch and linked closely to durable goods; a gift of a "helpful Electrostar household appliance" could after all "free your wife of the difficult cares and efforts of everyday housewifery."[86] The experience of Family Z from Kiel must have been typical. For Christmas 1954, the family bought their first large-scale consumer article, a "Marke Rapid" vacuum cleaner from Siemens, discounted by 30 percent for the holiday; in 1956 Herr Z found a "Braun Spezial" electric razor under the Christmas tree. Christmas 1958 brought another breakthrough, again measured by the ability to shop. No longer just "making it," the Family Z was "moving forward." After Herr Z found a better job, daily living conditions improved markedly. For Christmas, the family was able to purchase a television for 885 D-marks, two-thirds on credit (at this time the price was about one-tenth of the annual salary of a well-off professional).[87]

The triumphs of Herr Z in the late 1950s look modest indeed when compared to the consumer frenzy of 1965, when West Germans spent some 20 billion D-marks—15 percent more than the year before, and the equivalent of the annual federal military budget—on holiday shopping. According to the news magazine *Spiegel*, customers sought luxurious gifts without regard for price. "It's fabulous," a Hamburg fur dealer reported. "Sables, minks, Persian lambskins, it doesn't matter, it all goes!" The splurge was fueled in large part by "newly successful" young adults, the twenty-five to thirty-five-year-olds whose wallets bulged with profits earned over the past decade, but even auto mechanics willingly spent over 750 D-marks on watches. Diamond necklaces, pearls, and emeralds flew off the shelves; a jeweler in Hamburg claimed his profits had risen 30 percent from the year before. The central Volkswagen office in Stuttgart received numerous orders for the stylish Ghia-Coupé, to be delivered as gifts in the holiday season; and an Opel dealer in Hamburg, capitalizing on the Christmas spirit, gift-wrapped a Kadett coupe and placed it on his showroom floor (Figure 6.1). Shoppers bought television and stereo consoles priced between 1,000 and 10,000 D-marks, automatic dishwashers that cost 2,000 D-marks, "American '*Lounge-Chairs*'" for 1,700 D-marks, and "Hornback" handbags for 900 D-marks. West Germans shopped, *Spiegel* concluded, "as if the world or the currency was about to collapse, or a yet greater Economic Miracle was coming."[88]

Such tales about the dream worlds of consumer abundance inspired by holiday spending had important ideological valence in the Cold War context, revealed in one of the more clever state appropriations of Christmas well-being: the annual gift-package campaigns organized by West German officials for East Germans in "the zone." "Don't forget them," ran the text on a typical campaign poster. "Give them joy for Christmas. Your letter, your gift, your package: send it over there!"[89] Adenauer added his authoritative encouragement, praising in his 1956 holiday address "the flood of packages of all sizes . . . streaming into the captive part of Germany."[90] The campaigns were supposedly private, charitable concerns, publicly sponsored by Protestant and Catholic groups that collected donations from generous individuals. In reality, the West German authorities consciously used Christmas "gifts" for political ends. Throughout the 1950s and then especially after the building of the Berlin Wall in 1961, government officials worked behind the scenes to promote the drives, sometimes with financial support from the United States. By 1958 American embassy employees working with the West German Ministry of All-German Affairs were spending around 1 million D-marks a year to send Christmas packages to East Germans; West Germans could claim a tax break for the expenses involved in purchasing and mailing their "gifts." The goal of the campaigns, according to American embassy dispatches from Bonn, was "not to relieve suffering or provide the necessities of life for needy persons," but rather to demonstrate to underprivileged East Germans the high quality of Western goods and the superiority of life in the West. The best presents were accordingly "less essential and higher quality consumer goods." Campaign organizers asked West Germans to send packages in particular to East German youths, who might be "open-minded to Western ideology." As one embassy staff member surmised, "this kind of contact can have maximum impact, if it consists of gifts of items that young people are generally inclined to treasure and . . . would otherwise not be able to have."[91]

According to contemporary opinion polls, millions of Germans on both sides of the Iron Curtain were sending and receiving Christmas packages; from 1954 to 1960, about one-third of West German adults sent Christmas packages "over there" each year. Despite such high participation rates, pollsters for the Bielefeld-based public-opinion research institute EMNID expressed surprise that the rest of the population was ignoring the blandishments of their political leaders. Polls suggested that most West Germans took part in the campaigns for personal reasons. They mailed their packages to relatives or close friends, and in 1960 only 5 percent directed their "gifts" to persons unknown, presumably with the help of package drive officials.[92] Yet politics and personal connections were tightly linked. According to federal statistics, the number of packages sent east indeed increased dramatically after the building of the Berlin Wall, from 35.4 million in 1960 to an average of 50 million per year from 1961 to 1966.[93]

East German politicians recognized the intent behind this outpouring of Western generosity. "The Adenauer authorities could care less about assistance," an SED politburo member explained at a meeting in 1952 in reference to that year's package drive. "They want to exacerbate tensions and create unrest, while millions of people in West Germany live an impoverished existence with little or no support." SED officials publicly denounced Western intentions, carefully monitored Christmas packages from the West for "enemy material," and undertook package drives of their own to ease the "impoverished existence" of Germans in the West. Residents of the GDR, they claimed, sent twice as many Christmas packages to the West as vice versa.[94] Newspaper accounts reported that "profiteers" used the package exchange to smuggle controlled medicines and abortifacients into the East. In 1961 the package traffic reached a new high because of Western attempts to breach the newly built "anti-fascist protection wall." To educate the population about the West's duplicity, the East German customs office opened an exhibit on the illegal holiday traffic in the Ministry of Health.[95]

Christmas-package campaigns drew East and West Germans into complex relationships of reciprocal give-and-take. Shopping for and packaging gifts, and negotiating the requisite official forms and customs controls, required substantial energy; these annual gift exchanges reinforced family and ethnic ties and drew on familiar private traditions to ameliorate the tensions generated by heightened public conflict. Yet the response "over there" was decidedly mixed. When East Germans opened a package from the West, observes ethnographer Ina Dietzsch, they might experience complex emotions ranging from excitement and delight to shame, disappointment, and resentment.[96] Christmas packages met real needs for quality consumer goods in the East and reminded recipients of the United States–sponsored emergency Care Packages familiar from the immediate postwar years. As West German officials hoped, they hinted at the delights of consumer capitalism. "What a feast for the senses, when the long-awaited Christmas packet finally arrived and even the wrapping paper gave off this fine aroma," remembered one East

German recipient. The oranges, fine chocolates, coffee, soap, and perfume included in the typical holiday package smelled "like the West" or "the wide world."[97] The brand names of Western products resonated with East Germans, who bragged about getting not just coffee or chocolate, for example, but Tschibo and Kaba, "western coffee" and "western chocolate."[98] For West Germans, sending gifts of baking powder or hand-me-down clothing to relatives in the East "proved how bad supplies were in the GDR" and, for West Berliner Christian Härtel, showed that the Federal Republic "was now on the right side of history!"[99] Western "gifts" required appropriate expressions of gratitude and reciprocity, and packages sent from East to West typically contained books, prized Dresden *Weihnachtsstollen* (Christmas cake), handicrafts like fine glass and crystal from Jena, or carved wooden decorations from the Erzgebirge. East Germans at times experienced frustration when they tried to match the generosity of their wealthier Western contacts, and some grew angry at West German presumptions.[100]

Though Christmas had long been associated with excess and material abundance, the wave of consumerism that washed over the West German holiday in the Economic Miracle evoked a renewed round of cultural criticism. Familiar worries about commercialization and secularization took on an intensified tone and urgency, exacerbated by fears of Americanization and broader critiques of consumer society. Even apparently innocent decorations could evoke dismay. As one CDU city councilor in Düsseldorf grumbled, the ostentatious electric light displays in the downtown shopping district might entice buyers, but they created an "American Christmas panorama" that was "a slap in the face" to good German customs.[101] Chancellor Adenauer no doubt spoke for many when he decried the impact of the "the exaggerations and excessiveness of our era" on the holiday's cherished Christian values. "One sees with regret the exaggerated flood of lights in the streets and stores, which takes away from children but also from adults a good deal of the joy of the shining lights of Holy Eve," Adenauer lamented in 1955. "The excess of presents," he noted in a cutting reference to uncontrolled consumption, "almost crushes to death the joy of gifts selected with personal feeling." Yet Adenauer maintained the optimism of a good Christian Democrat: "God has given us the power to control these causes for concern," he concluded, and Germans could "protect the true and authentic core of Christmas: we should spread our joy out of gratitude that God's son (*Gottmensch*) was born for all mankind."[102] Critics on the left as well as the right took aim at the consuming desires animated by the postwar holiday. In his 1952 short story

"Christmas Not Just Once a Year," Heinrich Böll famously cast Christmas as a meaningless consumer ritual that symbolized West Germany's declining family morality and failure to confront the Nazi years. Authors such as Alfred Andersch, Hans Werner Richter, and Günter Grass also used the holiday in their novels and memoirs to problematize West Germany's "flight" into consumption.[103]

The arrival of West German television and its growing popularity in the early 1960s crystallized the impact of consumer culture on the holiday for audiences and culture critics alike. The Northwest German Broadcast Corporation openly exploited the seasonal spirit by broadcasting their first television show on Christmas Eve 1952, and they ran predictable holiday specials each year thereafter. For some critics, television wrought troubling changes in West German society; communities of faith and family, they feared, would increasingly give way to a society of alienated and atomized individuals, in thrall to the "silver screen" but unable to fully participate in civic life.[104] Television certainly changed the nature of holiday sociability. Like radio before it, TV rescripted the practices of holiday leisure time. Religious messages were hardly absent from the airwaves, but by 1954 reviewers were bitterly complaining about television's disruption of the "quiet, candle-lit day" of Christmas.[105] In 1962 a record-breaking audience of 11.5 million West Germans sat at home on Christmas Eve to watch the two-hour special *The Little Lord*, confirming the so-called vampire medium's ability to draw audiences away from normal routines and transform traditional family and religious observances. Though the show followed a documentary on the origins of the Christmas carol "Silent Night," a broadcast of a Protestant vespers service from the Three Kings Church in Frankfurt am Main, and a Christmas Symphony, *The Little Lord* was not about the baby Jesus, despite its title. Rather, *The Little Lord* told the story of a young aristocrat who challenged his stern father.[106] As cartoonist Wigg Siegl saw it (Figure 6.4), broadcast advertising trivialized the evangelical message of the holiday. In the television studio, even the birth of Jesus could be used to sell banal goods like baby diapers ("wrap him in swaddling clothes—Schnulli diapers!"). Satirists suggested that faith could never compete with the splendors of the mass media and consumer goods. Another cartoon showed Joseph leading Mary on a donkey past a Christmas tree lit by floodlights and surrounded with the big-ticket gifts that defined West German economic progress, including a television set, an automobile, and a refrigerator. "Let us move on," Joseph sighs. "After all, how can our Christmas miracle compare to that of the Germans?"[107]

Werbespot .... *(alttestamentarisch feierlich)* ... und wickelte ihn in Windeln — *(modern suggestiv)* ...Schnulliwindeln Jaaa, das sind Windeln! Sooo saugefroh, sooo gesäßtreundlich, sooo hautngen! — *(Knabenchor)* Schnulli! Schnulli! — *(ärztlich seriös)* ... im Feuchten siede' · Bakterien, darum ... *(Knabenchor)* Schnulli, Schnull' - *(Gong)* Der Unterleib wünscht Schnulli!'

FIGURE 6.4

"The private parts want Schnulli!" Anticommercialism Christmas
cartoon by Wigg Siegl. (*Simplicissimus*, no. 51, 1963)

In the 1960s, the commercialization of Christmas attracted sustained protest from the West German counterculture. The holiday was an easy target
for attacks on bourgeois family values and the hypocrisy of consumer society, and leftists dusted off old socialist carols and penned new satirical lyrics
for well-known standards. Between 1967 and 1970, a collective in Hamburg
published annual collections of *Garstigen Weihnachtslieder* (Nasty Christmas Carols), with lyrics that attacked imperialism, the Vietnam War, and
"consumer terror." As one version of the Christian classic "Oh Savior, Tear
the Heavens Open" had it:

> Oh Nixon, tear the heavens open
> Napalm rains down from on high
> Your bombers that take off in Guam
> Bless the folk of Viet Nam.[108]

The words to another carol captured the revolutionary ethos of the 68ers: "Advent, Advent, a department store's on fire—first one, then two, then three, then four, then the pigs knock on the door."[109]

Anti-Christmas protests were again in vogue. In one of the most renowned "actions," student leader Rudi Dutschke and members of the Sozialistischer Deutscher Studentenbund (Socialist German Student League) staged a raucous revolt in the Kaiser Wilhelm Memorial Church in Berlin on Christmas Eve, 1967. Dutschke's attempts to wrest the service from the pastor and harangue the congregation from the pulpit stalled when a fifty-nine-year-old disabled veteran hit him on the head with his crutch. The mainstream press echoed the veteran's reaction in its indignation at Dutschke's violation of sacred tradition.[110] The 68ers also reshaped the "bourgeois pieties" of family celebration. They "demystified" the Weihnachtsmann and Knecht Ruprecht and children in newly founded *Kinderläden* (storefront childcare collectives) participated in "anti-Christmas celebrations."[111] In Berlin in 1969, members of Kommune 2 encouraged their children to burn down their Christmas tree as a sign of commitment to alternative family values.[112] As Doris Foitzik sees it, the counterculture's attempt to break with the mainstream holiday was "both humorous and hurtful." The bourgeois norms of the holiday were deeply ingrained and difficult to leave behind. Earnest questions about the appropriateness of celebrating Christmas in committed left-wing circles evoked mixed reactions, and even the street actions and "anti-Christmas" protests drew on the festive spirit of the holiday.[113]

Like their West German counterparts, East Germans confronted the seemingly inescapable commodification of Christmas in the postwar decades. The familiar ideals of "Peace on Earth" and social harmony worked well enough with basic notions of a new socialist self. The celebration of material well-being, however, raised paradoxical dilemmas. With its extravagant rituals of shopping, gifting, and feasting, Christmas was rooted, after all, in the conspicuous consumer capitalism of the late nineteenth-century bourgeoisie. Commerce in the GDR, even during the holiday season, was supposed to ensure equitable provision and division of consumer goods to meet basic needs, not support individual material desires. In a socialist economy, state planning rather than the "free market" would determine profits, price, and supply and demand. Christmas called attention to these contradictions, and attempts to remake the holiday forced SED leaders to (re)shape socialist consumption norms in the capitalist-inflected language of market individualism and commodity abundance. "The regime's reliance on the language of individualistic mass-consumption and affluence of (capitalist) standards and cultural norms left over from before the war," historian Judd Stitziel explains, "exposes the degree to which it tried to compete with capitalism on capitalists' terms."[114]

The tensions between personal indulgence and more sober ideologies of equality played out in East German Christmas advertising, which linked the joys of consumer satisfaction to the collective achievements of the socialist state. Throughout the year, state-run retail outlets constituted an important symbolic realm for the representation of the egalitarianism that ostensibly defined social relations in the GDR. HO (*Handelsorganisation*) stores and Konsum consumer cooperatives—the "show windows of socialism"—were meant to demonstrate the material and ethical superiority of the socialist economy.[115] The symbolism of consumption was particularly freighted during the holiday season. *Neue Werbung* (New Advertising), the official East German magazine for advertising professionals, taught its readers that the best way to create a "Christmas mood" was to market prosperity in a socialist key. The show windows of the HO department stores in Berlin and Dessau—with their colorful display of consumer goods in "the treasure chest of your Christmas wishes" beneath a banner reading "Christmas—A Family Celebration—Under Assured Peace"—were models of socialist advertising.[116] Annual poster campaigns promised "Presents for the Holiday from your Konsum/The result of our peaceful reconstruction: Good Quality, Broad Selection." This slogan, from 1952, frames a happy gentleman shopper in front of a decorated tree on Stalinallee, the showcase boulevard in East Berlin. "Our rich offering of goods," read another poster from 1958, "the result of the successful labor of our workers for the victory of socialism!" Beyond the slogans, which called attention to the collective goals of the socialist economy, there was little to distinguish East German advertising from its Western counterpart.[117]

Stalinallee played a central role in socialist fantasies of consumer abundance. Though the stately neoclassical apartment buildings, department stores, and restaurants that lined the avenue were designed as a conscious rejection of Western "functionalism," their holiday trappings were quite familiar. On "Golden Sunday" in 1952, wrote Elsbeth Kupfer in *Neues Deutschland*, people massed along the broad sidewalks of "the first socialist street of the German capital city." Display apartments open to the public, fitted out with furniture and housewares from HO and Konsum stores, testified to the benefits of the socialist consumer regime. "All Berlin was up and running," Kupfer continued, including West Germans, who recognized a superior East Bloc bargain when they saw one; the crowds forced police to temporarily close the HO retail fair in the Stalinallee Sports Arena.[118] A photo spread in *Neues Deutschland* in 1951, which compared the holiday gifts of the Artur Raasch family of Christmases past, present, and future, made the argument clear. In 1948 Raasch lived alone in a modest apartment, and his *Weihnachtstisch* (Christmas table), reflecting the strained conditions, was laid with three books, a bottle of liquor, a tie, a package of HO flour, and a bottle of perfume. In 1951 the presents were basically the same, though there was more of everything, including a wife and a son. Best of all was the imagined future. By 1955 the Raasch family had moved into an apartment on Stalinallee, and the accompanying photo showed numerous presents, including clothes, a camera, ample liquor and food, children's toys, and, in a nice Christmas touch, a newborn child. That Raasch was a propagandist's invention hardly mattered; his story, like that of the Family Z in West Germany, showed that annual holiday celebrations marked time along the way to a prosperous individual and national future.[119]

The SED could hardly avoid East-West competition during the Christmas season; the success of the government's efforts to demonstrate the superiority of life under socialism depended in large part on the ability to provide appealing living standards vis-à-vis West Germany. *Neues Deutschland* compared the prices of gifts and holiday items in East and West to show that salaries and social security went further under socialism. "Christmas shopping like never before," bragged reporters in 1951, quoting an overwhelmed shopkeeper who said excitedly, "One needs four arms or even six to satisfy every customer in the days before Christmas." Official statistics for 1954 showed that East German retail outlets realized a praiseworthy 20 percent increase in holiday sales over the previous year—proof of the superiority of the five-year plan. The "Department Store of Peace" in Leipzig reportedly sold fifty-five tons of poultry, and shoppers across the nation bought record numbers of luxury items, shoes, "industrial goods," food and drink, and toys. "The goods available for Peace Christmas 1954 are more abundant and more diverse, and the quality of the products is better," one reporter boasted, an optimistic conclusion that tacitly revealed the anxiety engendered by inevitable comparisons to the West.[120]

Behind the scenes, state employees struggled to meet the expectations raised by rosy images of holiday abundance. Bothersome shortages and the government's sometimes frantic attempts to stock store shelves in time for the holidays revealed the contradictions of consumer provision in the GDR. Politbüro members certainly understood that East Germans wanted ample holiday goods. In 1950 they mandated cuts in the price of flour and ordered retailers to ensure that the shelves were stocked in state-run groceries. Butter and fat, eggs, wild game, coffee, and good tobacco products were in short supply, the Politbüro discovered, but local HOs could still offer "an array of Christmas specialties," including baked goods and pastries, sweets and chocolates, fruits and nuts, meats and fowl, and wine and spirits.[121] Though top leaders showed less concern for shortages as the decade went on and the economy stabilized, they continually chafed under comparisons to the West and struggled to guarantee that shoppers found at least basic goods during the holiday season.[122] Cash was important, too. Throughout the 1950s and early 1960s, government leaders issued annual directives regulating the payment of holiday bonuses, granting thirty-five GDR-marks for married couples, twenty-five for single East Germans, and ten for students.[123]

Party propagandists idealized holiday shopping in the East even as they denigrated Western consumer society. "The most beautiful and inward German holiday" belonged to *das Volk*—the people—wrote the editors of *Neues Deutschland* in December 1951. Like cultural critics in West Germany, East Germans decried the "Americanization" of the holiday, though the tone was more strident: "We will never permit the American cultural barbarians to replace the old German Christmas customs with gigantic Christmas packages filled with bottles of Coca-Cola, to debase German Christmas songs by turning them into American hits."[124] The perils behind the seductive façade of Western consumerism were cleverly pictured by a cartoon of a mock Nativity scene that appeared in the 1957 Christmas issue of the satire magazine *Eulenspiegel* (Figure 6.5). A naive East German lamb stares at a cradle filled with alluring consumer goods and labeled "Economic Miracle" while a West German politician and a businessman, represented as angels in crude caricatures, sing an insincere carol with the words, "Oh come ye little children ... to the manger in our stall." The text beneath the cradle reads: "Searching for specialists, designers, engineers from the East zone who can be bought cheap." In the gloom to the right and left of the crumbling façade lurk thugs holding clubs and a man in a military uniform. The specialists lured to the West by consumer goods, the cartoon suggested, would be sold out by a society dominated by class exploitation and ruled by unreconstructed Nazis.

How can we evaluate the appeal of Peace Christmas in the first decades of the GDR? Final conclusions are elusive, but the traditions of the socialist

FIGURE 6.5

"Oh come little children, come one and all, come to the
cradle, here in our stall!" The East German view of Christmas
in the West. (*Eulenspiegel*, 17 December 1957)

Christmas had deep roots in the working-class culture of the late Imperial
and Weimar years—still a living memory—and this ideological framework
may have resonated with committed socialists who sought alternatives to fascist or capitalist worldviews. The effects of consumer shortages are also worth
considering. Historian Ina Merkel contends that the relative scarcity of many
goods, including basic provisions, made their intermittent consumption
particularly satisfying. When paternalist state organizations provided extra
goods and wages in the holiday season, they may well have generated popular
approval. Finally, following Merkel, the state's efforts to provide goods to
cover basic needs and, when that failed, the privation shared by the general
population "had powerful egalitarian effects." As long as the regime could

provide the postwar generation with extensive social services, an equitable distribution of goods, and increasing levels of prosperity, it could generate a "basic consensus" and significant public support.[125] As a celebration of socialist equality and relative consumer abundance, and bolstered by its historical ideological framework, Christmas under the "red star" might well have been a meaningful holiday for some East Germans.

If so, ideology became less appealing in the decades that followed the construction of the Berlin Wall. Wildt's "uncanny dynamic of consumption" played out in the GDR as well. As products became increasingly diverse and East German wages and savings grew in the 1960s and 1970s, consumer practices moved away from the egalitarianism of the 1950s and began to serve as signs of social distinction and generational difference. The tangible economic successes of the East German 1960s were undermined by the shadow of the Berlin Wall, the seductive glitz of Western-style consumption, and the ongoing deferral of comparable levels of consumer satisfaction. Erich Honecker's tacit embrace of Western models of consumption and the retreat from attempts to create a socialist-style consumer culture in the 1970s further eroded the regime's legitimacy. "Suspended between pain and prosperity," as historian Katherine Pence puts it, East Germans over the years lost faith in the promise of socialism.[126] Christmas in the GDR, like its Western counterpart, became less ideological. Though visions of peace, freedom, and "building socialism" characterized the rhetoric of public celebration until the end, by the late 1960s, SED propagandists had moved away from the aggressive politicization that marked the holiday at the height of the Cold War.

The 1960s consolidated long-underway trends in sociability and celebration on both sides of the Wall. Growing commercialism and an expanding valorization of private life increasingly defined Christmas for East and West Germans alike. If the holiday became less socialist in the East, it became less Christian in the West. Opinion surveys undertaken by EMNID and the Allensbach Institute for Demography across the second half of the twentieth century repeatedly used Christmas to plumb the depths of popular piety, with discouraging results for those who cherished the holiday's Christian meaning. The long threatened and much bemoaned *Verweltlichung*, or secularization, of Christmas had finally taken place—in the 1960s rather than in the consumer rush of the 1890s or under the totalitarian pressures of the 1930s. In 1988, reported the Allensbach Institute, just 45 percent of West Germans still believed that the religious meaning of Christmas was its most important aspect; the balance considered the holiday a "western custom" in which faith was at best of secondary importance. Older respondents were somewhat more religious, as were Catholics compared to Protestants. For the majority, however, gifts, eating good food, and having "a beautiful Christmas tree" were all more memorable than attending a Christmas service. Secularization was accompanied by a revealing decline in the feelings of inwardness once associated with holiday rituals. Outward, worldly concerns—family arguments, unavoidable weight gain, boring television programs, and disappointing gifts—increasingly troubled the holiday spirit.[127] From 1963 to 1995, the number of Germans who cited the "Christmas mood" as the most important aspect of the holiday dropped from 12 to a mere 3 percent, a disturbing expression of the holiday's growing lack of depth.[128]

Equivalent statistics for the GDR are more difficult to come by. According to a survey of holiday observances undertaken by ethnographer/historian Christa Lorenz in 1984, East Germans also preferred to spend Christmas at home. Some few families still observed a Christian holiday, but most were concerned with domestic gifting and feasting rituals. Complaints about overcommercialization were common in East Germany, but no respondent admitted that their own observances were in any way political. State propaganda was a matter of public, not private, celebration. In the newly valorized culture of privacy, individualism, and materialism that dominated everyday life in East Germany in the 1970s and 1980s, Christmas looked a lot like it did in the Federal Republic.[129]

German pollsters continue to express surprise at the secularization of the holiday. From 1961 to 1995, according to EMNID, those who ranked at first place the holiday's "Christian meaning" (including, for example, "the child in the manger, a visit to church, a Christmas service, the Christmas message") dropped from 18 to 8 percent. Ten years later, when 84 percent of those polled placed family togetherness at the top of the list, the pollsters concluded that "Christmas has been transformed from a celebration of faith to a celebration of family." In 2005 only 56 percent of West Germans still believed in God, and in the former East German states, only 27 percent described themselves as believers. Barely half of the population still went to a Christmas service—compared with just one in ten on an ordinary Sunday—and EMNID concluded that "many Germans thus celebrate the birth of Christ without believing in God."[130] Yet on some level, the pollsters missed the point. Germans may no longer believe, but Christmas is the time when they act as if they do by demonstrating an enduring attachment to religious tradition. Attending Christmas services do doubt exemplifies the rise of a "cafeteria-style" approach to religious practice, where parishioners can choose to participate in a hierarchy of activities but reject church authority and lack any deep sense of faith.[131] At the same time, the desire to attend a church service precisely on Christmas Eve testifies to the centrality of the Christian heritage to what Jonathan Sheehan calls "the moral, spiritual, and educational architecture of what came to be called the West."[132] Christmas remains a decisive time to recognize and indeed ritualize this heritage, to pay off at least once a year the spiritual costs of rampant consumerism and individualization.

Tabulated responses to questions like "What is most important about Christmas?" or "Where will you spend Christmas Eve?" hardly capture the texture or emotional depth of individual family celebrations, but they are suggestive of large-scale changes in observance. "Consumerism was the 'ism' that won" during the short twentieth century, argues historian Gary Cross; it beat out other political, social, and religious philosophies because, according to Cross, consumption offers a more democratic means for people to "define self and community through the ownership of goods."[133] While I approach assertions about the democratic nature of consumer culture with some suspicion, the triumph of Christmas consumerism clearly gave family festivities a new center of gravity—the end result of a process of growing commodification dating back to the nineteenth century. The modest celebration observed by Mertens and Susannah in *The Murderers Are Among Us* indeed gestured toward the transition. The postwar decades saw the connections between self and society shift away from notions of community based on politics or faith to more private and individual assertions of family and the pleasures of domestic abundance, often scripted by mass-media products like radio and television and the more subtle messages embodied in consumer goods. In the last decades of the twentieth century, Germans relived one of the great ironies of the modern holiday: even as Christmas was finally and thoroughly commercialized, celebration offered Germans a way to preserve a sense of faith and family in the face of the profound social-cultural changes of the postwar decades. Commercialization and secularization undermined familiar forms of community. At the same time, celebrants adopted new vocabularies and practices rooted in consumer culture and private life as a means to express ever-more-tenuous notions of faith, family togetherness, and national belonging.

Conclusion
The Nation around the Christmas Tree

The Germans have quite a religious feeling for their *Weihnachtsbaum*, coming down, one may fancy, from some dim ancestral worship of the trees of the wood.

—⟶ Clement Miles, *Christmas in Ritual and Tradition* (1912)

IN DECEMBER 1996, when I was doing the initial research for this book, I took a job as one of the 500 Father Christmases working for the "Weihnachtsmann Campaign" organized by the Technical University in Berlin. On Christmas Eve, I paid "surprise" visits to five different families who had preordered the services of this secular saint. In full costume—red cloak, fake beard, black boots, and burlap sack—I bicycled through the district of Kreuzberg, filled my sack with presents left outside apartment doors by enthusiastic parents, announced my presence with a loud knock, and joined in the festivities. During this experience as participant-observer, I handed out presents, sang carols, and praised young children, who nervously recited Christmas poetry. I wondered at the extraordinary persistence of these family rituals, which seemed virtually unchanged since E. T. A. Hoffmann described them in *The Nutcracker* in 1816. The collections of familiar Christmas stories, poetry, and songs that turn up each year in German bookstores reinforce this highly burnished patina of stability. "How-to" books describe the origins of holiday customs in minute detail and explain the art of making old-fashioned decorations at home, so readers can experience a holiday "as beautiful as before."[1] Christmas Eve services continue to draw record attendance in German churches, and outdoor Christmas markets enliven German cities large and small. Television and radio specials, concerts, public decorations, the purchase of 26 million Christmas trees in 2006, which broke all previous records—all are symptoms of an enduring national tradition.[2]

The family rituals I observed on Christmas Eve appeared timeless, rooted perhaps, as British folklorist Clement Miles wrote in 1912, in some "dim ancestral worship" of the German forest.[3] The research I undertook for this book suggested otherwise. Historically speaking, Christmas is a relatively new invention, closely linked to the emergence of the modern sense of self. Over the past 200 years, its symbols and rituals have been sites of conflict and struggle, its observance pulled in sometimes radically different directions. Just as the idea of the nation is best understood as an imaginary or rhetorical formation that resists any single definition, available for mobilization by a variety of actors, so Christmas is a surprisingly open construct, used by Germans to support competing articulations of Volk and fatherland.[4] As the intimate ties between Christmas and German patriotism suggest, German identity is not just a product of manly militarism, parades and monuments, or political ideology. Feelings of cultural cohesion and national belonging are closely connected to the domestic cultures of everyday life, produced and reproduced in celebrations of Germany's favorite holiday.

Though always mutable, family festivity had significant continuities. Across the nineteenth century, the German bourgeoisie reshaped existing religious, aristocratic, and popular customs and invented the modern holiday. Its symbols, rituals, and moods—"made in Germany"—became an export product, sold to and shared with the Western and eventually the non-Western world as the definitive version of the holiday. Christmas ritualized middle-class identities and lifestyles, and Germans spoke with pride about the tender interior emotions generated by what they called the Christmas mood. Indeed, they were deeply invested in the holiday's image of timeless permanence, the better to construct alternate if parallel versions: the very stability of family customs encouraged repeated revision. By 1900 the mainstream middle-class Christmas celebrated a sentimentalized Prussian-Protestant German nationalism, linked to the pleasures of an emergent capitalist consumer society. Competing groups remade the holiday to meet their own social and political needs. War and political confrontation inspired highly charged variations on the basic theme. Yet even political radicals succumbed to the vision of social harmony and emotional depth at the core of the conventional holiday.

Traditions endured but were surprisingly permeable and productive, in large part because Christmas crossed boundaries and blurred experiences that are usually kept at least nominally separate: the sacred and the secular, the modern and the traditional, the commercial and the authentic, the public and the private. Put another way, Christmas was defined and delimited by changing articulations of politics, materialism, religion, and domesticity. All came together in the holiday season in creative, syncretic, and sometimes contradictory ways. Romantic author Ludwig Tieck's concern with the decay of the holiday's "childlike naturalness," already expressed in 1835, captured the anxiety generated by these cultural crossovers. Cultural critics typically bemoaned the effects of commercialization, which seemed to violate the holiday's most basic truths. As advertising experts and businessmen eagerly appropriated a festival based on gifts and abundance to sell all kinds of product, family observances centered on consumer splurges generated an ever-present litany of complaint. The rampant materialism embodied in excessive Kauflust, critics charged, trivialized the birth of Christ. The vapid pleasures of consumer culture corrupted authenticity, debased tradition, and destroyed piety.

Commercialization certainly changed popular celebration, but it hardly drained the holiday of meaning. Rather, consumer culture opened new avenues of feeling and identification, crystallized once a year in the holiday season. In many ways, the apparently timeless and traditional aspects of German Christmas were themselves inventions of modern mass-production and marketing schemes. A good German holiday was unimaginable without the proper tree, ornaments, candles, foods, and texts—all products of an advanced industrial society. Mass-produced goods and modern consumption practices segmented social hierarchies around taste and class and made visible the minute distinctions that defined identities and lifestyles.[5] They also standardized family rituals and spread the Christmas mood across all levels of society and thereby helped build a shared national culture rooted in things and feelings. The emotional community celebrated on Christmas Eve, when Germans presumably sang the same songs, ate the same foods, and opened similar gifts at the same time, was not just imagined. The material culture of Christmas brought Germans together in constellations of practice and feeling that could both sustain and contradict other sources of self-identity.

Modern cultures of consumption coexisted in an uneasy but mutually sustaining relationship with religion. Clergymen who worried that modern commerce degraded the holiday and spirituality alike missed half the story. They understood that the cult of domestic piety enjoyed by both Catholics and Protestants in the late 1800s hardly depended on formal liturgies or profound spirituality. Yet they failed to see the ways in which the grand ideas of reform theologies—whether Protestant, Catholic, or Jewish—nurtured the domestication of faith and the feminization of religion, trends encouraged and perhaps accelerated by middle-class family celebration. It proved a short step indeed from Schleiermacher's 1806 description of the holy family bonds realized in Christmas festivities to the sentimental domestic rituals that colonized lofty theologies and formal observances and sacralized middle-class lifestyles. Family rituals drew on and challenged official liturgies, but as the testimony recorded in this book suggests, celebrants often asserted that domestic piety was no less "deep" or moving than formal expressions of faith.[6] Changes in the way Germans thought about and practiced religion only made Christmas more important as a place where both the clergy and the laity could preserve some sense of the sacred in a modernizing world. It appears that Christmas helped remake and even preserve spirituality itself, in part by sentimentalizing and commercializing popular piety.

The relationship between religion and nationalism that circulated through the holiday was similarly complex. The "nationalization of the masses" did not so much secularize as reshape religious culture by channeling it through consumer goods and domestic practices that took on nationalist overtones.[7] Faith was fundamental to the feelings of community generated around the Christmas tree: mainstream celebrations repeatedly portrayed Germany as a Christian nation, unified in the celebration of the birth of Jesus. This was a powerful set of ideas and practices, and the national aspirations of German Protestants, Catholics, and Jews all drew sustenance from the cult of domestic piety, albeit in quite different ways.[8] In the end, secularization arrived not as a result of nineteenth-century modernization but in the 1960s, when an alarming crisis of faith accompanied the consolidation of a culture of affluence. Changes in family life, the flagging appeal of collective political ideologies, and the growing pluralism of German (and Western) society—all turned the 1960s into a hinge decade in which worshippers pulled away from formal religious observance.[9] Yet Christmas retained its religious edge even then. As the one day a year on which Germans still flock to church, the holiday helps keep Christian culture alive in a commercialized and apparently secularized world.

Germany's political leaders certainly recognized the opportunities and dangers inherent in a holiday that linked family, faith, and nation. During the Franco-Prussian and First and Second World Wars, political and civic elites expended immense effort to build a culture of War Christmas around family celebration. Their efforts testify to their deep appreciation of the holiday's appeal, as well as to their fear that the holiday gone wrong could generate widespread discontent. Social Democrats crafted proletarian festivities that challenged the class hierarchies of middle-class proprieties; National Socialists reinvented Christmas to naturalize the codes and values of the racial state; West German liberals and East German Communists used competing holidays to promote the collective values of hostile Cold War regimes. All sought to capitalize on Christmas's emotional repertoire and apparent ability to forge links between families and the national collective.

This book has continually grappled with the popular appeal of these political projects. Support for political appropriation is never easy to quantify, but one thing is clear: interpretations based on official versus vernacular frameworks hardly capture the subtle ways in which political culture both absorbed and penetrated everyday life. The dominant narratives promoted by political, civic, and religious leaders and the practices of popular celebration were mutually sustaining enterprises. The controversies that circulated around religious celebration in the Nazi and post–World War II years perhaps best exemplify the way that Christmas celebrations blurred public and private meanings, but they are hardly the sole example.[10] Politicized rituals no doubt smoothed the projection of state power into private life, especially when combined with compelling claims on consumption, family, or faith. At the same time, significant groups of Germans rejected inventions that strayed too far from the "traditional" humanitarian values they associated with the holiday.

As this political give-and-take suggests, "German Christmas" continually contends with an ever-present past, turning a shared history of Western society's central religious and family holiday into a specifically German story with uniquely dark overtones. German Christmas remains overdetermined, laden just below the surface with the violent ruptures and radical political experimentation of Germany's "shattered" twentieth century.[11] The ease with which National Socialists remade the holiday continues to trouble the German imagination, as public fascination with photographs of the Christmas party of camp guards at Auschwitz suggests.[12] The construction of counternarratives—whether liberal-Christian or antifascist—continues apace. Helma Sanders-Brahm's *Germany, Pale Mother* (1980) prominently features a War Christmas scene, with an original recording of the Stalingrad *Ringsendung* (ring broadcast)—intended to show that the holiday, like the mother and child of the film, was a victim of the Fatherland. Joseph Vilsmaier's film *Stalingrad* (1993) includes a War Christmas scene of miserable soldiers sold out by the Nazi leadership, indistinguishable from 1950s-era novels and films. Memories of the Nazi War Christmas are pertinent and contested, and not just in popular film. In his 1992 "Christmas address" to German troops deployed in Cambodia, general inspector of the German Bundeswehr Klaus Naumann remarked that "for the first time since 1944, German soldiers will spend Christmas in action outside the Heimat." Critics, sensitive to Germany's troubled history of military occupation, retorted that his words "sounded like 'War Christmas' 1992." Naumann was reprimanded by the minister of defense.[13] Perhaps it was no coincidence that the same year, thousands of Berliners joined hands to form a six-kilometer-long Christmas Eve *Lichterkette*, or chain of light, to protest "right-radical violence, antisemitism, and racism." Holding candles and lanterns, they lined the city streets from Unter den Linden to Theodor-Heuss Platz.[14]

Over the last fifteen years, Germans have increasingly come to terms with the conflicted history of their favorite holiday. Ingeborg Weber-Kellermann's influential cultural-social history of German Christmas, first published in 1978, paved the way for more critical studies by historians like Doris Foitzik, Richard Faber, and Esther Gajek. Their work on "the ideological penetration of the holiday of holidays" challenged assertions that Christmas was celebrated in a private niche, impervious to political manipulation.[15] Popular literature is also more open to the holiday's troubled past. As German Christmas is increasingly saturated with consumer images, political appropriations themselves generate their own nostalgic and marketable forms. In an ironic twist on the classic family Christmas book, journalist Rosemarie Köhler's *Erinnerungsbuch* (Memory Book) on Christmas in Berlin from 1945 to 1989 presents the Cold War as a defanged battle over Christmas trees and shopping malls and delivers on its promise of "many illustrations and reports from contemporaries."[16] Judith and Rita Breuer's richly illustrated exhibition catalog *Von Wegen Heilige Nacht!* (Forget Christmas Eve!) includes page after page of colorful propaganda images from the Kaiserreich, World War I, the Nazi era, and the GDR. The exhibit and catalog are meant to expose "false" versions of German Christmas and warn the public that neo-Nazis continue to have designs on the holiday.[17] The Breuers' concerns are justified: a quick Internet search reveals numerous websites that promote the texts and images of Nazi Christmas for apparently dubious purposes, without attribution or analysis. At the same time, the Breuers' book shows that even Nazi Christmas kitsch, with its sepia-toned "beauty," has a certain aesthetic and nostalgic appeal, the allure of which can override the rejection of a discredited history. These examples could be multiplied, but the point is that the German Christmas past continues to haunt the Christmas present—"sometimes more clearly, sometimes more opaquely, but rarely entirely unrecognizably," as Professor Alexander Tille put it in 1893.[18]

Given the tumult of Germany's twentieth century, it is no surprise that Germans cling to the *Gemütlichkeit und Geborgenheit* (coziness and comfort) promised by the holiday. Despite their loaded history, annual Christmas rituals offer Germans a powerful escape into a vision of community based on emotions and values that seem to have little to do with the politics of the past. Celebrations, Victor Turner pointed out long ago, allow "society to take cognizance of itself" by making evident the social bonds that give meaning to human activity.[19] As the famous anthropologist wrote in a telling sentence, "A celebratory performance rejoices in the key values and virtues of the society that produces it, and in a history whose high points of success and conquest (or even noble failure) exemplify qualities of moral and aesthetic excellence."[20] The history of German Christmas suggests that things are a bit more complicated, that Turner's holistic method produces a view of social-historical processes that is too static, stable, and systemic. Probing the tensions and struggles hidden by the formal qualities of ritual leaves one suspicious of assertions that celebration reproduces a coherent system of meaning, much less the moral excellence championed by Turner. Indeed, in *Christmas in Germany*, I have sought to uncover the particular appropriations masked by universal claims to show that symbols and celebrations are "contradictory, politically charged, changeable, and fragmented."[21] I have preferred to explore the conflicts surrounding German Christmas rather than take too seriously assertions that the holiday created *Frieden auf Erden und den Menschen ein Wohlgefallen* (Peace on Earth, Good Will to Men). At the same time, I have had to acknowledge the seriousness with which generations of Germans chased this dream.

Turner may seem like an old-fashioned optimist, certain in his conviction that ritual evokes broadly shared meaning and social virtue. His approach nonetheless explains much about why people become so invested in holidays in the first place. Rituals do help individuals find their place in social structures, however fragmented. Celebration does return to shared values, however conflicted. Moreover, as Turner explained, the "celebratory frame," shaped by the memory of past celebrations and anticipation for those to come, brings out "the innovative potential of participants." When they join in communal rituals grounded in music and singing, art and literature, stagecraft and decoration, and special food and drink, celebrants improvise on standard scripts and engage in creative acts of self-expression.[22] German Christmas had (and has) a potent emotional charge because it uses all these means to celebrate the enduring myths of middle-class family life. As the appeal of communities based on religious or collective political values fades into a postmodern consumer culture of fragments and appearances, Christmas remains a time out of time, a special holiday, indeed a "season" (*Weihnachtszeit*) for the rehearsal and consolidation of the familial bonds that we still see as the basis of our sense of community and social relations. As John Gillis put it, "Our obsession with family myths, rituals, and images is [explained by] the fact that we no longer have access to other locations on which we might map our deepest moral values."[23] No wonder German Christmas was so powerful, so popular, and so contested. Middle-class sentimentalism permeated the modern holiday, and this "immense repertory of sympathy and domesticity" gave participants a way to think about and express the intimate, interiorized feelings basic to modern subjectivities and modern Western culture writ large, even in times of rapid political or social change and uncertainty.[24]

The sentimental emotions of private life are hardly natural, God-given, or inherently good, though the holiday made them seem that way. Indeed, the history of Christmas explored in this book suggests instead that the ways in which we experience and express emotions are products of shared cultural-historical practices, not entirely reducible to biological urges, socioeconomic determinants, or ideological aspirations. The cult of sentimentalism is no product of nature but a cultivated middle-class project, nurtured by rituals and myths through modalities of consumerism, faith, and national politics. An investigation of the enduring attachment to sentimentalism should be central to the emerging history of emotions, and this book can be read, in part, as a contribution to a larger interdisciplinary endeavor that examines the ways emotions are evoked, authenticated, and defended.[25] I suspect that future studies will underscore the foundational importance of sentimentalism for the making of the modern interiorized self, showing that putatively natural feelings are also social constructs, malleable and open to appropriation in pursuit of all manner of ideological agendas.

Notes

AfWN   *Aufführungen für Weihnachten und Neujahr* (Mühlhausen i. Thürigen, various years)

BAB   Bundesarchiv-Berlin (Lichterfelde)

BA-FA   Bundesarchiv-Filmarchiv, Berlin

BA-MA   Bundesarchiv-Militärarchiv, Freiburg

BayHSA   Bayerische Hauptstaatsarchiv, Munich

DAF   Deutsche Arbeitsfront (German Worker's Front)

EOK   Evangelischer Oberkirchenrat (Protestant Upper Church Consistory)

EZA   Evangelisches Zentralarchiv, Berlin

KV   *Kölnische Volkszeitung*

LIZ   *Leipziger Illustrirte Zeitung*

MadR   *Meldungen aus dem Reich, 1938-45*, ed. Hans Boberach (Herrsching: Pawlak, 1984)

ND   *Neues Deutschland*

NSDAP   National Socialist Workers Party

OkR   Oberkonsistorialrat (Chief Consistorial Councilor, Protestant Church)

RMVP   Reichsministerium für Volksaufklärung und Propaganda (Reich Ministry for Popular Enlightenment and Propaganda)

SAPMO   Stiftungs Archiv für Partien und Massenorganizationen der DDR, Berlin

Sopade   *Deutschland-Berichte der Sozialdemokratischen Partei Deutschlands (Sopade), 1939–1940*, ed. Klaus Behnken (Frankfurt/Main: Petra Nettelbeck Zweitausendeins, 1980)

StA-M   Staatsarchiv München

TENT   Landesarchiv Berlin, PrBr Rep. 30, Theater Exemplar Neuer Teil

UA-EKO   Unternehmensarchiv-Eisenhüttenkombinat Ost, Eisenhüttenstadt

VB   *Völkischer Beobachter*

VZ   *Vossische Zeitung*

1 For a syncretic overview of recent work on ritual and performance, see Burke, "Performing History." For classic statements on how rituals and symbols "work," see Turner, ed., *Celebration*; Cohen, *The Symbolic Construction of Community*; Bell, *Ritual Theory, Ritual Practice*; and Lincoln, *Discourse and the Construction of Society*.

2 Fritzsche, *Stranded in the Present*.

3 Taylor, *Sources of the Self*, 198; also Seigel, *The Idea of the Self*; and Wahrman, *The Making of the Modern Self*. For a review of the scholarship, see Gregory S. Brown, "Am 'I' a 'Post-Revolutionary Self'?"

4 Taylor, *Sources of the Self*, 13.

5 Ibid., 204; Wahrman, *The Making of the Modern Self*, xiv–xv.

6 Restad, *Christmas in America*, 91–104; Mark Connelly, *Christmas*, 9–43. Christmas in the United States and Great Britain has been the subject of a number of impressive monographs in the last decade, including Nissenbaum, *The Battle for Christmas*; Marling, *Merry Christmas!*; and Waits, *Modern Christmas in America*. See also Pleck, *Celebrating the Family*; Litwicki, *America's Public Holidays*; and Schmidt, *Consumer Rites*. For Great Britain, see Bella, *The Christmas Imperative*; Weightman and Humphries, *Christmas Past*; and Golby and Purdue, *The Making of the Modern Christmas*. For a theoretical overview of and collection of essays on Christmas, see Daniel Miller, ed., *Unwrapping Christmas*.

7 "Weihnachten," *LIZ*, 21 December 1844, 391–92.

8 Brace, *Home-Life in Germany*, 224 (emphasis mine); Wylie, *The Germans*, 85; Miles, *Christmas in Ritual and Tradition*, 263.

9 Wylie, *The Germans*, 85, 106.

10 For a selection of the literature, see Stearns with Stearns, "Emotionology"; Biess, "Forum—History of Emotions"; Reddy, *The Navigation of Feeling*; and François, Siegrist, and Vogel, eds., *Nation und Emotion*. For a helpful overview, see Roeder, "Coming to Our Senses."

11 "Das Weihnachtsfest," *LIZ*, 21 December 1844, 385.

12 See, for example, Sewell, "The Concept(s) of Culture."

13 Rosenwein, "Worrying about Emotions in History," 842; Rosenwein, *Emotional Communities in the Middle Ages*.

14 Bausinger, *Folk Culture in a World of Technology*.

15 Auslander, "Beyond Words," 1117–18.

16 For overviews of the history and theory of consumer culture, see Confino and Koshar, "Regimes of Consumer Culture"; Geyer and Jarausch, "In Pursuit of Happiness"; Slater, *Consumer Culture and Modernity*; and De Grazia with Furlough, eds., *The Sex of Things*.

17 Steinhoff, "Christianity and the Creation of Germany," 295, 300. See also Helmut Walser Smith, ed., *Protestants, Catholics and Jews in Germany*; and Helmut Walser Smith, *German Nationalism and Religious Conflict*.

18 For two useful introductions to the vast literature on the religious history of modern Germany, see Nowack, *Geschichte des Christentums in Deutschland*; and Helmut Walser Smith, ed., *Protestants, Catholics and Jews in Germany*.

19 See Hettling and Nolte, eds., *Bürgerliche Feste*; and Düding, Friedemann, and Münch, eds., *Öffentliche Festkultur*. For other sophisticated analyses of national identity that focus on public space and symbols, see Koshar, *Germany's Transient Pasts*; and Tacke, *Denkmal im sozialen Raum*.

20 Confino, *The Nation as a Local Metaphor*, 73–93; Swett, "Celebrating the Republic without Republicans"; Behrenbeck, "The Nation Honours the Dead."

21 For example, Hardtwig, "Bürgertum, Staatssymbolik und Staatsbewußtseinn, 1871–1914." Such views accord with models of the German "Sonderweg" as represented by *The German Empire, 1871–1918*, the classic work by Hans-Ulrich Wehler.

22 Bausinger, "Anmerkungen zum Verhältnis von öffentlicher und privater Festkultur."

23 De Grazia and Furlough make this point in *The Sex of Things*, 1–10. For an important exception to the focus on public, masculine German nationalism, see Reagin, *Sweeping the German Nation*. For a still useful overview of scholarly approaches to nationalism, see Calhoun, *Nationalism*.

24 Blackbourn, *The Long Nineteenth Century*, 427; Michael B. Klein, *Zwischen Nation und Region*, 347.

25 Anderson, *Imagined Communities*; Hobsbawm, *Nations and Nationalism since 1780*; Hobsbawm and Ranger, *The Invention of Tradition*; Calhoun, *Nationalism*.

26 Tille, *Die Geschichte der deutschen Weihnacht*, ix. For more recent histories of the German holiday, see *Das Weihnachtsfest*, the influential study by Ingeborg Weber-Kellermann; Foitzik, *Rote Sterne*; and Faber and Gajek, eds., *Politische Weihnacht in Antike und Moderne*.

CHAPTER 1

1 Caroline to Wilhelm von Humboldt, 23 December and 29 December 1815, in Sydow, ed., *Wilhelm und Caroline von Humboldt in ihren Briefen*, 161, 163.

2 "Berlins erster Weihnachtsbaum," *ND*, 25 December 1946, 8.

3 Friedrich, ed., *Festive Culture in Germany and Central Europe*; see especially in that volume Brophy, "The Politicization of Traditional Festivals in Germany, 1815–48"; and Biskup, "The Transformation of Ceremonial." On the Bildungs-

bürgertum, see Sperber, "Bürger, Bürgerlichkeit, Bürgerliche Gesellschaft"; and also Weber-Kellermann, *Weihnachtsfest*, 110.

4 Miles, *Christmas Customs and Traditions*, 161–62, 227–34.

5 Taylor, *Sources of the Self*, 293.

6 Caroline to Wilhelm, 29 December 1815, in Sydow, ed., *Wilhelm und Caroline von Humboldt in ihren Briefen*, 163.

7 Goethe, "Sorrows"; Barthes, *A Lover's Discourse*, esp. 204–9.

8 Bausinger, *Typisch deutsch*, 65.

9 Bodelschwingh, *Aus einer hellen Kinderzeit*, 64–71.

10 Hettling and Nolte, "Bürgerliche Feste."

11 Elm, *Goldene Weihnachtsbuch*, 5.

12 On the Luther Bible, see Sheehan, *Enlightenment Bible*.

13 On Germany as a "Christian nation," see Steinhoff, "Christianity and the Creation of Germany."

14 Bock and Plöse, eds., *Aufbruch in die Bürgerwelt*; Weber-Kellermann, *Frauenleben im 19. Jahrhundert*; Blackbourn, *The Long Nineteenth Century*, chaps. 2 and 3.

15 Weber-Kellermann, *Weihnachtslieder*, 199–213.

16 Perrot, "Introduction," 2.

17 Taylor, *Sources of the Self*, 13–14, 106.

18 "Weihnachten," *LIZ*, 21 December 1844, 391.

19 On the centrality of Schleiermacher to "'the great spiritual revolution' of the nineteenth century," see Sheehan, *Enlightenment Bible*, 229–30; and Hübinger, *Kulturprotestantismus und Politik*.

20 Schleiermacher, *Die Weihnachtsfeier*; for an English translation, see Schleiermacher, *Christmas Eve*. Page numbers in text. I have relied on Tice's translations, though I have compared them to the German original and made slight changes where appropriate. Taylor outlines the connections between modern selfhood and Protestant theology in *Sources of the Self*, esp. 214–18.

21 See Schellong, "Schleiermachers 'Weihnachtsfeier.'"

22 For this translation I have drawn primarily on Schleiermacher, *Die Weihnachtsfeier*, 57; compare Tice, 82.

23 Quoted in Sheehan, *Enlightenment Bible*, 229.

24 Roper, *The Holy Household*, esp. 3–5.

25 Schellong, "Schleiermachers 'Weihnachtsfeier,'" 80.

26 Hölscher, "The Religious Divide," 36–37.

27 Quoted in Sheehan, *Enlightenment Bible*, 233.

28 Reddy, *The Navigation of Feeling*, 146; Schenk, *Mind of the European Romantics*.

29 E. T. A. Hoffmann, *Nußknacker und Mausekönig*, 5–6; for background, see McGlathery, *E. T. A. Hoffmann*, 118–21.

30 Gillis, "Ritualization of Middle-Class Family Life"; Gillis, *A World of Their Own Making*, esp. 99–104.

31 Budde, *Auf dem Weg ins Bürgerleben*, 82–84; also Frykman and Löfgren, *Culture Builders*; and Gillis, *A World of Their Own Making*, 108–9.

32 E. T. A. Hoffmann, *Nußknacker und Mausekönig*, 6.

33 Hamlin, *Work and Play*, 11, 17.

34 Gillis, *A World of Their Own Making*, 37; also Fritzsche, *Stranded in the Present*, esp. 160–61; Weber-Kellermann, "Excurs"; Rybczynski, *Home*.

35 Taylor, *Sources of the Self*, 290.

36 E. T. A. Hoffmann, *Nußknacker und Mausekönig*, 53.

37 Corbin, *The Foul and the Fragrant*, 176.

38 Steinhoff, "Christianity and the Creation of Germany," 291.

39 Nickel, *Die heiligen Zeiten und Feste*, 132–33, 134, 140–41.

40 Olfers, *Erblüht in der Romantik*, 47, 104.

41 From the 1860 *Mescheder Kreisblatt*, quoted in Sauermann, *Von Advent bis Dreikönige*, 108.

42 Kügelgen, *Bürgerleben*, 211, 519.

43 Martin-Fugier, "Bourgeois Rituals," 286.

44 Nissenbaum, *Battle for Christmas*, 176–203; Schmidt, *Consumer Rites*, 124.

45 Brace, *Home-Life in Germany*, 224–25; compare Nissenbaum, *Battle for Christmas*, 219–22.

46 Brace, *Home-Life in Germany*, 222.

47 For an introduction, see Russ, *German Festivals and Customs*; also the bibliography in Weber-Kellermann, *Weihnachtsfest*, 223–27.

48 For a concise history of the tree, see Kammerhofer-Aggermann, "Die Entstehung des bürgerlichen Weihnachtsfestes," esp. 100–108. For an early and still authoritative account, see Tille, "German Christmas and the Christmas Tree," 172.

49 Quoted in Weber-Kellermann, *Weihnachtsfest*, 107.

50 Quoted in ibid., 47.

51 Janz, *Bürger besonderer Art*, 77–82; Kammerhofer-Aggermann, "Die Entstehung des bürgerlichen Weihnachtsfestes," 102.

52 Sauermann, *Von Advent bis Dreikönige*, 108–12. On Danzig, see "Zur Geschichte des Weihnachtsbaum," *Pastoral-Blatt des Bistums Münster*, December 1886, 140.

53 Diary, Landesarchiv Berlin, Rep. 061 Familiennachlaß Schoepplenberg, Acc. no. 10, bd. 2 (1875–1892), 16; Weber-Kellermann, *Weihnachtsfest*, 118, 130–31.

54 Elm, *Goldene Weihnachtsbuch*, 64–65.

55 Siefker, *Santa Claus*, 157–58; Miles, *Christmas in Ritual and Tradition*, 219; Weber-Kellermann, *Weihnachtsfest*, 24–33.

56 On the United States, see Nissenbaum, *Battle for Christmas*, chap. 2.

57 See, for example, the cards in Wohlfart, *Der braven Kinder Weihnachtswünsche*.

58 See Weber-Kellermann, *Weihnachtsfest*, 98–101; and Weber-Kellermann, *Die Familie*, 302.

59 Kammerhofer-Aggermann, "Die Entstehung des bürgerlichen Weihnachtsfestes," 106.

60 "Protestantische Gebräuche unter den Katholiken," *Pastoral-Blatt des Bistums Münster*, December 1888, 134.

61 "Entchristlichung des Christfestes," *Pastoral-Blatt des Bistums Münster*, December 1883, 143.

62 "Zur Geschichte des Weihnachtsbaumes," *Pastoral-Blatt des Bistums Münster*, December 1886, 142.

63 "Eine Blume an der Krippe," *Katholische Volkszeitung*, 25 December 1894, n.p.

64 "Zur Geschichte des Weihnachtsbaumes," *Pastoral-Blatt des Bistums Münster*, December 1886, 142.

65 "Christnacht! Zum Weihnachts Feste," *KV*, 25 December 1897 (morning ed.), 1.

66 "Verfahren bei der Vination," *Pastoral-Blatt des Bistums Münster*, 16 November 1863, 121. See also the some 100 pages of instructions for services from Advent to Epiphany in Schott, *Das Meßbuch der heiligen Kirche*, 49–143.

67 Steinhoff provides a concise summary of general liturgical differences in "Building Religious Community," 282–83. On Catholic hierarchy, see Nowak, *Geschichte des Christentums in Deutschland*, 101.

68 Weber-Kellermann, *Weihnachtslieder*, 24–31, 125–81; Luther quote, 126.

69 Steinhoff, "Building Religious Community," 286.

70 Hölscher, "Die Religion des Bürgers," esp. 598.

71 Weber-Kellermann, *Das Buch der Weihnachtslieder*, 199–204, 258.

72 Bergen, "Hosanna or 'Hilf, O Herr Uns,'" 142.

73 Ziehnert, *Winterfreuden*, 2; also *Winterunterhaltungen für die reifere Jungend*. That Ziehnert's volume was intended as either a Christmas or New Year's gift reflected the aristocratic practice of gift giving at the year's end rather than at Christmas; gifting ceremonies were still new inventions.

74 Füller, *Erfolgreiche Kinderbuchauthoren des Biedermeier*, 6.

75 Schenda, *Volk ohne Buch*, 200–202.

76 Zalar, "The Process of Confessional Inculturation," 124; for Catholic reading materials, see, for example, advertisements in *Germania*, 9 December 1873, 9.

77 Friedrich Güll, "Weihnachts-Bilder"; Heger, ed., *Deutsches Weihnachtsbuch für die Jugend*; *Immergrünes Weihnachtsbuch für die Jugend*.

78 For typical advertisements, see *LIZ*, 6 December 1845, 366–67; quote from *LIZ*, 29 November 1845, 350.

79 Hohendahl, *Building a National Literature*, 329. On the rapid growth of Christmas books in the last third of the century, see Göbel and Verweyen, eds., *Weihnachten im Bilderbuch*.

80 Literacy spread rapidly in German-speaking lands, but the lower classes owned few books and read little until later in the century. Schenda, *Die Lesestoffe der Kleinen Leute*, 38; Graff, *The Legacies of Literacy*, esp. 260–94.

81 Elm, *Goldene Weihnachtsbuch*.

82 Lohmeyer, ed., *Deutsche Jugend*.

83 For a rather idealized version of a domestic celebration heavily influenced by Christian thought, see, for example, "Wie in einem christlichen Hause Weihnachten gefeiert wurde."

84 Marbach, *Die heilige Weihnachtszeit*, 4.

85 "Weihnachtsgedanken," *LIZ*, 25 December 1858, 417.

86 McLeod, "Weibliche Frömmigkeit—männliche Unglaube?"

87 McLeod, *Piety and Poverty*, 163. On feminization, also see Allen, "Religions and Gender in Modern German History," 190; Janz, *Bürger besonderer Art*, 76; and Marion A. Kaplan, *The Making of the Jewish Middle Class*, 76–77.

88 Budde, *Auf dem Weg ins Bürgerleben*, 412.

89 Holm, "Weihnachtslied eines Kindes," 4.

90 For example, "An den heiligen Christ! Ein Kinderbrief, mitgeteilt von D. Duncker," in Lohmeyer, ed., *Deutsche Jugend: Weihnachts-Album*, 95–96.

91 Quote from the typical poem "Christkindlein" in *Kinder-Lieder*, 5

92 Heger, *Deutsches Weihnachtsbuch*, 2.

93 Quoted in "Modern-Protestantische Weihnachten," *KV*, 25 December 1900 (morning ed.), 1.

94 Children's Christmas cards inevitably repeated images of angelic parades; see Wohlfart, *Der braven Kinder Weihnachtswünsche*.

95 In Blüthgen, *Weihnachtsbuch*.

96 See, for example, the 1859 poem and picture (the baby Jesus with lamb and toys resting beneath a decorated, candle-lit tree), "Jesuskind unter dem Weihnachtsbaum," in G. Süs, *Paradiesgarten für fromme und liebe Kinder*; reprinted in Göbel and Verweyen, eds., *Weihnachten im Bilderbuch*, 28–29.

97 Zalar, "The Process of Confessional Inculturation," 134.

98 "Weihnachts-Wache," *KV*, 25 December 1894 (morning ed.), 3.

99 "Eine Blume an der Krippe," *KV*, 25 December 1894, 1.

100 "Weihnachten," *KV*, 24 December 1910 (noon ed.), 1. See Allen, "Religions and Gender in Modern German History," 197.

101 "Eine Blume an der Krippe," *KV*, 25 December 1894, 1.

102 On popular magazines, see Graf with Graf, "Die Ursprünge der modernen Medienindustrie," esp. 27.

103 "Weihnachten," *KV*, 24 December 1910 (noon ed.), 1.

104 Quoted in Sauermann, *Von Advent bis Dreikönige*, 141.

105 Meyer, *Weihnachtsfest*, 127.

106 Dr. Ernst Klessmann, in Sauermann, *Von Advent bis Dreikönige*, 87. See the print of "Der Weihnachtsbaum" with secular and holy elements in "Der Weihnachtsbaum," *LIZ*, 25 December 1858, 425.

107 Blüthgen, *Weihnachtsbuch*.

108 For a similar argument on family literature in the United States, see Denning, *Mechanic Accents*, 78.

109 Kracauer, "Little Shopgirls Go to the Movies," 294. On literacy and reading cultures in northern Europe, see Graff, *The Legacies of Literacy*, esp. 260–94.

110 Beumer, "Die Söhne des Proletariers"; Stewart, *On Longing*, 23.

111 Some stories were written by the directors of charity missions in an attempt to encourage the generosity of potential donors; for example, "Die arme Familie." Also see Gutmann, "'Die Arme Frau Dortel am Weihnachtsabend,'" 102–3.

112 Wraner, "Einen Weihnachtsbaum bekam sie doch."

113 Kracauer, "Little Shopgirls Go to the Movies," 295.

114 Tieck, "Weihnacht-Abend," 944.

115 Kotzde, "Christnacht im Schnee," 49.

116 M. Mirbach, "'Friede den Menschen auf Erden, die eines guten Willens sind!' Eine Weihnachts-Geschichte," *KV*, 25 December 1894, 1–2; L. Budde, "Weihnachtsleid," *KV*, 25 December 1896, 5.

117 Jensen, "Eine Weihnachtsbescherung," 11, 13.

118 The Andersen story was first published in 1845 and was quickly translated into German; for a rather bizarre set of stories that develops a holiday cult of death, see Doering, ed., *Weihnachtsbüchlein*.

119 In Blüthgen, *Weihnachtsbuch*, 226–38.

120 C. Herlotzsohn, "Neue Weihnachtsbilder," *LIZ*, 26 December 1846, 411.

121 Kracauer, "Little Shopgirls Go to the Movies," 302.

122 Theodor Storm, "Unter dem Tannenbaum."

123 Shorske, *Fin-de-Siecle Vienna*; Mosse, *Nationalism and Sexuality*; Reagin, *Sweeping the German Nation*.

124 Theodor Storm, "Unter dem Tannenbaum," 12.

125 See the introduction to ibid., 1–10; quote on 9.

126 Theodor Storm, "Unter dem Tannenbaum," 27–28.

127 On the confessional ramifications of the national canon, see Helmut Walser Smith, *German Nationalism and Religious Conflict*, 20–37; Cramer, "The Cult of Gustavus Adolphus"; and Altgeld, "Religion, Denomination, and Nationalism in Nineteenth-Century Germany."

128 Marbach, *Die heilige Weihnachtszeit*, 123.

129 Ibid.

130 Cassel, *Weihnachten*, esp. 3–8.

131 Tille, "German Christmas," 168–69.

132 Meyer, *Weihnachtsfest*, 3.

133 Anthony D. Smith, *The Ethnic Origins of Nations*, 177; compare Hobsbawm and Ranger, *The Invention of Tradition*.

134 Marbach, *Die heilige Weihnachtszeit*, 2–4.

135 Ibid., 107, 115.

136 Lagarde, *Altes und Neues über das Weihnachtsfest*, 322. On Lagarde, see Stern, *The Politics of Cultural Despair*.

137 Tille, "German Christmas and the Christmas Tree," 168; Tille, *Yule and Christmas*; Tille, *Die Geschichte der Deutschen Weihnacht*. On Tille, see Manz, "Translating Nietzsche, Mediating Literature."

138 Quote in Kück and Sohnrey, *Feste und Spiele des deutschen Landvolks*, 28; also Mannhardt, *Wald- und Feldkulte*; Weinhold, *Weihnacht-Spiele und Lieder aus Süddeutschland und Schlesien*; Reitschel, *Weihnachten in Kirche, Kunst und Volksleben*.

139 "Altdeutsches Spielzeug," *LIZ*, 25 December 1880, 560; see Leroy, *Konstruktionen des Germanen in bildungsbürgerlichen Zeitschriften des deutschen Kaiserreiches*.

140 Blackbourn, *The Long Nineteenth Century*, 390–91.

141 "Eigenartige Weihnachtsgebräuche," *Vorwärts*, 24 December 1909.

142 I. Lautenbacher, "Die Weihnachtskrippe: Eine kunst- und kultur-historische Studie," *Frankfurter Zeitung und Handelsblatt*, 25 December 1885, 1.

143 Elm, *Goldene Weihnachtsbuch*, 1–5.

144 Ibid., 19–20.

145 Ibid., 20.

146 Ibid., 22.

147 See Cramer, "The Cult of Gustavus Adolphus."

148 "Friede den Menschen," *Germania*, 24 December 1874, 1.

149 "Gott mit uns!," *Germania*, 24 December 1875, 1.

150 "Der verwaisten Gemeinde Christnacht," *Germania*, 23 December 1876, 1.

151 Altgeld, "Religion, Denomination, and Nationalism," 54.

152 "Christnacht! Zum Weihnachts Feste," *KV*, 25 December 1897 (morning ed.), 1.

153 Wilhelm Frank, "Eine Nacht in Bethlehem," *KV*, 25 December 1909, 1; A. Baumstark, "Weihnachtsfeier im Jerusalem des fünften Jahrhunderts," *KV*, 25 December 1910, 1.

154 "Politische Weihnachtsgedanken," *KV*, 25 December 1898, 1.

155 "Modern-protestantische Weihnachten," *KV*, 25 December 1900 (morning ed.), 1.

156 "Weihnachten," *KV*, 25 December 1905 (morning ed.), 1.

157 Hull, *Absolute Destruction*, 103; Blackbourn, *The Long Nineteenth Century*, 374–79.

158 War Christmas is examined in depth in chapter 3.

159 Ganaway, *Toys, Consumption and Middle Class Childhood*.

160 E. T. A. Hoffmann, *Nußknacker und Mausekönig*, 7.

161 Hoffman von Fallersleben, "Der Weihnachtsmann"; reprinted in Wegehaupt, ed., *Weihnachten im alten Kinderbuch*, 57–58. On the song's reception, see Weber-Kellermann, *Weihnachtslieder*, 251–56.

162 "Das Spielzug der Kinder," *LIZ*, 19 December 1846, 395.

163 *Brockhaus' Conservations-Lexikon Bd. XV*, 76–79. I am grateful to Bryan Ganaway for sharing this source with me.

164 Hamlin, *Work and Play*, 41.

165 Advertisement for Christmas presents from Jandorf department store in *Berliner Morgenpost*, 29 November 1908.

166 Rudolf Stocknis, "Weihnachtswanderung durch Berlin. III," *VZ*, 17 December 1893.

167 Wallich, *Erinnerungen aus meinem Leben*, 32–33. On militarism and war toys, see Hamlin, *Work and Play*, 38–43.

168 Reagin, *Sweeping the German Nation*, esp. 55–61.

169 For example, Lohmeyer, ed., *Deutsche Jugend*; Troll, ed., *Deutsches Weihnachtsbuch*; Beckey, ed., *Deutsche Weihnachten*.

170 "Wie es die Franzosen am Rheine getrieben," in Beumer, ed., *Weihnachtsbuch*, 189–94; "Die Weihnachtspfeife: Eine Bismarckerinnerung von ***," in Beckey, ed., *Deutsche Weihnachten*, 22–23.

171 Falkenhausen, *Ansiedlerschicksale*, 32; also Prince, *Eine deutsche Frau im Innern Deutsch-Ostafrikas*, 63–67, 150–51, 203–4.

172 Falkenberg, "'Der Christbaum ist der schönste Baum,'" 4–11.

173 Steinhoff, "Christianity and the Creation of Germany," 300.

174 Eulenburg, "Weihnachtsmärchenspiel."

175 See Steakley, "Iconography of a Scandal."

176 See Hammer, *Deutsche Kriegstheologie*; Missalla, *"Gott mit uns."*

177 Eulenburg, "Weihnachtsmärchenspiel," 63.

178 Ibid., 76–77.

179 See Wurst, *Fabricating Pleasure*, esp. 347–51.

CHAPTER 2

1 Tönnies, *Custom: An Essay on Social Codes*. Hobsbawm and Ranger emphasize the cultural inventiveness of the late nineteenth-century middle classes in *Invented Traditions*; on fractures in Imperial festival culture, see Abrams, *Worker's Culture in Imperial Germany*.

2 Van Rahden, "Weder Milieu noch Konfession"; Richarz, "Der jüdische Weihnachtsbaum," 276.

3 Kaplan, *The Making of the Jewish Middle Class*, 76. As Sarna suggests in "Is Judaism Compatible with American Civil Religion?," Jews in the United States faced a similar "December dilemma."

4 "Des Erlösers Geburt," *Vorwärts*, 24 December 1905.

5 McLeod, *Piety and Poverty*, 28.

6 Gregor, Roemer, and Roseman, *German History from the Margins*, 7.

7 Spiel, *Fanny von Arnstein oder die Emanzipation*, 435. Spiel's account is often cited as evidence of the first Christmas tree in Vienna; see, for example, Richarz, "Weihnukka—Das Weihnachtsfest im jüdischen Bürgertum," 90.

8 Lässig, *Jüdische Wege ins Bürgertum*, 669 (emphasis in original).

9 Kaplan, "Redefining Judaism in Imperial Germany," 1; also van Rahden, "Weder Milieu noch Konfession."

10 Richarz, "Der jüdische Weihnachtsbaum," 280.

11 Quoted in Hopp, *Jüdisches Bürgertum in Frankfurt am Main im 19. Jahrhundert*, 178.

12 Bernstein, "Wie ich als Jude in der Diaspora aufwuchs"; quotes, 188–91.

13 Mühsam, *Ich bin ein Mensch gewesen*, 362.

14 Hopp, *Jüdisches Bürgertum*, 178–79.

15 "D. S. Berlin," *Im deutschen Reich: Zeitschrift des Centralvereins deutscher Staatsbürger jüdischen Glaubens*, January 1901, 50.

16 Cohn, *Verwehte Spuren*, 50.

17 Born, *Mein Leben*, 68–69.

18 Quoted in Richarz, "Der jüdische Weihnachtsbaum," 286 (emphasis in original).

19 Hirsch, *Der Weihnachtsbaum in der jüdischen Familie*, 4.

20 J. Ziegler, "Weihnachts-Bescheerung" [*sic*], *Allgemeine Zeitung des Judentums*, 20 December 1895, 604–5; A. Levy, "Post festum," *Allgemeine Zeitung des Judentums*, 3 January 1896, 4–6.

21 "Es war in jenen Tagen," *Allgemeine Zeitung des Judentums*, 25 December 1891, 614.

22 Kugelmann, "O Chanukka, o Chanukka!," 8–10.

23 Müller, "Lichter," 10.

24 *Allgemeine Zeitung des Judentums* (1896), quoted in Richarz, "Weihnukka," 90–91.

25 Mühsam, "Heilige Nacht."

26 Daxelmüller, "Chanukka," 41.

27 Herzl quoted in Friedlander, "Makkabi," 61; Cohn, *Verwehte Spuren*, 38. For an account of widespread Maccabee celebrations in Germany and the Austro-Hungarian Empire around 1900, see "Die Makkabäerfeier," *Die Welt*, 31 December 1897, 4–5.

28 "Zum Chanukka-Fest," *Die Jüdische Presse*, 11 December 1884, 505.

29 Quote from the *Tageblatt* (1903) in Joselit, "'Merry Chanuka," 312. See Pleck, *Celebrating the Family*, 97–98.

30 Kaplan, "Redefining Judaism in Imperial Germany," 5.

31 "Weihnachtsbäume und Chanukkageschenke," *Israelitische Wochenschrift: Zeitschrift für die Gesamtinteressen des Judentums*, no. 23 (1892), 417.

32 For Singer, see advertisements in *Israelitische Wochenschrift*, 15 December 1899, 786; and 20 December 1901, 802. M. Schneider's "grand Christmas sale" in *Frankfurter Israelitisches Familienblatt*, 28 November 1902, 7–8.

33 Zuckermann, "Du Wirst den Kindern heut die Lichter zünden," 41.

34 For example, Moritz Jung, "Chanukka-Betrachtung," *Der Israelit: Ein Central-Organ für das orthodoxe Judenthum*, 8 December 1898, 1809–10.

35 Ernst Müller, "Lichter," *Die Welt*, 14 December 1900, 10.

36 "Chanukah," *Jüdische Allgemeine Zeitung*, 11 December 1903, 589.

37 *The Jewish Encyclopedia* (1906), 316.; online at ⟨http://www.chazzanut.com/media/maoz.html⟩ (12 July 2006).

38 Geissmar, *Erinnerungen (1913)*, 457.

39 "Wochen-Chronik," *Israelitische Wochenschrift*, 777.

40 Quote from a Hanukkah celebration for Jewish school children in "Wochen-Chronik," *Israelitische Wochenschrift*, 8 December 1899, 778.

41 Popp, *Jugendgeschichte einer Arbeiterin*, 1, 2–3.

42 Bebel, "Ein Geleitwort," in Popp, *Jugendgeschichte einer Arbeiterin*, iii. On working-class autobiographies, see Kelly, *The German Worker*.

43 Lidtke, *The Alternative Culture*, 192.

44 "Zu Weihnachten," *Vorwärts*, 25 December 1892.

45 "Krisen-Weihnacht," *Vorwärts*, 25 December 1908.

46 "Entweihte Nacht," *Vorwärts*, 25 December 1901.

47 "Weihnachtsfest," *Vorwärts*, 25 December 1902.

48 "Weihnachtsbetrachtungen," *Vorwärts*, 25 December 1909.

49 "Weihnacht," *Vorwärts*, 25 December 1895.

50 Holt, "The Church Withdrawal Movement in Germany"; McLeod, *Piety and Poverty*, 25–26.

51 McLeod, *Piety and Poverty*, 28.

52 "Weihnachtsbetrachtungen," *Vorwärts*, 25 December 1909.

53 Ibid.

54 "Sonnenwende," *Vorwärts*, 25 December 1906.

55 A. F. Thiele, "Gewonnenes Spiel," *Vorwärts*, 25 December 1891.

56 Peter Nansen, "Ein Weihnachtsmärchen," *Unterhaltungsblatt des Vorwärts*, 25 December 1908, 997–98.

57 *Märchenbuch für die Kinder des Proletariats*; for *König Mammon*, see Bromme, *Lebensgeschichte eines modernen Fabrikarbeiters*, 32.

58 Zetkin, "An die Eltern!," n.p. The book was an edited edition of the supplements for children that appeared in the 1905–1906 editions of Zetkin's newspaper, *Die Gleichheit*.

59 Almsloh, "Was am Weihnachtsbaum erzhählt wird," 51–52.

60 Dithmar, *Arbeiterlieder 1844 bis 1945*, 181–95, 266–69.

61 Foitzik, *Rote Sterne*, 42.

62 Reprinted as *"Stille Nacht"* in the ten-pfennig booklet *Proletarische Weihnachtslieder* (Berlin: A. Hoffman, ca. 1927). See Dithmar, *Arbeiterlieder 1844 bis 1945*, 191–92; alternate versions in Weber-Kellermann, *Weihnachtslieder*, 217–24.

63 Foitzik, *Rote Sterne*, 43.

64 Advertisements for workers' celebrations in *Vorwärts*, 21 December 1877.

65 Advertisements for workers' celebrations in *Vorwärts*, 18 December 1892.

66 "Berliner Nachrichten: Weihnachtsglocken," *Vorwärts*, 25 December 1908.

67 "Lokales," *Vorwärts*, 24 December 1893.

68 For example, "Die Weihnachtsfeier für die Kinder der Ausgesperrten und Streikenden," *Vorwärts*, 25 December 1904.

69 "Verbotene Weihnachten," *Vorwärts*, 20 December 1903.

70 "Weihnachtstage in Crimmitschau," *Vorwärts*, 24 December 1903; "Weihnachtstage in Crimmitschau II," *Vorwärts*, 25 December 1903.

71 Nolan, *Social Democracy and Society*, 301; quoted in Abrams, *Worker's Culture in Imperial Germany*, 19.

72 Kelly, *The German Worker*, 4.

73 Lidtke, *The Alternative Culture*, 192.

74 Abrams, *Worker's Culture in Imperial Germany*, 22–23.

75 See, for example, "Aus Gross-Berlin: Fünf Minuten vor Weihnachten," *Vorwärts*, 22 December 1913, which exposed the experiences of workers in different jobs.

76 Moszeik, ed., *Aus der Gedankenwelt einer Arbeiterfrau von ihr selbst erzählt*, 15.

77 Bromme, *Lebensgeschichte eines modernen Fabrikarbeiters*, 234.

78 Huck, "Die Freiwilligen Sozialleistungen der Firma Siemens," 40–41.

79 Budde, *Auf dem Weg ins Bürgerleben*, 276. See also Walser, *Dienstmädchen*, esp. 17; and Ottmüller, *Die Dienstbotenfrage*, esp. 15.

80 Stillich, *Die Lage der weiblichen Dienstboten in Berlin*, 169–77. For the *Teller*, see Moszeik, ed., *Aus der Gedankenwelt*, 15.

81 "Weihnacht der Dienstboten," *Kieler Tagespost*, 22 December 1909; reprinted in Bejschowetz-Iserhoht, *Dienstboten zur Kaiserzeit*, 103–4.

82 In Berlin in 1899, for example, 85 percent of serving girls had been employed in their current positions for less than two years. Budde, *Auf dem Weg ins Bürgerleben*, 281.

83 Ibid., 412–13; Walser, *Dienstmädchen*, 83.

84 Viersbeck, *Erlebnisse eines Hamburger Dienstmädchens*, 25, 56–58, 89.

85 Ibid., 57.

86 Moszeik, ed., *Aus der Gedankenwelt*, 107.

87 Bromme, *Lebensgeschichte eines modernen Fabrikarbeiters*, 101.

88 Advertisement for Conrad Tack & Co., a shoe factory in Magdeburg with six-teen retail outlets in Berlin alone, in *Vorwärts*, 13 December 1904; advertisement for Maggi products, *Vorwärts*, 17 December 1905.

89 Gebhardt, *Blätter aus dem Lebensbilderbuch: Jugenderinnerungen*, 46.

90 Sauermann, *Von Advent bis Dreikönige*, 13, 150.

91 Abrams, *Worker's Culture in Imperial Germany*.

92 Quoted in Sauermann, *Von Advent bis Dreikönige*, 81.

93 Fischer, *Denkwürdigkeiten und Erinnerungen eines Arbeiters*, 175–78.

94 Stifter, "Weihnacht," in *Die Gartenlaube für Österreich*, vol. 1, no. 2 (1866); re-printed in Stifter, *Gesammelte Werke Bd. 6*, 573.

95 Spencer, "Policing Popular Amusements in German Cities," esp. 366–68.

96 On the general church interest in the protection of the holidays, see the files of the Evangelische Oberkirchenrat (EOK) on "Der Heilighaltung der Sonn- und Feiertage," EZA 7/2755, 2756, 2757, 2758, 2759, and 2766, which span the years from 1859 to 1924.

97 Article 266 of the *Amtsblatt der königlichen Regierung zu Potsdam und der Stadt Berlin*, n. 22, 2, June 1854; copy in EZA 7/2755, 194.

98 See "No. 962, Polizei-Verordnung. Die äußere Heilighaltung der Sonn- und Feiertage betr.," in *Amtsblatt der königlichen Regierung zu Coblenz*, n. 50, 15 De-cember 1853; copy in EZA 7/2755, 402–4.

99 Ibid.

100 Mark M. Smith, "Making Sense of Social History," 173.

101 "Polizeiverordnung über die äußere Heilighaltung der Sonn- und Feiertage," in *Bekanntmachungen des Königl. Polizei-Präsidiums*, 21 July 1911, in Landesarchiv Berlin Rep. 01–02, Acc. no. 2300 (Polizeiverordnung Abt. 6, no. 10, "Arbeit an Sonntagen und Feiertagen," 1889–1928), 149–50, 160.

102 McLeod, *Piety and Poverty*, 206.

103 Ibid., 10.

104 Ibid., 188–89.

CHAPTER 3

1 Brown and Seaton, *Christmas Truce*, 68, 80–86.

2 Niemann, *Das 9. königlich-Sächsisches Infanterie-Regiment N. 133 im Weltkrieg*, 32.

3 *The Christmas Truce* (2007), DVD produced by the History Channel. Quote from ⟨http://store.aetv.com/html/product/ind ex.jhtml?id=77626⟩ (19 Sep-tember 2008).

4 Jürgs, *Der kleine Frieden im großen Krieg*; "Singer Buys Rare World War I Let-ter," *New York Times*, 9 November 2006, B2; *Merry Christmas (Joyeux Noel)*, produced by Sony Pictures Classics, directed by Christian Carion, 2005. See

also "Alfred Anderson, 109, Last Man from Christmas Truce of 1914," *New York Times*, 22 November 2005, B9.

5 Weintraub, *Silent Night*; compare Brown and Seaton, *Christmas Truce*.

6 Mosse, *Fallen Soldiers*, 77; Fussell in Stansky, "Film Review," 593.

7 Wolfgang Kruse describes the Christmas truce as an expression of widespread antiwar sentiment and the growing popularity of socialism in the ranks in *Krieg und nationale Integration*; see also Ulrich and Ziemann, eds., *Frontalltag im Ersten Weltkrieg*. For an interpretation more focused on chance and spontaneity, see Foitzik, *Rote Sterne*, 38. For a view of the truce as a "celebration of history and tradition" and British "fair play," see Ecksteins, *Rites of Spring*, 190.

8 Mayer, "Kriegstagebuch," 73–74.

9 *Kriegsweihnachten*, n.p.

10 Augustinus Kilian, "Weihnachtsbrief an die Krieger im Felde!" (Limburg, 1916); ms in BAB, 92 Sachthem, Sammlung/273, 4.

11 "Des Christen Kriegsgebet zur Weihnachtszeit," *Weihnachten im Kriege*, n.p. See also *Feldpredigten*, the Catholic journal edited by Cardinal Faulhaber, published 1916–18.

12 Kühne, *Kameradschaft*. On the *Leidensgemeinschaft*, see Reimann, *Der große Krieg der Sprachen*, 120–21; on the return to tradition as a way of dealing with the war, see Winter, *Sites of Memory*.

13 Weber-Kellerman, *Weihnachtsfest*, 118–19.

14 "Eine große Bitte an alle deutschen Kinder," *Gartenlaube* 47, December 1870, 792; also the cover of *LIZ*, 24 December 1870. See Foitzik, *Rote Sterne*, 32–34.

15 Private diary of Johann Adam Lippert, *Erinnerungen an den Krieg 1870/71*, ms. in BayHSA Abt. IV (Militärarchive), Kriegsbriefe 279.

16 Gottfried Bürklein to Friedrich Bürklein, 24 December 1870, in BayHSA Abt. IV (Militärarchiv), Kriegsbriefe 250.

17 Quoted in *Unserm Kaiser!*, 144.

18 Leibig, *Erlebnisse eines freiwilligen bayerischen Jägers*, 204.

19 Frankenberg, *Kriegstagebücher*, 290–93.

20 Kühnhausen, *Kriegs-Erinnerungen*, 217.

21 Rogge, *Bei der Garde*, 111.

22 Karl Horn, "Aufzeichnungen aus dem Feldzuge 1870–71 als freiwilliger kgl. bayr. Feldgeistlicher," quoted in Kermann, "Der deutsch-französische Krieg von 1870/71 aus der Sicht eines pfälzischen Militärgeistlichen," 212.

23 Kretschmann, *Kriegsbriefe aus den Jahren 1870/71*, 236.

24 Rogge, *Bei der Garde*, 110.

25 Hammer, *Deutsche Kriegstheologie*, 22, n. 23.

26 Leibig, *Erlebnisse eines freiwilligen bayerischen Jägers*, 204.

27 Emonts, *Unserer Jäger Freud und Leid*, 115.

28 Ibid., 117–21

29 On popular attitudes toward the war, see Rohkrämer, "Gesinnungsmilitarismus der 'kleinen Leute' im Deutschen Kaiserreich"; and Blackbourn, *The Long Nineteenth Century*, 379.

30 Tanera, *Ernste und heitere Erinnerungen eines Ordonnanzoffiziers im Jahre 1870/7.*

31 *Unserm Kaiser!*, 144–48.

32 See, for example, the holiday issues of various soldier's newspapers from circa 1910 in BA-MA, MSg2/5042, MSg2/1994, MSg2/5169, MSg2/1974.

33 For example, G. Hofang, "Weihnachten in der Kaserne," *LIZ*, 25 December 1880, 553, 555–56.

34 For an exposé of late nineteenth-century military propaganda from the perspective of an "ordinary soldier," see Rehbein, *Das Leben eines Landarbeiters*, 168–69.

35 These titles represent only a handful of the numerous holiday scripts with military themes. Otto Deuker, "Der Weihnachtsabend in der Hauptmannsküche. Charakterszene für zwei Herren und eine Dame," handwritten ms. (1899), TENT 1115; Julius Vogel, *Am Weihnachtsabend oder Auf der Hauptwache, Scherz in 1 Akt mit Gesang* (Mülheim a.d. Ruhr, 1904), TENT 3180; Martin Böhm and G. Margot, *Friede auf Erden oder des alten Soldaten Weihnachtsengel, Genrebild in 1 Akt von Martin Böhm und G. Margot* (1908), TENT 4356; Martin Böhm, *Kriegers Weihnachten. Genrebild mit Gesang in 1 Akt von Martin Böhm* (Berlin, 1909), TENT 4660; Paul R. Lehnhard, "Majors Weihnachts-Überraschungen," *AfWN*, no. 26 (ca. 1912); Edmund Braune, "Des alten Kriegers Weihnachtsabend," *AfWN*, no. 41 (ca. 1913).

36 Martin Böhm, *Weihnachten unter Kaiser Wilhelm II. Genrebild in 1 Akt von Martin Böhm* (Berlin, 1910), TENT 4959, 2. Böhm had his own Berlin-based publishing house specializing in theater scripts and wrote a number of Christmas melodramas with nationalist/militarist themes, which played at Concordia Festsäle and the Reichshallen-Theater. For a partial list of Böhm's Christmas plays, see previous note.

37 Ibid.

38 Ibid., 15.

39 Ebner, "Kriegserlebnisse"; Hirth, "'Herr Pfarrer, Sie werden ein strammer Soldat.'" On war theology, see Hammer, *Deutsche Kriegstheologie*; and Meier, "Evangelische Kirche und Erster Weltkrieg," 724.

40 Keppler, Faulhaber, and Donders, eds., *Feldpredigten*, no. 1 (1916), 1.

41 Hürten, "Die katholische Kirche im Ersten Weltkrieg."

42 "Weihnachts-Beilage der Germania," *Germania*, 25 December 1914 (morning ed.).

43 Augustinus Kilian, "Weihnachtsbrief an die Krieger im Felde!" (Limburg, 1916), BAB, 92 Sachthem, Sammlung/273, 4.

44 *Kriegs-Korrespondenz des Evangelischen Preßverbandes für Deutschland (E.V.)*, 27
    November 1914, EZA 7/2873, n.p. For EOK attempts to provide religious mate-
    rial for pastors and soldiers in the field, see EZA 7/2873, 7/2877, 7/2899.

45 EZA 7/2877, 20–29.

46 *Ein Weihnachtsfeldpostbrief unsern lieben Limbacher Kriegern.*

47 Bamberger, *Andachtsbüchlein für die jüdischen Krieger*; Picht, "Zwischen Vater-
    land und Volk."

48 Letters summarized in Ebner, "Kriegserlebnisse," 184–88. Ebner also copied sev-
    eral of his own letters into the diary.

49 Ibid., 186.

50 Ibid., 183.

51 Ibid., 202.

52 Mayer, "Kriegstagebuch," 73.

53 Ebner, "Kriegserlebnisse," 203.

54 Ibid., 204–5.

55 Ibid., 207, 189.

56 Ibid., 201.

57 Ibid., 208.

58 Ibid., 183–84.

59 Ibid., 55, 714; on flagging enthusiasm for the war in general, see Hammer, *Kriegs-
    theologie*, 259–60.

60 Statistics in Ebner, "Kriegserlebnisse," 845. According to his own count, Ebner
    also heard confession 43,811 times and gave Holy Communion 81,728 times.

61 After 1917, seven film units from the newly established Bild- und Filmamt pro-
    duced official photos of "life at the front" and bought private photos for pub-
    lic distribution. Excellent collections of both official and personal photos from
    WWI, including dozens of shots of Christmas, are in the BayHSA Abt. IV Mi-
    litärarchiv and the BfZ in Stuttgart. For an overview of war photography on the
    German side, see Dewitz, "Geschichte der Kriegsphotographie."

62 "Weihnachtsfest der deutschen Truppen im Schützengraben in Polen," BayHSTA
    Abt. IV Militärarchiv, BS- 58. This photo, like other photos from this shoot, at
    times appears as an "authentic" picture of German celebrations, as in Eksteins,
    Rites of Spring.

63 Dewitz, "Geschichte der Kriegsphotographie," 171.

64 Behlert, ed., *Weihnachtsfeier A. O. K.*

65 *Weihnachtsfeier im Feindesland. Zugleich eine vaterländische Gedenkfeier in der
    Kirche zu Frémicourt. Heiligabend 1914. 8th Artillerie (F) Munitions-Kolonne
    des Grande-Corps*, Staatsbibliothek Munich; the remarkable collections of First
    World War "gray literature" at the Deutsche Bücherei in Leipzig contains nu-
    merous examples of such material.

66 Binding, *A Fatalist at War*, 85.

67 Merck, *Briefe aus dem Felde*, 19.

68 Richert, *Beste Gelegenheit zum Sterben*, 198. For a description of soldiers' lack of enthusiasm for "war theology," see Ulrich and Ziemann, eds., *Frontalltag im Ersten Weltkrieg*.

69 Quoted in Wolfgang Kruse, "Krieg und Klassenheer," 542.

70 Stumpf's diary was published as part of the Reichstag Investigating Committee's investigation of the reasons for Germany's wartime collapse. Stumpf, *World War I Diary*.

71 Ibid., 58.

72 Ibid., 146.

73 Ibid., 275–77.

74 Such instances were remarkable enough to be noted in memoirs. See Meier, "Evangelische Kirche," esp. 718; for an example, see Mayer, "Kriegstagebuch," 77.

75 Mayer, "Kriegstagebuch," 72, 82–84, 330.

76 Picht, "Zwischen Vaterland und Volk."

77 Sulzbach, *Zwischen Zwei Mauern*, 44, 54–55.

78 Martin Friedländer, "Das Chanukka-Feldpostpaket," *Jüdische Presse*, 11 December 1914.

79 Dr. Baeck, "Die Kraft der Wenigen. Zum Chanukkafest 1915. Ein Gruss an die jüdischen Soldaten im deutschen Heere vom Verband der Deutschen Juden"; reprinted in *Der Schild*, 20 December 1935, 1–2. On the political goals of Jewish organizations, see Picht, "Zwischen Vaterland und Volk."

80 Letter of Christian Brautlecht, from "Chiry, west of Noyon," 25 December 1914, in Witkop, *Kriegsbriefe gefallener Studenten*, 150. Realizing the broad appeal of War Christmas, Witkop included some fifteen Christmas letters in the collection.

81 Quoted in Leed, *No Man's Land*, 189.

82 "Weihnacht 1915," *Der Schützengraben*, December 1915, 58. On the trench press, see Lipp, *Meinungslenkung im Krieg*; on the "Heimat of feeling" generated by Christmas, see Foitzik, *Rote Sterne*, 28.

83 Reimann, *Der große Krieg der Sprachen*, 56.

84 In sum, about 28.7 billion pieces of mail were sent in both directions during the war; statistics in Metken, "'Ich hab' diese Karte im Schützengraben geschrieben.'" Numerous studies on soldier's letters and the requisite interpretative methodologies have been published in the last decades; for a selection, see Knoch, "Feldpost"; Schikorsky, "Kommunikation über das Unbeschreibbare"; and Ulrich, *Augenzeugen*. Christmas greetings from various civic groups are in the collection of the Deutsche Bücherei, Leipzig.

85 Statistics in Stahr, "Liebesgaben für den Ernstfall," 89; see also Hegel, "'Jede Liebesgabe hilft mit zum Siege.'"

86 "Weihnachtsbitte für unsere Helden," poster from the Liebesgabenausschuß Braunschweig, 1915, BayHSA Plakate Sammlung, 16510; "Weihnachtsfreude unsern Märken!" poster from the Staatliche Abnahmestelle freiwilliger Gaben für das III, Armeekorps, Berlin, 1915; reprinted in *Das Plakat* (January 1916).

87 "Weihnachtsbitte für unsere Helden" poster from the Liebesgabenausschuß Braunschweig, 1915, BayHSA Plakate Sammlung, 16510.

88 Milhaly, *Kriegstagebuch*, 126, 151–52, 206; for similar stories, see Hämmerle, ed., *Kindheit im Ersten Weltkrieg*, 147.

89 Hegel, "'Jede Liebesgabe hilft mit zum Siege,'" 16–17.

90 Binding, *A Fatalist at War*, 37.

91 Ulrich, *Augenzeugen*, 305. On the close connections between official and vernacular rhetoric, see also Schikorsky, "Kommunikation über das Unbeschreibbare"; and Reimann, *Der große Krieg der Sprachen*.

92 Schikorsky, "Kommunikation über das Unbeschreibbare."

93 Merck, *Briefe aus dem Felde*, 22–24.

94 Binding, *A Fatalist at War*, 85–86.

95 Meyer to Sophie, 19 December 1915, in Probst and Kaldewei, eds., *Ewig Dein*, 50. See Knoch, "Erleben und Nacherleben," esp. 203–4.

96 For two famous collections of letters published during the war, see Pniower and others, eds., *Briefe aus dem Felde*; and Witkop's classic *Kriegsbriefe*. For an analysis of these and other collections, see Ulrich, *Augenzeugen*.

97 Metken, "'Ich hab' diese Karte im Schützengraben geschrieben,'" 138–39; BayHSA Abt. IV has a fine collection of War Christmas cards.

98 Binding, *A Fatalist at War*, 37.

99 Cohen, *Symbolic Construction of Community*, esp. 12–15.

100 Mayer, "Kriegstagebuch," 92.

101 "Rede des Divisionspfarrers Meier bei einer Militaer-Weihnachtsfeier in der Kirche zu Lens," pamphlet, no pub. data, 1914, Erzbischöfliches Archiv, Freiburg, Nachlass Mayer.

102 "Kriegers Weihnachtsgesang 1914," pamphlet (Liebenzell: Schriftenverlag der Liebenzeller Mission/Württemberg, 1914).

103 Franz Grundner, "Weihnachts-Lied. Beim Anzünden des Kristbaumes im Schützengraben zu singen," *Der Drahtverhau: Schützengraben-Zeitung der 3. Kopm. bayr Ldw. Inf. Rg. No.1*, December 1915, n.p.

104 "Kriegs-Tannenbaumlied," *Der Schützengraben*, December 1915, 64.

105 See, for example, *48 Weihnachtslieder für Soldaten*. For a typical Evangelical songbook, see Röthig, *Weihnachtslieder im Felde*; for a Catholic example that includes prayers like "The Christian's War-Prayer for Christmas Time," see *Weihnachten im Kriege*.

106 Bauer's memoirs are excerpted in Blaumeiser and Blimlinger, eds., *Alle Jahre wieder*, 63–64.

107 Stumpf, *World War I Diary*, 277–78.

108 On bodily emotions, see Connerton, *How Societies Remember*. For an interesting take on the complex emotional and ideological work of music, see Brown and Volgsten, eds., *Music and Manipulation*.

109 Reimann, *Der große Krieg der Sprachen*, 117.

110 Ebner, *Kriegserlebnisse*, 208.

111 Letter of Richard Kutzner, 25 December 1914, in Witkop, *Kriegsbriefe*, 185; Hettling and Jeismann, "Weltkrieg als Epos."

112 "Eine Kinder-Weihnachtsbescherung im Felde," *Der Schützengraben*, December 1915, 60.

113 Sulzbach, *Zwischen Zwei Mauern*, 54–55.

114 Quoted in Ziemann, *Front und Heimat*, 237–38.

115 Gertrud Bäumer, "Heimatchronik," *Die Frau*, vol. 25, no. 4 (January 1918), 138–34; Davis, *Home Fires Burning*.

116 Gertrud Bäumer, "Heimatchronik," *Die Frau*, vol. 25, no. 5 (February 1918), 173.

117 Von-Ed, "Kriegsweihnacht im deutschen Hause," 1–2 (emphasis in original).

118 Nora, "Between Memory and History."

119 See Confino's discussion of popular memory and loss in "The Nation as Local Metaphor."

120 Leed, *No Man's Land*, 120.

121 Eliade, *Myths, Rites, Symbols*, 94.

122 Ibid., 2–3.

123 "Weihnachten 1914," *Weser-Zeitung*, quoted in Foitzik, *Rote Sterne*, 27.

124 Flex, "Weihnachtsmärchen des fünfzigsten Regiments"; Mosse, *Fallen Soldiers*, esp. 75–79. See Becker, "From Death to Memory," 32–49.

125 Willibald Seemann, "Soldatentod am Weihnachtsabend," *Das Reichsbanner*, 23 December 1928, 364. For other examples, see the Christmas issues of *Das Reichsbanner. Zeitung des Reichsbanner Schwarz-Rot-Gold*, the newspaper of the Social Democratic paramilitary group, especially in the late 1920s and early 1930s.

126 World War I Jewish pilots were similarly called "Makkabäer der Lüfte"; *Der Schild. Zeitschrift des Reichsbundes jüdischer Frontsoldaten*, 27 December 1935, n.p.

127 *Gefallene Deutsche Juden*, 92–93.

128 Barthes, *Mythologies*, 148.

129 Hans Zöberlein, "Weihnachten in der Siegfriedstellung. Ein Unvergeßliches Kriegserlebnis," *VB*, 25/26/27, December 1930.

130 Barthes, *Mythologies*, 129.

CHAPTER 4

1 "Weihnachten," *Die Reklame*, 20 October 1893, 213.

2 H. Ahlsmann to Provinzial Kirchenrat, Berlin, 16 November 1928, EZA 14/865, n.p. The Reichstag debate is in *Verhandlungen des Reichstags*, 3485–506. For more

on the popular responses to the bill, see the press clippings and letters in EZA 14, Konsistorium Berlin Brandenburg/865; and Spiekermann, "Freier Konsum und Soziale Verantwortung."

3　*Verhandlungen des Reichstags*, 3487–88.

4　Ibid., 3489.

5　Ibid., 3498.

6　Ibid., 3492.

7　Ibid., 3493.

8　Ibid., 3495.

9　Ibid., 3499.

10　"Der Ladenschluß am Heiligabend," in *Lichterfelder Lokal Anzeiger*, 8 October 1931.

11　On the collapse of the "bourgeois stylistic regime" around 1900, see Auslander, *Taste and Power*; for an overview of twentieth-century German mass media, see Schildt, "Das Jahrhundert der Massenmedien."

12　Strasser, McGovern, and Judt, eds., *Getting and Spending*; De Grazia with Furlough, eds., *The Sex of Things*, esp. 4.

13　Geyer, "In Pursuit of Happiness," 286; Abrams, *Worker's Culture in Imperial Germany*, 21. See also Stihler, *Die Entstehung des modernen Konsums*; and Saldern, "Massenfreizeitkultur im Visier."

14　*Staatsbürger Zeitung*, 14 December 1898.

15　Cross, *An All-Consuming Century*, 1–5.

16　Lerner, "Consuming Pathologies," 48–49.

17　Sahlins, *Culture and Practical Reason*, 216. See Hausen's discussion of consumerism and symbolic meaning in "Mothers, Sons, and the Sale of Symbols and Goods," esp. 378–79.

18　Sauermann, *Von Advent bis Dreikönige*, 146–49.

19　Blackbourn, *The Long Nineteenth Century*, 313.

20　See Bausinger, *Folk Culture in a World of Technology*.

21　See Käthe Wohlfahrt's home page at ⟨https://shop.wohlfahrt.com/⟩ (19 May 2009).

22　Vaupel, "Eine Runde Sache," 11–19; and Leichsenring, "Erzgebirgische Weihnachtspyramiden," 3–4.

23　On ornaments and prices, see the advertisements in Elm, *Goldene Weihnachtsbuch*, 101–4. Wage estimates in Berghahn, *Modern Germany*, 270.

24　"Lokales," *VZ*, 23 December 1887.

25　Wohlfart, *Der braven Kinder Weihnachtswünsche*.

26　"Weihnachten," *Die Reklame*, 20 October 1893, 213.

27　"Die Weihnachtssaison," *Die Reklame*, 22 October 1894, 229.

28　Ibid., 229–30.

29　"Weihnachten," *Die Reklame*, 20 October 1893, 214.

30 "Deine Reklame soll sein . . . Die 10 wichtigsten Gebote," *Seidels Reklame*, December 1914, 517–18.

31 "Weihnachtsplakate," *Seidels Reklame*, December 1913, 389.

32 Ibid., 390, 392.

33 "Schaufenster," *Seidels Reklame*, December 1913, 395.

34 Rellstab, *Der Weihnachtswanderer von Alt-Berlin*, 169.

35 Rudolf Stocknis, "Weihnachtswanderung durch Berlin. III," *VZ*, 17 December 1893.

36 L.V.A., "Weihnachtswanderung durch Berlin VI," *VZ*, 24 December 1893.

37 The pages of December issues of *Vorwärts* are full of advertisements for holiday entertainment; see, for example, 25 December 1906.

38 Spencer, "Policing Popular Amusements in German Cities," 378–79.

39 See advertisements in the December issues of *Vorwärts* from 1900 to 1910.

40 Theater was arguably the primary source of public entertainment before the rise of the electronic mass media, and though historians have concentrated on the production of famous or avant-garde plays (for example, Jelavich, *Munich and Theatrical Modernism*), simple melodramas far outweighed modern pieces in the playbills of the era. The Landesarchiv-Berlin has a vast collection of handwritten and printed theater scripts and censor comments from the late Kaiserreich, which includes over 200 Christmas plays; LaB, PrBr Rep. 30, Theater Exemplar Neuer Teil, no. 1–3015a and no. 3016–6981. In addition, various publishing houses concentrated on theater pieces and issued annual collections of Christmas scripts. See, for example, *Aufführungen für Weihnachten und Neujahr* (Mühlhausen im Thüringen: G. Danner, various publication dates); and *J. Rademachers Vereinsbühne* (Bonn: J. Rademacher, various publication dates).

41 Lipinski, *Friede auf Erden! Oder*," 21. See theater advertisements, *Vorwärts*, 25 December 1902. For another example of a "proletarian" Christmas play, see Diedrich, *Wintersonnenwende*.

42 Quoted in Rüden, *Sozialdemokratisches Arbeitertheater*, 95. See also Foitzik, *Rote Sterne*, 44.

43 Short summaries of the plays listed here (and dozens of other Christmas plays) in the December issues of *Aufführungen für Weihnachten und Neujahr* (Mühlhausen im Thüringen, various years).

44 Meinhold, "Die Liebe ist das Himmelreich."

45 "Weihnachten," *KV*, 25 December 1903 (morning ed.), 1.

46 The entire article is reproduced in "Modern-protestantische Weihnachten," *KV*, 25 December 1900 (morning ed.), 1 (emphasis in original).

47 "Wie geht's dem deutschen Weihnachtsmann?," *Vorwärts*, 25 December 1897.

48 "Der Große Weihnachtsbummel des goldenen Sontags," *Vorwärts*, 22 December 1909.

49 On Nuremberg, see Nestmeyer, "Zwei Engel für Liebel." On Christmas markets in Germany and Berlin, see "ChristmasMarketTours.com/Atlas Cruises and Tours," ⟨http://www.christmasmarkettours.com/⟩ (27 August 2006); and "Weihnachtsmarkt Deutschland 2007," ⟨http://www. weihnachtsmarkt-deutschland .de/2007/⟩ (19 May 2009).

50 For a rosy view of the annual markets, see Weber-Kellermann, *Das Weihnachtsfest*, 70–83. More critical scholars explain public fairs as fields where the bourgeoisie engaged in the repression of popular forms of festivity, or where popular festivity challenged and destabilized middle-class hegemony. See, for example, Christa Lorenz, *Berliner Weihnachtsmarkt*; and Stallybrass and White, *The Politics and Poetics of Transgression*. On contact zones, see Pratt, *Imperial Eyes*, 6–7.

51 Lorenz, *Berliner Weihnachtsmarkt*, 19, 25.

52 Weber-Kellermann, *Das Weihnachtsfest*, 70; Lorenz, *Berliner Weihnachtsmarkt*, 26; Paulsen, "Weihnachten in Berlin," 113–14.

53 Seyfried, *Chronik von Berlin*; quoted in Paulsen, "Weihnachten in Berlin," 115.

54 Tieck, "Weihnacht-Abend," 907.

55 Ibid., 908–9.

56 Ibid.

57 Ibid., 907.

58 Ibid., 909–10; on confectionary displays, see Paulsen, "Weihnachten in Berlin," 116–17.

59 Lorenz, *Berliner Weihnachtsmarkt*, 86.

60 Ibid., 96–99; Hans Ostwald, "Weihnachts- und Neujahrssitten in Berlin von Ehedem," *LIZ*, 11 December 1924, 898.

61 *Führer durch den Berliner Weihnachtsmarkt 1934*, 2–4.

62 Nestmeyer, "Zwei Engel für Liebel," 92; Helmhagen, *Nürnberg im Zauber des Christkindlesmarktes*, 13; Haid, *The Christmas Market of Nuremberg*, 17.

63 "Weihnachtsmarkt—ein Volksfest," *Berlin Börsen-Zeitung*, 7 December 1934, in DAF clipping file, BAB NS 5 VI/17393.

64 *Führer durch den Berliner Weihnachtsmarkt 1934*, 6, 12 (emphasis in original).

65 Lorenz, *Berliner Weihnachtsmarkt*, 134–36.

66 "Theuerung und Weihnachtsverkehr," *VZ*, 24 December 1889 (evening ed.), 1.

67 Michael B. Miller, *The Bon Marché*; Schmidt, *Consumer Rites*. For contemporary accounts of the development of the German department store, see Lux, *Studien über die Entwicklung der Warenhäuser in Deutschland*; Wagner, *Über die Organisation der Warenhäuser*; Colze, *Berliner Warenhäuser*; and Göhre, *Das Warenhaus*.

68 Colze, *Berliner Warenhäuser*, 16–17, 56, 76; Gerlach, *Das Warenhaus in Deutschland*, 77, 62.

69 Göhre, *Das Warenhaus*, 101.

70 On the critics, see Lerner, "Consuming Pathologies."

71 Wagner, *Organisation der Warenhäuser*, 4, 51–52.

72 Göhre, *Das Warenhaus*, 51.

73 Fritzsche, *Reading Berlin*, 142.

74 "Berliner Weihnachten," *Kölnische Zeitung*, 20 December 1896; Wagner, *Organisation der Warenhäuser*, 9–11, 14–15, 56.

75 "Lokales," *Vossische Zeitung*, 19 December 1887.

76 *Die Welt am Sonntag*, 9 December 1901. Attempts to use the second Advent as a "copper Sunday" apparently failed to catch on, in Berlin at least; see, for example, Wylie, *The Germans*, 91.

77 *Der Kleine Journal*, 9 December 1901; for Christmas shoplifters, see Lerner, "Consuming Pathologies," 46.

78 "Was das Weihnachtsfest den Kindern bedeutet," *Vorwärts* 24 December 1901; "Der Große Weihnachtsbummel des goldenen Sontags," *Vorwärts*, 22 December 1909.

79 Schmidt, *Consumer Rites*, 169.

80 Göhre, *Das Warenhaus*, 124–25.

81 Ibid., 142.

82 Stallybrass and White, *The Politics and Poetics of Transgression*, 38.

83 Göhre, *Das Warenhaus*, 19. On the preferences of the "little man," see Colze, *Berliner Warenhäuser*, 10.

84 "Weihnachtsbescherung für die Kinder der Arbeitslosen," *Vorwärts*, 18 December 1913. On ritualized spending as an act of self-transformation, see Pleck, *Celebrating the Family*, 246.

85 See, for example, the advertisement for the KDW in *Vorwärts*, 14 December 1913, n.p.

86 Göhre, *Das Warenhaus*, 72; Colze, *Berliner Warenhäuser*, 16.

87 Göhre, *Das Warenhaus*, 65.

88 Ibid., 73.

89 Lux, *Entwicklung der Warenhäuser*, 34.

90 Colze, *Berliner Warenhäuser*, 51.

91 Göhre, *Das Warenhaus*, 126–27.

92 "Der Goldene Sonntag," *Die Staatsbürger Zeitung*, 20 December 1903. I am grateful to Paul Lerner for sharing this and other sources from his research on Germany's department stores.

93 "Eine dringende Mahnung an die Weihnachtseinkäufer," *Die Staatsbürger Zeitung*, 9 December 1904.

94 Lerner, "Consuming Pathologies," 50.

95 See the short report in *Vorwärts*, 24 December 1891 (Beilage).

96 On anti-Semitic Christmas flyers, see the series of reports in *Im deutschen Reich: Zeitschrift des Centralvereins deutscher Staatsbürger jüdischen Glaubens* January 1898, 51; March 1904, 173–74; July 1904, 438–40.

97 For example, "Weihnachtsvorbereitungen," *Emelka-Woche*, no. 48 (19 December 1929), BA-FA Wochenschauen 502; "Weihnachtsvorbereitungen," *Emelka-Woche*, no. 51 (11 December 1929), in BA-FA Wochenschauen 503; "Weihnachtsmarkt auf dem Potsdamer Platz in Berlin," *Deulig-Tonwoche*, no. 50 (14 December 1932), BA-FA, DTW 50/1932.

98 "Der Silberne Sonntag," *Berliner Börsen-Zeitung*, 12 December 1932 (evening ed.), 5; Fritzsche, *Reading Berlin*, 147, 164.

99 Langwadt, *Das Weihnachtsgeschäft im Warenhaus*, 8, 44.

100 "Der Silberne Sonntag," *Berliner Börsen-Zeitung*, 12 December 1932 (evening ed.), 5.

101 Langwadt, *Das Weihnachtsgeschäft im Warenhaus*, 44.

102 Fallada, *Little Man—What Now?*, 184.

103 Zille cartoon in Lorenz, *Berliner Weihnachtsmarkt*, 123.

104 Peukert, *The Weimar Republic*.

105 "Rote Weihnachten!," *Berliner Morgenpost*, 25 December 1918, 1.

106 Lange, "Heimatchronik," 155; "Rote Weihnachten!," *Berliner Morgenpost*, 25 December 1918, 1.

107 Theodor Kappstein, "Weihnachtsgedanken," *LIZ*, 12 December 1918, 4.

108 Rudolf Eucken, "Betrachtungen zum Weihnachtsfest 1924," *LIZ*, 11 December 1924, 880.

109 Kappstein, "Weihnachtsgedanken," 4.

110 "Zueignung," *Der Weihnachtsbaum der deutscher Frau*. On the Weimar-era demographic revolution and related changes in social values and behavior, see Peukert, *Weimar Republic*, 7–9, 86–101.

111 "Weihnacht bei Müttern," *Berliner Morgenpost*, 22 December 1918, n.p.

112 Rudolf Mühlhausen, "Den deutschen Frauen das Dankbare Vaterland," *LIZ*, 12 December 1918, 18; Daniel, *The War from Within*.

113 "Weihnachtliche Heiratswelle," *Berliner Börsen-Zeitung*, 11 December 1932 (morning ed.), 15.

114 Paul Zinck, "Weihnachts- und Sylvesterbräuche," *LIZ*, 13 December 1923, 402.

115 "Weihnachtssitten und Weihnachtsbräuche," in *Der Weihnachtsbaum der deutscher Frau*, n.p.; Paul Zinck, "Deutsches Weihnachtsgebäck," *LIZ*, 11 December 1924, 886.

116 Compare Reagin, *Sweeping the German Nation*.

117 See Jochens, *Deutsche Weihnacht*.

118 Kupferberg in *LIZ*, 11 December 1919; Cutex in *Berliner Illustrirte Zeitung*, 15 December 1929, 2267.

119 Langwadt, *Das Weihnachtsgeschäft im Warenhaus*, 36; Swett, Wiesen, and Zatlin, eds., *Selling Modernity*.

120 Bertold Ert, "Weihnachtsstimmung," *Seidels Reklame* 12 December 1926, 551.

121 Langwadt, *Das Weihnachtsgeschäft im Warenhaus*, 48, 49–50.

122 Ibid., 40.

123 Karl Maäs, "Das Weihnachts-Inserat," *Die Reklame*, December 1920, 391.

124 *Berliner Illustrirte Zeitung*, 15 December 1929, 2274.

125 Karl Escher, "Spenden und Spender," *LIZ*, 11 December 1924, 892–83.

126 Quote from an advertisement for Kaloderma shaving cream in *Berliner Illustrirte Zeitung*, 8 December 1929, 2204. On prewrapped gifts, see Langwadt, *Das Weihnachtsgeschäft im Warenhaus*, 40.

127 Quotes from advertisement for Orange-Lavender Eau de Cologne (*Kölnisch Wasser Lavendel-Orangen*) in *Berliner Illustrirte Zeitung*, 30 November 1929, 2167.

128 Maäs, "Das Weihnachts-Inserat," 391; 1931 quote in Jochens, *Deutsche Weihnacht*, 64.

129 Greta Daeglau, "Haushalt-Strategie für die Feiertage. Von der Vorbereitung des 'Bunten Tellers' und anderer Genüsse. Teil I," *Berliner Börsen-Zeitung* 11 December 1932 (morning ed.), 13; and Greta Daeglau, "Haushalt-Strategie für die Feiertage. Festtagsmenüs und Abendplatten, Gästempfang und Zwischenmahlzeit. Teil II," *Berliner Börsen-Zeitung*, 18 December 1932 (morning ed.), 5.

130 Marßolek and Saldern, *Radiozeiten*.

131 Braun, "Weihnachtliche Impressionen," 101.

132 "Radio-Weihnachten 1923: Unterhaltung einer Weihnachtsgesellschaft durch das neue Rundfunk-Konzert vermittelst eines im Zimmer aufgestellten Telefunken-Empfängers mit Lautsprecher," *LIZ*, 13 December 1923, 405.

133 Jochens, *Deutsche Weihnacht*, 64, 76.

134 Advertisement for the Saba-Superhet radio in *Berliner Lokal-Anzeiger*, 4 December 1932, n.p. See Resper, "Was man für Weihnachten wissen muß!" and "Welchen Radioapparat kaufe ich zu Weihnachten?," *Berliner Lokal-Anzeiger*, 4 December 1932, n.p.; and Lacey, *Feminine Frequencies*.

135 *Die Sendung*, 7 December 1928, n.p.

136 Ibid., 20–26 December 1925, 21–22.

137 Ibid., 21 December 1928, XII.

138 Geyer, "Germany, or, the Twentieth Century as History," 679.

139 Applegate and Potter, "Germans as the 'People of Music.'" The importance of Weimar-era radio (and Christmas music in general) for German nationalism is overlooked in this otherwise suggestive collection.

140 This reconstruction of typical holiday broadcasts is drawn primarily from national broadcast schedules in December issues of *Die Sendung* (for example, 14–21 December 1924; 21–28 December 1924; 12–19 December 1925; 20–26 December 1925; 7 December 1928; 14 December 1928; 21 December 1928). For in-depth descriptions of individual broadcasts, see December issues of *Deutsche Welle*. For workers' radio, see the journal *Arbeiterfunk: Offizielles Organ des Arbeiter-Radio-Band Deutschlands* and Lacey, *Feminine Frequencies*, 35–38. For

a fascinating take on radio and (West) German identity, see Badenoch, *Voices in the Ruins*.

141 Richard Wetz, "Mein Weihnachtsoratorium," *Der Rundfunk-Hörer*, 13 December 1929, 5.

142 Georg Pfister, "Beiträge zu einer kirchlichen Volkskunde," conference presentation at III. Pastoralkonferenz zum katholischen Brauchtum, Munich, 27 November 1929; ms. in Archiv des Erzbistums München und Freisung, Munich, Religiöse Volksbräuche (Knf. Thesen), 1929.

143 Robert Hösel, "Put Money in Your Purse," *Seidels Reklame*, December 1926, 549–50 (emphasis in original).

144 Emil W. Frauenhof to OKR Charlottenburg, EZA 7/2769, n.p. (emphasis in original); on postsentimental holidays, see Pleck, *Celebrating the Family*, esp. 1–5, 242–49.

145 "Eine Weihnachtsbotschaft des Kanzlers," *Frankfurter Zeitung*, 25 December 1931.

146 Nissenbaum, *Battle for Christmas*. On economic conditions in Weimar, see Tooze, *Wages of Destruction*, esp. 135–47.

147 Foitzik, *Rote Sterne*, 66–67.

148 Weber-Kellermann, *Das Buch der Weihnachtslieder*, 249.

149 "Kein Frieden mit dem Klassenfeind! Nicht trügerische Kirchenglocken—Sturmgeläute zum revolutionären Kampf!," *Die Rote Fahne*, 25 December 1927.

150 Paul Körner, "'Gnadenbringende Weihnachtszeit.' Mutter und Kind ohne Unterwäsche—Wochenbett auf dem Hängeboden—Proletarier-Weihnachten," *Die Rote Fahne*, 25 December 1928.

151 "Weihnacht der Armen," pamphlet by Zentralstelle der Proletarischen Freidenker, Berlin, 1930, n.p.

152 "Polizeimaßnahmen für den Heiligen Abend," *Berlin Lokal-Anzeiger*, 24 December 1932, 1; W. Schulz to Generalsuperintendent, Evangelisches Konsistorium Berlin-Brandenburg, 12 January 1931, EZA 14/865, n.p.

153 A copy of the original flyer from December 1930 and a letter describing events from Pastor W. Schulz to Generalsuperintendent Evangelische Konsistorium, Berlin, 12 January 1931, EZA 14/865, n.p.

154 All quotes from Oberpfarrer G. Pächtner, "Bericht über Störung des Weihnachts-Heiligenabends durch kommunistische Demonstranten," Tagebuch, no. 3043/30, 29 December 1930, EZA 14/865, n.p.

155 Muth-Klingerbrun, "Youngdeutsche Weihnacht," *Illustrierter Beobachter*, 20 December 1930.

156 "Wider das undeutsche Festefeiern," *VB*, 24 December 1927.

157 "Im Zuchthaus des Warenhausjuden," *Illustrierter Beobachter*, 20 December 1929.

158 "Anschläge auf Warenhäuser," *VZ*, 20 December 1932; "Der Silberne Sonntag," *Berliner Börsen-Zeitung*, 12 December 1932, 5.

159 Fritzsche, *Rehearsals for Fascism*; quote from Bergerson, *Ordinary Germans in Extraordinary Times*, 6; on Aryanization, see Friedländer, *Nazi Germany and the Jews*, esp. 232–39, 257–61.

160 I am grateful to Sven Reichardt for his collaboration on a paper titled "Storm Troopers and the Nazification of Christmas," which we presented at the annual conference of the German Studies Association in 1997. Much of the following material on the SA draws on this paper. See also Reichardt, "Gewalt im SA-Milieu," 164–77; and Reichardt, *Faschistische Kampfbünde*, 420, 449–58.

161 This composite draws on several accounts of SA celebrations in the late Weimar period, including a letter from SA man Max Liebscher, BAB, NS 26/323, n.p.; "Weihnachtsfeiern im Gau Berlin," *Der Angriff*, 20 December 1932; "Weihnachtsfeiern," *Der Angriff*, 22 December 1932. Articles in *Der SA-Mann*, 31 December 1932; and press clippings on SA Christmas celebrations gathered by the Munich police in 1931 and 1932, StA-M, Polizeidirektion 6808.

162 "Weihnachtsfeier des Sturmen I der S.A. München am 3. Dezember 1927 im Fäustlegarten," StA-M, Polizeidirektion 6809, Police Report, no. 595, 75.

163 "Weihnachtsfeier der S.A. Solln," *Münchner Landzeitung*, 15 December 1931.

164 "Julnacht," in *Der S.A.-Mann*, 21 December 1929.

165 Heinrich Anacker, "SA-Weihnacht 1930."

166 "Erhöhte 'Tätigkeit' der S.A.," *VZ*, 20 December 1932; "Schüsse im S.A.-Lokal," *VZ*, 24 December 1932; "Nächtliche Nazi Überfälle," *Vorwärts*, 24 December 1932; "Drei SA.-Feuerüberfälle auf Arbeiter," *Die Rote Fahne*, 25 December 1932.

167 Gerhard Pantel, "Der S.-A. zum Heiligabend," *Der Angriff*, 22 December 1929; compare "Neue nationalsozialistische Blutopfer im Zeichen des 'Weihnachtsfriedens,'" *VB*, 29 December 1931.

168 Götz, "Eines S.A.-Mannes Weihnacht," *VB*, 25/26/27 December 1932.

169 "Erhöhte 'Tätigkeit' der S.A.," *VZ*, 20 December 1932.

170 "Polizeimaßnahmen für den Heiligen Abend," *Berlin Lokal-Anzeiger*, 24 December 1932, 1; "Die Auswirkungen der Amnestie," *Berlin Lokal-Anzeiger*, 21 December 1932, 1.

CHAPTER 5

1 Ozuof, *Festivals and the French Revolution*; Geldern, *Bolshevik Festivals*; Petrone, *Life Has Become More Joyous, Comrades*. See also Mosse, *The Nationalization of the Masses*; Wilson, "Festivals in the Third Reich"; Vondung, *Magie und Manipulation*; and Friedrich, ed., *Festive Culture in Germany and Europe*.

2 Berezin, *Making a Fascist Self*. On the Nazi "intelligentsia," the numerous university-educated followers of the "movement," see Peukert, *Weimar Republic*, 94.

3 Kremer, "Neuwertung 'überlieferter' Brauchformen?," 3005; Burleigh and Wippermann, *The Racial State*.

4 Auguste Reber-Gruber, "Deutsche Weihnachten," *Nationalsozialistische Mädchenerziehung: Amtliche Zeitschrift des Nationalsozialistischen Lehrerbundes für weibliche Erziehung und Bildung* (December 1936), 310.

5 Friedrich Schulze-Langendorff, "Weihnachtsfeuer, Weihnachtsfreude," *VB*, 24 December 1927, 5.

6 Herbert A. E. Müller, "Tanne und Gral: Deutsche Weihnachts- u. Lichtgedanken," *VB*, 22 December 1928, 3.

7 Frodi Ingolfson Wehrmann, "Wintersonnenwende—Schicksalswende," *VB*, 24 December 1925, 4.

8 By taking seriously the "positive" appreciation of Nazi culture by ordinary Germans, this chapter documents narratives and practices of consent and challenges assertions that popular support for the Nazis depended primarily on coercion. On the benefits Nazi cultural policy offered "Aryans," see Baranowski, *Strength through Joy*; Koshar, *German Travel Cultures*; Proctor, *The Nazi War on Cancer*; and Behnken, ed., *Inszenierung der Macht*. For two studies that frame the issue of popular support for Nazism around issues of consent and coercion, respectively, see Fritzsche, *Germans into Nazis*; and Gellately, *Backing Hitler*. Corey Ross questions the popularity of the nazification of Christmas, concluding that the holiday "was a time for private authenticity over public conformity," in "Celebrating Christmas," 342; for similar conclusions, see also Weber-Kellermann, *Weihnachtsfest*, 57, 127. My analysis of the public response draws in part on popular-opinion reports by the Social Democratic Party in exile and the Nazi Security Service (SD), as well as personal accounts. See Behnken, ed., *Sopade*; Boberach, ed., *MadR*. For a discussion of the bias in these documents, see Kershaw, *Popular Opinion and Political Dissent in the Third Reich*, 8–9.

9 Koonz, *The Nazi Conscience*, 3. See also Berezin, *Making the Fascist Self*.

10 "Weihnachtsfeier der Nationalsozialistischen Deutschen Arbeitspartei im 'Hofbräuhausfestsaal,'" StA-M Polizeidirektion 6700. For the Nazi take on events, see "Die Weihnachtsfeier der Nationalsozialistischen Deutschen Arbeiterpartei München," *VB*, 11 January 1922.

11 In 1933, citing the economic importance of the holiday, Nazi authorities cynically banned public demonstrations against Jewish department stores; see "Störungen des Weihnachtsgeschäfts untersagt," *Frankfurter Zeitung*, 17 December 1933. For renewed protests in 1934, see Behnken, ed., *Sopade*, 35.

12 For an introduction to the growing literature on church-state relations in the Nazi years, see Bergen, "Nazism and Christianity: Partners and Rivals?"

13 As Klaus Vondung concluded in his groundbreaking study of Nazism as a political religion, the systemic transformation of German national culture sought

by National Socialists was firmly in place by 1940. See Vondung, *Magie und Manipulation*, 116–17; compare Reichel, *Der schöne Schein des Dritten Reiches*.

14 Gajek, "Weihnachten im Dritten Reich"; Gajek, "Nationalsozialistische Weihnacht"; Foitzik, *Rote Sterne*, esp. 104–40; Ross, "Celebrating Christmas," 329; and Hobsbawm and Ranger, eds., *The Invention of Tradition*.

15 See, for example, the work of Nazi ethnographer and Working Group member Hans Strobel, whose articles on the Germanic legacy of Christmas appeared throughout the Nazi years. On Strobel as Nazi ethnographer, see Freund, "Volk, Reich und Westgrenze"; and Lixfeld, *Folklore and Fascism*.

16 Foitzik includes an in-depth review of *Die neue Gemeinschaft* and the Nazi organizations that shaped Christmas in *Rote Sterne*, 92–104.

17 For a description of these celebrations with guidelines for ritual observance, see "Deutsche Weihnacht," a special issue of *Die neue Gemeinschaft*; I am grateful to Doris Foitzik for her generosity in sharing with me copies of this and other sources.

18 Ibid., 6–7 (emphasis in original).

19 Lüdtke, "The 'Honor of Labor,'" 98.

20 Markmiller, "Beobachtungen zum Fest- und Brauchwesen der NS-Zeit."

21 On home evenings, see "Heimabend des BDM: Weihnachtsarbeiten für das Winterhilfswerk," *Illustrierter Beobachter*, 24 December 1936. On the DAF, see *Vorweihnachtliche Feier*. On school celebrations, see Siebold, "Die deutsche Schulfeier als Forderung und Aufgabe," esp. 7; Gerstner, "Weihnachtliche Lichtfeier"; and Manger, *Mittwinter*. On the SS, see "Lichtsprüche der SS," 1936 to 1944, BAB, NS 19/2240.

22 See, for example, Weimar-era newsreel segments on "Weihnachts-Vorbereitungen" from 1926, 1929, and 1932, respectively, in BA-FA Wochenschauen 1364, BA-FA Wochenschauen 503, and BA-FA Wochenschauen DTW50/1932.

23 On the media dictatorship, see Rentschler, *Ministry of Illusion*, esp. 16. On audiovisual space, see Geyer, "Germany, or, the Twentieth Century as History," 679. For introductions to radio and film in the Nazi period, see, respectively, Lacey, *Feminine Frequencies*; and Rentschler, *The Ministry of Illusion*. Also see Bergerson, "Listening to Radio in Hildesheim"; and Reichel, *Der schöne Schein des Dritten Reiches*.

24 Susman, "The Culture of the Thirties," 158.

25 Marling, *Merry Christmas*, 184–86.

26 For Nazi era radio programs, see *Sieben Tage. Funkblätter mit Program*. On the 1937 broadcast, see *Sieben Tage*, 19 December 1937, n.p.

27 Hernandez, "Sacred Sound and Sacred Substance."

28 An example in BA-FA, Wochenschauen DTW 209/1935. On regionalism and national identity, see Applegate, *A Nation of Provincials*; and Confino, *The Nation as Local Metaphor*.

29 BA-FA Wochenschauen, UTW 275/1935, Ufa-Tonwoche, no. 275, 11 December 1935; UTW 278/1935, Ufa-Tonwoche, no. 278, 30 December 35.

30 BA-FA Wochenschauen, UTW 225/1934, Ufa-Tonwoche, no. 225, 24 December 1934.

31 "Deutschland für dich, du für Deutschland: Berliner S.A.- Standarte beschert 6000 arme Kinder—Weihnachtsansprache Dr. Goebbels," *VB*, 25–26 December 1934, 3.

32 Loah, "Kinderszenen im Kriege," 175.

33 Gebhardt, *Der zweifache Weg*, 276.

34 Ibid., 169. For a small but exemplary selection of Gebhardt's literary output, see Gebhardt, ed., *Der freie deutsche Rhein*; and Gebhardt, ed., *Stoffe für die Schulfeier am Verfassungstage (11. August)*. And for a collection of materials for a variety of patriotic holidays, see Gebhardt, *Vorsprüche und Festgedichte zu Veranstaltungen in Kriegervereinen*.

35 Gebhardt, *Der zweifache Weg*, 104–5.

36 Florus Bardt (pseud. of Gebhardt), *Des Lehrers Weihnachtsfeier in der Schulklasse*, 9.

37 Gebhardt, *Der zweifache Weg*, 228, 268, 271.

38 Ibid., 103.

39 The original text is Gebhardt, ed., *Festliche Tage der Schule*; for the revised fourth edition of this book (the publisher also changed names to suit the times), see Gebhardt, ed., *Festliche Tage der Schule im Dritten Reich*, 14–15. For other Nazi festivities penned by Gebhardt, see Gebhardt, ed., *Kraft durch Freude*; and A. Rolf (pseud. of Gebhardt), ed., *Unser Saarland wieder Deutsch und Frei!*

40 Weber-Kellermann, *Weihnachtslieder*, 307.

41 Basic biographical details in Wistrich, *Wer war Wer im Dritten Reich*, 17–18. See also the exchange of letters between Klaus Vondung and Baumann from 1968, Institut für Zeitgeschichte, Munich, ZS2224, Baumann, Hans; and Baird, *Hitler's War Poets*.

42 For one example, see Engelmann, ed., *Hohe Nacht der klaren Sterne!* For collections of Baumann's songs, see Baumann, *Der helle Tag*; and Baumann, *Bergbauernweihnacht*.

43 Baumann's lyrics are reprinted in Weber-Kellermann, *Weihnachtslieder*, 309–10. The melody can be heard at ⟨http://www.ingeb.org/Lieder/hohenach.html⟩ (8 May 2009).

44 Pudelko, "Zur Frage des Weihnachtsliedes," 157.

45 Bertlein, "Hans Baumann, der Künder der jungen Generation," 127–28.

46 *Der Verlorene Sohn* (1934), dir. Luis Trenker, produced by Deutsche Universal-Film AG. Available from Facets Video in Chicago; for an in-depth analysis of *The Prodigal Son*, see Rentschler, *Ministry of Illusion*, 73–98.

47 For the contemporary response and *Film-Kurier* quote, see Rentschler, *Ministry of Illusion*, 79–81.

48 Ibid., 76.

49 For a discussion of Nazi "incitement" to sexuality, see Herzog, *Sex after Fascism*. My interpretation of the film draws on Sontag, "Fascinating Fascism"; and Schulte-Sasse, "Leni Riefenstahl's Feature Films and the Question of a Fascist Aesthetic."

50 Ludwig Müller, "'Friede auf Erden': Eine Weihnachts-Botschaft des Reichsbischofs Müller," *VZ*, 24 December 1933.

51 Vorländer, *Die NSV*, 382; Kaplan, *Between Dignity and Despair*, 49.

52 "Sonderdruck. Einsatz der Hitler-Jugend für das Winterhilfswerk des Deutschen Volkes 1936/37," in *Reichsbefehl der Reichsjugendführung der NSDAP*, 27 November 1936, BAB, NS37/1017; also see material on the WHW in EZA 7/2771.

53 Figures from Wolf, *Das Winterhilfswerk des Deutschen Volkes*; reprinted in Vorländer, *Die NSV*, 235.

54 BA-FA Wochenschauen, DTW 209/1935 Deulig-Tonwoche, no. 209, 30 December 1935; BA-FA Dokumentarfilme, NS-Herrschaft 620, "Echo der Heimat, Folge 5," 1937.

55 "Aufwärts aus eigener Kraft!," *VB*, 27 December 1933.

56 Statistics in Vorländer, *Die NSV*, 44, 47.

57 "Lage- und Stimmungsbericht des Hauptamtes für Volkswohlfahrt," December 1936, 2, BAB, NS 22/845. See also Angele Brown, "Vom 'germanischen Julfest' zum 'Totenfest,'" 23–30.

58 *Rechenschaftsbericht, Winter-Hilfswerk des Deutschen-Volkes 1934/35*, BAB, R 18/5600; *Rechenschaftsbericht, Winter-Hilfswerk des Deutschen-Volkes 1935/1936*, BAB, R 22/843.

59 Bruno Nelissen Haken, "Festfreude—Keiner Steht Abseits!," *Berliner Lokal-Anzeiger*, 21 December 1933.

60 Behnken, ed., *Sopade*, 169.

61 Ibid.

62 Hirche, *Der "Braune" und der "Rote" Witz*, 125. For other WHW jokes, see Hillenbrand, *Underground Humor in Nazi Germany*, 89–90.

63 Behnken, ed., *Sopade*, 173.

64 John Connelly, "The Uses of National Community," 928.

65 Historian Herbert Vorländer concludes that Winter Relief was one of the most popular aspects of Nazi rule in *Die NSV*, 175–86.

66 Quoted in Sauermann, ed., *Weihnachten in Westfalen um 1900*, 113–14.

67 Rosenberg, *Der Mythos des XX. Jahrhunderts*, quoted in Mosse, *Nazi Culture*, 40. On the appeal of fascist respectability, see Mosse, *Nationalism and Sexuality*.

68 Saldern, "Victims or Perpetrators?," 151.

69 Reber-Gruber, "Frau und Feier!—Ein Aufruf," 9.

70 Schnidtmann-Leffler, "Frau und Volkstum," 225.

71 Dora Hansmann, "Adventszeit—magische Zeit: Vom heidnischen Dämonzauber und von unseren Adventsbräuchen," *Die Deutsche Frau*, supplement to *VB*, 6 December 1936. See also Breuer and Breuer, *Von wegen Heilige Nacht*, 81–82.

72 *Weihnachtsfibel für das deutsche Haus*, 6.

73 Schultz, "Auch an seinem Heim erkennt man den National Sozialisten!," 16–18.

74 *Vorweihnachtliche Feier*; quotes on 10, 52.

75 *Weihnachtsfibel für das deutsche Haus*; quotes on 6, 7, 13.

76 The cover of the catalog *Herzenswünsche Erfüllen* (1935) reprinted in Breuer and Breuer, *Von wegen Heilige Nacht*, 70. On the exclusionary aspects of German capitalism, see Baranowski, *Strength through Joy*, 25–39; and Kaplan, *Between Dignity and Despair*, 3.

77 Jakob, "Wirtschaftpropaganda!," 5. See also *Braune Weihnachtsmesse Chemnitz*; and *Braune Weihnachtsmesse Dresden*.

78 De Grazia, *Irresistible Empire*, 126.

79 Glaser, "Ohne besondere Vorkommnisse," 48–49.

80 Private conversation with Karl-Heinz Schoeps, professor of German Literature, University of Illinois, 1997. On Nazi carols in general, see Weber-Kellermann, *Weihnachtslieder*, 306–26.

81 See holiday advertisements in the *Völkischer Beobachter* before 1933; and for a rare photo of a private Christmas tree decorated with swastika-shaped electric lights, see Rühlig and Steen, eds., *Walter*, n.p. On the persistent popularity of Nazi kitsch, see Friedländer, *Reflections of Nazism*.

82 On the law, see StA-M Pol. Dir. 6958. For examples of outlawed Christmas kitsch, see StA-M Pol. Dir. 6971, 6967, 6982; and "Patentierte SA.-Weihnachtsmänner," *Der SA-Mann*, 16 December 1938.

83 Boberach, ed., *MadR*, 1822, 3044, 3145, 4502, 4577.

84 Ibid., 1859, 3123, 6203.

85 Behnken, ed., *Sopade*, 1392, 1400.

86 Statistics in Koonz, *Mothers in the Fatherland*, 183. Saldern asserts that "these women [NSF members], and especially those who were leaders, accepted the role allotted to them by the Nazi system" ("Victims or Perpetrators?," 151).

87 "Ausrichtung und Vorschläge zur Feiergestaltung in der Weihnachtszeit," Reichsfrauenführung, Abteilung Kultur, Erziehung, Schulung (Berlin), an alle Gaufrauenschaftsleiterinnen, Abteilungsleiterinnen der Abteilung Kultur, Erziehung, Schulung, and Schrifttumsreferentinnen, 20 November 1936, BAB, NS 44/44.

88 *Monatsbericht der Reichsleitung der NSDAP, Reichsfrauenführung für die Monate November/December 1938*, BAB, NS 22/924, 10.

89 Saldern, "Victims or Perpetrators?," 151.

90 "Ausrichtung und Vorschläge"; see also Rundschreiben No. F/40, Feiergestaltung "Vorweihnacht," Gaufrauenschaftsleitung München-Oberbayern, Abteilung

Jugendgruppen, Kultur, Erziehung, Schulung, an alle Kreis Frauenschaftsleite-
rinnen, Kreis Kulturreferentinnen, Kreis Jugendgruppenführerinnen, Orts Frau-
enschaftsleiterinnen, Orts Jugendgruppenführerinnen und Kinderscharleiterin-
nen, 12 November 1937, BAB, NS 44/52.

91   "Ausrichtung und Vorschläge."

92   Behnken, ed., *Sopade*, 1308–9.

93   *Monatsbericht der Reichsleitung der NSDAP, Reichsfrauenführung für die Monate
     November/Dezember 1936*, BAB, NS 22/924, 2–3.

94   *Monatsbericht der Reichsleitung der NSDAP, Reichsfrauenführung für die Monate
     November/Dezember 1938*, BAB, NS 22/924, 7.

95   *Monatsbericht der Reichsleitung der NSDAP, Reichsfrauenführung für die Monate
     November/Dezember 1936*, BAB, NS 22/924, quotes on 5, 2–3, 3.

96   Quoted in Besier, *Die Kirchen und das Dritte Reich*, 248.

97   Steigmann-Gall argues for the close connections between Christians and Nazis
     in *The Holy Reich*. For a more traditional interpretation that concentrates on
     church-state conflict, see Besier, *Die Kirchen und das Dritte Reich*. For an intro-
     duction to the extensive literature on Christianity in Nazi Germany, see Evans,
     "Forum on Richard Steigmann-Gall, *The Holy Reich*."

98   Bergen, *Twisted Cross*, 9. For a summary of the German Christians, see 5–17.

99   Ibid., 48.

100 Wilhelm Bauer, *Feierstunden Deutscher Christen*, 49–50; compare Bergen,
     Twisted Cross, 47.

101 Bauer, *Feierstunden Deutscher Christen*, 44–48.

102 Ibid., 200.

103 Quoted in Bergen, *Twisted Cross*, 163.

104 The rally is preserved for posterity in a twenty-two-minute "educational docu-
     mentary" as "Die erste Weihnachtsfeier der Reichsbahndirektion Berlin im Drit-
     ten Reich," 1934, BA-FA, Dokumentarfilm 427. Reimers includes a copy of the
     script in "Der Führer als völkische Erlösergestalt." For film stills, see the *Völki-
     scher Beobachter*, 19 December 1933. On "positive Christianity," see Steigmann-
     Gall, *The Holy Reich*, 14.

105 Quotes from Reimers, "Der Führer als völkische Erlösergestalt," 172–73, 174.

106 Bauer, *Feierstunden Deutscher Christen*, 139–45, 197–203.

107 Bergen, *Twisted Cross*, 48, 170.

108 Pfarrer Kurt Everth to the Kammern des Deutschen Evangelischen Kirche, 6
     November 1936, EZA 1/C3/296, 58.

109 Superintendent von Scheven, Provinzialkirchenausschluß für die Kirchenpro-
     vinz Pommern to Gauleitung Pommern der NSDAP, 19 December 1936, EZA
     7/2272. This was not an isolated example. Another report in this file complained
     that similar songs were sung at NSV celebrations in Mecklenburg.

110   Eckhardt, Gaugeschäftsführer NSDAP Gauleitung Pommern, to von Scheven, Provinzialkirchenausschuß für die Kirchenprovinz Pommern, 22 December 1936, EZA 7/2272.

111   See Pfarrer Joachim Braun (Berlin) to EOK Berlin, Präsident Dr. Werner, 13 December 1938; Evangelisches Konsistorium der Mark Brandenburg to Oberkirchenrat, 22 December 1938; both in EZA 7/3199.

112   See reports on church holiday activities in Boberach, ed., *Berichte des SD und der Gestapo über Kirchen und Kirchenvolk in Deutschland*.

113   *Monatsbericht der Reichsleitung der NSDAP, Reichsfrauenführung für die Monate November/Dezember 1936*, BAB NS 22/924, 1–3.

114   "The Pope's Christmas Broadcast: Warning against Nazism and Communism," *London Times*, 28 December 1936, 9.

115   Faulhaber, *Judentum, Christentum, Germanentum*. Also see "Kanzelerklärung Faulhabers," 10 December 1941; and "Faulhaber an die Geistlichen im Wehrdienst," 30 November 1942; both in *Akten Kardinal Michael von Faulhabers*, 858–59, 955–57.

116   See, for example, the mingling of nationalist, traditional Protestant, and racial themes in the works collected in Lilje, ed., *Evangelische Weihnacht*.

117   Benzing-Vogt, "Vom Kind in der Krippe zum Kind in der Wiege."

118   Quoted in Foitzik, *Rote Sterne*, 117.

119   "O du fröhliche, o du selige . . . ," *Der Allemanne*, 22 December 1936; quoted in "Neue Weihnachtslieder?," *Katholisches Wochenblatt*, 10 January 1937, DAF clipping file "Weihnachtsfeste, Weihnachtsbräuche 12/23–1/37," BAB NS 5 VI/17393.

120   Moritz-Henning, ed., *Nun brennen viele Kerzen*.

121   Bauer, *Feierstunden Deutsche Christen*, 201.

122   Quoted in Bergen, *Twisted Cross*, 50; see also 168–71.

123   "Neue Weihnachtslieder?," *Katholisches Wochenblatt*, 10 January 1937, DAF clipping file "Weihnachtsfeste, Weihnachtsbräuche," 12/23–1/37, BAB NS 5 VI/17393; Ludendorff and Ludendorff, *Weihnachten im Lichte der Rassenerkenntnis*. Falk's original lyrics read: "Oh you joyful, oh you blessed, mercy bringing Christmas time!/The world was lost, Christ is born/Rejoice, rejoice oh Christendom."

124   Reprinted from *Die HJ* in "Eine Schandtat in Versen: Wildgewordene Dichterin entweiht unsere Weihnachtslieder," *Rhein NSZ Front*, 29 December 1936, DAF clipping file "Weihnachtsfeste, Weihnachtsbräuche 12/23–1/37," BAB NS 5 VI/17393.

125   From Rarkowski's 1939 Christmas sermon; quoted/translated in Zahn, *German Catholics and Hitler's Wars*, 157.

126   From Faulhaber's 1941 Christmas address; quoted/translated in ibid., 114.

127   D. Hymmen, "Weihnachtsansprache an die Gemeinden," *Gesetzblatt der Deutschen Evangelischen Kirche*, Ausgabe B (Altpreußen), 21 December 1943, 64 (emphasis in original).

128 Wieneke, "Grußwort des Evangelischen Oberkirchenrats zu Weihnachten 1944," Entwurf, EZA 7/3199.

129 Protestant pastors could be equally direct: a pastor in Thundorf opened a Christmas sermon with a direct attack on attempts to promote Rosenberg's redefinition of Christmas as a Germanic holiday in a local farmer's newspaper. See Boberach, ed., *MadR*, 1930.

130 Gröber, *Weihnachtshirtenbrief für die Kinder*, 4.

131 Lewy, *The Catholic Church and Nazi Germany*, 292.

132 See the extensive report on church use of music in Boberach, ed., *MadR*, 6207–12; quotes, 6211–12.

133 "Die Kirche in der Weihnachtszeit . . .," SD-Abschnitt Kiel, 16 February 1944, BAB, NS6/106, 43–50.

134 Hermann Sauer, "Gutachten über Verantwortung und Möglichkeiten der Kirche für Kriegsweihnachten," 15 October 1939, 1–1a, EZA 7/3199; quotes on 1–1a, 10–11, 4 (all emphases in original).

135 Werner to Kerrl, Reichsminister für die kirchlichen Angelegenheiten, 13 November 1939, EZA 7/3199, n.p.

136 A copy of the letter with Kerrl's cover page in BAB, R43 II/1266, 68–71.

137 The possibility of a separate religious broadcast was also suggested; see "Richtlinien für die Gestaltung der Weihnachtsfeiern in der Wehrmacht," 14 December 1939, BAB, NS6/329, 157.

138 "Runderlass des EOK an die Ev. Gemeinden betr. Einsatz zu Weihnacht," EOI 2901/39, October 1939, EZA 7/3199, n.p.

139 According to file notes dated 31 January 1940, EZA 7/3199, n.p.

140 "Runderlass des EOK an die Ev. Gemeinden betr. Einsatz zu Weihnacht," EOI 2901/39, October 1939, EZA 7/3199, n.p.

141 See the catalog of songbooks and discussion of the Christian mission of the Quempas in *Vom Quempas-Weihnachtssingen*. For EOK recommendations, see D. Hymmen to Obersten Behörden der deutschen evangelischen Kirchen, 13 April 1940, EZA 7/3199.

142 Summaries of reports collected by the EOK from across Germany in EZA 7/3199.

143 Boberach, ed., *MadR*, 597–98.

144 Ibid., 1879.

145 Oberleutnant Eberhard Eilers to OkR Wieneke, 13 January 1944 and 3 January 1945, EZA 7/3199.

146 Akten Vermerk, 23 January 1945, EZA 7/3199, n.p.

147 Renese, EK der Kirchenprovinz Grenzmark, Posen-Westpreussen, Schneidemühl, to EOK-Berlin, 22 December 1939, EZA 7/3199, n.p.; "Auf die Verfügung vom 26.2.40 K I, no. 1170 betr. christliche Weihnachtsfeiern in städtischen Krankenanstalten," EZA 7/3199, n.p.

148 Letter from Konsistorialrat Scherrer, EK der Kirchenprovinz Schlesien, to the EOK, 16 January 1942, EZA 7/3199, n.p.

149 Weineke to Ministerialdirektor Fritzsche, RMVP, 4 April 1945, EZA 7/3084, n.p.

150 "Vorbereitungen für die 'Volksweihnacht 1940,'" *Deutsche Wochenschau*, no. 536, 51 (11 December 1940), BA-FA, DW 536/1940.

151 For a small selection of annual War Christmas newsreels, see "Weihnachten an der Front, u.a.," *Ufa-Tonwoche*, no. 485, 52 (20.12.39), BA-FA, UTW 485/1939; "Weihnachtsvorbereitungen an der Front und in der Heimat," *Deutsche Wochenschau*, no. 589, 52, 1941 (17 December 1941), BA-FA, DW 589/1941; and "Kriegsweihnacht," *Deutsche Wochenschau*, no. 539, 2, 1941 (2 January 1941), BA-FA, DW 539/1941.

152 "Weihnachtsvorbereitungen an der Front und in der Heimat," *Deutsche Wochenschau*, no. 642, 1, 1943 (21 December 1942) BA-FA, DW 642/1943.

153 For example, Boberach, ed., *MadR*, 603, 1888, 3135, 4600, 4633.

154 For an extensive account of War Christmas propaganda, see Foitzik, *Rote Sterne*, 146–54.

155 Boberach, ed., *MadR*, 3136.

156 Ibid., 3140–41.

157 Ibid., 3136.

158 Goebbels quotes in "Das Endergebnis der Wollsammlung," *VB*, 15 January 1942. See also Partei-Kanzlei Rundschreiben, no. 159/41, Sammlung von Woll- und Wintersachen zur Versorgung der Soldaten, 20 December 1941, BAB, NS6/335, 170; "Ein Aufruf des Führers," *VB*, 21 December 1941; and "32 Millionen Stück," *VB*, 5 January 1942.

159 Boberach, ed., *MadR*, 3165, 3120, 3138.

160 Ibid., 3151.

161 Ibid., 3150.

162 Boberach, "Stimmungsschwung," 61.

163 "Durch Kampf und Arbeit zum Sieg und zum Frieden: Reichsminister Dr. Goebbels sprach zu den Deutschen an der Front, in der Heimat und in aller Welt," *VB*, 25/26/27 December 1942, 1–2, 2.

164 Ibid., 2. For a recording of the broadcast, see "Weihnachtsringsendung von allen Fronten," 24 December 1942, Deutsches Rundfunkarchiv, Frankfurt/M, Archivnummer 2570043. For background information, see Reichel, *Der Schöne Schein des Dritten Reiches*, 170–71. Selections from the similar "Deutsche Weihnacht 1940," 24 December 1940, on the compact disk *Heimat, deine Sterne Vol. 7, Kriegsweihnacht 1940*, UraCant, 2030, n.d.

165 Boberach, ed., *MadR*, 4587, 4599.

166 Ibid., 4598, 4600.

167 Ibid., 4600.

168 Ibid., 4599.

169 Ibid., 4577.

170 Letter from Frau E. L., Innsbruck, 25 December 1943, in Buchbender and Sterz, eds., *Das andere Gesicht des Krieges*, 128. See the letter from Herr H. K., Berlin, noting that the family would not celebrate Christmas that year at all (127–28).

171 Wilson, "Festivals and the Third Reich," 288.

172 Kriegstagebuch, Festung Stalingrad, Quartermaster's Reports 22 November 1942–21 January 1943, BA-MA RH20-6/794, 49–53.

173 Partei-Kanzlei Rundschreiben 438/44, Versorgung der Bevölkerung mit Weihnachtsbäumen, 9 December 1944, BAB, NS6/349, 33.

174 Partei-Kanzlei Bekanntgabe 459/44: Verhalten von Wehrmachtsangehörigen bei politischen und militärischen Veranstaltungen, 16 December 1944, BAB, NS6/349, 90–91.

175 "Unsere Feiern zur Weihnachtszeit: Deutsche Kriegsweihnacht," *Kulturpolitisches Mitteilungsblatt der Reichspropagandaleitung der NSDAP Hauptkulturamt*, 1 November 1943.

176 Like Baumann and other Nazi cultural workers, Scheller shaped a successful if dubious postwar writing career; see "Personalien: Thilo Scheller," 48.

177 Liese, *Licht muß wieder werden*.

178 A copy of the pamphlet and a letter from the RMVP about its distribution in EZA 7/3199. The poem with guidelines for domestic observances was reprinted in a number of Nazi Christmas books; see, for example, "Weihnachten in der Familie," 133–38.

179 For an account from World War I, see Mihaly, . . . *da gibt's ein Wiedersehen*, 113.

180 Boberach, ed., *MadR*, 4557.

181 "Weihnachtsansprache Goebbels" and "Weihnachts-Ringsendungen," 28 December 1944, BAB, R 055/1290, 268–69.

182 Handwritten comments, 6 January 1943, EZA 1/C3/296, 58.

183 Kästner, "Weihnachtsschwarzmarkt in Berlin," 16.

184 "Nationalsozialistische Weihnacht," *VB*, 24/25/26 December 1933.

CHAPTER 6

1 *Die Mörder sind unter uns* (1946); produced by DEFA and directed by Wolfgang Staudte. All quotes are from the film's English subtitles. For a selection of the vast literature on how Germans continue to process their responsibility for the crimes of the Nazi period, see Maier's classic *The Unmasterable Past*; Confino, *Germany as a Culture of Remembrance*; Confino and Fritzsche, eds., *The Work of Memory*; Moeller, *War Stories*; and Herf, *Divided Memory*.

2 See Moeller, *War Stories*; and Kaes, *From Hitler to Heimat*, 10–11.

3 "Die Mörder sind unter uns," *Telegraf,* 17 November 1946; Walter Lennig, "Ein film der deutschen Wirklichkeit," *Berliner Zeitung,* 17 November 1946; "Der erste deutsche Nachkriegsfilm," *Spandauer Volksblatt,* 16 November 1946; all in *Die Mörder sind unter uns* clipping file, BA-FA 11628, vol. 1.

4 On continuities between the pre– and post–World War II policies of German communists, see Weitz, *Creating German Communism, 1890–1990.*

5 Confino and Koshar, "Regimes of Consumer Culture," 135–61; Geyer "In Pursuit of Happiness," 269–314.

6 Irtl, "Aufbruch aus der Stunde Null," 73.

7 Kästner, "Weihnachtsschwarzmarkt in Berlin"; "Aus nichts—aber mit Liebe," *Neue Berliner Illustrierte,* 2 December 1945, 15; "Wie wir unsern Weihnachts-baum 'finanzierten,'" *Neue Berliner Illustrierte,* 3 December 1947, 4–5.

8 Casdorff, *Weihnachten 1945.* Other examples of this memory work include the museum exhibition "Aus nichts, aber mit Liebe: Friedensweihnacht 1945," Kulturhistorisches Museum in der Kloster zum Heiligen Kreuz in Rostock, 1995–96; and "Friedensweihnacht '45," FAKT television special, Channel 1 ARD, broadcast 17 December 2007, ⟨http://www.mdr.de/fakt/5099881.html⟩ (9 June 2008).

9 Roundletter from Lokies, Kammer für Erziehung und Unterricht beim Evangelischen Bischof von Berlin, to die Herrn Vorsitzenden und Sachbearbeiter der Erziehungsausschüsse, Berlin, 27 November 1946; Böhm and Gabenau, "Wie Feiern wir Weihnachten?," roundletter from Amt für Gemeindeaufbau, Evangelische Kirchenleitung der Kirchenprovinz Berlin-Brandenburg, to die Herrn Pfarrer unseres Aufsichtsbereichs, 19 November 1946; both in EZA 7/3199, n.p.

10 "Zum 1. Advent. Der Rat der Evangelischen Kirche in Deutschland, Stuttgart"; copy in EZA 7/3199, n.p.

11 Roundletter, August Marahrens, 8 December 1945, EZA 7/3199, n.p.. On Marahrens's support for the Nazis, see Hockenos, *A Church Divided,* 33.

12 Hockenos, *A Church Divided,* 171.

13 Kirby, "The Cold War, the Hegemony of the United States and the Golden Age of Christian Democracy," 285–86.

14 "Weihnachtsbotschaft des Papstes," *Der Tagesspiegel,* 27 December 1945, n.p.

15 Dr. Benn, Kanzlei der Evangelischen Kirche in Deutschland, Berlin to Kirchenleitung in Berlin, Magdeburg, Greifswald, Görlitz, the Kirchenleitung der östlichen Provinzialkirchen, 18 December 1946; letters in response in EZA 7/3199, "Das Weihnachtsfest," Dec. 1938–Jan 1963, n.p.

16 "Vorschläge für ein 'Volksdemokratisches Weihnachten.' Sowjetzonaler Gewerkschaftsbund hat einen 'neuen tieferen Sinn' des Festes entdeckt," press release, Evangelischer Pressedienst (EPD), 24 November 1956, EZA 7/3199, "Das Weihnachtsfest," Dec. 1938–Jan 1963; other reports on GDR dechristianization campaigns in the same file.

17 Adenauer, *Nachdenken über die Werte*, n.p. The very existence of this book—a special "numbered edition" limited to 1,000 copies—testifies to the uncanny nature of the (German) Christmas past.

18 Quoted in Foitzik, *Rote Sterne*, 205.

19 "Weihnachten wird offiziel zum 'friedlichen Tannenfest.' Advent in der Zone/ Alte Symbole verschwinden," EPD press release, 8 December 1958, EZA 7/3199.

20 *Die Welt*, 23 December 1961; quoted in Foitzik, *Rote Sterne*, 207.

21 "Funktionäre: no. 240 packt aus," *Der Spiegel*, 14 October 1958, 42–44.

22 Adenauer, *Nachdenken über die Werte*, n.p.

23 Ibid.

24 Härtel and Kabus, "Zwischen Gummibärchen und *Playboy*," 19. For the trustees, see Kruez, *Das Kuratorium Unteilbares Deutschland*; and Foitzik, *Rote Sterne*, 210–11.

25 On the Belsen children, see "KZ Kinder" in *Welt im Film* (*WiF*), BA-FA *WiF* 30/1945. For the Marshall Plan scene, see BA-FA *WiF* 290/1950. For other harmonious scenes of "Christmas preparations," see *WiF* 80/1946; *WiF* 81/1946; *WiF* 133/1947; *WiF* 185/1948; *WiF* 237/1949; *WiF* 238/1949; and Blick in die Welt 51/1950.

26 Moeller, *War Stories*, 7.

27 "Aufruf an das bayerische Volk!," issued by the Bayerische Staatsregierung, 1946, BayHStA/MArb 2246; see also "Weihnachtsaktion 1952 des Jugendrotkreuzes der DRK-Landverbände Nordrhein-Westfalen für bedürftige Kinder in Bayern," BayHStA/MArb 2107; "Bericht über die Weihnachtsfeier von München-Riem," BayHStA/MArb 1698.

28 Adenauer, *Nachdenken über die Werte*, n.p.

29 These three images with text are reprinted in Breuer and Breuer, *Von wegen Heilige Nacht*, 180, 182, and 186–88, respectively.

30 "Adventsfeier der Heimatvertriebenen," *Miesbacher Merkur*, 17 December 1951; "Schlesische Weihnacht am Tegernsee," *Tegernseer Zeitung*, 20 December 1951. These and other accounts in a clipping file on expellee celebrations, BayHStA/ MArb 1698.

31 "Betrifft: Weihnachtsbetreuung im Landkreis Fürstenfeldbruck," report from Kuhn, Leiter des Landratsamt Fürstenfeldbruck Flüchtlingsamtes to Frl. Below, Regierung von Oberbayern, 3 January 1952, BayHStA/MArb 1698.

32 Bund der Vertriebenen, ed., "Ein große Freud verkünd ich euch—Ein Arbeitsbrief zu Advents- und Weihnachtszeit"; cited in Breuer and Breuer, *Von wegen Heilige Nacht*, 191.

33 Frank Biess, "'Everybody Has a Chance,'" 219.

34 Recent studies of postwar East and West Germany society have explored narratives that cast Germans as victims of the war and National Socialism. See, for example, Biess, *Homecomings*; Moeller, *War Stories*; and Bartov, "Defining

Enemies," 771–816, 788. On the Battle of Stalingrad itself, see Eschebach, "'Das Opfer deutscher Männer,'" 37–41. For a full discussion of the drawing, see Perry, "Madonna of Stalingrad," 7–27; and Martin Kruse, ed., *Stalingrad-Madonna*.

35 Attending the dedication ceremony in 1983 were Reuber's surviving children, Hohenzollern Prince Louis Ferdinand (in his role as chair of the Memorial Church Board of Trustees), and publisher Axel Springer, whose efforts were instrumental in the transfer of the drawing; "Symbol für die Sehnsucht nach Geborgenheit," *Hamburger Abendblatt*, 27/28 August 1983.

36 Ibid.

37 "Madonna aus Berlin soll nach Stalingrad," *Berliner Morgenpost*, 25/26 December 1988.

38 Martin Kruse, "Ein Frühvollendeter," 6.

39 "'Stalingrad-Madonna' hat tiefen Eindruck hinterlassen," *Berliner Morgenpost*, 21 November 1983. Compare to readers' letters in *Welt am Sonntag*, 2 October 1983. For the attendant's comments, see "Madonna aus Berlin soll nach Stalingrad," *Berliner Morgenpost*, 25/26 December 1988. The myth of the drawing was kept alive after its dedication by articles in the annual Christmas issues of Berlin papers and by church attempts to give a copy of the drawing to the archbishop of Volgograd (former Stalingrad) in 1988.

40 Bahr and Bahr, *Kriegsbriefe gefallenen Studenten*, 194, 200. For another eyewitness account that confirms Reuber's story, see Jochen Kummer, "Weihnachten in Stalingrad," *Welt am Sonntag*, 22 November 1992, 29.

41 Wette, "Massensterben als 'Heldenepos,'" 274, n. 35.

42 "Allgemeiner Stimmungsbericht. Auszug aus Tätigkeitsbericht der Feldpostprüfstelle bei Pz. A. O. K. 4 für Januar 1943," BA-MA, RW 4/264: 10–13. For a rather different view, see the letters collected in Golovchansky and others, eds., *Ich will raus aus diesem Wahnsinn*; Ryback, "Stalingrad: Letters From the Dead"; Blaumeister and Blimlinger, eds., *Alle Jahre Wieder*, 172–79.

43 Pötzsch, *Die Madonna von Stalingrad*, 16, 19.

44 Schröter was flown out of the "cauldron" and assigned the task of writing a report on the battle for public distribution by the propaganda ministry. He was allowed access to official reports of the battle; some of the materials he collected are in the Federal Military Archive's famed "Stalingrad file" (BA-MA RW 4/264). In 1943 Goebbels labeled Schröter's work "unbearable for the German people" and canceled its publication; Schröter's 1953 memoir is a revised version of his report. Quotes here are from the English translation, *Stalingrad*: on Christmas, 132–37; quotes, 135–37. For background on Schröter, see Wette, "Das Massensterben als 'Heldenepos,'" 55.

45 See, for example, firsthand accounts by participants in the battle in BA-MA, RW 4/264. Three of the censorship reports on soldiers' mail from Stalingrad contained in this file are reprinted in Wette, "'Unsere Stimmung ist auf dem

Nullpunkt angekommen.'" See also Bergen, "German Military Chaplains in the Second World War."

46 For a contemporary account, see Schwab-Felisch, "Die Literature der Oberge-freiten," 644–51. See also Pfeifer, *Der deutsche Kriegsroman*; Baron, "Stalingrad als Thema der deutschsprachigen Literatur," 226–32; and Schäfer, "'Alle fluchten, alle funktionierten,'" 42–49.

47 Bernig, *Eingekesselt*, 281–82.

48 Gerlach, *Verratene Armee*; quotes on 195–96, 210. For an English translation, see Weidenfeld, *The Forsaken Army*; translations here are mine.

49 Gerlach, *Verratene Armee*, 179, 208.

50 Broszat, "Literatur und NS-Vergangenheit," 121.

51 Doris Foitzik, whose description of Cold War holiday propaganda is unparalleled, argues that the politicization of Christmas in East Germany was undertaken for the most part in response to western rhetoric; see *Rote Sterne*, chaps. 5 and 6.

52 Berliner Ausstellungs- und Werbebetriebe VEB, "Der Berliner Weihnachtsmarkt 1957: Ergebnisse—Erfahrungen—Lehren," 28 February 1958, LAB Sta. Rep. 113, no. 45 (Berliner Weihnachtsmarkt 1958), 13. For detailed accounts of typical attractions, see the architect's drawing plan of the market layout in Dewag Filiale, Berlin, Abteilung Ausstellungen, "Berliner Weihnachtsmarkt, 1954," LAB Sta. Rep. 113, no. 45. I am grateful to Katherine Pence for pointing out this material.

53 See Port, *Conflict and Stability in the German Democratic Republic*; and Ross, *Constructing Socialism at the Grass-Roots*, esp. chap. 6.

54 "Der Berliner Weihnachtsmarkt 1957," 1, 12.

55 Quoted in Kaminsky, *Wohlstand, Schönheit, Glück*, 10.

56 "Der Berliner Weihnachtsmarkt 1957," 12, 5.

57 Ibid., 6, 12.

58 Foitzik, *Rote Sterne*, 171–74; Lorenz, "Frieden, Freude, Völkerfreundschaft," 254–57.

59 Möller and Mählert, "NS-Zeit und Kriegserfahrung als gemeinsamer Ausgangspunkt."

60 H. L., "Vorweihnacht," *ND*, 15 December 1946, 1.

61 G. Schrl., "Galgen neben Weihnachtsbaum. Feierstunde der Lichtenberger 'OdF,'" *ND*, 24 December 1946, 6; Walter Bartel, "Kinder hinter Stacheldraht," *ND*, 25 December 1947, 5; "Fragten sie damals auch nach christlicher Nächstenliebe? Was ehemalige KZ-Insassen über Weihnachtsfeiern berichten/Bonn will den Henkern 'Mitleid' zeigen," *ND*, 21 December 1955, 2; Robert Siewert, "Weihnachten 1938 im Konzentrationslager Buchenwald," *ND*, 24 December 1955, 3.

62 Otto Grotewohl, "Friede auf Erden!," *ND*, 25 December 1946, 1. On the GDR holiday, see Foitzik, *Rote Sterne*, chap. 5; Lorenz, "Frieden, Freude, Völkerfreund-

schaft," 253–76; Ross, "Celebrating Christmas," 323–42; and Köhler, *Weihnachten in Berlin, 1945–1989.*

63 Herbert Gute, *Von Neujahr bis Sylvester: Die Fest-, Feier-, und Gedenktage im Ablauf des Jahres* (1959); cited in Lorenz, "Frieden, Freude, Völkerfreundschaft," 254.

64 For a copy of the poem, see "Ein neuer Stern ist erwacht," *ND*, 25 December 1946, 1; Ross, "Celebrating Christmas," 331–32; and Foitzik, *Rote Sterne*, 178–79.

65 "Fernsehen," *ND*, 27 December 1961, 4.

66 Ross, "Celebrating Christmas," 213.

67 "Friede auf Erden—Friede in Deutschland," *ND*, 25 December 1963, 1; John Stave, "Die Letzte Woche," *ND*, 21 December 1963, Beilage, n.p.

68 Pollack, "Von der Volkskirche zur Minderheitskirche."

69 "Sonstige Weihnachtsfeiern," 21 October 1959, Brandenburgisches Landeshauptarchiv Rep 731-127, 9. I am grateful to Timothy C. Dowling for sharing with me his research notes on the Stalinstadt Christmas; see Dowling, "Stalinstadt/ Eisenhüttenstadt."

70 "Protokoll, Arbeitsbesprechung der Abtl. Sozial u. Kultur, 19. XII.1951," UA-EKO, A-654; "Protokoll über der Weihnachtsfeier der EKO am 3.12.1952 stattgefundene 2. Besprechung zur Ausgestaltung," 3 December 1952, UA-EKO, A-654.

71 "Der Weihnachtsmann war da/Eisenhüttenstadt, Weihnachten 1966," Stadtarchiv Eisenhüttenstadt, S67; also "Weihnachtsfeier am 4. Dezember 1965," Stadtarchiv Eisenhüttenstadt, S67.

72 Bräuer, *Die ersten drei Jahrzehnte*, 213–14.

73 Ibid., 218, 349–51.

74 Ibid., 77–79.

75 "Doktor Dibelius heuchelte in Fürstenberg (West)," *Neuer Tag*, 21 April 1954; reprinted in Bräuer, *Die ersten drei Jahrzehnte*, 80.

76 Bräuer, *Die ersten drei Jahrzehnte*, 337–41; 497–501. See Pollack, "Von der Volkskirche zur Minderheitskirche," 271–94.

77 Pollack, "Von der Volkskirche zur Minderheitskirche," 271–94.

78 Ross, *The East German Dictatorship*, 117.

79 *Ach du fröhliche* (1962), produced by DEFA, directed by Günter Reisch, BA-FA, SP 02477/10.

80 Quote from "ach, du fröhliche . . .," *Progress Film Program*, 85 (1962), n.p.

81 "Ein neues Zeitalter hat begonnen," *ND*, 24/25 December 1962, 1.

82 "Stalinallee: Stalin's Miracle Mile in Red Berlin," *Life Magazine*, 22 December 1952, 27–30. For an overview of the avenue, see Nicolaus and Obeth, *Die Stalinallee*. Empty East Berlin store windows in *Der Spiegel*, 24 December 1952, 3. Uta Poiger convincingly argues for "the political significance . . . of cultural choices" in *Jazz, Rock, and Rebels*, 207, 226–28.

83 Erhardt, "Was steht zur Debatte?," 7. For background on the social effects of the Economic Miracle, see Niethammer, "War die bürgerliche Gesellschaft in Deutschland 1945 am Ende oder am Anfang?," esp. 530.

84 Wildt, *Vom kleinen Wohlstand*, 62.

85 Ibid., 41–49.

86 Advertisement for Electrostar GMBH in *Der Spiegel*, 5 December 1956, 67.

87 Wildt, *Vom kleinen Wohlstand*, 54–55. Wage statistics in Berghahn, *Modern Germany*, 270.

88 "Weihnachtsgeschäft: Das Viele Geld," *Der Spiegel*, 22 December 1965, 19–20.

89 "Vegiß sie nicht!" (1962) in Plakatsammlung: Institut für Zeitungsforschung der Stadt Dortmund, fiche 34/image 43.

90 Adenauer, *Nachdenken über die Werte*, n.p.

91 Quotes and a fine description of the U.S. activities behind the package campaigns in Poiger, *Jazz, Rock, and Rebels*, 132–33.

92 "Der Kontakt zur Bevölkerung Mitteldeutschlands," *EMNID-Information* 50 (1960), 4–6; "Der Kontakt mit der Ostzonenbevölkerung," *EMNID-Information* 51 (1957), 7–8.

93 Lindner, "Dein Päckchen nach drüben," 30.

94 Politbüro Protokolle "Paketsendungen aus Westdeutschland," 20 December 1952, SAPMO IV 2/2-254, 7; Politbüro Protokolle "Kirchenfrage/Paketaktion der evangelischen und katholischen Kirchen," 22 December 1953, SAPMO J IV 2/2–338, 4; Foitzik, *Rote Sterne*, 209–10.

95 Rei., "Weihnachtspäckchen so oder so? Vorbildliche Leistungen der Post/Schieber versuchen, Festverkehr zu stören," *ND*, 20 December 1961, 8. On this and other attempts to publicize DDR attitudes toward the package campaigns, see Hergeth, "'Die Popularisierung der Maßnahmen.'"

96 Dietzsch, "Geschenkpakete—ein fundamentales Mißverständnis."

97 Härtel and Kabus, "Zwischen Gummibärchen und *Playboy*," 9.

98 Dietzsch, "Geschenkpakete—ein fundamentales Mißverständnis," 112.

99 Härtel and Kabus, "Zwischen Gummibärchen und *Playboy*," 19.

100 Dietzsch, "Geschenkpakete—ein fundamentales Mißverständnis," 117.

101 "Weihnachtsrummel: Es muß auch flimmern," *Der Spiegel*, 16 December 1953, 6.

102 Adenauer, *Nachdenken über die Werte*, n.p.

103 Böll, "Christmas Not Just Once a Year," 419–38; "Nicht nur zur Weihnachtszeit," *Der Spiegel*, 24 December 1952, 26–27. On other postwar authors, see Perry, "Mastering the (Christmas) Past."

104 See Perry, "Healthy for Family Life."

105 "Tagebuch des Fernsehers," *Frankfurter Allgemeine Zeitung*, 24 December 1954.

106 Eurich and Würzberg, *30 Jahre Fernsehalltag*, 92; *Hör Zu!*, 23–29 December 1962, 52–53.

107 *Der Spiegel*, 28 December 1955, 10.

108 Foitzik, *Rote Sterne*, 239–40.

109 Köhler, *Weihnachten in Berlin*, 108.

110 "Wo Kaiser Wilhelm II. saß und Rudi Dutschke auf die Kanzel stieg," *Die Welt*, 20 November 93; Köhler, *Weihnachten in Berlin*, 108; Foitzik, *Rote Sterne*, 246–47.

111 Foitzik, *Rote Sterne*, 251.

112 Herzog, *Sex after Fascism*, 161.

113 Foitzik, *Rote Sterne*, 251.

114 Stitziel, *Fashioning Socialism*, 22.

115 Merkel, "Wer nie vorm Konsum Schlange stand," 83.

116 "Auf dem Wege zu besseren Schaufenstern: Dekorationen und Gestaltungen zum Weihnachtsfest," *Neue Werbung: Zeitschrift für Theorie und Praxis der Werbung*, November 1956, 27–30.

117 Posters in Jüllig, "Deutsch-deutsche Weihnachten."

118 Elsbeth Kupfer, "Am Goldenen Sonntag in Berlin," *ND*, 23 December 1952, 6; "Die erste sozialistische Straße . . .," *ND*, 28 December 1952, 1.

119 "Der Weihnachtstisch einer Berliner Familie," *ND*, 25 December 1951, 3.

120 "Bilanz der Weihnachtseinkäufe," *ND*, 25 December 1949, 5; Weihnachtseinkäufe wie noch nie," *ND*, 25 December 1951, 3; "Noch nie gab es ein solches Weihnachtsgeschäft," *ND*, 24 December 1954, 1. On general East-West competition, see Merkel, *Utopie und Bedürfnis*, 413.

121 "Zusätzliche Versorgung der Bevölkerung zum Weihnachtsfest mit Nahrung und Genußmitteln durch die HO. (Weihnachtsteller der Bevölkerung)/Anlage, no. 1 zum Protokoll, no. 20 vom 28 November 1950," SAPMO-BA DY30/IV2/2/120 (Protokolle der Sitzungen des Politbüros), 31–35.

122 Harsch, *Revenge of the Domestic*, 283.

123 "Weihnachtszuwendungen 1954," SAPMO-BA DY30/JIV2/2/391 (Protokolle der Sitzungen des Politbüros), 23–24; "Weihnachtszuwendungen 1961," *ND*, 19 November 1961, 2.

124 "Die deutsche Weihnacht," *ND*, 25 December 1951, 1.

125 Merkel, *Utopie und Bedürfnis*, 312, 160. On popular support for the SED state, see Port, *Conflict and Stability in the German Democratic Republic*, esp. 1–10; and Wierling, "The Hitler Youth Generation in the GDR."

126 Pence, "The Myth of a Suspended Present," 137.

127 "Weihnachten: Religiöses Fest oder altes Brauchtum? Schenken bereitet den meisten besonders viel Freude," *Allensbacher Berichte* 31 (1988): 1–8.

128 "Weihnachten 1995: Besinnung bleibt auf der Strecke, *Umfrage & Analyse (TNS-Emnid)*, 11/12 (1995), 78.

129 Betts, *Building Socialism at Home*, esp. 118–22; compare Foitzik, *Rote Sterne*, 191–93.

130 "Das Weihnachtsfest gehört der Familie, *Emind-Informationen* 50/51 (1961), 3;
"Weihnachten 1995: Besinnung bleibt auf der Strecke, *Umfrage & Analyse (TNS-Emnid)*, 11/12 (1995): 76–79; "Die andere Bedeutung der Weihnacht, *Umfrage & Analyse (TNS-Emnid)*, 11/12 (2005) 32.

131 Ruff, *Wayward Flock*, 84–85.

132 Sheehan, *Enlightenment Bible*, x.

133 Cross, *All-Consuming Century*, 1, 5.

CONCLUSION

1 Breuer and Breuer, *Weihnachten so schön wie früher*.

2 Bender, "Es grünt so grün."

3 Miles, *Christmas Ritual and Tradition*, 264.

4 Calhoun, *Nationalism*, 8.

5 Bordieu, *Distinction*; Auslander, *Taste and Power*.

6 For a famously harsh critique of the erosive effects of sentimentalism on faith, see Douglas, *Feminization of American Culture*.

7 The classic version of the secularization argument is Mosse, *Nationalization of the Masses*.

8 On the importance of multiconfessionalism, see Smith and Clark, "The Fate of Nathan."

9 McLeod, *The Religious Crisis of the 1960s*, 258, 265.

10 See Lüdtke, "The 'Honor of Labor,'" esp. 71–74.

11 Maier, *Unmasterable Past*; Jaurausch and Geyer, *Shattered Past*.

12 Neil A. Lewis, "In the Shadow of Horror, Auschwitz Guards Frolic," *New York Times*, 19 September 2007.

13 "Naumann eingekesselt: Generalinspekteur ärgert Rühe," *Die Tageszeitung*, 11 March 1993, 4. My thanks to Christian Gerlach for calling this event to my attention.

14 "Lichterketten gegen Gewalt in Berlin," *Frankfurter Allgemeine Zeitung*, 28 December 1992, 5.

15 Tille, *Die Geschichte der deutschen Weihnacht*, ix. For more recent histories of the German holiday, see the influential study by Weber-Kellermann, *Das Weihnachtsfest*; Foitzik, *Rote Sterne*; and Faber and Gajek, eds., *Politische Weihnacht in Antike und Moderne*.

16 Weber-Kellermann, *Das Weihnachtsfest*; Foitzik, *Rote Sterne*; Faber and Gajek, *Politische Weihnacht in Antike und Moderne*.

17 Köhler, *Weihnachten in Berlin*. See also Jochens, *Deutsche Weihnacht*.

18 Breuer and Breuer, *Von Wegen Heilige Nacht*.

19 Turner, ed., "Introduction," 24.

20 Ibid., 14. The most famous statement of this approach is Geertz, *The Interpretation of Cultures*.

21 Sewell, "The Concept(s) of Culture," 45; Clifford, *Predicament of Culture*; Bell, *Ritual Theory, Ritual Practice*.

22 Turner, "Introduction," 11–12.

23 Gillis, *A World of Their Own Making*, xvii.

24 Howard, "What Is Sentimentality?," 76.

25 Serious study of sentimentalism is generally undertaken by literary critics; it is time for historians to pick up the ball. See Howard, "What Is Sentimentality?"; and Dobson, "Reclaiming Sentimental Literature." For a historian's take, see Christina Klein, *Cold War Orientalism*, esp. 15–17. On the still-nascent character of the study of emotions by historians of modern Germany, see Biess, "Forum— History of Emotions."

Bibliography

ARCHIVAL/LIBRARY COLLECTIONS

Berlin, Germany
    Bildarchiv Preussischer Kulturbesitz
    Bundesarchiv
    Bundesarchiv-Filmarchiv
    Evangelisches Zentralarchiv
    Landesarchiv Berlin
    Staatsbibliothek Berlin Haus I: Kinderbuch Abteilung
    Stiftungs Archiv für Parteien und Massenorganizationen der DDR
Eisenhüttenstadt, Germany
    Stadtarchiv Eisenhüttenstadt
    Unternehmensarchiv-Eisenhüttenkombinat Ost
Frankfurt/Main, Germany
    Deutsches Rundfunkarchiv
Freiburg, Germany
    Bundesarchiv-Militärarchiv
    Erzbischöfliches Archiv
Leipzig, Germany
    Deutsche Bücherei
    Stadtarchiv Leipzig
Munich, Germany
    Archiv des Erzbistums München und Freising
    Bayerisches Hauptstaatsarchiv (Kriegsarchiv)
    Bayerisches Hauptstaatsarchiv (Nachlässe und Sammlungen)
    Bayerisches Hauptstaatsarchiv (Neue Bestände)
    Siemens-Museum/Archiv
    Staatsarchiv München
Stuttgart, Germany
    Bibliothek für Zeitgeschichte

PRIMARY SOURCES: NEWSPAPERS AND POPULAR MAGAZINES

Allgemeine Zeitung des Judentums
Der Angriff
Berliner Börsen-Zeitung
Berliner Illustrirte Zeitung
Berliner Lokal-Anzeiger
Berliner Morgenpost
Der Drahtverhau: Schützengraben-Zeitung
Feldpredigten
Frankfurter Allgemeine Zeitung
Frankfurter Israelitisches Familienblatt
Frankfurter Zeitung und Handelsblatt
Die Frau
Die Gartenlaube
Germania
Gesetzblatt der Deutschen Evangelischen Kirche
Hamburger Abendblatt
Illustrierter Beobachter
Der Israelit: Ein Central-Organ für das orthodoxe Judenthum
Israelitische Wochenschrift: Zeitschrift für die Gesamtinteressen des Judentums
Die Jüdische Presse
Jüdische Allgemeine Zeitung
Katholische Volkszeitung
Katholisches Wochenblatt
Der Kleine Journal

Kölnische Volkszeitung
Kölnische Zeitung
Lichterfelder Lokal Anzeiger
Leipziger Illustrirte Zeitung
London Times
Münchner Landzeitung
Neue Berliner Illustrierte
Neues Deutschland
New York Times
Pastoral-Blatt des Bistums Münster
Das Plakat
Das Reichsbanner
Die Reklame
Die Rote Fahne
Der Rundfunk-Hörer
Der SA-Mann
Der Schild
Der Schützengraben
Seidels Reklame
Die Sendung
Sieben Tage: Funkblätter mit Program
Die Staatsbürger Zeitung
Der Tagesspiegel
Telegraf
Völkischer Beobachter
Vorwärts
Vossische Zeitung
Die Welt
Die Welt am Sonntag

PRIMARY SOURCES: PRINTED MATERIAL

Adenauer, Konrad. *Nachdenken über die Werte: Weihnachtsansprachen.* Edited by Walter Berger. Buxheim: Martin, 1976.

Almsloh, Ernst. "Was am Weihnachtsbaum erzählt wird." In *Für unsere Kinder: Weihnachtsbuch der Gleichheit,* edited by Klara Zetkin, 51–52. Stuttgart: Paul Singer, 1906.

Anacker, Heinrich. "SA-Weihnacht 1930." In *Die Trommel. SA Gedichte*. Munich: Franz Eher, 1930.

Aufführungen für Weihnachten und Neujahr. Mühlhausen in Thürigen: G. Danner, various publication dates.

Bahr, Walter, and Hans W. Bahr. *Kriegsbriefe gefallener Studenten 1939–1945*. Tübingen, 1952.

Bamberger, M. L. *Andachtsbüchlein für die jüdischen Krieger und deren Angehörige*. Berlin: H. Itzkowski, 1914.

Bauer, Wilhelm. *Feierstunden Deutscher Christen*. Weimar: Verlag Deutsche Christen, 1935.

Baumann, Hans. *Bergbauernweihnacht: Lieder*. Wolfenbüttel: Georg Kallmeyer, 1942.

———. *Der helle Tag*. Potsdam: Ludwig Voggenreiter, n.d., ca. 1938.

Beckey, Heinrich, ed. *Deutsche Weihnachten*. Lengerich i/W: Bischof & Klein, 1912.

Behlert, Karl, ed. *Weihnachtsfeier A. O. K. Bugarmee, Heeresgruppe von Linsingen, H. QU. Jablon, 1915*. Meiningen: Junghanss & Koritzer, 1915.

Behnken, Klaus, ed. *Deutschland-Berichte der Sozialdemokratischen Partei Deutschlands (Sopade), 1939–1940*. 7 vols. Frankfurt/Main: Petra Nettelbeck Zweitausendeins, 1980.

Bertlein, Hermann. "Hans Baumann, der Künder der jungen Generation." *Die deutsche Schulfeier*, April 1939, 126–32.

Beumer, Philipp Jacob. "Die Söhne des Proletariers." In *Weihnachtsbuch für die reifere Jugend, zugleich ein Vorlesebuch für Schule und Haus*, edited by Philipp Jacob Beumer, 173–88. Weisel: A. Bagel, 1869.

Binding, Rudolf. *A Fatalist at War*. Translated by Ian F. D. Morrow. London: George Allen & Unwin, 1929.

Blaumeiser, Heinz, and Eva Blimlinger, eds. *Alle Jahre wieder . . . Weihnachten zwischen Kaiserzeit und Wirtschaftswunder*. Vienna: Böhlau, 1993.

Blüthgen, Victor. *Das Weihnachtsbuch: Allerlei Weihnachtliches in Vers und Prosa. Mit 7 Kunstbeilagen und zahlreichen Textbildern*. Leipzig: Ernst Kiels Nachfolger, 1899.

Boberach, Heinz, ed. *Berichte des SD und der Gestapo über Kirchen und Kirchenvolk in Deutschland, 1934–1944*. Mainz: Matthias-Grünewald, 1971.

———, ed. *Meldungen aus dem Reich: Die geheimen Lageberichte des Sicherheitsdienstes der SS, 1934–1945*. 17 vols. Herrsching: Pawlak, 1984.

Bodelschwingh, Friedrich von. *Aus einer hellen Kinderzeit*. Bethel bei Bielefeld: Anstalt Bethel, 1952.

Böll, Heinrich. "Christmas Not Just Once a Year." In *The Stories of Heinrich Böll*, translated by Leila Vennewitz, 419–38. New York: Alfred A. Knopf, 1989.

Born, Max. *Mein Leben: Die Erinnerungen des Nobelpreisträgers*. Munich: Nymphenburger, 1975.

Brace, Charles Loring. *Home-Life in Germany*. New York: Charles Scribner, 1853.

Bräuer, Heinz. *Die ersten drei Jahrzehnte der evangelischen Friedenskirchgemeinde Eisenhüttenstadt. Erinnerungen.* 2nd edition. Privately printed, 2000. Available at ⟨http://friedenskirchengemeinde.huettenstadt.de/download/BUCH.pdf⟩. 31 January 2010.

Braun, Alfred. "Weihnachtliche Impressionen." In *Weihnachtsgeschichten aus Berlin,* edited by Gundel Paulsen, 100–105. Husum: Husum, 1993.

Breuer, Judith, and Rita Breuer. *Von wegen Heilige Nacht! Das Weihnachtsfest in der politischen Propaganda.* Mülheim an der Ruhr: Verlag an der Ruhr, 2000.

———. *Weihnachten so schön wie früher, Alte Zimmerdekoration zum Selberbasteln.* Mülheim an der Ruhr: Verlag An der Ruhr, 2000.

Bromme, Moritz William Theodor. *Lebensgeschichte eines modernen Fabrikarbeiters.* Edited by Bernd Neumann. Frankfurt/Main: Athenäum, 1971; orig. published, 1905.

Buchbender, Ortwin, and Reinhold Sterz, eds., *Das andere Gesicht des Krieges: Deutsche Feldpostbriefe, 1939–1945.* Munich: C. H. Beck, 1983.

Cassel, Paulus. *Weihnachten, Ursprünge, Bräuche und Aberglauben. Ein Beitrag zur Geschichte der christlichen Kirche und des deutschen Volkes.* Berlin: Ludwig Rauh, 1861.

"Des Christen Kriegsgebet zur Weihnachtszeit." In *Weihnachten im Kriege: Weihnachtsgebete u. -Lieder; Auch für Soldaten, Lazarette u. dgl.* Essen: Fredebeul & Koenen, 1914.

Cohn, Willy. *Verwehte Spuren.* Cologne: Böhlau, 1995.

Colze, Leo. *Berliner Warenhäuser.* Berlin: Hermann Seemann Nachfolger, 1908.

De Lagarde, Paul. *Altes und Neues über das Weihnachtsfest.* Göttingen: Dieterichsche Universitätsbuchhandlung, 1891.

"Deutsche Weihnacht." Special edition of *Die neue Gemeinschaft: Das Parteiarchiv für nationalsozialistische Feier- und Freizeitgestaltung,* edited by Reichspropagandaleitung, Amtsleitung Kultur. Munich: Franz Eher, 1937.

"Die arme Familie." In *Weihnachtsgeschichten und Weihnachtslieder: Eine Weihnachtsgabe für die Jugend,* 2–10. Schreiberhau: Rettungshaus zu Schreiberhau, 1857.

Dithmar, Reinhard. *Arbeiterlieder 1844 bis 1945.* Berlin: Luchterhand, 1993.

Doering, Heinrich, ed. *Weihnachtsbüchlein: Dichtungen und Legenden zur Feier des Christfestes.* Leipzig: Renger'sche Buchhandlung, 1846.

"D. S. Berlin." *Im deutschen Reich: Zeitschrift des Centralvereins deutscher Staatsbürger jüdischen Glaubens,* January 1901, 50.

Ebner, Jakob. "Meine Kriegserlebnisse." 4 vols. Ms. in Erzbischöfliches Archiv-Freiburg, Nachlass Ebner, 53–55.

Elm, Hugo. *Das Goldene Weihnachtsbuch. Beschreibung und Darstellung des Ursprungs, der Feier, der Sitten, der Gebräuche, Sagen und des Aberglaubens der Weihnachtszeit und gleichzeitig Anleitung zur sinnigen Schmücken des Christbaumes, der Pyramide, sowie zur Anlegung der Krippen und Weihnachtsgärten.* Halle: G. Schwetschke'scher Verlag, 1878.

Emonts, J. W. *Unserer Jäger Freud und Leid. Kriegserinnerungen 1870/71 nach dem Tagebuch eines bayerischen Jägers*. Kaiserslauten: August Gotthold, 1887.

Engelmann, Katrin, ed. *Hohe Nacht der klaren Sterne! Ein Weihnachts- und Wiegenliederbuch*. Wolfenbüttel and Berlin: Reichsjugendführung/Georg Kallmeyer, 1938.

Eulenburg, Philpp Graf zu. "Ein Weihnachtsmärchenspiel." In *Das Weihnachtsbuch. Erzählungen, Märchen, Gedichte und Lieder. Mit 38 Illustrationen und 7 Musikstücken*, edited by Philipp Graf zu Eulenberg, 57–79. Stuttgart: Deutsche Verlags-Anstalt, 1892.

Falkenhausen, Helene von. *Ansiedlerschicksale: Elf Jahre in Deutsch Südwestafrika, 1893–1904*. Berlin: Dietrich Reimer, 1905.

Fallada, Hans. *Little Man—What Now?* Translated by Susan Bennett. London: Libris, 1996; orig. published, 1932.

Faulhaber, Michael von. *Judentum, Christentum, Germanentum: Adventspredigten gehalten in St. Michael zu München 1933*. Munich: Huber, 1934.

Fischer, Carl B. *Denkwürdigkeiten und Erinnerungen eines Arbeiters*. Leipzig: Eugen Diederichs, 1903.

Flex, Walter. "Das Weihnachtsmärchen des fünfzigsten Regiments." In *Walter Flex Gesammelte Werke*, 151–72. Munich: C. H. Beck, 1936.

48 Weihnachtslieder für Soldaten. Stuttgart: Holland und Josenhaus, 1914.

Frankenberg, Fred Graf. *Kriegstagebücher von 1866 und 1870/71*. Edited by Heinrich v. Poschinger. Stuttgart: Deutsche Verlags-Anstalt, 1896.

Führer durch den Berliner Weihnachtsmarkt 1934. Edited by Arbeitsgemeinschaft zur Belebung der Berliner Innenstadt e.V. Berlin: Behag, 1934.

Gebhardt, Florentine. *Blätter aus dem Lebensbilderbuch: Jugenderinnerungen*. Berlin: Max Gelle, 1930.

———— [Florus Bardt, pseud.]. *Des Lehrers Weihnachtsfeier in der Schulklasse. Eine Feier mit Ansprachen, Deklamationen, Gesängen, Spielen, Reigen u. Märchen für a) Oberstufe b) Mittelstufe c) Unterstufe geeignet für einfache und gehobene Schulverhältnisse*. Berlin: Kribe-Verlag, 1926.

————. *Vorsprüche und Festgedichte zu Veranstaltungen in Kriegervereinen*. Berlin: Kribe-Verlag, 1928.

————. *Der zweifache Weg. Lebenserinnerungen, dritter Teil*. Berlin: published as manuscript by M. E. Gebhardt, 1942.

————, ed. *Festliche Tage der Schule. Eine reichhaltige Sammlung von Gedichten und Aufführungen für Schule und Lehrerhaus*. Berlin: Kribe-Verlag, 1922.

————, ed. *Festliche Tage der Schule im Dritten Reich: Eine reichhaltige Sammlung von Gedichten und Aufführungen für Schule und Lehrerhaus*. Berlin: Neuer Berliner Buchvertrieb, 1933.

————, ed. *Der freie deutsche Rhein. Praktischer Stoff für Rheinlandfeiern*. Berlin: Kribe Verlag, 1930.

————, ed. *Kraft durch Freude: Vier Feiern für Deutsche Abende und andere national-sozialistische Veranstaltungen in Schule und Gemeinde des 3. Reiches*. Berlin: Neuer Berliner Buchvertrieb, n.d., ca. 1934.

————, ed. *Stoffe für die Schulfeier am Verfassungstage (11. August): Gedichte, Deklamationen, Wechselgespräche, Festspiele, Inschriften für Heldendenkmäler usw*. Berlin: Kribe-Verlag, 1926.

———— [A. Rolf, pseud.], ed. *Unser Saarland wieder Deutsch und Frei! Drei Feiern für Schule und Verein*. Berlin: Neuer Berliner Buchvertrieb, 1934.

Gefallene Deutsche Juden. Frontbriefe, 1914–1918. Edited by Reichsbund Jüdischer Frontsoldaten e. V. Berlin: Vortrupp, 1935.

Geissmar, Clara. *Erinnerungen (1913)*. In *Jüdisches Leben in Deutschland. Bd. 1: Selbstzeugnisse zur Sozialgeschichte im Kaiserreich 1780–1871*, edited by Monika Richarz, 452–61. Stuttgart: Deutsche Verlags-Anstalt, 1976.

Gerlach, Heinrich. *Die Verratene Armee: Ein Stalingrad Roman*. Munich: Nymphenburger, 1957.

Gerstner, Hermann. "Weihnachtliches Lichtfeier," *Die Deutsche Schulfeier* 2 (1937): 303–10.

Glaser, Hermann. "Ohne besondere Vorkommnisse." In *Jugend im Dritten Reich*, edited by Hermann Glaser and Axel Silenius, 48–63. Frankfurt/Main: Tribüne, 1975.

Goethe, J. W. "The Sorrows of Young Werther." In *Goethe's Collected Works*, vol. 11, translated by Victor Lange, 5–87. New York: Suhrkamp, 1988.

Göhre, Paul. *Das Warenhaus*. Frankfurt/Main: Rütten & Loening, 1907.

Golovchansky, Anatoly, Valentin Oipov, Anatoly Prokopenko, Ute Daniel, and Jürgen Reulecke, eds. *Ich will raus aus diesem Wahnsinn: Deutsche Briefe von der Ostfront 1941–1945; aus sowjetischen Archiven*. Hamburg: Rowohlt, 1993.

Granzow, Klaus. *Tagebuch eines Hitlerjungen 1943–1945*. Bremen: Carl Schünemann, 1965.

Gröber, Conrad. *Weihnachtshirtenbrief für die Kinder*. Freiburg: Herder Drucker, 1939.

Güll, Friedrich. "Weihnachts-Bilder." Special volume of *Jugend Bibliothek. Erster Jahrgang, Drittes Bändchen. Weihnachtsbuch*, edited by Gustav Rieritz. Berlin: M. Simion, 1840.

Hämmerle, Christa, ed. *Kindheit im Ersten Weltkrieg*. Vienna: Böhlau, 1993.

Heger, Moritz, ed. *Deutsches Weihnachtsbuch für die Jugend. Für Kinder von acht bis elf Jahren. Mit 4 Kupfern*. Dresden: Meinhold & Sohne, 1851.

Hirsch, Samson Raphael. *Der Weihnachtsbaum in der jüdischen Familie: Offenes Sendschreiben an den Berliner Correspondenten des "Jeschurun, Monatsblatt von S. R. Hirsch."* Hamburg: Herold'schen Buchhandlung, 1855.

Hoffmann, E. T. A. *Nußknacker und Mausekönig*. Stuttgart: Reclam 2001.

Hoffmann, Rudolf, ed. *Der deutsche Soldat; Briefe aus dem Weltkrieg. Vermächtnis*. Munich: Albert Langen/Georg Müller, 1937.

Holm, Mia. "Weihnachtslied eines Kindes." In *Hänschen an den Weihnachtsmann: Ein Bilderband mit Märchen, Geschichten, und lustigen Schwänken für Mädchen unf Buben im Alter von 7-10 Jahren*, edited by Hermann Schaffstein, 4. Cologne: Schaffstein, 1904.

Hoppe, Rudi. *Weihnachten im Kriege: Sonderdruck für die Gestaltung v. Julfeiern und weihnachtlichen Abenden in d. SS.* Berlin: Der Reichsführer SS, SS Hauptamt, 1942.

Immergrünes Weihnachtsbuch für die Jugend. Leipzig: E. Mengler, 1850.

Irtl, Josef. "Aufbruch aus der Stunde Null." In *Weihnachten 1945: Ein Buch der Erinnerungen*, edited by Claus Hinrich Casdorff, 72–80. Frankfurt/Main: Athenäum, 1989.

Jakob, Berthold. "Wirtschaftpropaganda!" In *Braune Weihnachts-Verkaufsmesse für Industrie, Handwerk, Handel und Gewerbe in den Ausstellungshallen am Holstentor.* Lübeck: Wullenwever-Druck, 1933.

J. Rademachers Vereinsbühne. Bonn: J. Rademacher, various publication dates.

Jürgs, Michael. *Der kleine Frieden im großen Krieg: Westfront 1914: Als Deutsche, Franzosen und Briten gemeinsam Weihnachten feierten.* Munich: Bertelsmann, 2003.

Kästner, Erich. "Weihnachtsschwarzmarkt in Berlin." In *Weihnachtsgeschichten aus Berlin*, edited by Gundel Paulsen, 15–17. Husum: Husum, 1993.

Killy, Walther, ed. *Bürgerleben: Die Briefe an den Bruder Gerhard 1840–1867.* Munich: C. H. Beck, 1990.

Kotzde, Wilhelm. "Christnacht im Schnee." In *Deutsches Weihnachtsbuch. Teil II: Erzählungen. Für die Jugend von 12. Jahre ab*, edited by Alexander Troll, 38–50. Berlin: Johannes Räde/Literarische Vereinigung des Berliner Lehrervereins, 1904.

Kremer, Hannes. "Neuwertung 'überlieferter' Brauchformen?" *Die Neue Gemeinschaft* 3 (1937): 300s. Translated by Randall L. Bytwerk, the German Propaganda Archive, ⟨http://www.calvin.edu/academic/cas/gpa/feier37.htm⟩. 16 October 2006.

Kretschmann, Hans von. *Kriegsbriefe aus den Jahren 1870/71.* Edited by Lily Braun. Stuttgart: Greiner & Pfeiffer, 1904.

Kriegsweihnachten 1914. Grosses Hauptquartier. Berlin: A. Winser, ca. 1915.

Kück, Eduard, and Heinrich Sohnrey. *Feste und Spiele des deutschen Landvolks.* Berlin: Deutsche Landbuchhandlung, 1911.

Kügelgen, Wilhelm von. *Bürgerleben: Die Briefe an den Bruder Gerhard 1840–1867.* Edited by Walther Killy. Munich: C. H. Beck, 1990.

Kühnhausen, Florian. *Kriegs-Erinnerungen eines Soldaten des könglich bayerischen Infanterie-Leib-Regiments 1870–71.* Partekirchen: L. Wenzel, 1896.

Lahme, Georg. *Aufbruch zu Hitler.* Dortmund: Fuchs, 1933.

Langwadt, Claudius. *Das Weihnachtsgeschäft im Warenhaus.* Bottrop: Wilhelm Postberg, 1932.

Leibig, Oskar. *Erlebnisse eines freiwilligen bayerischen Jägers im Feldzuge 1870/71.* Nördlingen: C. H. Beck, 1886.

Liese, Hermann, ed. *Deutsche Kriegsweihnacht.* 4th ed. Munich: Hauptkulturamt in der Reichspropagandaleitung der NSDAP/Franz Eher, 1944.

———, ed. *Licht muß wieder werden.* Berlin: Hauptkulturamt der NSDAP Reichspropagandaleitung, 1943.

Lilje, Hanns, ed. *Evangelische Weihnacht: Ein Buch von Weihnachtsglaube, Weihnachtskunst und Weihnachtssitte.* Berlin: Im Furche-Verlag, 1939.

Lipinski, Richard. *Friede auf Erden! Oder: Die Ausweisung am Weihnachts-Abend: Soziales Bild in 2 Aufzügen.* Berlin: Hoffmann, 1895.

Loah, Ruth. "Kinderszenen im Kriege." In *Kindheit und Jugend unter Hitler,* edited by Helmut Schmidt, 171–87. Berlin: Siedler, 1992.

Lohmeyer, Julius, ed. *Deutsche Jugend: Weihnachts-Album.* Berlin: Leonhard Simion, 1885.

Ludendorff, Erich, and Mathilde Ludendorff. *Weihnachten im Lichte der Rassenerkenntnis.* Munich: Ludendorff Verlag, 1933.

Ludwig, Julie. "Weihnachten im Schnee: Eine Erzählung aus den Bergen." In *Deutsche Jugend: Weinachts-Album,* edited by Julius Lohmeyer, 70–82. Berlin: Leonhard Simion, 1885.

Lux, Käthe. *Studien über die Entwicklung der Warenhäuser in Deutschland.* Jena: Gustav Fischer, 1910.

Manger, Bruno. *Mittwinter. Deutsche Weihnacht in Geschichte, Glauben und Brauch.* Halle: Hermann Schroedel, 1936.

Marbach, Johannes. *Die heilige Weihnachtszeit nach Bedeutung, Geschichte, Sitten und Symbolen.* Frankfurt/Main: J. D. Sauerländer, 1865; 1st ed., 1858.

Märchenbuch für die Kinder des Proletariats. Berlin: Baake, 1893.

Mannhardt, Wilhelm. *Wald- und Feldkulte: Der Baumkultus der Germanen und ihrer Nachbarstämme.* Berlin: Gebrüder Borntraeger, 1905; 1st ed., 1875.

Mayer, Fridolin. "Kriegstagebuch 1914–1918." Ms. in Erzbischöfliches Archiv-Freiburg, Nachlass Mayer.

Merck, Theodor Q. *Briefe aus dem Felde.* Hamburg: Druckerei des Rauhen Hauses, 1919.

Meyer, Arnold. *Das Weihnachtsfest: seine Entstehung und Entwicklung.* Tübingen: J. C. B. Mohr/Paul Siebeck, 1913.

Mihaly, Jo. *. . . da gibt's ein Wiedersehen! Kriegstagebuch eines Mädchens, 1914–1918.* Freiburg: F. H. Lerle, 1982.

Miles, Clement. *Christmas in Ritual and Tradition, Christian and Pagan.* Detroit: Gale Research, 1986; orig. published, 1912.

Moritz-Henning, Ernst, ed. *Nun brennen viele Kerzen: Neue Lieder um die Weihnacht.* Potsdam: Ludwig Voggenreiter, 1937.

Moszeik, Carl, ed. *Aus der Gedankenwelt einer Arbeiterfrau von ihr selbst erzählt.* Lichterfelde-Berlin: Edwin Runge, 1909.

Mühsam, Erich. "Heilige Nacht." In *Ausgewählte Werke, Bd. 1: Gedichte. Prosa. Stücke.* Berlin/East: Volk und Welt, 1978, 41.

Mühsam, Paul. "Ich bin ein Mensch gewesen." Undated ms. in Leo Baeck Institute, New York. In *Jüdisches Leben in Deutschland. Bd. 2: Selbstzeugnisse zur Sozialgeschichte im Kaiserreich,* edited by Monika Richarz, 357–64. Stuttgart: Deutsche Verrlags-Anstalt, 1979.

Naegele, Bert. *Jene zwölf Jahre . . . Erzählung eines Zeitzeugen.* Berlin: Desktop published by the author in Staatsbibliothek II, 1993.

Nickel, Marcus Adam. *Die heiligen Zeiten und Feste nach ihrer Geschichte und Feier in der katolische Kirche, Teil 1: Der Weihnachtsfestkreis.* Mainz: C. G. Kunze, 1835.

Niemann, Johannes. *Das 9. königlich-Sächsisches Infanterie-Regiment N. 133 im Weltkrieg, 1914–1918.* Hamburg, 1969. In BA-MA Bibliothek, NVI c 133b.

Olfers, Hedwig von. *Erblüht in der Romantik, gereift in selbstloser Liebe/aus Briefen zesammengestellt v. II 1816–1891.* Berlin: Ernst Siegfried Mittler und Sohn, 1914.

"Personalien: Thilo Scheller," *Der Spiegel,* 20 August 1958, 48.

Plakolb, Max. "Eine Distel als Weihnachtsbaum." In *Alle Jahre Wieder . . . : Weihnachten zwischen Kaiserzeit und Wirtschaftswunder,* edited by Heinz Blaumeister and Eva Blimlinger, 172–79. Wien: Böhlau, 1993.

Plivier, Theodor. *Stalingrad.* Translated by Richard and Clara Winston. New York: Appleton-Century-Crofts, 1948.

Pniower, Otto, Georg Schuster, Richard Sternfeld, L. E. Dillinger, and Elisabeth von Ostrowski, eds. *Briefe aus dem Felde. Für das deutsche Volk im Auftrage der Zentralstelle zur Sammlung von Feldpostbriefen im Märkischen Museum zu Berlin.* Oldenburg: Gerhard Stalling, 1916.

Popp, Adelheid. *Jugendgeschichte einer Arbeiterin.* Munich: Ernst Reinhardt, 1909.

Pötzsch, Arno. *Die Madonna von Stalingrad: Ein Gedanken vor der Weihnachts-madonna von Stalingrad.* Hamburg: H. H. Nölke, 1946.

Prince, Magdalene von. *Eine deutsche Frau im Innern Deutsch-Ostafrikas: Elf Jahre nach Tagebuchblättern erzählt.* Berlin: Ernst Siegfried Mittler und Sohn, 1908.

Probst, Adolf Gerd, and Gerhard Kaldewei, eds. *Ewig Dein. Feldpostkarten des Fritz Meyer, 1915–1917.* Bielefeld: Westfallen, 1985.

Proletarische Weihnachtslieder. Berlin: A. Hoffman, ca. 1927.

Pudelko, Walther. "Zur Frage des Weihnachtsliedes." *Die Musik, Monatsschrift* 31, no. 3 (December 1938): 145–57.

Rauch, Karl, and Carl H. Erkelenz, eds. *Nacht unter Sternen: Weihnachtsbuch für den deutschen Soldaten in Norwegen.* Oslo: Wehrmachtbefehlshaber Norwegen/ Wehrmacht-Propagandagruppe, 1943.

Reber-Gruber, Auguste. "Deutsche Weihnachten." *Nationalsozialistische*

Mädchenerziehung: Amtliche Zeitschrift des Nationalsozialistischen Lehrerbundes für weibliche Erziehung und Bildung (December 1936): 310.

———. "Frau und Feier!—Ein Aufruf." *Die Deutsche Schulfeier* 1, no. 1 (October 1936): 9.

Rehbein, Franz. *Das Leben eines Landarbeiters.* Edited by Karl Winfried Schafhausen. Darmstadt: Leuchterhand, 1973; orig. published, 1911.

Reitschel, Paul. *Weihnachten in Kirche, Kunst und Volksleben.* Bielefeld and Leipzig: Velhagen & Klasing, 1902.

Rellstab, Ludwig. *Der Weihnachtswanderer von Alt-Berlin: Auszüge aus Ludwig Rellstabs Weihnachtswanderungen in der Vossischen Zeitung 1826–1859.* Edited by Paul S. Ulrich. Berlin: Berliner Wissenschafts-Verlag, 2002.

Richert, Dominik. *Beste Gelegenheit zum Sterben: Meine Erlebnisse im Kriege 1914–1918.* Edited by Angelika Tramitz and Bernd Ulrich. Munich: Knesebeck and Schuler, 1989.

Rogge, D. Bernhard. *Bei der Garde. Erlebnisse und Eindrücke aus dem Kriegsjahre 1870/71.* Hannover: C. Meyer, 1895.

Rohrer, Fritz, ed. *Kinder-Lieder: Weihnachten 1883.* Zurich: F. Lohbauer, 1883.

Röthig, Bruno. *Weihnachtslieder im Felde. Für Männerchor gesetzt.* Rheydt: Ausschuß der Evangelischen Militärseelsorge im Felde zu Rheydt, 1915.

Schleiermacher, Friedrich. *Christmas Eve: Dialogue on the Incarnation.* Translated by Terrence N. Tice. Richmond, Va.: John Knox Press, 1967.

———. *Die Weihnachtsfeier: Ein Gespräch.* Basel: Benno Schwabe & Co., n.d.; orig. published, 1806.

Schnidtmann-Leffer, Elisabeth. "Frau und Volkstum, Brauch und Sitte/Eine weihnachtliche Betrachtung." *Deutsche Frauen-Kultur* 12, no. 38 (1934): 225–27.

Schott, Anselm. *Das Meßbuch der heiligen Kirche.* Freiburg/Breisgau: Herder, 1926; 1st ed., 1884.

Schröter, Heinz. *Stalingrad.* Translated by Constantine Fitzgibbon. New York: Ballantine Books, 1958.

Schultz, Wolfgang Schultz. "Auch an seinem Heim erkennt man den National Sozialisten!" *Die Hoheitsträger* 3 (1939): 16–18. Translated by Randall L. Bytwerk, the German Propaganda Archive, ⟨http://www.calvin.edu/academic/cas/gpa/interiordecoration.htm⟩. 16 October 2006.

Schwab-Felisch, Hans. "Die Literatur der Obergefreiten." *Der Monat* 4 (1952): 644–51.

Siebold, Karl. "Die deutsche Schulfeier als Forderung und Aufgabe." *Die Deutsche Schulfeier* 1, no. 1 (October 1936): 7.

Stillich, Oskar. *Die Lage der weiblichen Dienstboten in Berlin.* Berlin: Akademischer Verlag für Soziale Wissenschaften, 1902.

Storm, Gertrude. *Theodor Storm: Ein Bild seines Lebens v. I & II.* Berlin: Curtius/Gebr. Paetel, 1912.

Storm, Theodor. *Unter dem Tannenbaum.* In *Werke Bd. II*, 7–28. Stuttgart: J. G. Cott'sche, n.d.

———. *Unter dem Tannenbaum/Wenn die Äpfel reif sind.* Edited by W. Ehlers and W. Duggen. Leipzig: Juluis Beltz, 1930.

Stumpf, Richard. *War, Mutiny, and Revolution in the German Navy: The World War I Diary of Seaman Richard Stumpf.* Edited and translated by Daniel Horn. New Brunswick: Rutgers University Press, 1967.

Sulzbach, Herbert. *Zwischen Zwei Mauern: 50 Monate Westfront.* Berg Am See: Kurt Vowinckel, 1986.

Süs, Gustav. *Paradiesgarten für fromme und liebe Kinder.* Dresden: Meinhold, 1859.

Sydow, Anna von, ed. *Wilhelm und Caroline von Humboldt in ihren Briefen Bd.5.* Berlin: Ernst Siegfried Mittler und Sohn, 1907.

Tanera, Carl. *Ernste und heitere Erinnerungen eines Ordonnanzoffiziers im Jahre 1870/71.* Munich: C. H. Beck, 1896.

Tieck, Ludwig. "Weihnacht-Abend." In *Schriften in zwölf Bänden*, vol. 11, edited by Uwe Schweikert, 907–48. Frankfurt/Main: Deutscher Klassiker, 1988.

Tille, Alexander. "German Christmas and the Christmas Tree." *Folklore* (June 1892): 166–82.

———. *Die Geschichte der Deutschen Weihnacht.* Leipzig: E. Kiel, 1893.

———. *Yule and Christmas: Their Place in the Germanic Year.* London: David Nutt, 1899.

Tönnies, Ferdinand. *Custom: An Essay on Social Codes.* Translated by A. Farrell Borenstein. New York: Free Press, 1961; orig. published, 1909.

Troll, Alexander, ed. *Deutsches Weihnachtsbuch. Teil II: Erzählungen. Für die Jugend von 12. Jahre ab.* Berlin: Johannes Räde/Literarische Vereinigung des Berliner Lehrervereins, 1904.

Unserm Kaiser! Als Festgabe zum Regierungsjubiläum. Kriegserinnerungen der Veteranen des Kreis-Krieger-Verbandes Bochum-Land. Bochum: Wilhelm Stumpf, 1913.

Verhandlungen des Reichstags, IV. Wahlperiode 1928, Bd. 426. Stenographische Berichte. Berlin: Reichsdruckerei, 1930.

Viersbeck, Doris. *Erlebnisse eines Hamburger Dienstmädchens.* Munich: Ernst Reinhardt, 1910.

Voigt, O. H., ed. *Frohe Weihnacht 1943. 2 Batterie, Lehrregiment (Mot.).* N.p., 1943.

Volk, Ludwig, ed. *Akten Kardinal Michael von Faulhabers, 1917–1945.* Mainz: Matthias Grünewald, 1975.

Vom Quempas-Weihnachtssingen. Kassel: Bärenreiter, ca. 1940.

Von-Ed, Ida. "Kriegsweihnacht im deutschen Hause." *Deutsche Kriegsnachrichten*, edited by Kriegspresseamt (19 December 1917): 1–2.

Vorweihnachtliche Feier. Edited by Amt "Feierabend" der NS.-Gemeinschaft "Kraft durch Freude," Abteilung Volkstum/Brauchtum. Berlin: Verlag der DAF, 1938.

Wagner, H. *Über die Organisation der Warenhäuser: Kaufhäuser und der großen Spezialgeschäfte.* Leipzig: Poeschel, 1911.

Wallich, Hildegard. *Erinnerungen aus meinem Leben.* Altenkirchen: Dieckmann, 1970.

"Weihnacht der Armen." Pamphlet by Zentralstelle der Proletarischen Freidenker. Berlin, 1930.

Weihnachten im Kriege. Weihnachtsgebete und -Lieder. Auch für Soldaten, Lazarette und Dergleichen. Essen: Fredebeul & Koenen, 1914.

Ein Weihnachtsfeldpostbrief unsern lieben Limbacher Kriegern mit deutschem Gruß und Händedruck gewidmet vom Kirchenvorstand zu Limbach. Limbach: J. R. Ulbricht, 1914.

Weihnachtsfibel für das deutsche Haus. Berlin: Reichsausschuß für volkswirtschaftliche Aufklärung, 1934.

Weihnachtsgrüße (Ein praktisches Verteilheftchen für Weihnachtsfeiern). Charlottenburg: Der Bote, 1927.

Weihnachtsgrüße (Ein praktisches Verteilheftchen für Weihnachtsfeiern). Charlottenburg: Der Bote, 1930.

Weihnachtsgruss der Gemeinschaft in —— an —— (Schema). Stuttgart: Buchhandlung d. Dtsch Philadelphiavereins, 1917.

Weihnachts-Kameradschaftsabend. 6 Kompanie Armee Nachrichten Regiment 549. N.p., 1939.

Weinhold, Karl. *Weihnacht-Spiele und Lieder aus Süddeutschland und Schlesien.* Vienna: Wilhelm Braumüller, 1875.

Weitzkel, Fritz, ed. *Die Gestaltung der Feste im Jahres- und Lebenslauf in der SS-Familie.* Düsseldorf: SS-Oberabschnitt West, n.d.

"Wie in einem christlichen Hause Weihnachten gefeiert wurde." In *Weihnachtsbuch für die reifere Jugend, zugleich ein Vorlesebuch für Schule und Haus,* edited by Philipp Jacob Beumer, 9–14. Weisel: A. Bagel, 1869.

Winterunterhaltungen für die reifere Jungend. Nuremberg: Campe, 1823.

Witkop, Philipp. *Kriegsbriefe gefallener Studenten.* Munich: Georg Miller, 1928.

Wraner, H. "Einen Weihnachtsbaum bekam sie doch." In *Hänschen an den Weihnachtsmann: Ein Bilderband mit Märchen, Geschichten, und lustigen Schwänken für Mädchen und Buben im Alter von 7 bis 10 Jahren,* 6–7. Edited by Hermann Schaffstein. Cologne: Schaffstein, 1904.

Wylie, Ida A. R. *The Germans.* Brooklyn: Bobbs-Merrill, 1911.

Zetkin, Klara. "An die Eltern!" In *Für unsere Kinder: Weihnachtsbuch der Gleichheit,* edited by Klara Zetkin. Stuttgart: Paul Singer, 1906.

Ziehnert, Amadeus. *Winterfreuden zur Unterhaltung und Belustigung für Kinder jedes Alters; ein Weihnachts- und Neujahrsgeschenk.* Pirna: Carl August Friese, ca. 1820.

"Zueignung." In *Der Weihnachtsbaum der deutscher Frau.* Hannover: Verband Deutsche Frauenkleidung und Frauenkultur, 1920.

Abrams, Lynn. *Worker's Culture in Imperial Germany: Leisure and Recreation in the Rhineland and Westphalia*. New York: Routledge, 1992.

Allen, Ann Taylor. "Religion and Gender in Modern German History: A Historiographical Perspective." In *Gendering Modern German History: Themes, Debates, Revisions*, edited by Karen Hagemann and Jean H. Quataert, 190–207. New York: Berghahn Books, 2007.

Altgeld, Wolfgang. "Religion, Denomination, and Nationalism in Nineteenth-Century Germany." In *Protestants, Catholics and Jews in Germany, 1800–1914*, edited by Helmut Walser Smith, 49–65. New York: Berg, 2001.

Anderson, Benedict. *Imagined Communities*. London: Verso, 1983.

Applegate, Celia. *A Nation of Provincials: The German Idea of Heimat*. Berkeley: University of California Press, 1990.

Applegate, Celia, and Pamela Potter. "Germans as the 'People of Music': Genealogy of an Identity." In *Music and German National Identity*, edited by Celia Applegate and Pamela Potter, 1–35. Chicago: University of Chicago Press, 2002.

Auslander, Leora. "Beyond Words." *American Historical Review* 110 (October 2005): 1015–45.

———. *Taste and Power: Furnishing Modern France*. Berkeley: University of California Press, 1996.

Baird, Jay W. *Hitler's War Poets: Literature and Politics in the Third Reich*. Cambridge: Cambridge University Press, 2007.

Baranowski, Shelly. *Strength through Joy: Consumerism and Mass Tourism in the Third Reich*. Cambridge: Cambridge University Press, 2004.

Baron, Ulrich. "Stalingrad als Thema der deutschsprachigen Literatur." In *Stalingrad: Mythos und Wirklichkeit einer Schlacht*, edited by Wolfgang Wette and Gerd R. Ueberschär, 226–332. Frankfurt/Main: Fischer, 1992.

Barthes, Roland. *A Lover's Discourse: Fragments*. New York: Noonday, 1993.

———. *Mythologies*. New York: Hill and Wang, 1972.

Bartov, Omer. "Defining Enemies, Making Victims: Germans, Jews, and the Holocaust." *American Historical Review* 103 (June 1998): 771–816.

———. *Hitler's Army: Soldiers, Nazis, and War in the Third Reich*. New York: Oxford University Press, 1992.

Bausinger, Hermann. "Anmerkungen zum Verhältnis von öffentlicher und privater Festkultur." In *Öffentliche Festkultur: Politische Feste in Deutschland von der Aufklärung bis zum Ersten Weltkrieg*, edited by Dieter Düding, Peter Friedemann, and Paul Münch, 390–401. Reinbeck bei Hamburg: Rowohlt, 1988.

———. *Folk Culture in a World of Technology*. Translated by Elke Dettmer. Bloomington: University of Indiana Press, 1990.

———. *Typisch deutsch: Wie deutsch sind die Deutschen?* Munich: C. H. Beck, 2002.

Becker, Annette. "From Death to Memory: The National Ossuaries in France after the Great War." *History and Memory* 5 (Fall/Winter 1993): 32–49.

Behnken, Klaus, ed. *Inszenierung der Macht: Ästhetische Faszination im Faschismus.* Berlin: Nishen, 1987.

Behrenbeck, Sabine. "The Nation Honours the Dead: Remembrance Days for the Fallen in the Weimar Republic and the Third Reich." In *Festive Culture in Germany and Europe from the Sixteenth to the Twentieth Century*, edited by Karin Friedrich, 303–21. Lewiston, N.Y.: Edwin Mellen, 2000.

Bejschowetz-Iserhoht, Marion. *Dienstboten zur Kaiserzeit: Weibliches Hauspersonal in Kiel 1871–1918.* Kiel: Gesellschaft für Kieler Stadtgeschichte, 1984.

Bell, Catherine. *Ritual Theory, Ritual Practice.* New York: Oxford University Press, 1992.

Bella, Leslie. *The Christmas Imperative: Leisure, Family, and Women's Work.* Halifax, Nova Scotia: Fernwood, 1992.

Bender, Justus. "Es grünt so Grün." *Die Zeit*, 20 December 2006, 64.

Benzing-Vogt, Irmgard. "Vom Kind in der Krippe zum Kind in der Wiege: Das Weihnachtslied der NS-Zeit." *Neue Musikzeitung* (December/January 1997–1998): 49–51.

Berezin, Mabel. *Making the Fascist Self: The Political Culture of Interwar Italy.* Ithaca: Cornell University Press, 1997.

Bergen, Doris L. "German Military Chaplains in the Second World War and the Dilemmas of Legitimacy." In *The Sword of the Lord: Military Chaplains from the First to the Twenty-First Century*, edited by Doris L. Bergen, 165–86. Notre Dame: University of Notre Dame Press, 2004.

———. "Hosanna or 'Hilf, O Herr Uns': National Identity, the German Christian Movement, and the 'Dejudaization' of Sacred Music in the Third Reich." In *Music and German National Identity*, edited by Celia Applegate and Pamela Otter, 140–54. Chicago: University of Chicago Press, 2002.

———. "Nazism and Christianity: Partners and Rivals? A Response to Richard Steigmann-Gall, *The Holy Reich: Nazi Conceptions of Christianity, 1919–1945.*" *Journal of Contemporary History* 42, no. 1 (2007): 25–33.

———. *The Twisted Cross: The German Christian Movement in the Third Reich.* Chapel Hill: University of North Carolina Press, 1996.

Bergerson, Andrew. "Listening to Radio in Hildesheim, 1923–1953." *German Studies Review* 24, no. 1 (2001): 83–113.

———. *Ordinary Germans in Extraordinary Times: The Nazi Revolution in Hildesheim.* Bloomington: Indiana University Press, 2004.

Berghahn, Volker R. *Modern Germany: Society, Economy, and Politics in the Twentieth Century.* Cambridge: Cambridge University Press, 1983.

Bernig, Jörg. *Eingekesselt: die Schlacht von Stalingrad im deutschsprachigen Romanen nach 1945.* New York: Peter Lang, 1997.

Besier, Gerhard. *Die Kirchen und das Dritte Reich, Bd.3, Spaltungen und Abwehr-kämpfe 1934 bis 1937*. Berlin: Propyläen, 2001.

Betts, Paul. *The Authority of Everyday Objects: A Cultural History of West German Industrial Design*. Berkeley: University of California Press, 2004.

———. "Building Socialism at Home: The Case of East German Interiors." In *Socialist Modern: East German Everyday Culture and Politics*, edited by Katherine Pence and Paul Betts, 96–132. Ann Arbor: University of Michigan Press, 2008.

Biess, Frank. "'Everybody Has a Chance': Nuclear Angst, Civil Defence, and the History of Emotions in Postwar West Germany." *German History* 27 (April 2009): 215–43.

———. "Forum: History of Emotions." *German History* 28 (March 2010): 67–80.

———. *Homecomings: Returning POWs and the Legacies of Defeat in Postwar Germany*. Princeton: Princeton University Press, 2006.

Biskup, Thomas. "The Transformation of Ceremonial: Ducal Weddings in Brunswick, c. 1760–1800." In *Festive Culture in Germany and Central Europe from the Sixteenth to the Twentieth Century*, edited by Karen Friedrich, 169–86. Lewiston, N.Y.: Edwin Mellen, 2000.

Blackbourn, David. *The Long Nineteenth Century: A History of Germany, 1780–1918*. New York: Oxford University Press, 1998.

Blackbourn, David, and Geoff Eley. *The Peculiarities of German History: Bourgeois Society and Politics in Nineteenth-Century Germany*. New York: Oxford University Press, 1991.

Boberach, Heinz. "Stimmungsschwung in der deutschen Bevölkerung." In *Stalingrad: Mythos und Wirklichkeit einer Schlacht*, edited by Wolfgang Wette and Gerd R. Ueberschär, 61–66. Frankfurt/Main: Fischer, 1992.

Bock, Helmut, and Renate Plöse, eds. *Aufbruch in die Bürgerwelt: Lebensbilder aus Vormärz und Biedermeier*. Münster: Westfälisches Dampfboot, 1994.

Bordieu, Pierre. *Distinction: A Social Critique of the Judgement of Taste*. Translated by Richard Nice. Cambridge, Mass.: Harvard University Press, 1996.

Brooks, Peter. *The Melodramatic Imagination: Balzac, Henry James, Melodrama, and the Mode of Excess*. New Haven: Yale University Press, 1976.

Brophy, James. "The Politicization of Traditional Festivals in Germany, 1815–48." In *Festive Culture in Germany and Central Europe from the Sixteenth to the Twentieth Century*, edited by Karen Friedrich, 73–106. Lewiston, N.Y.: Edwin Mellen, 2000.

Broszat, Martin. "Literatur und NS-Vergangenheit." In *Nach Hitler: Der schweirige Umgang mit unserer Geschichte*, edited by Hermann Graml and Klaus-Dietmar Henke, 121–30. Munich: R. Olderbourg, 1987.

Brown, Angele. "Vom 'germanischen Julfest' zum 'Totenfest'—Weihnachten und Winterhilfswerk-Abzeichen im Nationalsozialismus." *Deutsches Historisches Museum Magazin* 5 (Winter 1995): 23–30.

Brown, Gergory S. "Am 'I' a 'Post-Revolutionary Self'? Historiography of the Self in the Age of Enlightenment and Revolution." *History and Theory* 47 (May 2008): 229–48.

Brown, Malcolm, and Shirley Seaton. *Christmas Truce.* New York: Hippocrene Books, 1984.

Brown, Steven, and Ulrick Volgsten, eds. *Music and Manipulation: On the Social Uses and Social Control of Music.* New York: Berghahn Books, 2006.

Budde, Gunilla-Friederike. *Auf dem Weg ins Bürgerleben: Kindheit und Erziehung in deutschen und englischen Bürgerfamilien 1840–1914.* Göttingen: Vandenhoeck & Ruprecht, 1994.

Burke, Peter. "Performing History: The Importance of Occasions." *Rethinking History* 9 (March 2005): 35–52.

Burleigh, Michael, and Wolfgang Wippermann. *The Racial State: Germany, 1933–1945.* Cambridge: Cambridge University Press, 1991.

Calhoun, Craig. *Nationalism.* Minneapolis: University of Minnesota Press, 1997.

Carter, Erica. *How Modern Is She? Postwar West German Reconstruction and the Consuming Woman.* Ann Arbor: University of Michigan Press, 1997.

Casdorff, Claus Hinrich. *Weihnachten 1945: Ein Buch der Erinnerungen.* Frankfurt/ Main: Athenäum, 1989.

Clifford, James. *The Predicament of Culture: Twentieth-Century Ethnography, Literature, and Art.* Cambridge, Mass.: Harvard University Press, 1988.

Cohen, Anthony P. *The Symbolic Construction of Community.* New York: Routledge, 1993.

Confino, Alon. *Germany as a Culture of Remembrance: Promises and Limits of Writing History.* Chapel Hill: University of North Carolina Press, 2006.

———. "The Nation as Local Metaphor: Heimat, National Memory, and the German Empire, 1871–1918." *History and Memory* 5, no. 1 (Spring/Summer 1993): 42–86.

———. *The Nation as a Local Metaphor: Württemberg, Imperial Germany, and National Memory, 1871–1918.* Chapel Hill: University of North Carolina Press, 1997.

Confino, Alon, and Peter Fritzsche, eds. *The Work of Memory: New Directions in the Study of German Society and Culture.* Urbana-Champaign: University of Illinois Press, 2002.

Confino, Alon, and Rudy Koshar. "Regimes of Consumer Culture: New Narratives in Twentieth-Century German History." *German History* (June 2001): 135–61.

Connelly, John. "The Uses of National Community: Letters to the NSDAP Kreislei- tung Eisenach, 1939–1940." *Journal of Modern History* 68 (December 1996): 899–930.

Connelly, Mark. *Christmas: A Social History.* London: I. B. Tauris, 1999.

Connerton, Paul. *How Societies Remember.* Cambridge: Cambridge University Press, 1989.

Corbin, Alain. *The Foul and the Fragrant: Odor and the French Social Imagination.* Cambridge, Mass.: Harvard University Press, 1986.

———. *The Lure of the Sea: The Discovery of the Seaside in the Western World, 1750–1840.* Translated by Jocelyn Phelps. Berkeley: University of California Press, 1994.

Cramer, Kevin. "The Cult of Gustavus Adolphus: Protestant Identity and German Nationalism." In *Protestants, Catholics and Jews in Germany, 1800–1914,* edited by Helmut Walser Smith, 97–120. New York: Berg, 2001.

Cross, Gary. *An All-Consuming Century: Why Commercialism Won in America.* New York: Columbia University Press, 2000.

Daniel, Ute. *The War from Within: German Working-Class Women in the First World War.* Oxford: Berg, 1997.

Davis, Belinda. *Home Fires Burning: Food, Politics, and Everyday Life in World War I Berlin.* Chapel Hill: University of North Carolina Press, 2000.

Daxelmüller, Christoph. "Chanukka—ein jüdisches Fest zwischen Tradition und Anpassung." *Volkskunst* 4 (November 1988): 41–48.

De Grazia, Victoria. "Introduction." In *The Sex of Things: Gender and Consumption in Historical Perspective,* edited by Victoria de Grazia with Ellen Furlough, 1–10. Berkeley: University of California Press, 1996.

———. *Irresistible Empire: America's Advance through 20th-Century Europe.* Cambridge, Mass.: Harvard University Press, 2005.

Denning, Michael. *Mechanic Accents: Dime Novels and Working-Class Culture in America.* London: Verso, 1987.

Dewitz, Bodo von. "Zur Geschichte der Kriegsphotographie des Ersten Weltkrieges." In *Die letzten Tage der Menschheit: Bilder des Ersten Weltkrieges,* edited by Ranier Rother, 163–76. Berlin: Deutsches Historisches Musuem/ARS Nicolai, 1994.

Dietzsch, Ina. "Geschenkpakete—ein fundamentales Mißverständnis: Zur Bedeutung des Paketaustausches in persönlichen Briefwechseln." In *Das Westpaket: Geschenksendung, keine Handelsware,* edited by Christian Härtel and Petra Kabus, 105–17. Berlin: Christoph Links, 2000.

Dodson, Joanne. "Reclaiming Sentimental Literature." *American Literature* 69, no. 2 (1997): 263–88.

Douglas, Ann. *The Feminization of American Culture.* New York: Farrar, Straus, and Giroux, 1977.

Dowling, Timothy. "Stalinstadt/Eisenhüttenstadt: A Model for (Socialist) Life in the German Democratic Republic, 1950–1968." Ph.D. diss., Tulane University, 1999.

Düding, Dieter, Peter Friedemann, and Paul Münch, eds. *Öffentliche Festkultur: Politische Feste in Deutschland von der Aufklärung bis zum Ersten Weltkrieg.* Reinbeck bei Hamburg: Rowohlt, 1988.

Ecksteins, Modris. *Rites of Spring: The Great War and the Birth of the Modern Age.* London: Black Swan, 1990.

Eliade, Mircea. *Myths, Rites, Symbols: A Mircea Eliade Reader*, vol. 1, edited by Wendell C. Beane and William G. Doty. New York: Harper, 1976.

Eschebach, Insa. "'Das Opfer deutscher Männer': Zur Funktion des Opferbegriffs in der Rezeptionsgechichte der Schlacht um Stalingrad." *Sozialwissenschaftliche Informationen (SOWI)* 22 (January/February/March 1993): 37–41.

Eurich, Claus, and Gerd Würzberg. *30 Jahre Fernsehalltag: Wie das Fernsehen unser Leben verändert hat*. Reinbeck bei Hamburg: Rowohlt, 1980.

Evans, Richard, ed. "Forum on Richard Steigmann-Gall, *The Holy Reich*." *Journal of Contemporary History* 41, no. 1 (2007): 5–78.

Faber, Richard, and Esther Gajek, eds. *Politische Weihnacht in Antike und Moderne: Zur ideologischen Durchdringung des Fests der Feste*. Würzburg: Königshausen & Neumann, 1997.

Falkenberg, Regine. "'Der Christbaum ist der schönste Baum . . .'—Baumschmuck im Wandel der Zeit." *Deutsches Historisches Museum Magazin* 5 (Winter 1995): 4–11.

Foitzik, Doris. *Rote Sterne, braune Runen: Politische Weihnachten zwischen 1870 und 1970*. Münster: Waxmann, 1997.

François, Etienne, Hannes Siegrist, and Jakob Vogel, eds. *Nation und Emotion: Deutschland und Frankreich im Vergleich 19. und 20 Jahrhundert*. Göttingen: Vandenhoeck & Ruprecht, 1995.

Freund, Wolfgang. "Volk, Reich und Westgrenze: Wissenschaften und Politik in der Pfalz, im Saarland und im annektierten Lothringen, 1925–1945." Ph.D. diss., University of Saarbrücken, 2002.

Friedlander, Michal S. "Makkabi—Das Branding eines jüdischen Helden." In *Weih-nukka: Geschichten von Weihnachten und Chanukka*, edited by Cilly Kugelmann, 55–67. Berlin: Stiftung Jüdisches Museum Berlin/Nicolaische Verlagsbuchhand-lung, 2005.

Friedländer, Saul. *Nazi Germany and the Jews*. Vol. 1, *The Years of Persecution, 1933–1939*. New York: Harper Collins, 1997.

———. *Reflections of Nazism: An Essay on Kitsch and Death*. New York: Harper & Row, 1984.

Friedrich, Karin, ed. *Festive Culture in Germany and Europe from the Sixteenth to the Twentieth Century*. Lewiston, N.Y.: Edwin Mellen, 2000.

Fritzsche, Peter. *Germans into Nazis*. Cambridge, Mass.: Harvard University Press, 1998.

———. *Life and Death in the Third Reich*. Cambridge, Mass.: Harvard University Press, 2008.

———. *Reading Berlin 1900*. Cambridge, Mass.: Harvard University Press, 1996.

———. *Stranded in the Present: Modern Time and the Melancholy of History*. Cambridge, Mass.: Harvard University Press, 2004.

Frykman, Jonas, and Orvar Löfgren. *Culture Builders: A Historical Anthropology of Middle-Class Life*. New Brunswick: Rutgers University Press, 1987.

Füller, Klaus Dieter. *Erfolgreiche Kinderbuchauthoren des Biedermeier: Von der Erbauung zur Unterhaltung*. Frankfurt/Main: Peter Lang, 2006.

Gajek, Esther. "Nationalsozialistische Weihnacht." In *Politische Weihnacht in Antike und Moderne: Zur ideologischen Durchdringung des Fests der Feste*, edited by Richard Faber and Esther Gajek, 118–215. Würzburg: Königshausen & Neumann, 1997.

———. "Weihnachten im Dritten Reich: Der Beitrag der Volkskundler an den Veränderungen des Weihnachtsfestes." *Ethnologia Europa* 20 (1990): 121–40.

Ganaway, Bryan. *Toys, Consumption and Middle Class Childhood in Imperial Germany, 1871–1918*. New York: Peter Lang Publishers, 2009.

Geertz, Clifford. *The Interpretation of Cultures: Selected Essays*. New York: Basic Books, 1973.

Geldern, James von. *Bolshevik Festivals, 1917–1929*. Berkeley: University of California Press, 1993.

Gellately, Robert. *Backing Hitler: Consent and Coercion in Nazi Germany*. New York: Oxford University Press, 2001.

Gerlach, Siegfried. *Das Warenhaus in Deutschland: Seine Entwicklung bis zum ersten Weltkrieg in historisch-geographischer Sicht*. Stuttgart: Steiner, 1988.

Geyer, Michael. "Germany, or, the Twentieth Century as History." *South Atlantic Quarterly* 96 (Fall 1997): 663–702.

———. "In Pursuit of Happiness: Consumption, Mass Culture, and Consumerism." In *Shattered Past: Reconstructing German Histories*, by Konrad H. Jarausch and Michael Geyer, 269–314. Princeton: Princeton University Press, 2003.

Gillis, John R. "Ritualization of Middle-Class Family Life in Nineteenth-Century Britain." *International Journal of Politics, Culture, and Society* 3 (Winter 1989): 213–35.

———. *A World of Their Own Making: Myth, Ritual, and the Quest for Family Values*. New York: Basic Books, 1996.

Göbel, Karin, and Annemarie Verweyen, eds. *Weihnachten im Bilderbuch: Kleine Schriften der Freunde des Museums für Deutsche Volkskunde, Heft 10*. Berlin: Freunde des Museums für Deutsche Volkskunde, 1987.

Golby, John M., and A. W. Purdue. *The Making of the Modern Christmas*. Athens: University of Georgia Press, 1986.

Graf, Andreas, with Susanne Graf. "Die Ursprünge der modernen Medienindustrie: Familien- und Unterhaltungszeitschriften der Kaiserzeit (1870–1918)." Originally published in *Geschichte des deutschen Buchhandels im 19. und 20. Jahrhundert*, edited by Georg Jäger (2003). A revised/expanded version available at ⟨http://www.zeitschriften.ablit.de/graf/default.htm⟩. 19 June 2008.

Graff, Harvey J. *The Legacies of Literacy: Continuities and Contradictions in Western Society and Culture*. Bloomington: Indiana University Press, 1987.

Gregor, Neil, Nils Roemer, and Mark Roseman, eds. *German History from the Margins*. Bloomington: Indiana University Press, 2006.

Gutmann, Hans-Martin. "'Die arme Frau Dortel am Weihnachtsabend': Eine Erzählung Johann Hinrich Wicherns aus dem Jahre 1848 in sozialgeschichtlichen Kontext." In *Politische Weihnacht in Antike und Moderne: Zur ideologischen Durchdringung des Fests der Feste*, edited by Richard Faber and Esther Gajek, 87–118. Würzburg: Königshausen & Neumann, 1997.

Haid, Erika. *The Christmas Market of Nuremberg: An Insider's Guide*. Nuremberg: Erika Haid, 1999.

Hamlin, David D. *Work and Play: The Production and Consumption of Toys in Germany, 1870–1914*. Ann Arbor: University of Michigan Press, 2007.

Hammer, Karl. *Deutsche Kriegstheologie (1870–1918)*. Munich: Kösel, 1971.

Hardtwig, Wolfgang. "Bürgertum, Staatssymbolik und Staatsbewußtseinn 1871–1914." *Geschichte und Gesellschaft* 16 (1990): 269–95.

Harsch, Donna. *Revenge of the Domestic: Women, the Family, and Communism in the German Democratic Republic*. Princeton: Princeton University Press, 2007.

Härtel, Christian, and Petra Kabus. "Zwischen Gummibärchen und *Playboy*: Ein innerdeutscher Dialog." In *Das Westpaket: Geschenksendung, keine Handelsware*, edited by Christian Härtel and Petra Kabus, 9–24. Berlin: Christoph Links, 2000.

Hausen, Karin. "Mothers, Sons, and the Sale of Symbols and Goods: The 'German Mother's Day,' 1923–33." In *Interest and Emotion: Essays on the Study of Family and Kinship*, edited by Hans Medick and David Warren Sabean, 371–414. Cambridge: Cambridge University Press, 1984.

Hegel, Andrea von. "'Jede Liebesgabe hilft mit zum Siege'—Weihnachtsliebesgaben und Wohltätigkeitsveranstaltungen für die Soldaten im Ersten Weltkrieg." *Deutsches Historisches Museum Magazin* 5 (Winter 1995): 15–19.

Helmhagen, Egon. *Nürnberg im Zauber des Christkindlesmarktes*. Nuremberg: A. Hofmann, 1994.

Herf, Jeffrey. *Divided Memory: The Nazi Past in the Two Germanys*. Cambridge, Mass.: Harvard University Press, 1997.

Hergeth, Andreas, "'Die Popularisierung der Maßnahmen': Zollorgane werben für ihren Einsatz." In *Das Westpaket: Geschenksendung, keine Handelsware*, edited by Christian Härtel and Petra Kabus, 83–96. Berlin: Christoph Links, 2000.

Hernandez, Richard L. "Sacred Sound and Sacred Substance: Church Bells and the Auditory Culture of Russian Villages during the Bolshevik *Velikii Perelom*." *American Historical Review* 109 (December 2004): 1475–1504.

Herzog, Dagmar. *Sex after Fascism: Memory and Morality in Twentieth-Century Germany*. Princeton: Princeton University Press, 2005.

Hettling, Manfred, and Michael Jeismann. "Der Weltkrieg als Epos. Philipp Witkops 'Kriegsbriefe gefallener Studenten.'" In *Keiner fühlt sich hier mehr als Mensch*, edited by Gerhard Hirschfeld, Gerd Krumeich, and Irina Renz, 175–98. Essen: Klartext, 1993.

Hettling, Manfred, and Paul Nolte. "Bürgerliche Feste als symbolische Politik im 19. Jahrhundert." In *Bürgerliche Feste: Symbolische Formen politischen Handelns im 19. Jahrhundert*, edited by Manfred Hettling and Paul Nolte, 7–36. Göttingen: Vandenhoeck & Ruprecht, 1993.

———, eds. *Bürgerliche Feste: Symbolische Formen politischen Handelns im 19. Jahrhundert*. Göttingen: Vandenhoeck & Ruprecht, 1993.

Hillenbrand, F. K. M. *Underground Humor in Nazi Germany, 1933–1945*. London: Routledge, 1995.

Hirche, Kurt. *Der "Braune" und der "Rote" Witz*. Düsseldorf: Econ, 1964.

Hirth, Cornel F. "'Herr Pfarrer, Sie werden ein strammer Soldat': Die Kriegstagebücher des Oberpfarrers Dr. Jakob Ebner." *Badische Heimat* 81, no. 3 (September 2001): 470–73.

Hobsbawm, Eric. *Nations and Nationalism since 1780: Programme, Myth and Reality*. Cambridge: Cambridge University Press, 1994.

Hobsbawm, Eric, and Terence Ranger. *The Invention of Tradition*. Cambridge: Cambridge University Press, 1983.

Hockenos, Matthew D. *A Church Divided: German Protestants Confront the Nazi Past*. Bloomington: Indiana University Press, 2004.

Hohendahl, Peter Uwe. *Building a National Literature: The Case of Germany*. Translated by Renate Baron Franciscono. Ithaca: Cornell University Press, 1989.

Hölscher, Lucien. "Die Religion des Bürgers: Bürgerliche Frömmigkeit und protestantische Kirche im 19. Jahrhundert." *Historische Zeitschrift* 250 (1990): 595–630.

———. "The Religious Divide: Piety in Nineteenth-Century Germany." In *Protestants, Catholics and Jews in Germany, 1800–1914*, edited by Helmut Walser Smith, 33–47. New York: Berg, 2001.

Holt, Niles. "The Church Withdrawal Movement in Germany." *Journal of Church and State* 32, no. 1 (1990): 37–48.

Hopp, Andrea. *Jüdisches Bürgertum in Frankfurt am Main im 19. Jahrhundert*. Stuttgart: Franz Steiner, 1997.

Howard, June. "What Is Sentimentality?" *American Literary History* 11, no. 1 (1999): 63–81.

Hübinger, Gangolf. *Kulturprotestantismus und Politik: Zum Verhältnis von Liberalismus und Protestantismus im wilhelminischen Deutschland*. Tübingen: Mohr, 1994.

Huck, Klaus Joachim. "Die Freiwilligen Sozialleistungen der Firma Siemens." Diplom thesis, Ludwig-Maximilians-University, Munich, 1965.

Hull, Isabel V. *Absolute Destruction: Military Culture and the Practices of War in Imperial Germany*. Ithaca: Cornell University Press, 2005.

Hürten, Heinz. "Die katholische Kirche im Ersten Weltkrieg." In *Der Erste Weltkrieg: Wirkung, Wahrnehmung, Analyse*, edited by Wolfgang Michalka, 725–35. Munich: Piper, 1994.

James, Harold. *A German Identity, 1770–1990*. New York: Routledge, 1987.

Janz, Oliver. *Bürger besonderer Art: evangelische Pfarrer in Preussen 1850–1914*. Berlin: Walter de Gruyter, 1994.

Jelavich, Peter. *Munich and Theatrical Modernism: Politics, Playwriting, and Performance, 1890–1914*. Cambridge, Mass.: Harvard University Press, 1985.

Jochens, Birgit. *Deutsche Weihnacht: Ein Familienalbum 1900–1945*. Berlin: Nicolai, 1996.

Joselit, Jenna Weissman. "'Merry Chanuka': The Changing Holiday Practices of American Jews, 1880–1950." In *The Uses of Tradition: Jewish Continuity in the Modern Era*, edited by Jack Wertheimer, 303–25. New York: Jewish Theological Seminary of America/Harvard University Press, 1992.

Jüllig, Carola. "Deutsch-deutsche Weihnachten." *Deutsches Historisches Museum Magazin* 5 (Winter 1995): 31–36.

Kaes, Anton. *From Hitler to Heimar: The Return of History as Film*. Cambridge, Mass.: Harvard University Press, 1989.

Kaminsky, Annette. *Wohlstand, Schönheit, Glück: Kleine Konsumgeschichte der DDR*. Munich: C. H. Beck, 2001.

Kammerhofer-Aggermann, Ulrike. "Die Entstehung des bürgerlichen Weihnachts-festes." In *"Stille Nacht! Heilige Nacht!" Zwischen Nostalgie und Realität*, edited by Thomas Hochradner with Silvia Steiner-Span, 100–108. Salzburg: Freunde der Salzburger Geschichte, 2002.

Kaplan, Marion A. *Between Dignity and Despair: Jewish Life in Nazi Germany*. New York: Oxford University Press, 1998.

———. *The Making of the Jewish Middle Class: Women, Family, and Identity in Imperial Germany*. New York: Oxford University Press, 1991.

———. "Redefining Judaism in Imperial Germany: Practices, Mentalities, and Community." *Jewish Social Studies* 9, no. 1 (October 2002): 1–33.

Kelly, Alfred. *The German Worker: Working-Class Autobiographies from the Age of Industrialization*. Berkeley: University of California Press, 1987.

Kermann, Joachim. "Der deutsch-französische Krieg von 1870/71 aus der Sicht eines pfälzischen Militärgeistlichen." *Archiv für mittelrheinische Kirchengeschichte* 40 (1988): 189–220.

Kershaw, Ian. *Popular Opinion and Political Dissent in the Third Reich: Bavaria, 1933–1945*. Oxford: Clarendon Press, 1991.

Kirby, Dianne. "The Cold War, the Hegemony of the United States and the Golden Age of Christian Democracy." In *World Christianities c. 1914–c. 2000*, edited by Hugh McLeod, 285–303. Cambridge: Cambridge University Press, 2006.

Klein, Christina. *Cold War Orientalism: Asia in the Middlebrow Imagination, 1945–1961*. Berkeley: University of California Press, 2003.

Klein, Michael B. *Zwischen Nation und Region: Identitätsstrukturen im Deutschen Kaiserreich (1871–1918)*. Stuttgart: Franz Steiner, 2005.

Knoch, Peter. "Erleben und Nacherleben: Das Kriegserlebnis im Augenzeugenbericht und im Geschichtsunterricht." In *Keiner fühlt sich hier mehr als Mensch*, edited by Gerhard Hirschfeld, Gerd Krumeich, and Irina Renz, 119–219. Essen: Klartext, 1993.

———. "Feldpost—eine unentdeckte Quellengattung." *Geschichtsdidaktik* 11, no. 2 (1986): 154–71.

Köhler, Rosemarie. *Weihnachten in Berlin, 1945–1989: Ein Erinnerungsbuch mit vielen Abbildungen und Berichten von Zeitzeugen*. Berlin: Eichborn, 2003.

Koonz, Claudia. *Mothers in the Fatherland: Women, the Family, and Nazi Politics*. New York: St. Martin's Press, 1987.

———. *The Nazi Conscience*. Cambridge, Mass.: Harvard University Press, 2003.

Koshar, Rudy. *German Travel Cultures*. New York: Berg, 2000.

———. *Germany's Transient Pasts: Preservation and National Memory in the Twentieth Century*. Chapel Hill: University of North Carolina Press, 1988.

Kotkin, Stephen. *Magnetic Mountain: Stalinism as a Civilization*. Berkeley: University of California Press, 1995.

Krakauer, Siegfried. "The Little Shopgirls Go to the Movies." In *The Mass Ornament: Weimar Essays*. Translated and edited by Thomas Y. Levin, 291–304. Cambridge, Mass.: Harvard University Press, 1995.

Kreuz, Leo. *Das Kuratorium Unteilbares Deutschland: Aufbau, Programmatik, Wirkung*. Oplanden: Leske und Budrich, 1980.

Kruse, Martin. "Ein Frühvollendeter." In *Die Stalingrad-Madonna: Das Werk Kurt Reubers als Dokument der Versöhnung*, edited by Martin Kruse. Hannover: Lutherisches Verlagshaus, 1992.

———, ed. *Die Stalingrad-Madonna: Das Werk Kurt Reubers als Dokument der Versöhnung*. Hannover: Lutherisches Verlagshaus, 1996.

Kruse, Wolfgang. "Krieg und Klassenheer. Zur Revolutionierung der deutschen Armee in Ersten Weltkrieg." *Geschichte und Gesellschaft* 22, no. 4 (1996): 530–61.

———. *Krieg und nationale Integration: Eine Neuinterpretation des sozialdemokratischen Burgfriedensschlusses 1914/15*. Essen: Klartext, 1994.

Kugelmann, Cilly. "O Chanukka, o Chanukka! Eine historische Verortung des Chanukka-Dilemmas." In *Weihnukka: Geschichten von Weihnachten und Chanukka*, edited by Cilly Kugelmann, 8–10. Berlin: Stiftung Jüdisches Museum Berlin/Nicolaische Verlagsbuchhandlung, 2005.

Kühne, Thomas. *Kameradschaft: Die Soldaten des nationalsozialistischen Krieges und das 20. Jahrhundert*. Göttingen: Vandenhoeck & Ruprecht, 2006.

Lacey, Kate. *Feminine Frequencies: Gender, German Radio, and the Public Sphere, 1923–1945*. Ann Arbor: University of Michigan Press, 1996.

Lässig, Simone. *Jüdische Wege ins Bürgertum: Kulturelles Kapital und sozialer Aufstieg im 19. Jahrhundert*. Göttingen: Vandenhoeck & Ruprecht, 2004.

Leed, Eric J. *No Man's Land: Combat and Identity in World War I*. Cambridge: Cambridge University Press, 1979.

Leichsenring, Claus. "Erzgebirgische Weihnachtspyramiden." *Glück Auf: Beiträge zur Folklorepflege* 29/30 (1987): 3–88.

Lerner, Paul. "Consuming Pathologies: Kleptomania, Magazinitis, and the Problem of Female Consumption in Wilhelmine and Weimar Germany." *Werkstatt Geschichte* 42 (2006): 45–56.

Leroy, Esther. *Konstruktionen des Germanen in bildungsbürgerlichen Zeitschriften des deutschen Kaiserrreiches*. Frankfurt/Main: Peter Lang, 2004.

Lewy, Guenter. *The Catholic Church and Nazi Germany*. Cambridge, Mass.: Da Capo, 2000.

Lidtke, Vernon L. *The Alternative Culture: Socialist Labor in Imperial Germany*. New York: Oxford University Press, 1985.

Lincoln, Bruce. *Discourse and the Construction of Society: Comparative Studies of Myth, Ritual, and Classification*. New York: Oxford University Press, 1989.

Lindner, Bernd. "'Dein Päckchen nach drüben': Der deutsch-deutsche Paketversand und seine Rahmenbedingungen." In *Das Westpaket: Geschenksendung, keine Handelsware*, edited by Christian Härtel and Petra Kabus, 25–44. Berlin: Christoph Links, 2000.

Lipp, Anne. *Meinungslenkung im Krieg: Kriegserfahrungen deutscher Soldaten und ihrer Deutung 1914–1918*. Göttingen: Vendenhoeck & Ruprecht, 2003.

Litwicki, Ellen M. *America's Public Holidays*. Washington, D.C.: Smithsonian Institute, 2000.

Lixfeld, Hannjost. *Folklore and Fascism: The Reich Institute for German Volkskunde*. Bloomington: Indiana University Press, 1994.

Lorenz, Christa. *Berliner Weihnachtsmarkt: Bilder und Geschichten aus 5 Jahrhunderten*. Berlin: Berlin-Information, 1987.

———. "Frieden, Freude, Völkerfreundschaft: Weihnachten in der GDR." In *Politische Weihnacht in Antike und Moderne: Zur ideologischen Durchdringung des Fests der Feste*, edited by Richard Faber and Esther Gajek, 253–76. Würzburg: Königshausen & Neumann, 1997.

Lüdtke, Alf. "The 'Honor of Labor': Industrial Workers and the Power of Symbols under National Socialism." In *Nazism and German Society, 1933–1945*, edited by David Crew, 67–109. New York: Routledge, 1994.

Maier, Charles S. *The Unmasterable Past: History, Holocaust, and German National Identity*. Cambridge, Mass.: Harvard University Press, 1988.

Manz, Stefan. "Translating Nietzsche, Mediating Literature: Alexander Tille and the Limits of Anglo-German Transfer." *Neophilologus* 97, no. 1 (January 2007): 117–34.

Marling, Karal Ann. *Merry Christmas! Celebrating America's Greatest Holiday*. Cambridge, Mass.: Harvard University Press, 2000.

Marßolek, Inge, and Adelheid von Saldern, eds. *Radiozeiten: Herrschaft, Alltag, Gesellschaft (1924–1960)*. Potsdam: Verlag für Berlin-Brandenburg, 1999.

Martin-Fugier, Anne. "Bourgeois Rituals." In *A History of Private Life*, vol. 4, *From*

the Fires of Revolution to the Great War, edited by Michelle Perrot and translated
by Arthur Goldhammer, 260–337. Cambridge, Mass.: Harvard University Press,
1990.

McGlathery, James M. *E. T. A. Hoffmann.* New York: Twayne, 1997.

McLeod, Hugh. *Piety and Poverty: Working-Class Religion in Berlin, London and
New York, 1870–1914.* New York: Holmes & Meier, 1996.

———. *The Religious Crisis of the 1960s.* Oxford: Oxford University Press, 2007.

———. "Weibliche Frömmigkeit—männlicher Unglaube? Religion und Kirchen im
bürgerlichen 19. Jahrhundert." In *Bürgerinnen und Bürger: Geschlechterverhältnisse
im 19. Jahrhundert*, edited by Ute Frevert, 134–56. Göttingen: Vandenhoeck und
Ruprecht, 1988.

Meier, Kurt. "Evangelische Kirche und Erster Weltkrieg." In *Der Erste Weltkrieg.
Wirkung, Wahrnehmung, Analyse*, edited by Wolfgang Michalka, 691–724.
Munich: Piper, 1994.

Merkel, Ina. *Utopie und Bedürfnis: Die Geschichte der Konsumkultur in der DDR.*
Cologne: Böhlau, 1999.

———. "Wer nie vorm Konsum Schlange stand . . ." In *KONSUM: Konsumgenossenschaften in der DDR*, edited by Andreas Ludwig, 81–96. Berlin: Das Dokumentati-
onszentrum Alltagskultur der DDR, 2006.

Metken, Sigrid. "'Ich hab' diese Karte im Schützengraben geschrieben . . .': Bildpost-
karten im Ersten Weltkrieg." In *Die letzten Tage der Menschheit: Bilder des Ersten
Weltkrieges*, edited by Ranier Rother, 137–48. Berlin: Deutsches Historisches
Musuem/ARS Nicolai, 1994.

Miller, Daniel. "A Theory of Christmas." In *Unwrapping Christmas*, edited by Daniel
Miller, 3–37. Oxford: Clarendon Press, 1993.

———, ed. *Unwrapping Christmas.* Oxford: Clarendon Press, 1993.

Miller, Michael B. *The Bon Marché: Bourgeois Culture and the Department Store.*
Princeton: Princeton University Press, 1981.

Missalla, Heinrich. *"Gott mit uns": Die deutsche katholische Kriegspredigt, 1914–1918.*
Munich: Kösel, 1968.

Moeller, Robert, G. *War Stories: The Search for a Usable Past in the Federal Republic of
Germany.* Berkeley: University of California Press, 2001.

Möller, Frank, and Ulrich Mählert. "NS-Zeit und Kriegserfahrung als gemeinsamer
Ausgangspunkt und als Steinbruch der beiden deutschen Gründungserzählungen:
Ein Gespräch mit Prof. Dr. Norbert Frei, Jena." In *Abgrenzung und Verflechtung:
Das geteilte Deutschland in der zeithistorischen Debatte*, edited by Frank Möller
and Ulrich Mählert, 15–28. Berlin: Metropol, 2008.

Mosse, George. *Fallen Soldiers: Reshaping the Memory of the World Wars.* New York:
Oxford, 1990.

———. *Nationalism and Sexuality: Middle-Class Morality and Sexual Norms in
Modern Europe.* Madison: University of Wisconsin Press, 1985.

————. *The Nationalization of the Masses: Political Symbolism and Mass Movements in Germany from the Napoleonic Wars through the Third Reich*. New York: H. Fertig, 1975.

————. *Nazi Culture: Intellectual, Cultural, and Social Life in the Third Reich*. New York: Schocken, 1981.

Nestmeyer, Ralf. "Zwei Engel für Liebel." *Die Zeit*, 27 November 2003, 92.

Nicolaus, Herbert, and Alexander Obeth. *Die Stalinallee: Geschichte einer deutschen Straße*. Berlin: Verlag Bauwesen, 1997.

Niethammer, Lutz. "War die bürgerliche Gesellschaft in Deutschland 1945 am Ende oder am Anfang?" In *Bürgerliche Gesellschaft in Deutschland: Historische Einblicke, Fragen, Perspektiven*, edited by Lutz Niethammer, 515–32. Frankfurt/Main: Fischer, 1990.

Nissenbaum, Stephen. *The Battle for Christmas*. New York: Knopf, 1996.

Nolan, Mary. *Social Democracy and Society: Working Class Radicalism in Düsseldorf, 1890–1920*. Cambridge: Cambridge University Press, 1981.

Nora, Pierre. "Between Memory and History: Les Lieux de Mémoire." In *Representations* 26 (Spring 1989): 7–25.

Nowak, Kurt. *Geschichte des Christentums in Deutschland: Religion, Politik und Gesellschaft vom Ende der Aufklärung bis zur Mitte des 20. Jahrhunderts*. Munich: C. H. Beck, 1995.

Ottmüller, Uta. *Die Dienstbotenfrage: Zur Sozialgeschichte der doppelten Ausnutzung von Dienstmädchen im deutschen Kaiserreich*. Münster: Verlag Frauenpolitik, 1978.

Ozouf, Mona. *Festivals and the French Revolution*. Cambridge, Mass.: Harvard University Press, 1988.

Paulsen, Gundel. "Weihnachten in Berlin." In *Weihnachtsgeschichten aus Berlin*, edited by Gundel Paulsen, 112–19. Husum: Husum, 1993.

Pence, Katherine. "The Myth of a Suspended Present: Prosperity's Painful Shadow in 1950s East Germany." In *Pain and Prosperity: Reconsidering Twentieth-Century German History*, edited by Paul Betts and Greg Eghigian, 137–59. Stanford: Stanford University Press, 2003.

Perrot, Michelle. "Introduction." In *A History of Private Life*, vol. 4, *From the Fires of Revolution to the Great War*, edited by Michelle Perrot and translated by Arthur Goldhammer, 1–5. Cambridge, Mass.: Harvard University Press, 1990.

Perry, Joe. "Healthy for Family Life: Television, Masculinity, and Domestic Modernity during West Germany's Miracle Years." *German History* 25 (December 2007): 560–95.

————. "The Madonna of Stalingrad: Mastering the (Christmas) Past and West German National Identity after World War II." *Radical History Review* 83 (Spring 2002): 6–27.

————. "Mastering the (Christmas) Past: Manhood, Memory, and the German 'War Christmas.'" *Thematica: Historical Research and Review* 2 (1995): 57–76.

———. "The Nazification of Christmas: Politics and Popular Celebration in the Third Reich." *Central European History* 38 (December 2005): 572–605.

Perry, Joe, and Sven Reichardt. "'Unfrieden auf Erden' or 'Brücke zur Gemeinschaft'? Storm Troopers and the Nazification of Christmas, 1921–1938." Paper presented at the German Studies Association Conference, 27 September 1997.

Petrone, Karen. *Life Has Become More Joyous, Comrades: Celebrations in the Time of Stalin*. Bloomington: University of Indiana Press, 2000.

Peukert, Detlev J. K. *Inside Nazi Germany: Conformity, Opposition, and Racism in Everyday Life*. New Haven: Yale University Press, 1987.

———. *The Weimar Republic: The Crisis of Classical Modernity*. Translated by Richard Devenson. New York: Hill and Wang, 1992.

Pfeifer, Jochen. *Der deutsche Kriegsroman 1945–1960: Ein Versuch zur Vermittlung von Literatur und Sozialgeschichte*. Königstein: Scriptor, 1981.

Picht, Clemens. "Zwischen Vaterland und Volk. Das deutsche Judentum im Ersten Weltkrieg." In *Der Erste Weltkrieg: Wirkung, Wahrnehmung, Analyse*, edited by Wolfgang Michalka, 736–56. Munich: Piper, 1994.

Pleck, Elizabeth H. *Celebrating the Family: Ethnicity, Consumer Culture, and Family Rituals*. Cambridge, Mass.: Harvard University Press, 2000.

Poiger, Uta. *Jazz, Rock, and Rebels: Cold War Politics and American Culture in a Divided Germany*. Berkeley: University of California Press, 2000.

Pollack, Detlef. "Von der Volkskirche zur Minderheitskirche: Zur Entwicklung von Religiösität und Kirchlichkeit in der DDR." In *Sozialgeschichte der DDR*, edited by Hartmut Kaelble, Jürgen Kocka, and Hartmut Zwahr, 271–94. Stuttgart: Klett-Cotta, 1994.

Port, Andrew I. *Conflict and Stability in the German Democratic Republic*. Cambridge: Cambridge University Press, 2007.

Pratt, Mary Louise. *Imperial Eyes: Travel Writing and Transculturation*. London: Routledge, 1992.

Proctor, Robert N. *The Nazi War on Cancer*. Princeton: Princeton University Press, 1999.

Rahden, Till van. "Weder Milieu noch Konfession: Die situative Ethnizität der deutschen Juden im Kaiserreich in vergleichender Perspektive." In *Religion im Kaiserreich: Milieus—Mentalitäten—Krisen*, edited by Olaf Blaschke and Frank-Michael Kuhlemann, 409–34. Gütersloh: Chr. Kaiser, 1996.

Reagin, Nancy R. *Sweeping the German Nation: Domesticity and National Identity in Germany, 1870–1945*. Cambridge: Cambridge University Press, 2006.

Reddy, William M. *The Navigation of Feeling: A Framework for the History of Emotions*. Cambridge: Cambridge University Press, 2001.

Reichardt, Sven. *Faschistische Kampfbünde: Gewalt und Gemeinschaft im italienischen Squadrismus und in der deutschen SA*. Cologne: Böhlau, 2002.

Reichel, Peter. *Der schöne Schein des Dritten Reiches: Faszination und Gewalt des Faschismus*. Frankfurt/Main: Fischer Taschenbuch, 1996.

Reimann, Aribert. *Der große Krieg der Sprachen: Untersuchungen zur historischen Semantik in Deutschland und England zur Zeit des Ersten Weltkriegs.* Essen: Klartext, 2000.

Reimers, Karl F. "Der Führer als völkische Erlösergestalt: Die Berliner NS-Weihnachtskundgebung 1933 im offiziellen Filmbericht." *Geschichte in Wissenschaft und Unterricht* 19 (March 1968): 164–75.

Rentschler, Eric. *The Ministry of Illusion: Nazi Cinema and Its Afterlife.* Cambridge, Mass.: Harvard University Press, 1996.

Restad, Penne. *Christmas in America: A History.* New York: Oxford University Press, 1995.

Richarz, Monika. "Der jüdische Weihnachtsbaum—Familie und Säkularisierung im deutschen Judentum des 19. Jahrhunderts." In *Geschichte und Emanzipation: Festschrift für Reinhard Rürup*, edited by Michael Grüttner, Rüdiger Hachtmann, and Heinz-Gerhard Haupt, 275–89. Frankfurt/Main: Campus, 1999.

———. "Weihnukka—Das Weihnachtsfest im jüdischen Bürgertum." In *Weihnukka: Geschichten von Weihnachten und Chanukka*, edited by Cilly Kugelmann, 86–99. Berlin: Stiftung Jüdisches Museum Berlin/Nicolaische Verlagsbuchhandlung, 2005.

———, ed. *Jüdisches Leben in Deutschland. Bd. 1: Selbstzeugnisse zur Sozialgeschichte im Kaiserreich 1780–1871.* Stuttgart: Deutsche Verlags-Anstalt, 1976.

Roeder, George H., Jr. "Coming to Our Senses." *Journal of American History* 81, no. 3 (December 1994): 1112–22.

Rohkrämer, Thomas. "Der Gesinnungsmilitarismus der 'kleinen Leute' im Deutschen Kaiserreich." In *Der Krieg des kleinen Mannes: Eine Militärgeschichte von unten*, edited by Wolfram Wette, 95–109. Munich: Piper, 1995.

Roper, Lyndal. *The Holy Household: Women and Morals in Reformation Augsburg.* Oxford: Clarendon Press, 1989.

Rosenwein, Barbara H. *Emotional Communities in the Early Middle Ages.* Ithaca: Cornell University Press, 2006.

———. "Worrying about Emotions in History." *American Historical Review* 107 (June 2002): 821–45.

Ross, Corey. "Celebrating Christmas in the Third Reich and the GDR: Political Instrumentalization and Cultural Continuity under the German Dictatorships." In *Festive Culture in Germany and Europe from the Sixteenth to the Twentieth Century*, edited by Karen Friedrich, 323–42. Lewiston, N.Y.: Edwin Mellen, 2000.

———. *Constructing Socialism at the Grass-Roots: The Transformation of East Germany, 1945–65.* New York: St. Martin's, 2000.

———. *The East German Dictatorship: Problems and Perspectives in the Interpretation of the GDR.* New York: Oxford University Press, 2002.

Rüden, Peter von. *Sozialdemokratisches Arbeitertheater (1848–1914): ein Beitrag zur Geschichte des politischen Theaters.* Frankfurt/Main: Athenäum, 1973.

Ruff, Mark Edward. *The Wayward Flock: Catholic Youth in Postwar West Germany, 1945–1965*. Chapel Hill: University of North Carolina Press, 2005.

Rühlig, Cornelia, and Jürgen Steen, eds. *Walter: Leben und Lebensbedingungen eines Frankfurter Jungen im III. Reich*. Frankfurt/Main: Historisches Museum Frankfurt/Main, 1983.

Russ, Jennifer M. *German Festivals and Customs*. London: Oswald Wolf, 1982.

Ryback, Timothy W. "Stalingrad: Letters from the Dead." *New Yorker*, 1 February 1993, 58–71.

Rybczynski, Witold. *Home: A Short History of an Idea*. New York: Viking, 1986.

Sahlins, Marshall. *Culture and Practical Reason*. Chicago: University of Chicago Press, 1976.

Saldern, Adelheid von. "Massenfreizeitkultur im Visier. Ein Beitrag zu den Deutungs- und Einwirkungsversuchen während der Weimarer Republik." *Archiv für Sozialgeschichte* 33 (1993): 21–58.

———. "Victims or Perpetrators? Controversies about the Role of Women in the Nazi State." In *Nazism and German Society, 1933–1945*, edited by David Crew, 141–65. New York: Routledge, 1994.

Sarna, Jonathan D. "Is Judaism Compatible with American Civil Religion? The Problem of Christmas and the 'National Faith.'" In *Religion and the Life of the Nation: American Recoveries*, edited by Rowland A. Sherrill, 152–73. Urbana: University of Illinois Press, 1990.

Sauermann, Dietmar. *Von Advent bis Dreikönige: Weihnachten in Westfalen*. Münster: Waxmann, 1996.

———, ed. *Weihnachten in Westfalen um 1900. Berichte aus dem Archiv für westfälische Volkskunde*. Münster: Volkskundliche Kommission für Westfalen, 1976.

Schäfer, Jörgen. "'Alle fluchten, alle funktionierten': Die Schlacht um Stalingrad in deutschen Romanen der Nachkriegszeit." *Sozialwissenschaftliche Informationen (SOWI)* 22 (January/February/March 1993): 42–49.

Schellong, Dieter. "Schleiermachers 'Weihnachtsfeier': Ein Dokument des evangelischen Bürgertums zum Anfang des 19. Jahrhunderts." In *Politische Weihnacht in Antike und Moderne: Zur ideologischen Durchdringung des Fests der Feste*, edited by Richard Faber and Esther Gajek, 75–86. Würzburg: Königshausen & Neumann, 1997.

Schenda, Rudolf. *Die Lesestoffe der Kleinen Leute: Studien zur populären Literatur im 19. und 20. Jahrhundert*. Munich: C. H. Beck, 1976.

———. *Volk ohne Buch: Studien zur Sozialgeschichte der populären Lesestoffe 1770–1910*. Frankfurt/Main: Vittorio Klostermann, 1970.

Schenk, H. G. *The Mind of the European Romantics: An Essay in Cultural History*. Oxford: Oxford University Press, 1979.

Schikorsky, Isa. "Kommunikation über das Unbeschreibbare. Beobachtungen zum Sprachstil von Kriegsbriefen." *Wirkendes Wort* 44, no. 2 (1992): 295–315.

Schildt, Axel. "Das Jahrhundert der Massenmedien: Ansichten zu einer künftigen Geschichte der Öffentlichkeit." *Geschichte und Gesellschaft* 27, no. 2 (2001): 177–206.

Schmidt, Leigh Eric. *Consumer Rites: The Buying and Selling of American Holidays.* Princeton: Princeton University Press, 1995.

Scholder, Klaus. *The Churches and the Third Reich.* Vol. 1, *Preliminary History and the Time of Illusions, 1918–1934.* Translated by John Bowden. Philadelphia: Fortress Press, 1988.

Shorske, Carl E. *Fin-de-Siecle Vienna: Politics and Culture.* New York: Alfred A. Knopf, 1980.

Schulte-Sasse, Linda. "Leni Riefenstahl's Feature Films and the Question of a Fascist Aesthetic." *Cultural Critique* 18 (Spring 1991): 123–48.

Seigel, Jerrold. *The Idea of the Self: Thought and Experience in Western Europe since the Seventeenth Century.* Cambridge: Cambridge University Press, 2005.

Sewell, William H., Jr. "The Concept(s) of Culture." In *Beyond the Cultural Turn,* edited by Victoria E. Bonnell and Lynn Hunt, 35–54. Berkeley: University of California Press, 1999.

Sheehan, Jonathan. *The Enlightenment Bible: Translation, Scholarship, Culture.* Princeton: Princeton University Press, 2005.

Siefker, Phyllis. *Santa Claus, Last of the Wild Men: The Origins and Evolution of Saint Nicholas, Spanning 50,000 Years.* Jefferson, N.C., and London: McFarland, 1997.

Slater, Dan. *Consumer Culture and Modernity.* Cambridge, UK: Polity Press, 1997.

Smith, Anthony D. *The Ethnic Origins of Nations.* Oxford: Basil Blackwell, 1986.

Smith, Helmut Walser. *German Nationalism and Religious Conflict: Culture, Ideology, Politics, 1870–1914.* Princeton: Princeton University Press, 1995.

Smith, Helmut Walser, and Chris Clark. "The Fate of Nathan." In *Protestants, Catholics and Jews in Germany, 1800–1914,* edited by Helmut Walser Smith, 3–29. New York: Berg, 2001.

Smith, Mark M. "Making Sense of Social History." *Journal of Social History* 37 (Fall 2003): 165–86.

Sontag, Susan. "Fascinating Fascism." In *Under the Sign of Saturn,* edited by Susan Sontag, 71–105. New York: Vintage, 1981.

Spencer, Elaine Glovka. "Policing Popular Amusements in German Cities: The Case of Prussia's Rhine Province, 1815–1914." *Journal of Urban History* 16 (August 1990): 366–68.

Sperber, Jonathon. "Bürger, Bürgerlichkeit, Bürgerliche Gesellschaft: Studies of the German (Upper) Middle Class and Its Sociocultural World." *Journal of Modern History* 69 (June 1997): 271–97.

Spiekermann, Uwe. "Freier Konsum und Soziale Verantwortung: Zur Geschichte des Ladenschlusses in Deutschland im 19. und 20. Jahrhundert." *Zeitschrift für Unternehmergeschichte* 49, no. 1 (2004): 26–44.

Spiel, Hilde. *Fanny von Arnstein oder die Emanzipation: Ein Frauenleben an der Zeitenwende, 1758–1818.* Frankfurt/Main: S. Fischer, 1962.

Stahr, Heinrick. "Liebesgaben für den Ernstfall: Das Rote Kreuz in Deutschland zu Beginn des Ersten Weltkriegs." In *August 1914: Ein Volk zieht in den Krieg,* edited by Berliner Geschichtswerkstätte e. V, 83–91. Berlin: Dirk Nishen/Berliner Geschichtswerkstätte e. V., 1989.

Stallybrass, Peter, and Allon White. *The Politics and Poetics of Transgression.* Ithaca: Cornell University Press, 1986.

Stansky, Peter. "Film Review: 'The Great War and the Shaping of the 20th Century.'" *American Historical Review* 102 (April 1997): 593.

Steakley, James D. "Iconography of a Scandal: Political Cartoons and the Eulenberg Affair in Wilhelmine Germany." In *Hidden From History: Reclaiming the Gay and Lesbian Past,* edited by Martin Bauml Duberman, Martha Vicinus, and George Chauncey Jr., 233–63. New York: New American Library, 1989.

Stearns, Peter N., with Carol Z. Stearns. "Emotionology: Clarifying the History of Emotions and Emotional Standards." *American Historical Review* 90 (October 1985): 813–36.

Steigman-Gall, Richard. *The Holy Reich: Nazi Conceptions of Christianity, 1919–1945.* Cambridge: Cambridge University Press, 2003.

———. "Rethinking Nazism and Religion: How Anti-Christian were the 'Pagans'?" *Central European History* 36, no. 1 (2003): 75–105.

Steinhoff, Anthony J. "Building Religious Community: Worship Space and Experience in Strasbourg after the Franco-Prussian War." In *Protestants, Catholics and Jews in Germany, 1800–1914,* edited by Helmut Walser Smith, 267–96. New York: Berg, 2001.

———. "Christianity and the Creation of Germany." In *World Christianities c. 1815–c. 1914,* vol. 8, edited by Sheridan Gilley and Brian Stanley, 282–300. Cambridge: Cambridge University Press, 2006.

Stern, Fritz. *The Politics of Cultural Despair: A Study in the Rise of the Germanic Ideology.* Berkeley: University of California Press, 1961.

Stewart, Susan. *On Longing: Narratives of the Miniature, the Gigantic, the Souvenir, the Collection.* Baltimore: John Hopkins University Press, 1984.

Stitziel, Judd. *Fashioning Socialism: Clothing, Politics, and Consumer Culture in East Germany.* New York: Berg, 2005.

Stihler, Ariane. *Die Entstehung des modernen Konsums: Darstellung und Erklärungsansätze.* Berlin: Duncker & Humblot, 1998.

Strasser, Susan, Charles McGovern, and Matthias Judt, eds. *Getting and Spending: European and American Consumer Societies in the Twentieth Century.* Cambridge: Cambridge University Press, 2000.

Susman, Warren. "The Culture of the Thirties." In *Culture as History: The Transformation of American Society in the Twentieth Century*, edited by Warren Susman, 150–83. New York: Pantheon, 1984.

Swett, Pamela. "Celebrating the Republic without Republicans: The Reichsverfassungstag in Berlin, 1929–1932." In *Festive Culture in Germany and Europe from the Sixteenth to the Twentieth Century*, edited by Karin Friedrich, 281–302. Lewiston, N.Y.: Edwin Mellen, 2000.

Swett, Pamela E., S. Jonathan Wiesen, and Jonathan R. Zatlin, eds. *Selling Modernity: Advertising in Twentieth-Century Germany*. Durham: Duke University Press, 2007.

Tacke, Charlotte. *Denkmal im sozialen Raum: Nationale Symbole in Deutschland und Frankreich im 19. Jahrhundert*. Göttingen: Vandenhoeck & Ruprecht, 1995.

Taylor, Charles. *Sources of the Self: The Making of the Modern Identity*. Cambridge, Mass.: Harvard University Press, 1989.

Tooze, Adam. *The Wages of Destruction: The Making and Breaking of the Nazi Economy*. New York: Penguin, 2006.

Turner, Victor. "Introduction." In *Celebration: Studies in Festivity and Ritual*, edited by Victor Turner, 11–32. Washington, D.C.: Smithsonian Institution Press, 1982.

———, ed. *Celebration: Studies in Festivity and Ritual*. Washington, D.C.: Smithsonian Institution Press, 1982.

Ulrich, Bernd. *Die Augenzeugen: Deutsche Feldpostbriefe in Kriegs- und Nachkriegszeit 1914–1933*. Essen: Klartext, 1997.

Ulrich, Bernd, and Benjamin Ziemann, eds. *Frontalltag im Ersten Weltkrieg. Wahn und Wirklichkeit*. Frankfurt/Main: Fischer Taschenbuch, 1994.

Vaupel, Elisabeth. "Eine Runde Sache: Technikhistorisches zur Christbaumkugel." *Kultur & Technik: Zeitschrift des Deutschen Museums München* 12, no. 1 (1989): 11–19.

Vondung, Klaus. *Magie und Manipulation: Ideologischer Kult und politische Religion des Nationalsozialismus*. Göttingen: Vandenhoeck & Ruprecht, 1971.

Vorländer, Herbert. *Die NSV. Darstellung und Dokumentation einer nationalsozialistischen Organisation*. Boppard am Rhein: Boldt, 1988.

Voss, Kaija. *Berliner Weihnacht*. Berlin: be.bra, 2003.

Wahrman, Dror. *The Making of the Modern Self: Identity and Culture in Eighteenth-Century England*. New Haven: Yale University Press, 2006.

Waits, William B. *The Modern Christmas in America*. New York: New York University Press, 1993.

Walser, Karin. *Dienstmädchen: Frauenarbeit und Weiblichkeitsbilder um 1900*. Frankfurt/Main: Extrabuch, 1985.

Weber-Kellermann, Ingeborg. *Das Buch der Weihnachtslieder: 151 deutsche Advents- und Weihnachtslieder. Kulturgeschichte, Noten, Texte*. Mainz: Schott, 1994.

———. "Excurs: Die deutsche Bürgerfamilie und ihre weihnachtlichen Verhaltens- muster." In *Die Familie: Geschichte, Geschichten und Bilder*, 300–325. Frankfurt/ Main: Insel, 1984.

———. *Frauenleben im 19. Jahrhundert: Empire und Romantik, Biedermeier, Gründerzeit*. Munich: C. H. Beck, 1983.

———. *Das Weihnachtsfest: Eine Kultur und Sozialgeschichte der Weihnachtszeit*. Luzern and Frankfurt: Bucher, 1978.

Wedel, Hasso von. *Die Propagandatruppen der deutschen Wehrmacht*. Neckargemünd: Kurk Vowinckel, 1962.

Wegehaupt, Heinz, ed. *Weihnachten im alten Kinderbuch*. Leipzig: Ed. Leipzig, 1992.

Wehler, Hans-Ulrich. *The German Empire, 1871–1918*. Providence, R.I.: Berg, 1991.

Weidenfeld, George. *The Forsaken Army*. New York: Harper and Row, 1971.

Weightman, Gavin, and Steve Humphries. *Christmas Past*. London: Sidgwick and Jackson, 1987.

Weintraub, Stanley. *Silent Night: The Story of the World War I Christmas Truce*. New York: Free Press, 2001.

Weitz, Eric D. *Creating German Communism, 1890–1990: From Popular Protest to Socialist State*. Princeton: Princeton University Press, 1997.

Wette, Wolfram. "Das Massensterben als 'Heldenepos': Stalingrad in der NS- Propaganda." In *Stalingrad: Mythos und Wirklichkeit einer Schlacht*, edited by Wolfram Wette and Gerd R. Ueberschär, 43–60. Frankfurt/Main: Fischer, 1992.

———. "'Unsere Stimmung ist auf dem Nullpunkt angekommen': Berichte von Feldpostprüfstellen über die 'Kessel-Post.'" In *Stalingrad: Mythos und Wirklichkeit einer Schlacht*, edited by Wolfram Wette and Gerd R. Ueberschär, 90–101. Frankfurt/Main: Fischer, 1992.

Wierling, Dorothee. "The Hitler Youth Generation in the GDR: Insecurities, Ambitions, and Dilemmas." In *Dictatorship as Experience: Toward a Socio-Cultural History of the GDR*, edited by Konrad H. Jarausch, 307–23. New York: Berghan, 1999.

Wildt, Michael. *Vom kleinen Wohlstand: Eine Konsumgeschichte der fünfziger Jahre*. Frankfurt/Main: Fischer, 1996.

Wilson, William J. "Festivals in the Third Reich." Ph.D. diss., McMaster University, 1994.

Winter, Jay. *Sites of Memory, Sites of Mourning: The Great War in European Cultural History*. New York: Oxford University Press, 1995.

Wistrich, Robert. *Wer war Wer im Dritten Reich: Anhänger, Mitläufer, Gegner aus Politik, Wirtschaft, Militär, Kunst und Wissenschaft*. Munich: Harnack, 1983.

Wohlfart, Roland. *Der braven Kinder Weihnachtswünsche: Weihnachtsglückwunschbriefe des 19. und 20. Jahrhunderts*: Berlin: Staatliche Museen Preußischer Kulturbesitz, 1991.

Wurst, Karin. *Fabricating Pleasure: Fashion, Entertainment, and Cultural Consumption in Germany, 1780–1830*. Detroit: Wayne State University Press, 2005.

Zahn, Gordon, *German Catholics and Hitler's Wars: A Study in Social Control*. New York: Sheed & Ward, 1962.

Zalar, Jeffrey T. "The Process of Confessional Inculturation: Catholic Reading in the 'Long Nineteenth Century.'" In *Protestants, Catholics and Jews in Germany, 1800–1914*, edited by Helmut Walser Smith, 121–52. Cambridge: Cambridge University Press, 2006.

Index

Page numbers in italics indicate illustrations

Christmas and, 139, 148–49, 174–75; 1920s and, 171–72, 176–77; Nazi response to, 211–13; social class and, 168–69; social effects of, 142, 285; urge to buy and (see *Kauflust*); wartime (1917) mood and, 133–34; West Germany and, 266, 268–75; World War II shortages and, 229, 233–34

Copper Sunday, 166–67

Corbain, Alain, 27

Cornelius, Peter: *Christmas Cycle*, 178

Counterculture, West German, 274–75

Craft workers, 141, 142

Crèche. *See* Nativity scene

Cross, Gary, 282

Daeglau, Greta, 176

Dannhauer, Johann Konrad: *The Milk of the Catechism*, 32

Darwin, Charles, 71

"Dead Soldiers' Homecoming, The" (Scheller), 235, 237

Death, cult of, 234–37; Christmas and, 52–53, 135, 237; German (Nazi) War Christmas and, 234–35, *236*, 237; theme of rebirth and, 135, 237; War Christmas myths and, 135–36

December festivals, 14, 32, 43, 79; Christmas outdoor markets and, 156–65; Nazi versions of, 195–96. *See also* Winter solstice

De-Christianization: Communists and, 245, 261–62, 264; Jewish Christmas and, 68; Nazis and, 6, 10–11, 191, 193, 198–99, 215–27, 229, 237, 287. *See also* Secularization

Decorations and ornaments, 20, 27, 144, 156, 176, 246; Christmas room and, 28; Christmas tree and, 24, 30, 32, 33–34, 56, 62; East Germany and, 262, 265, 272; homemade, 215, 226,

283; mail-order sources for, 33; mass production of, 5, 145, 146, *146*, 155; militaristic, 62; Nazi symbols as, 186, 210–11, 213, 215, 217, 218, 226, 238; nutcracker's importance as, 145; War Christmas practices and, 100, 110. *See* t*also* Lights

De Grazia, Victoria, 212

Dehn, Günther, 92

Demon Night festival (Tyrol), 203–5

Denmark, 54

Department Store of Peace (Leipzig), 277

Department stores, *138*, 165–71; advertising by, 165, 166, 168, 170, 175; anti-Semitic campaign against, 143, 165–66, 170, 185, 192; Aryanization of, 185; catalogs of, 166, 211; Christmas outdoor markets vs., 162–63, 164–65, 167–68; class-based customers of, 168–69; development of, 165–66; display windows of, 139, 147, 150–51, *151*, 161, 163, 170, 175, 180, 277; early closing hours and, 141–42; East Berlin and, 268, 276; enthusiasm for, 167; Nazi boycotts of, 184, 192; resentment of, 141–42, 143, 165–66, 169–70; services of, 166; small shopkeepers vs., 140, 142, 169–70; temporary employees of, 169; West Berlin and, 266

Deutsche Bücherei (Leipzig), 122

Deutsche Kriegsweihnachten (German War Christmas Book), 235, *236*

"Deutschland über Alles" (anthem), 118, 131

Dibelius, Otto (bishop of Berlin-Brandenburg), 244–45, 263–64

Dickens, Charles: *A Christmas Carol*, 30

Dietzsch, Ira, 271

Displaced persons, 243, 248

Doctor of Stalingrad, The (Konsalik), 255

135–36; winter solstice and, 79, 81, 191, 194

Socialism. *See* East Germany; Social Democrats

Socialist German Student League, 275

Socialist Unity Party (East Germany), 242, 258, 260–61, 262, 264; "Christmas Miracle" and, 266, *267*; consumer consumption and, 275–76, 278

Social strata, 5, 27, 285; Christmas activities and, 152–53, 159; Christmas shopping and, 141–42, 143; Christmas story portrayals of, 16, 18–19, 48, 51–53; department store choice and, 168–69; department store workers and, 169; downward mobility and, 171; fictionalized upward mobility and, 51–52; German Jews and, 69; German polarization and, 118; Imperial German divisions and, 68; War Christmas divisions and, 113–14, 115, *115*, *116*, 117–19, 135. *See also* Bildungsbürgertum; Middle-class values; Working class

Society for German God Consciousness, 22

Sollmann, Wilhelm, 140–41

Solstice rituals. *See* Winter solstice

Songs: Hanukkah, 74, 75; Nazi, 202, 202–3, 214, 220, 221; patriotic, 131. *See also* Carols and hymns

Sopade (Social Democratic Party in exile), 208, 213, 214–15

Soviet Union. *See* Cold War

Sozialistischer Deutscher Studentenbund, 275

SPD. *See* Social Democrats

Spee, Friedrich: "Oh, Savior, Tear Open the Heavens," 221

Spiegel, Der (news magazine), *240*, 246, 269–70

Sputnik tree ornaments, 265

SS (paramilitary unit), 197, 213, 227

Stalin, Joseph, 260

Stalinallee (East Berlin), 268, 276–77

Stalingrad (film), 287

Stalingrad (Plivier), 255

Stalingrad, Battle of (1941), 231–32, 234; postwar legend of, 250–56, *251*, 287; "ring broadcast" and, 232–33, 287

Stalingrad— "To the Last Round" (Schröter), 254–55

Stalinstadt/Eisenhüttenenstadt, 262–65

Staudte, Wolfgang, 239, 241, 242

Steinhoff, Anthony J., 39

Stifter, Adalbert, 23, 48, 90

Stillich, Oskar, 86–87

Stitziel, Judd, 276

Stocknis, Rudolf, 60–61

Stolz, Alban, 37

Storm, Theodor, 23, 62; *Unter dem Tannenbaum*, 53–54

Storm troopers. *See* SA

Street fairs. *See* Christmas markets

Streicher, Jules, 213

Streizelmarkt (Dresden), 156

Strength through Joy (KdF), 192

Strzelewicz, Boleslaw, 81–82

Stumpf, Richard, 118–19

Sturmabteilung. *See* SA

Stuttgart Declaration of Guilt (1945), 244–45

Sulzbach, Herbert, 119, 132–33

Sumptuary laws, 85, 90–92, 153; Advent Sunday shopping and, 166; Christmas Eve store hours and, 91, 139–42, 171

Swastika tree ornaments, 186, 213, 217

Tanera, Carl, 97; *Serious and Humorous Memories of an Ordnance Office in 1870/71*, 101

Tannenbaum. *See* Christmas tree